The New Boys of Summer

The New Boys of Summer

Baseball's Radical Transformation in the Late Sixties

PAUL HENSLER

ROWMAN & LITTLEFIELD
Lanham • Boulder • New York • London

Published by Rowman & Littlefield
A wholly owned subsidiary of The Rowman & Littlefield Publishing Group, Inc.
4501 Forbes Boulevard, Suite 200, Lanham, Maryland 20706
www.rowman.com

Unit A, Whitacre Mews, 26-34 Stannary Street, London SE11 4AB

British Library Cataloguing in Publication Information Available

Library of Congress Cataloging-in-Publication Data
Names: Hensler, Paul, 1956– author.
Title: The new boys of summer : baseball's radical transformation in the late
    sixties / Paul Hensler.
Description: Lanham : Rowman & Littlefield, [2017] | Includes bibliographical
    references and index.
Identifiers: LCCN 2017009588 (print) | LCCN 2017029964 (ebook) | ISBN
    9781538102602 (electronic) | ISBN 9781538102596 (hardback : alk. paper)
Subjects: LCSH: Baseball—United States—History—20th century.
Classification: LCC GV863.A1 (ebook) | LCC GV863.A1 H469 2017 (print) | DDC
    796.35709046—dc23
LC record available at https://lccn.loc.gov/2017009588

Printed in the United States of America

For Donna

Contents

Preface

The decade of the 2010s has been marked by commemorations of many memorable events—good and bad—that occurred fifty years prior. From the formation of what would become classic rock 'n' roll groups to the tumultuous and tragic incidents of assassination and war, the 1960s were among the most compelling years in our nation's history; a period during which the innocence of Americana and American life was torn away to expose a country that at times was in abject upheaval. It has been argued that the beginning of the sixties was simply an extension of the 1950s and that the *real* 1960s did not commence until halfway through that decade. The obvious demarcation implied is that the sixties figuratively began when US Marines landed en masse in South Vietnam in March of 1965 to wage yet another battle in the continuing Cold War.

On the American home front, society was undergoing a series of dynamic changes that also took root during the fifties. The clamor for civil rights continued to intensify, and culture in the United States experienced shifts—seismic at times—as consumerism blossomed from coast to coast. Caught up in this sea change, for better or worse, was Major League Baseball, which was forced not only to meet the demands of fans nationwide but also to keep up with the times and face direct challenges posed to its status as the national pastime. Baseball faced stiff competition from other professional sports, especially football, and could no longer afford to be complacent in assuming that a nearly century-long tradition of action on the diamond was always going to be foremost in the mind of the American fan. The manner in which baseball addressed those challenges would determine the degree to which it would succeed or fail in the coming years. Indeed, as the end of the 1960s drew near and with the search for a new commissioner to replace the dethroned William Eckert underway, the *Sporting News* opined that the major leagues had to develop "a new master plan for the game's survival."[1]

Keeping in mind the plight of baseball and the zeitgeist of the late 1960s, I have chosen to examine key issues confronting the game, with special attention paid to those occurring in the time frame of two vital years: 1968 and 1969. At a 2008 historical symposium, "The Legacy of 1968," I presented a paper that gave an overview of baseball during that turbulent year. Within the pages of this book, however, I probe more deeply the aspects that held currency in the transformation of the game at the dawn of the 1970s.

The brief opening chapter touches on three events that occurred late in the 1968 baseball season and place the era in an appropriate context with regard to the state of the game. Thereafter, each chapter is devoted to an individual topic that will help the reader gain a better understanding of the forces that shaped baseball as the calendar changed from 1968 to 1969 and why they were so significant. Despite this self-imposed two-year limit, I believe that the delineation of these subjects offers valuable insight to the game's status, and taken collectively they demonstrate that in 1968 baseball ended its mid-twentieth-century stodginess and in 1969 began to more than hold its own against the trials imposed upon it by other sports and remain at the forefront of America's sporting culture.

This success came at a price and would be attained with difficulty, yet baseball brought itself into a new modern era and solidified its foundation for future gains in the ensuing decades. That said, however, there are instances in which a broader time frame becomes more informative. Particularly for the topics of labor, stadium construction, and information technology, stepping back to the earlier part of the 1960s provides a better context rather than trying to start the narrative—as well as the clock, so to speak—nearer to the end of the decade.

But 1968 and 1969 provided their own share of feats and deeds that have secured their places in history. To explain the shifts taking place in baseball during these two formative years, this book will cover a host of subjects. Following the introductory chapter, major factors significantly impacting the national pastime are presented, beginning with the expansion of both the American and National leagues for the 1969 season, which restored major-league baseball to Kansas City and introduced it to venues on the Pacific Coast as well as in Canada. A chapter outlining the general conditions for expansion is followed by separate chapters detailing the manner in which each league executed its plan to add new teams.

After the ousting of the maligned William Eckert as baseball commissioner in late 1968, Bowie Kuhn was soon named as his replacement, and the installation of Kuhn became pivotal in rescuing baseball from its torpor. On the labor front, strife between players and owners dated back to the earliest days of baseball's founding. Marvin Miller's naming as the director of the Major League Baseball Players Association was instrumental to the cause of those he was hired to serve and set the stage for future battles with the ranks of ownership. Meantime, the culture of baseball was affected by events at home and abroad. Domestic racial issues, the war in Vietnam, assassinations of prominent public figures, youthful rebellion, drug use, and the growing medium of television each placed their imprint on the game just as the national pastime was about to celebrate its centennial.

Baseball also bade farewell to some longtime members of its fraternity following the 1968 season, as a new crop of star players and managers stepped onto the big stage. Expansion spawned not only new teams but also new divisions, creating hope for clubs thirsting to escape the second division and contend for a postseason playoff berth. The new divisional alignment in both leagues was accompanied by major changes in rules governing key aspects of the game that were implemented in 1969. Baseball desperately sought to revitalize offensive output as an antidote to the dearth of run production in 1968, which became known as "The Year of the Pitcher."

These significant updates would be played out in new, modern stadiums that were slowly replacing their outdated predecessors. *Multipurpose* became an operative word for these arenas, and the covering of new playing fields with a material called AstroTurf punctuated the coming age of plastics. Lastly, rapid developments in information technology facilitated the processing of increasingly large amounts of data. Baseball moved into a computer age that opened new avenues for marketing the game to fans near and far, and also led to the breakthrough debut of Macmillan's *The Baseball Encyclopedia*.

These issues exemplify the fits and starts that attended Major League Baseball's crossing of a threshold, its movement from a pair of old-style, ten-team leagues into a new divisional era that would later transform into the game we know today. An earlier generation of players became venerated as the Boys of Summer, and they continue to hold their rightful place in the game's legend and lore. But in the late 1960s an updated version of those characters made its own mark as radical transformation placed indelible stamps upon the national pastime. While the playing of the game itself remained familiar, baseball nonetheless took on a new appearance through dint of modernization. The narrative of this book will resonate with those who witnessed these happenings firsthand as well as those who wish to learn more about how baseball braved the trials it faced at the close of one of America's most dynamic decades.

Acknowledgments

The creation of any historical literary work is not done in a vacuum, and this book is no different in that regard. While the author is charged with handling the heavy lifting, the supporting cast behind the scenes provides an invaluable service on several key fronts that add so much to the success of the project. Assistance can come from near and far, in big and small measures, and at various stages along the way. All of it, you can rest assured, is greatly appreciated by me.

In the earliest days of the formulation of this book, Eugene Leach, history and American studies professor emeritus at Trinity College in Hartford, Connecticut, and Jean Hastings Ardell of the Society for American Baseball Research (SABR) were happy to review and make suggestions about the opening of the book, which can at times be an onerous challenge to any author. The official historian for Major League Baseball, John Thorn; fellow SABRite and Connectican Bill Ryczek; and author Paul Dickson were also present at this time.

On the journey of researching, Francie Berger, Cheryl Chamberlin, and Lisa Kuraska at my local library—Hall Memorial Library in Ellington, Connecticut—were kind in handling interlibrary loan requests. Jacob Pomrenke of SABR was helpful with that group's information, and Frank Houdek, professor emeritus at Southern Illinois University Law School and a colleague at the annual Cooperstown Symposium on Baseball and American Culture, directed me to some valuable material for the last chapter. A rewarding detour during work on race, war, and politics put me in touch with Martin Gedra of the National Archives in College Park, Maryland, while Jessica Pigza and Tal Nadan at the New York Public Library's Brooke Russell Astor Reading Room for Rare Books and Manuscripts efficiently handled my appointment there. My thanks also to Brad Snyder at the University of Wisconsin–Madison, as well as Michelle McCarthy and Marika Hashimoto at New York University's Tamiment Library.

With deserved and due respect to the above, I still have to save my loudest applause for those at the A. Bartlett Giamatti Center at the National Baseball Hall of Fame and Museum in Cooperstown, New York. For those doing any kind of research in the field of baseball, there is no finer repository of information than that which lies under the auspices of librarian Jim Gates and research manager Matt Rothenberg, but here I give special recognition to manuscript archivist Claudette Scrafford and research assistant Cassidy Lent, who cheerfully and deftly handled my research ventures to Cooperstown. My thanks also at the Hall of Fame to John Horne and Kelli Bogan, whose photographs enhance the narrative of these pages.

Regarding feedback to confirm that I got the story right in key sections of the narrative where my expertise is not as strong as it is in others, I tip my hat to Ed Edmonds, professor emeritus of law at the University of Notre Dame, and David Bohmer, professor emeritus at DePauw University—both also Cooperstown Symposium confreres—who kindly answered my critiquing requests. A nod also goes to Kevin FitzMaurice for lending his technical expertise to assist the marketing aspect of this book.

One slightly different credit is worth sharing as well. During the course of my work on this book, I undertook several minor side projects for SABR, and these diversions fortuitously put me in contact with Bill Nowlin, who has written and edited more about baseball than I could ever hope to dream about. My work on these essays meant that Bill was first to review these works, and given the very positive feedback I received from him in all cases, I gained more and more confidence in my writing, whatever the subject might be. Also, I express my appreciation for those at my publisher, Rowman & Littlefield, who helped greatly with their editorial assistance. Jessica McCleary, Meg French, and Mike Kopf were invaluable to smoothing out the rough spots and blemishes that found their way into the narrative no matter how hard I tried to keep them to a minimum.

And—last but not least—are kudos due two women whose roles in this project were central to its success. Christen Karniski, acquisitions editor at Rowman & Littlefield, was always quick and informative with her replies to my various questions, but any good husband knows that his wife is the true Polaris, providing the beacon of all good things. Donna, my spouse of thirty years and counting, has been my biggest booster behind all the work that has been devoted to this book, which serves as a wonderful springboard to keep moving forward.

CHAPTER 1

At the Threshold

At Tiger Stadium in Detroit on the afternoon of September 14, 1968, the home team's starting pitcher, on the precipice of history, paced anxiously in his dugout in the bottom of the ninth. Down by a score of 4–3, the Tigers staged an emotional two-run rally climaxed by Willie Horton's single that allowed a joyful Mickey Stanley to score the winning run against the Oakland Athletics. The Tigers' victory was their ninety-fifth of the season, but the greater significance concerned the game's winning pitcher.

Entering that day's contest with a record of twenty-nine wins and five losses, Dennis Dale McLain was on the verge of becoming the first pitcher in thirty-four years to reach the thirty-win plateau. Horton's late heroics added to a surreal, redemptive season experienced by the Tigers following the team's effort of 1967, when they came up short in one of the wildest pennant races of all time.

But as the 1968 campaign progressed, it held an increasingly special aura for the Tigers as they sought their first American League (AL) pennant since 1945. In a postgame curtain call, both Denny McLain and the hometown fans were in a forgiving mood on this heady afternoon. Just four months earlier, McLain had decried Detroit supporters as "the biggest front-running fans in the world . . . the worst in the league."[1] But the best remedy for healing such a rift—a command performance by the villain-turned-hero—was clearly demonstrated. Demanding an encore by the game's latest thirty-game winner, the cheering crowd was rewarded when McLain emerged from the dugout and returned the love with waves and blown kisses. In the elation of the moment, all was forgiven.

Ten days after McLain's milestone achievement, the New York Mets were in the process of closing out their final road trip of the 1968 season at Atlanta Stadium, and settling near their accustomed place in the standings: the basement

1

of the National League (NL). Under manager Gil Hodges, who had come to Shea Stadium after four-plus seasons at the helm of the Washington Senators, the Amazin' Mets were destined only to equal their modest ninth-place finish of 1966, yet the seventy-three wins they achieved in 1968 would prove to be the most in the franchise's young history.

During his inaugural campaign in New York, Hodges began to skillfully shepherd a bevy of youthful talent percolating up from the Mets' farm system. But the quietly fretting, chain-smoking skipper complained of chest pains in the early innings of the September 24 game against the Braves. Retreating to the visitors' clubhouse, he was examined by trainer Gus Mauch and Braves physician Dr. Harry Rogers, both of whom convinced Hodges that he should be taken to Crawford W. Long Hospital. With a diagnosis revealing a coronary thrombosis, a lengthy recovery was in the foreseeable future for Hodges. A rumored upcoming trade that would place Dick Allen, the peevish slugger of the Philadelphia Phillies, in a Mets uniform to bolster the offense, impressed as counterintuitive to Hodges's rehabilitation.

After returning to his home in Brooklyn late in the year, Hodges gradually improved his health through weight loss, cessation of smoking, and a change in diet. Repairing to Florida for the rest of the winter enabled him to embark on a walking program and prepare for the 1969 season. With spring training just two months away, Hodges drew inspiration from Danny Murtaugh and Birdie Tebbetts, big-league managers who had also suffered heart attacks, and he was given a clean bill of health to resume a limited regimen of his accustomed tasks. "I won't pitch batting practice again," Hodges announced, "but I will manage the club."[2]

The commissioner of Major League Baseball plodded through the end of 1968, hardly buoyed by the various missteps he had made during the year. William Eckert's most recent gaffe was his decision on October 6 to allow the fourth game of the World Series between the St. Louis Cardinals and Detroit Tigers to be played despite a persistent rain that delayed the beginning of the contest and interrupted it again in the third inning. Cardinals ace Bob Gibson complained about "all that mud on my shoes, and it was heavy out there."[3] Rather than displaying the best that baseball had to offer during the Fall Classic, its showcase event devolved into a stilted game of chicken between the contestants.

The Cardinals opened with a pair of runs in the top of the first inning, added two more tallies in their half of the third, and did everything possible to speed the contest up so as to make it an official game. Meanwhile, the Tigers countered by stalling for time in the hope that the poor weather would force the commissioner's hand to call a merciful end to the contest. Oblivious to the rain that drenched many in attendance, including Vice President Hubert Humphrey,

Eckert insisted that the game continue and then virtually muzzled the umpires after the final out was made by permitting postgame interview access to only two reporters: Murray Chass of the Associated Press and Milt Richman of UPI. In a change of bad-weather policy for the Series, the umpires, who normally had full control over temporarily halting play and postponing the game, had ceded their authority to the commissioner.

Eckert, depicted by one scribe as "conscientious and sincere but totally uninformed for baseball's highest position," had already overseen Major League Baseball's lame reaction to a pair of historic blows suffered by the United States earlier in the year.[4] Baseball's ham-fisted reaction to the slayings of Dr. Martin Luther King Jr. and presidential candidate Robert Kennedy were shameful entries in Eckert's dossier, now joined by his presiding over a World Series contest made farcical by the Cardinals' speedup tactics and the Tigers' delaying shenanigans.

—⁂—

The Charles Dickens trope—"It was the best of times, it was the worst of times"—also applies to the years of 1968 and 1969. This was a volatile era during which visions of a better America were thought to have vanished, and a time when the world as a whole was jolted by unrest. With a full fifty years having passed since the landmark year of 1968, a similar statement can be made about the national pastime.

Upheavals in American politics, economics, society, and culture during 1968 also had an impact on Major League Baseball, some of them in ways not envisioned during the early part of the 1960s. The King and Kennedy assassinations, increasingly vociferous protests against the Vietnam War, continuing racial tension, and a deepening divide between older and younger Americans—labeled the "generation gap"—fostered doubt, mistrust, and uncertainty as to what direction the country was heading. As if the nation needed a respite from the tragedies and unrest of the previous twelve months, some relief was provided as the year drew to a close. NASA's Apollo 8 mission was launched on December 21 and succeeded in becoming the first manned space flight to orbit the moon. During a live television broadcast, commander Frank Borman along with fellow astronauts Bill Anders and Jim Lovell took the opportunity to read poignant verses from the book of Genesis while in lunar orbit, after which the crew "fired their rockets and headed back to this planet of blue seas, rich vegetation, and endless strife."[5]

An argument can be advanced that with America having survived the throes of 1968, our nation could endure and persevere under any conditions. Reeling but still standing, the United States began 1969 with a new administration in Washington headed by Richard M. Nixon, yet the bugbear of Vietnam refused to go away.

A program called "Vietnamization" aimed to turn the American role of running the war over to the South Vietnamese, but this shift in policy had difficulty gaining traction because of the heavy reliance of South Vietnam on all manner of American aid. The Cold War, far from over, also continued, yet through all the angst of war and fear of the threats posed by Communism, the United States reveled in what was perhaps the greatest technical achievement of the twentieth century. In July Apollo 11 completed the mission, envisioned by the late President John F. Kennedy, of landing a man on the moon and returning him safely to Earth. The apotheosis of the American spirit was on full display for the entire world to see, and this accomplishment delivered a healthy boost to an American morale that had been greatly damaged in 1968.

By and large, racial violence had settled down because the riots of earlier in the decade had forced local governments to address more forthrightly the problems concerning minorities. A rise in black voter registration also encouraged some African Americans in more heavily populated areas to run for office, but African Americans continued to feel the sting of discrimination. Jim Crow was not going away quickly despite civil rights legislation enacted in 1964 and 1965.

The conclusion of the 1960s also witnessed another inescapable change in the culture of American society. Since the 1950s, more and more women had been breaking the mold of gender stereotyping, and by 1963 they were further emboldened by the release of Betty Friedan's opus, *The Feminine Mystique*. In the world of collegiate sports, women's athletics struggled in vain for equality with men's programs in the years before Title IX was enacted. However, many colleges that had formerly been male-only institutions opened their doors for coeducational enrollment by the end of the decade, signaling a key victory for the women's rights movement.

The United States was hardly at peace by the end of 1969, but the country was in a less frenetic condition compared to 1968. A long, slow turning of the corner in race relations was in progress, yet moving into a new decade would still entail the shouldering of burdens acquired in the old decade, primarily the war in Vietnam and the fallout from the protests against it. Over these two years, baseball was enduring its own transformation that was affected by contemporaneous issues in America as well as demands that forced it to confront the modern age into which it was inexorably moving.

—〰—

To this day Denny McLain remains the last pitcher to win thirty games in one season and may be the last ever to do so. Since 1968 the evolution of baseball and the science of pitching have conspired to limit a pitcher's opportunity to achieve so many victories. It can only be left to speculation whether, had Gil Hodges not recovered from his late-season heart attack, another manager would have been capable of leading the Mets to the astounding success they reaped in 1969. That triumph had a salubrious effect on baseball's largest market, where interest had been waning since the end of the great Yankee dynasty in 1964. Bumbling commissioner William Eckert was unseated in December of 1968, and the installment of his successor proved to be one of baseball's most critical turning points. Few would foresee Eckert's replacement becoming a Hall of Fame inductee, and even fewer might have guessed that baseball would gainfully meet the challenges of its primary competitor, professional football.

Moving from 1968 into 1969, baseball reached a juncture at which an old version of the national pastime gave way to a new, modern era punctuated by other changes that were radical in nature. The post-1968 version of baseball proved equal to the task of holding forth despite the difficulties it faced at that point in its history. The road it traveled to remain a favorite among fans contained perils and uncertainties, but baseball also garnered rewards once it crossed that chronological threshold.

CHAPTER 2

The Demand to Expand

Major League Baseball's inaugural expansion of 1961 and 1962 had been executed in what can charitably be termed a haphazard manner. On October 17, 1960, the National League announced plans to add a pair of franchises for the 1962 season: one in New York, as a corrective to the dual departure in 1957 of the Brooklyn Dodgers and New York Giants, the other in Houston, which would be a brand-new venue for major-league baseball. Barely one week later the American League stunned the baseball world by revealing its own expansion plan for 1961, which would add teams in Washington, DC (to replace the Senators, who had earlier fled west to become the Minnesota Twins), and Los Angeles, allowing the AL to establish its own foothold in the Southern California market. Although both leagues intended to bring the national pastime to a broader fan base by 1962, the *New York Times* commented that "the American Leaguers apparently were determined to beat the National League to the punch" by employing "lightning moves" to stake their claim first.[1]

While baseball maintained its status as the preeminent national sport through the 1950s, the dawn of the 1960s saw competition from other athletic enterprises begin to erode the national pastime's grip on the American public. In 1960 the formation of the American Football League (AFL) not only created competition for the established National Football League (NFL) but also unwittingly set the stage for a future merger between the two. By decade's end this combined force, along with the growing interest in collegiate football, was relegating baseball's popularity to second-class status.

As 1967 was drawing to a close, baseball team owners may have felt increasingly ill at ease watching the birth of the American Basketball Association (ABA), the addition of new clubs to the National Basketball Association (NBA), expansion in the NFL and the AFL, and the doubling in size of the National Hockey League (NHL). With more sporting endeavors diverting fans' attention and potentially siphoning money away from the national pastime, baseball was at last compelled to take decisive action to modernize or be condemned by loss of revenue and market share among sports enthusiasts.

The Scramble to Choose Sites

Within baseball's realm, Charlie Finley of the Kansas City Athletics created a heightened sense of urgency to force the American League to take action regarding the addition of new teams. After years of trying to find a new city for his team, Finley at last struck a deal to shift the Athletics to Oakland for the 1968 season.[2]

The American League, whose owners needed to sanction the move, convened a special meeting on October 18, 1967, to hear Finley's case for transferring. A contingent from Kansas City, which included Mayor Ilus Davis and Missouri senator Stuart Symington, was invited to make an argument for keeping the club. Working to the advantage of the Kansas City interests were the support that Athletics fans showed, despite Finley's alleged indifference to the team, and the city's $42 million bond issue that would allow construction of the Jackson County sports complex (later called the Harry S. Truman Sports Complex), thus providing a new stadium for the baseball team as a replacement for the dated Municipal Stadium.

With claims of "substantial financial losses" and "danger of bankruptcy" should his team be forced to remain in Kansas City, Finley bolstered his argument by presenting a study that indicated a move to be in his best interests. After a first ballot by AL team owners fell one short of the seven favorable votes Finley needed for the approval he sought, a second poll produced the 7–1 outcome— with two abstentions—permitting him to abscond to the West Coast. A change in position by New York Yankees president Michael Burke tipped the vote in Finley's favor.[3] The American League promised to fill the void in Kansas City by putting an expansion club there within three years.

Clearly enraged by the loss of the team and the proposed three-year wait for its replacement, Symington vented to his colleagues on the floor of the Senate, condemning Finley as "the All-American disgrace to sport" and threatening to strip baseball of its exemption from federal antitrust laws. Davis stated his intent to seek an injunction to prevent the Athletics' departure due to the anticipated length of time before the city would be awarded a new team. But because of the diligence in the senator's endeavors to keep the Athletics from moving and his good standing with many American League owners—to say nothing of his political standing as a former candidate for United States president in 1960— Symington brokered a deal with the AL to have a new team installed in Kansas

City after a vacancy of only one year. Team owners had "pledged an irrevocable covenant" to Davis that a new team would be awarded to Kansas City by March 1, 1968, and made ready to take the field for the opening of the 1969 season.[4] The major proviso was a commitment by the expansion team's owner—unknown at that time—to a long-term lease for the new stadium before construction commenced. By mid-January 1968 Ewing Kauffman emerged from among several parties as the owner of the new Kansas City franchise.

The naming of a replacement for the departed Athletics compelled the American League to add a companion franchise to maintain an even number of teams. Finley had already explored the Pacific Northwest as a potential new site for the Athletics before opting for Oakland. However, Finley's attempt piqued the interest of the American League to pursue Seattle as a venue for major-league baseball. Columnist Dick Young reported that the National League likewise intended to court Seattle for expansion and was trying to direct the AL toward the greater Dallas–Fort Worth metropolis, which had also been the focus of Finley's attention just a few years earlier.[5] Groups from Seattle and Dallas–Fort Worth were given the opportunity—on short notice—to make presentations at the same October meeting where Finley was given approval to move to Oakland. A Seattle contingent, led by Pacific Coast League president Dewey Soriano, his brother Max, and William Daley, won the franchise over the Dallas group headed by AFL mogul Lamar Hunt, whose Dallas Texans moved in 1963 to become recast as the Kansas City Chiefs. The owners of the new Seattle and Kansas City franchises were assessed $5.25 million each to enter the American League, an amount based on a fee of $175,000 for each of the thirty players to be drafted from the rosters of the ten existing AL clubs.

Swift action on the part of the American League to address the void in Kansas City left the National League temporarily high and dry. Seattle was prime among the sites considered by the NL, but with the Emerald City no longer available, the Senior Circuit was "somewhat paralyzed, and nettled, by the unexpected loss of the Seattle territory. "The National League had been content to let expansion occur at a pace of its choosing, with 1971 set as an almost casual deadline. But with its hand now forced by the Junior Circuit, the NL jumped into the fray so as not to lose more ground. In mid-April 1968 the league followed suit, despite feeling that it was "stampeded" into taking the decision to add two clubs, and there was also fear that a greater initial number of AL teams would create an imbalance over the National League and secure for the AL an upper hand in acquiring more playing talent.[6] Nearly six weeks later the NL announced the selection of sites for its newest franchises, Montreal and San Diego. The new ownership groups would have to pay $10 million each to enter the league, nearly twice the amount charged by the American League, with the franchise fee of $4 million augmented by a fee of $200,000 for each of the thirty players that each new team would draft from other NL teams. While San Diego's entry was sanctioned by Los Angeles Dodgers owner Walter O'Malley and drew little criticism—the city's new 50,000-seat stadium was ready for a tenant—the awarding of a team to Montreal provoked anguish among the bidders who lost out.

The *Milwaukee Sentinel*'s blaring headline of May 28—NO NL TEAM FOR CITY—made no attempt to conceal the disappointment felt by many who hoped for a new franchise to replace the Braves after their controversial departure to Atlanta at the close of the 1965 season. "Early speculation had created an air of optimism among local backers who were banking heavily on the program Milwaukee presented to the league—a stadium of major league size, proven baseball enthusiasm, and adequate financing," the newspaper reported.[7] The vivid display of support included nine Chicago White Sox contests hosted in Milwaukee that attracted 264,297 fans in 1968, which provided a significant contribution to the total of 803,775 the White Sox drew for the entire season. But there was lingering animosity over the legal wrangling that resulted from the Braves' shift to Atlanta, and with unanimity required among the existing National League clubs to approve the awarding of a new franchise, most NL owners believed that Braves president Bill Bartholomay was firm in his objection to adding a club in the Braves' prior city.

Just as Bartholomay was loath to see baseball in Milwaukee, so too was Houston Astros owner Judge Roy Hofheinz opposed to the granting of a National League team to a venue just two hundred miles from where his team played. Lamar Hunt pursued a franchise for the greater Dallas–Fort Worth region, which also featured a new stadium that was able to be expanded with a second tier. But Hofheinz stood his ground, to the dismay of the Dallas promoters, one of whom bitterly remarked, "We think baseball made a mistake to let one man . . . stand in the way of what's good for baseball."[8]

The third party that failed in its attempt to secure an expansion club was a group from Buffalo, New York, whose chief spokesman was attorney Bob Swados. One week before the NL named the new teams, expectations ran high in Buffalo when the Erie County Legislature agreed to terms with Major Leagues for Buffalo, Inc., for a lease on a proposed new $50 million domed stadium. A further enticement to adding a new club in Buffalo was the team's ability to draw on the eighth-largest regional television market in North America, which included Toronto, Ontario. Swados was confident his group would bring baseball to another outpost on the shores of Lake Erie—"They're not going to turn down a domed stadium in the Buffalo market, period," he averred—but he was disabused of his grand notion when the final selections were announced.[9] A huge disadvantage that played hob with the Swados group pertained to War Memorial

Stadium, which was situated in an undesirable section of Buffalo. Use of this ballpark would have been necessary until the new stadium could be completed, and the National League expressed its disapproval by choosing to avoid the city entirely.

As the NL was debating the choice of cities, a radical proposal was advanced by Jim Toomey, a front office assistant with the St. Louis Cardinals. In Toomey's plan a pair of twelve-team leagues would exist for the 1969 season, but then in 1970 the National League would be pared to its original eight teams, the American League would follow suit, and a third league would be created from all the expansion clubs—including those eventually chosen for San Diego and Montreal—created since 1960. Interleague play would become a new feature, with scheduling still adhering to a 162-game format.[10] While this idea did not come to pass, it nonetheless hinted at changes to baseball's structure—three divisions and interleague contests—that would occur decades later.

Embarking on their journeys into Major League Baseball, Montreal and San Diego represented geographic extremes, the former being the first franchise north of the United States border, the latter taking up residence in the nation's southwestern-most major city. The San Diego ownership group was limited in its membership because financing of the team was firmly in the hands of C. Arnholt Smith, a local banker and businessman who was a friend of Richard Nixon. Partnering with Smith was longtime Dodgers executive E. J. "Buzzie" Bavasi, who served as the general manager of the Dodgers under Walter O'Malley and now joined San Diego as club president.

In Montreal the initial backing for the expansion club seemed to be as solid as that of its new National League companion. However, the Canadian ownership stumbled early and often after the city was granted the franchise. Entrepreneurs from various businesses—including construction, distilling, and print media—pooled resources in the hopes of fulfilling its financial obligations to the NL, but two major drawbacks arose quickly and nearly doomed the club. The loss of a major contributor and a second lesser partner by late July kept the group from raising all the necessary funding—to say nothing of the handicap posed by the difference in value between the Canadian and American dollar—which meant the Montreal financiers were saddled with a roughly 8 percent deficit. In addition, the city lacked a stadium suitable for major-league baseball with only two tenuous options available to use until a bona fide ballpark could be constructed. The money problem was resolved, but lingering controversy over the stadium issue was another great concern. As 1968 progressed with time running out to find a playing venue to open the 1969 season, there was fear that Montreal might lose its brand-new team to Milwaukee before it could assemble its roster.[11] The stadium crisis was finally averted when agreement was reached in mid-October to hastily renovate Jarry Park.

To Split or Not to Split

Disputes over finances and stadiums were not the only problems confronting baseball's expansion. With the leagues now comprising a dozen teams each, decisions had to be made about whether to split the circuits into two six-team divisions or operate as single twelve-team entities. As if to emphasize the differences between the leagues, it was no surprise that the AL and NL were at odds over how the divisional issue should be handled.

Proceeding with purpose, the American League announced that it would form two new divisions with a geographical alignment. An added round of postseason playoffs—a best three-out-of-five series—between the winners of each division would determine the league champion. The Junior Circuit quickly sequestered its clubs in the Northeast—Boston, New York, Baltimore, Washington, Cleveland, and Detroit—into the new AL East, while the remaining six teams in the Midwest and on the Pacific Coast—Chicago, Minnesota, Kansas City, Seattle, Oakland, and California—were placed in the AL West.

Twins owner Calvin Griffith mused on the practicality of having two divisions, each with its own respective pennant race, rather than simply incorporating the two expansion clubs into a unified twelve-team entity. "It was a situation where after expansion we'd have too many losers [in one league]," said Griffith. Never shy about tending to the finances of his business, Griffith saw better opportunities for profits when the number of losers could be minimized and the number of potential pennant races in each league doubled. Because of his seniority among American League club owners, Griffith had a choice as to which division he preferred his team to be placed in. Being part of the AL East would have the benefit of playing more games against teams that were better established as well as avoiding—to a lesser degree—the relative inconvenience of traveling to the West Coast and abiding a two-hour time zone change for those road games. At the time the split was made, Griffith voted against placing his team in the AL West, favoring the placement of Kansas City in the East and Detroit in the West. But he later reflected—and with much hindsight, since the Twins were only a year removed from having nearly won the AL crown in 1967—that placement in the West provided the benefit of competing in a division hobbled by the presence of both new expansion teams. "I thought it would be better for the Twins to be in the West. We had a better chance of winning," said Griffith, who, with his eye on the bottom line, added, "If you win, you're gonna make money. . . . It turned out to be pretty darn good for us."[12]

These assignments made sense when one looked a map of the United States, but not all club owners agreed with the arrangement. Also objecting to their placement in the West were the Chicago White Sox, who would rather have competed directly against five mainline eastern teams. The ChiSox felt especially jilted because, while they were the only AL West club to have remained in the same city for more than fourteen years, the lack of seniority on the part of owners Arthur and John Allyn hampered their ability to determine their choice of division.

The next issue concerned the number of regular-season games to be played. One plan called for a balanced schedule in which each team would face its eleven opponents in seven home games and seven road games, for a total of 154 contests. However, the format adopted in late May 1968 mandated eighteen games against each of the five divisional rivals and eleven games against each team in the other division, for a total of 156. This shortening of the regular season from its usual 162 games made an accommodation for the new playoff series to determine the AL champion without compromising the approximate—and accustomed—start date of the World Series. Once again trying to make their voice heard, the White Sox requested the balanced schedule so that Chicago would have fewer contests on the West Coast—twenty-one road games instead of twenty-seven—which would in turn lessen the impact on local viewers and listeners following the action of late-night games in Anaheim, Oakland, and Seattle.

In the Senior Circuit adherence to the tradition of a single league regardless of the number of teams appeared to be the order of the day. When National League owners met, their daylong convention produced a united front. NL president Warren Giles, who "adamantly opposed expansion" at this time but "recognized the necessity of the two leagues coordinating all their efforts for their mutual benefit," announced that his league would remain a single group of twelve teams with no separation by division, and there was genuine concern that the National and American leagues would operate in a diverse manner. Commissioner William Eckert was willing to allow the leagues to take different tacks for 1969 and then review how each fared before possibly forcing the NL to split into two divisions. Still, the commissioner "impressed upon the two Leagues the urgent need to move ahead jointly and uniformly," and, showing some semblance of business acumen, implored them to consider that "the long term advantage in resolving their problems would be far more important than any short term advantages that some clubs would have." Giles stated his case against divisions, contending that it would look bad for a team without the best won-loss record at season's end to advance to the World Series. But American League president Joe Cronin was vociferous in opining that under a one-league scheme, there existed the potential for far too many also-rans that would hurt the stability of the game. "You can't sell a twelfth-place team!" Cronin barked, emphasizing the point that poorly performing clubs that had little hope of moving ahead of so many competitors stood to lose not only ballgames but also market value.[13]

In late June at a meeting of Major League Baseball's Executive Council hosted by Commissioner Eckert in New York, the National League heard the arguments for the divisional format, and it was recommended that the American League follow the 162-game schedule in use since 1961 rather than its proposed 156 contests. By July 10, the NL—controversially—saw the wisdom of divisional formatting, and the AL upheld the full complement of a 162-game season that scheduled eighteen games against intradivision opponents and twelve contests against teams in the other division.

M. Donald Grant, chairman of the board of the New York Mets, was thought to be staunchly opposed to splitting the NL, but he instead offered a novel approach to a divisional format. His proposal called for two groups of teams to be determined based on the record of the previous season. One division would include the club finishing at the top of the league, along with those clubs with the third-, fifth-, seventh-, ninth-, and eleventh-best records; the other would have those teams with the second-, fourth-, sixth-, eighth-, tenth-, and twelfth-best records. By reseeding the divisions each year and playing a balanced or mixed schedule—165 games (fifteen against eleven opponents) or 162 (fifteen contests versus eight opponents, another fourteen against three opponents)— Grant theorized that his method "would never develop a weak division" because of the annual shuffling process.[14]

Grant's proposition was not used, but the National League did elect to use unbalanced scheduling and created two divisions that did not hew entirely to geographic orientation. Although they were labeled as East and West, there was obvious disparity, notably in the West division. The East was formed with New York, Philadelphia, Montreal, and Pittsburgh, along with Midwestern entries St. Louis and Chicago. Although the West contained the expected trio of Pacific Coast franchises—Los Angeles, San Francisco, and San Diego—as well as Houston, the inclusion of Atlanta and Cincinnati, both in the eastern time zone, may have been a surprise. However, the Braves were glad to have the Dodgers and Giants in their division, since they were among the most popular teams who visited Atlanta Stadium, and the Mets had the good luck to find themselves in the East with the Cubs, presaging the fateful pennant race that would unfold in 1969.

Having tackled the selection of new teams and logistics of divisional formats, the next order of business dealt with the stocking of the expansion rosters. The AL and NL conducted their respective drafts within each league in mid-October, with Kansas City and Seattle choosing from among their ten AL counterparts, Montreal and San Diego picking from their ten NL brethren. Each existing team was allowed to protect fifteen players, while the remaining "leftovers, outcasts, and marginal players" were exposed to the new clubs. Upon losing a player to an expansion team, a club could then add more players to its protected list, and a computer was provided by IBM for use by the American League to "provide the interested parties . . . with a wealth of instant information," including updated lists of protected players and the burgeoning rosters of the expansion teams as they made their selections.[15]

Picks by Montreal and Seattle leaned toward veteran players who could more readily compete at the major-league level, but Kansas City and San Diego favored younger players and "unknown kids" who would be counted on to produce in the future.[16] At the completion of six rounds in each league, the four teams were as fully staffed as they could be at that point in their brief existence, and they were then at liberty to adjust their rosters via trade. With personnel infrastructures in place, the expansion clubs' pennant aspirations would be put to the test come the spring of 1969, but the clubs could be forgiven if little was expected despite all the effort they were devoting to establishing themselves.

The first big-league expansions of 1961 and 1962 yielded four teams whose seasons, by the end of 1968, were littered with loss totals in the nineties, not least among them the Washington Senators, with four years of one hundred losses or more, and the New York Mets, who reached the dubious century mark in defeats on five occasions. Some team owners had sounded an alarm over the caliber of talent available even before the expansion drafts took place, and there was genuine concern that if minor-league systems were stretched too thin, they would not be able to cultivate and supply players capable of performing at the highest level. Even as Opening Day of 1968 loomed, the *Sporting News* presciently mused, "Is major league baseball expanding too fast?"[17] As it turned out, the answer was not long in coming. Montreal still suffered from financial and stadium difficulties, and Seattle was about to embark on a maiden voyage that lasted all of one year. Bob Carpenter, owner of the Philadelphia Phillies, had counseled a patient approach to expansion, especially in the National League, to allow more time to be devoted to ensuring that those interests who sought new franchises could pass muster. His plea, however, was ignored.

In any event, baseball plunged ahead, patience be damned. There were teams to be added, politicians to be appeased, leagues to be split, new franchise fees—in the tens of millions of dollars—to be reaped by the existing clubs, and baseball's diminishing popularity to be confronted. Had Stuart Symington not raised a fuss about the loss of baseball in Kansas City upon Charlie Finley's abdication in 1967, the expansion script might have been written differently—or certainly at another time.

CHAPTER 3

American League Expansion
ONE UP, ONE DOWN

The American League expansion clubs of 1969 came to represent the apotheosis and nadir of a new franchise's survival. In Kansas City a well-grounded local owner implemented a sound business plan with an eye on long-term success, and the community at once welcomed the fresh start of major-league baseball and bade good riddance to Charlie Finley, the reviled owner of the departed Athletics. Given new life, the enthusiasm at Municipal Stadium was palpable. But in Seattle it appeared that baseball clamored more for the city than the other way around. Denizens of the Pacific Northwest had to be persuaded that they wanted big-league baseball, and this uncomfortable arrangement quickly produced an embarrassing failure that left a bad taste in the mouths of many who were connected to this venture, be they fans, players, municipal leaders, or baseball executives. This debacle was rectified in the mid-1970s when the Seattle Mariners were born, but a long, tortuous road was traversed before baseball placed a stake firmly on the shore of Puget Sound.

A "Refreshing Personality" in Kansas City

Stuart Symington's tirade on the floor of the United States Senate on October 19, 1967, marked the denouement of his bitter farewell to Charlie Finley. The pledge he secured from American League club owners to ensure the return of a major-league club to Kansas City for the 1969 season was not a hollow gesture on the part of the AL, but once the franchise was granted came the heavy lifting of building the organization from the ground up, beginning with finding an owner committed to providing long-term stability. As 1967 drew to a close, five parties with vested interests in the Kansas City area were vying for the right to become the franchisee.

At the annual winter meetings in December, held this year in Mexico City, the league's Screening Committee entertained presentations from each group. Bankers Crosby Kemper Sr. and Richard Stern offered to purchase the club outright with an option to resell three-quarters of the team's stock to the general public, which created an incentive for fans to take title—at least in a limited way—of their new team. This plan would spread ownership across a broad spectrum of citizens, not unlike the method of financial backing used by the Green Bay Packers of the NFL. A second consortium, consisting of ten well-known entrepreneurs and respected leaders in local affairs, was fronted by E. F. Hutton vice president John Latshaw and offered to form either a corporation or a partnership, whichever the American League preferred. Single-ownership proposals were put forth by numerous well-heeled aspirants. Alex Barket was another local banker who dreamed of delivering a winning team to Kansas City, with construction company mogul Tudie Patti at his side to help him run the team. And another securities dealer, Paul Hamilton, expressed his desire to become the new club's owner. Also in the running was a pharmaceutical magnate with deep pockets and a penchant for racehorses. Ewing Kauffman, president of Marion Laboratories, was known for "his resourcefulness and dynamic personality," according to one observer, and his $50 million in Marion assets was sure to garner the attention of the Screening Committee.[1]

In early January 1968, at a ninety-minute session convened at the Hotel Muehlebach in Kansas City, the committee presented its findings to the American League owners and their representatives—a group that included Oakland vice president Jim Cutler substituting for Charlie Finley, who, coincidentally or not, was unable to attend due to supposed conflicts on his schedule. Emerging victorious from the pack was a native of Cass County, Missouri, whose seemingly endless ambition made him a successful businessman and, later in his life, a philanthropist. To understand the roots of Kansas City's new club owner is to understand how the new team would anchor itself as one of baseball's most stable franchises.

—⁂—

Born in 1916, Ewing Kauffman spent his formative years as a teenager during the Great Depression and came to appreciate the value of resourcefulness to survival in difficult times. Instilled with a work ethic and vital "self-assurance and love of learning" imparted especially by his mother, Kauffman took advantage of educational opportunities while diligently handling several roles at a laundry. He later had a brief foray into life insurance sales, but unlike Charlie Finley, who thrived in the insurance business, Kauffman found this to be an uncomfortable career path. The entry of the United States into World War II swept Kauffman into military service as a signalman with the navy, during which time he became

"Mr. K"—Ewing Kauffman, pharmaceutical entrepreneur and be-
loved owner of the Kansas City
Royals. *National Baseball Hall of
Fame Library, Cooperstown, NY.*

well versed with games of chance and reaped financial rewards—nearly $90,000 by his own estimation—from participation in card games.[2]

Upon returning to Kansas City after the war and reuniting with his wife—Ewing and Marguerite Blackshire had been secretly married prior to his naval stint—Kauffman realized that the wealth he had accumulated meant that there was no sense of urgency to return immediately to work. Taking his time to find employment to his liking, in 1947 he answered a help-wanted advertisement for a pharmaceutical salesman with Lincoln Laboratories of Decatur, Illinois. So adept did Kauffman become in this role that he quickly became the top vendor at Lincoln, much to the consternation of some company executives who felt he was making too much in commissions. In fact his earnings exceeded the salary of Lincoln's president, so Kauffman's sales territory was reduced in an effort to curb his income and soothe the ego of the embarrassed company prexy. Kauffman took umbrage at the move and acted to prevent any further insult by departing Lincoln to start his own company.

The volatility of Kauffman's risk in this new enterprise was assuaged by his success as a salesman for Lincoln, which had enabled him to gain the confidence of physicians to whom he had previously sold many products. With this customer base on hand, Kaufmann forged ahead in June 1950 as "the one and only salesman of Marion Laboratories," focusing not only on oral medications but also those requiring syringes. Using his own middle name for that of his upstart business, he admitted use of the word "laboratories" was overreaching at the time, since he really was acting as a salesman for existing products developed by other pharmaceutical concerns. After six months operating Marion out of his home, Kauffman experienced growing pains—in a positive sense—and was forced to relocate the business. Challenged by the need to build a qualified staff of salesmen, Kauffman carefully selected Jean Sperry and Bob Pruitt to join Marion. During his selection process Kauffman sometimes went so far as to interview the wife of a potential salesman in order to better evaluate the candidate and determine how willing the spouse might be to encourage her husband to succeed as a salesman. Even the jargon used to spur his staff to greater accomplishments was shot through with "the vocabulary of trench warfare, where salesmanship [was] equated with patriotism, and malingering with desertion."[3]

As business and profits climbed, Kauffman eventually turned Marion into a stock company and allowed it to venture into the creation of its own products, including one called OS-CAL, which was derived from calcium found in oyster shells. Sales blossomed throughout the 1950s, and Marion continued to expand its territory in the Midwest, relying on its sales force to vend what it considered to be products of the highest quality. But the burgeoning gains bore a tragic result for Kauffman when his wife passed away in what authorities ruled—perhaps charitably—an accidental death. Whether Marguerite felt pressured by an inability to keep pace with her indefatigable husband or became withdrawn as a reaction to Marion's increasing public presence in the business and medical community, she was found dead inside the family car, which was parked in an enclosed garage with its engine on. Now a widower with two children as 1960 drew to a close, Ewing Kauffman struggled to cope with the shock of his loss.

Just months after Marguerite's death, Kauffman's life took a dramatic turn when he met Muriel McBrien at a trade conference in Florida. A widow herself, and the well-educated daughter of accomplished Torontonian parents, Muriel was gainfully pursued by Kauffman. The couple married in February 1962, and each partner played well off the other's gregariousness, with Muriel receiving Ewing's blessing to become involved in the arts scene around the greater Kansas City area. As if to shun the elitism attendant with their accumulating wealth and increasing visibility in the community, they adopted the colloquial monikers of "Mr. K." and "Mrs. K." A bonhomie of what one company secretary termed "Marion Spirit" imbued the firm with "a caring environment" and made working under Kauffman a rewarding experience for many of his employees.[4] At the end of 1962 Marion introduced a new product called PAVABID, which further cemented the firm's reputation in the pharmaceutical industry. The company became publicly traded in August 1965, and by the end of the decade Marion Laboratories had grown to such proportions that it was listed on the New York Stock Exchange.

Kauffman's devotion to his company left little time for involvement in civic or recreational diversions, and his passion for baseball was reserved rather than avid. As Charlie Finley was wrangling his way out of Kansas City in late 1967, Cleveland Indians president Gabe Paul spoke at a local business meeting and described the importance of having a big-league franchise in one's municipality. Present at that meeting to hear those words, Kauffman, perhaps feeling a bit philanthropic, offered to put up $1 million toward acquiring a new team to replace the departing Athletics. At that moment he was the sole party interested in bringing baseball back to Kansas City, but by the time the winter meetings convened in Mexico City in early December, Kauffman was now contending with the consortiums of Stern-Kemper, Latshaw, Barket, and Hamilton.

Relishing any new challenge he encountered, Kauffman gave serious consideration to building a baseball team from scratch, as he had built Marion Laboratories. He made an exploratory trip to Anaheim, California, to visit the Angels, a club that seemed to provide a template for him to follow. The Angels were a newer but relatively successful franchise that had just moved into a new stadium in 1966 and offered Kauffman a better model to follow rather than that of an old-line, established team such as the Red Sox or Yankees. Impressed by the operation in Anaheim, Kauffman was further implored to pursue buying the Kansas City team by his wife Muriel, who thought baseball would offer Ewing a salubrious diversion from the pharmaceutical business.

Also driving Kauffman was the snub he felt he had suffered at the hands of the other potential Kansas City team buyers, who obviously were aware that he was the first to make known his interest in a new club but then failed to offer him the chance to join one of their groups. Deciding to go it alone and upstage the other bidders, Kauffman employed his best salesmanship to convince the American League that he was the most suitable prospect. With Hamilton having dropped out, the Screening Committee convened on January 10, 1968, and privately tendered its recommendation to American League president Joe Cronin. The next day the league owners gathered to decide which of the remaining four candidates would be selected.

At the end of a meeting lasting seventy-five minutes, Kauffman emerged victorious and pledged his commitment to Kansas City and its fan base. "This city will never again lose major league baseball," the new owner declared, and he reinforced his point by announcing that he had entered into a covenant with municipal officials stipulating that "in the event of my death my estate would be bound to offer the club for sale locally." The *Kansas City Times* heralded the selection for the assets—tangible and intangible—inherent in Kauffman. "Single ownership, financial responsibility, organizational ability, and reputation" were key attributes that swayed the AL moguls when it came time for them to vote, and Yankee chairman Michael Burke called Kauffman "a refreshing personality," alluding to his contrast with Kansas City's prior team owner.[5]

But the euphoria of capturing the franchise faded quickly as Kauffman set about to lay the cornerstone and foundation for his new enterprise. The community at large had varying opinions of the owner: Was he "easygoing and jovial," or would he assume the haughty attitude of one spoiled by the success of his rags-to-riches life? An acquaintance noted, "It's easy to like him and a little risky to hear him out. . . . He is very persuasive."[6] Yet his opulently decorated Falcon corporate jet served as a vivid reminder of the rewards of his hard work.

Kauffman determined from the outset that there would be no confluence of his pharmaceutical company and his baseball venture, and he likewise was intent on keeping his own club ownership obligations separate from the operation of the team. He sought the best available executives to set up the front office, and following the naming of the club's board of directors days after taking ownership, Kauffman tapped Cedric Tallis as general manager and executive vice president. Tallis had been Kauffman's personal guide during his visit to Anaheim, and, taken by Tallis's scope of knowledge, Kauffman brought him aboard to direct the formation of the organization's infrastructure.

Tallis was charged with assembling the minor-league system to underpin the franchise, a scouting department to seek prospects, and the coaching staff to run the team at the major-league level. Although some of his better dealings remained in the future, Tallis later demonstrated his baseball acumen in astounding fashion by trading for players in 1969 and through the early 1970s—Amos Otis, Lou Piniella, Cookie Rojas, Freddie Patek, John Mayberry, and Hal McRae among them—who set the stage for the team's solid performance later that decade. Within three weeks of Tallis's hiring, Charlie Metro and Lou Gorman joined the organization to deal with player procurement and development.

While the Kansas City media gushed with enthusiasm over the prospect of major-league baseball's reprise—"We're All Steamed Up!" was the headline of a cheeky editorial cartoon that heralded the return of baseball to the city—there was genuine proof to back up all the shouting. In early March, fans were solicited for their ideas on what the team's nickname should be. In a period of two weeks, more than seventeen thousand proposals were submitted to a special "Name the Team" post office box. Each fan was asked to explain how he or she came up with the moniker, and the team hoped that it would have some pertinence to "the geographical, historical, or industrial significance of the area." After sifting through entries that included animals, Native American tribes, twists on Ewing Kauffman's name or his pharmaceutical business, as well as "phrases likely to be used in the description of a ball game [but that] had unfortunate double meanings," the club's board of directors selected "Royals" as the team name. The local newspaper approved the choice by explaining, "The title has special meaning for this city, where the Royal Livestock and Horse Show is the distinctive annual civic event that salutes this community's cow town and agricultural origins."[7]

Vital to the stability of the franchise were the plans already in motion to build a new ballpark to replace antiquated Municipal Stadium. Dutton Brookfield, the chairman of the Jackson County Sports Complex Authority, was looking forward to the day when the $102 million bond issue passed in June 1967 would finally yield "a dual sports complex which will be meaningful not only to this area, but also to the entire world of professional athletics." In early June 1968 Kauffman signed a four-year lease to use the existing forty-five-year-old stadium until the team's new ballpark was ready for play, and construction on the new stadium began in July. In early September a former American League Most Valuable Player was named the first field manager: Joe Gordon, an All-Star second baseman with the Yankees and Indians who had been serving as a scout for the California Angels since 1962. At the same time as Gordon was taken on, the club had just embarked on its inaugural season-ticket sales campaign, and within three weeks more than sixty-three hundred had been sold, setting an American League record.[8] The pace at which events were transpiring, as well as the fervor demonstrated by those who opened their wallets to purchase season tickets, boded well for the new franchise and a fan base that was anxious to extirpate the memory of Charlie Finley.

As 1968 progressed Cedric Tallis was busy on a number of fronts. Tasks consuming much of the general manager's time included signing on with a cooperative farm club in Dubuque, Iowa; creating a scouting network; preparing for both the amateur draft in June and major-league expansion draft in October; establishing a base camp for spring training in 1969; promoting the team to encourage ticket sales; and negotiating media contracts for radio and television coverage. The Royals built their team with an eye to the future by opting for players whose average age was younger than that of their expansion counterparts, the Seattle Pilots. Lou Piniella was acquired from the Pilots near the end of spring training and demonstrated his skill at the plate throughout the season to win 1969 Rookie of the Year honors in the American League.

The first draft of Tallis's opus resulted in a team whose reception by Kansas Citians was welcoming and enthusiastic. With 17,688 fans in attendance on April 8, 1969, Ewing Kauffman was given a standing ovation when he addressed the crowd and again "promised the fans [that] the Royals would be their team as long as he lives." The banner day was capped by the Royals' win over the Minnesota Twins in twelve innings, 4–3, as the newcomers embarked on a season in which they finished a surprising fourth in the American League West, with sixty-nine wins, and fell only one short of a record number of victories for a first-year team. Ending the season with a four-game winning streak, the Royals and their followers were brimming with optimism and looked forward to improving on their unexpectedly bright inaugural year. The day after the final game, the *Kansas City Star* told its readers, "Virtually all of the players commented last night they would be willing to go to spring training after a short rest," while the *Times* editorially praised the Royals' "ability and appeal that turned 1969 into a thoroughly satisfactory season."[9]

Just as the Royals' expansion draft choices favored youth, for the most part, the team also felt a need to create a method to cultivate fresh talent that would be brought into the organization in the years to come. Thirsting to win at baseball in the same way he won while gambling in the navy, Ewing Kauffman boasted that the Royals would field a championship team by the middle of the 1970s. The owner exuded confidence because he viewed the young players and their coaches coming into the minor-league system as the bedrock of the organization. Naturally it would take time for instruction to have an impact on player development, but feeling that the business model relevant to inculcating his drug salesmen could be applied to his minor-league system, Kauffman created a unique institution whose mission was to hasten the delivery of major-league-ready players to the Royals. The owner believed that the availability of homegrown talent would make the Royals worthy of contending for the World Series by 1975.

With Kauffman in the forefront, the club announced in September 1969 the creation of an institution that, it was hoped, would give the Royals an advantage in preparing young, untested players for a spot on their big-league roster. Kansas City's Baseball Academy was developed as an operation whose goal was not only to cater to the development of its players on the field but also to bring into the organization those individuals whose key traits—"speed of foot . . . good eyesight . . . fast reflex actions . . . and body balance"—were augmented with a more deeply rooted intangible factor: "a strong need to achieve something of significance."[10] Dr. Raymond Reilly, who had earlier worked with several government agencies as a research psychologist, was directed by Kauffman to pattern his player profile modeling on the Cincinnati Reds, an interesting choice of major-league teams, considering the Reds were soon to blossom into the Big Red Machine, albeit with the help of some shrewd trades. This melding of physical and mental characteristics—especially the latter—was consistent with Kauffman's philosophy as applied to the salesmen who plied their trade for Marion Laboratories.

Kauffman's innovation earned him the derision of those who compared the academy to Bill Veeck's radical stunt of employing the diminutive Eddie Gaedel, but the Royals owner was sincere in attempting to find young men whose playing ability and mentality fit a profile Kauffman was confident would lead to a successful career in Kansas City. In the event, the academy opened in August 1970 under the direction of Syd Thrift and operated for barely four years, with future second baseman Frank White its sole notable graduate. At the time, however, Kauffman's vision of the Baseball Academy demonstrated the type of thinking, unconventional in the baseball world, that he was willing to use to turn a fledgling expansion club into a championship team.

—⚏—

Although the Kansas City Royals fell short of meeting Kauffman's timetable for becoming a true championship team—they didn't win their first World Series until 1985—they established themselves as a force to be reckoned with after experiencing growing pains in the early years of the franchise. Beginning in 1976 the Royals dominated the American League West, winning the division crown four of the next five years, and captured the AL pennant in 1980. Cedric Tallis was instrumental in using the trade route to bring in key players such as Amos Otis, Freddie Patek, and Hal McRae to form the cornerstone of those great teams, while homegrown talent in the form of Frank White and George Brett rose from the ranks of the minor-league system to join them. Serving as a comfortable setting for many of their deeds was Royals Stadium, which opened in 1973 and quickly earned a reputation as one of the finest ballparks in baseball.

But none of this would have been possible if not for the work of Ewing Kauffman, the entrepreneur and visionary who entered the world of baseball for the sake of returning a major-league franchise to the city he dearly loved. The passionate attention Kauffman brought to his team gave it the stability and backbone to endure, but the Kansas City franchise also benefited from another intangible factor: the owner's commitment to founding his own baseball tradition and keeping his team where it was born.

The elation expressed by Kansas Citians over their franchise stood in stark contrast to the reception accorded its expansion partner on the West Coast, whose own brief existence was riddled with difficulties and suffered an ignominiously swift decline that left it quickly scrambling to find a new home after just one fateful season in the Pacific Northwest.

The Short, Sad Voyage of the Seattle Pilots

It was both by accident and by design that Seattle, Washington, earned its place at the table of legitimate major American cities. Its geographic location made it an unwitting jumping-off point to Alaska as the United States expanded in the nineteenth century, and as aviation technology grew during the twentieth century so too did Boeing Aircraft, a locally founded enterprise that would become a world leader in aviation technology. Serving as a backdrop to the city were the physical assets of the region. Seattle is surrounded by several national parks and forests as well as the beautiful waters of Puget Sound, all of which beckon boaters, hikers, and others who enjoy outdoor activities. The Seattle area was conflicted about what its rightful status should be—a city expanding with the times, or a place that sought to retain its bucolic charm and attachment to the natural splendor of its environment. "In short," one historian noted, "Seattle was an emerging metropolis, but its citizens did not exactly throb with a passion for growth."[11]

Boeing's landmark contribution to the aviation world, the model 707 jet-liner, was introduced in the mid-1950s and revolutionized long-distance travel, making formerly outlying destinations—such as Seattle—much more accessible. Although the success of the company had a significant impact on the region's economy, this good fortune did not directly translate into a resource that facilitated an upturn in other issues relevant to the city of Seattle. Boeing's workforce included well-paid engineers and very technically proficient laborers, but the company itself "was not a source of corporate dollars or open-handed magnates who would fund an opera company, a new hospital—or a baseball team."[12] A solid middle class comprised the backbone of Seattle's demographic structure, yet few with deep pockets were willing to step forward to assist in philanthropic endeavors.

This mindset was manifest in the realm of local politics, and city officials generally preferred to distance themselves from projects that otherwise would have allowed Seattle to move closer toward achieving status as a large, renowned American city. Seattle was not immune to social ills of the day or other unpleasantness plaguing urban regions across the United States, but its smaller physical size and relative geographic isolation offered a degree of protection from the full brunt of problems that impacted other municipalities.

Civic leaders were conflicted over the fate of their metropolis: Should Seattle be allowed to grow to its full potential and achieve major-league status, or should complacency in the city's solitude remain the overriding mindset for guiding their actions? The idea to host a regional fair in 1959 eventually grew into the project to host the 1962 World's Fair, thus proving that initiatives to put the region's best foot forward could grow into something larger than what was originally envisioned. The fair, which had been looked upon with some skepticism, became a resounding success that ultimately turned a profit of $1 million and validated the financial backing and sweat equity that local enterprises invested in the endeavor. The buildings constructed for the fair became part of the vital infrastructure that later hosted various sporting and cultural events, and the fair also provided a huge boost to the morale of the region while giving it confidence to elevate its image and stature.

Minor-league baseball had long been a staple of the Seattle sports scene, and the 1962 World's Fair lit the spark that spurred interest in culture and the arts. The city's two major newspapers were enthusiastic about sports, but Husky football at the University of Washington and hydroplane races were the favorites among spectator sports. However, when talk of big-league baseball coming to Seattle arose in the 1960s, a municipal group known as Choose an Effective City Council set its priorities on improving social programs rather than focusing attention on landing a major-league team. With the Dodgers and Giants having moved west in 1957, it seemed possible that baseball could be lured to the Pacific Northwest. If a new stadium—possibly a domed one—could be built, then perhaps baseball would be eager to fill it during the anticipated 1962 expansion that would follow the first phase of expansion in 1961. But when a stadium bond issue was conflated with other ballot initiatives in the fall of 1960, the vote fell far short of the requisite 60 percent needed for approval. The tepid response of the region's populace thwarted efforts to attract big-league baseball and pro football.

In the autumn of 1964 the Cleveland Indians gave serious consideration to shifting their franchise to Seattle. But several stadium-related factors—disputes over construction of a new stadium or renovation of Sicks' Stadium, which was named after brewer Emil Sick and his family—combined with the nagging problem of weak local support to doom the Indians' effort. The opening of new stadiums in the mid-1960s caught the attention of some Seattle sportswriters, who told their readers that recently constructed arenas such as the Houston Astrodome and Atlanta Stadium were instrumental in drawing teams to their new home cities. The National Football League was also considering expansion but deemed a new stadium—or a city's firm commitment to building one in the very near future—imperative to the granting of a franchise.

In the summer of 1966 the city of Seattle was engaged in a chicken-and-egg scenario. Seattle would commit to building a multipurpose stadium under the condition that pro football and/or Major League Baseball guaranteed that one or more new teams would remain for at least several decades. But the sports leagues were reluctant to award franchises to cities with currently inadequate stadium facilities. NFL commissioner Pete Rozelle counseled patience to see if Seattle voters might approve a bond issue that would deliver a new stadium for the benefit of both baseball and football.

Despite support from many civic and labor organizations, political leaders, and the sporting media, this latest effort failed, with less than 52 percent of voters approving the measure when at least 60 percent was required. The bottom line was that "the people of Seattle were not ready to add the $6.50 per year to their property tax bill required to bring pro sports to their city."[13] Both the NFL and Major League Baseball were, for the time being, out in the cold. Ironically, it would take a less popular sport—basketball—to provide a boost to the hopes of those dreaming of higher ambitions. The birth of the NBA's Supersonics in time for the 1967–1968 season demonstrated that a professional sports league believed that the denizens of the Pacific Northwest would turn out in adequate numbers to justify its decision to grant the city a franchise. Seattle was slowly coming of age after all.

Charlie Finley, owner of the Kansas City Athletics, contemplated a move to Seattle, but this attempt in September 1967 also came to grief when no agreement could be reached between Finley and Seattle officials over who would pay for the necessary expansion and renovations to Sicks' Stadium. In October, when American League club owners met in Chicago to determine whether Finley could move to Oakland, they not only considered the future of baseball in Kansas City but also entertained proposals from other cities seeking to join the ranks of the American League.

Yet another stadium referendum was slated for early 1968 in Seattle, and perhaps this third time would be the charm to convince baseball that the Pacific Northwest was at last ready for the major leagues. The National League coveted Seattle as a possible third site on the West Coast, and the AL desired a complementary far western home to give the Angels some scheduling equilibrium. Despite the previous failures of potential moves involving the Indians and Athletics to Seattle, the Emerald City remained a treasure in the eyes of Junior Circuit owners. Thus, if Finley was to be approved for his transfer to Oakland, it was in the league's best interest to bring Seattle into its fold, giving the AL a third club on the Pacific Coast. Both Finley and Michael Burke, president of the Yankees, expressed the high priority the league placed on staking a claim in Seattle before the National League did likewise.

On October 17, 1967, readers of the *Seattle Post-Intelligencer* were blandly informed on the bottom of the final page of the sports section that a small group of local civic leaders would make their pitch to acquire a team for the city. The next day, an announcement came from the owners' gathering in Chicago of three simultaneous events: Finley was approved for his requested relocation to Oakland; a new club was granted for Kansas City to replace the departing Athletics, a move which was meant to placate Stuart Symington; and Seattle was chosen to be the expansion partner of the new Kansas City team. The new clubs were intended to commence operating by 1971 at the latest.

However, seemingly before the ink dried on newsprint reporting the expansion plans, cautionary notes were being sounded: A ballot initiative the following February would prove crucial to the viability of retaining the franchise just granted to Seattle. John Owen of the *Post-Intelligencer* reported that another scheduled vote was pending to determine whether King County taxpayers would be willing to shoulder the burden of constructing a new multipurpose stadium, and although the newspaper cheerily trumpeted the good news with a banner headline—"Seattle to Get A.L. Baseball by 1971"—the accompanying page one above-the-fold story noted the sober caveat: "League OKs Team If City Has Stadium."[14]

Ownership of the new club was destined to fall to a small consortium headed by the Soriano brothers and a former owner of the Cleveland Indians. Max Soriano was once a pitcher with his eye on a career in baseball who instead became an attorney for the Pacific Coast League, while his sibling Dewey cut his teeth as a hurler for the Triple-A Seattle Rainiers, spent two decades as owner or general manager for several minor-league clubs in the greater Seattle area, and was currently serving as president of the Pacific Coast League. Joining them was William Daley, who had owned the Tribe from 1955 to 1962 and had been among the principals exploring the possible shift of the Indians to Seattle in 1964. It was during this venture that Daley and Dewey Soriano solidified their relationship, and by 1968 "it was Daley who provided the bankroll" despite his reputation as one who spent sparingly.[15] Daley's status as an out-of-town financier, rather than a locally based potential part-owner, was a source of worry.

Despite the ostensibly firm financial ground on which the new team stood, small cracks developed that would later wreak havoc. Several American League owners expressed concern that the Sorianos were the sole promoters in Seattle, but the AL was willing to give them the benefit of the doubt because of their past baseball experience. "They had voted a franchise to a city without a major league stadium, in an area that had not pursued a team avidly, and with an ownership group that was, at best, financed by a penny-pincher and, at worst, insufficiently capitalized."[16] At first glance, the problems of the new Seattle team were thought to be no worse than the typical issues that beset any nascent baseball enterprise, but the specter of the funding vote for a new stadium—and its prior two failures—continued to loom over the operation.

James Ellis, a local lawyer, was instrumental in moving Seattle to a higher civic level. Late in 1965, he stated that a general plan of action—including construction of a rapid transit system, park and other infrastructure improvements, as well as a multipurpose stadium—was vital to upgrading the municipality. Dubbed "Forward Thrust," the plan comprised thirteen separate initiatives whose overall aim was to provide a coherent developmental plan for moving King County into the future. With the new stadium one of the ballot's linchpins, the American League faced a significant loss if the electorate could not be convinced in February 1968 to approve funding for the facility, especially after having already been granted an expansion team. Seeking to avoid the embarrassment of possible revocation of the franchise by the American League if the voters rejected the stadium initiative, proponents of big-league baseball enlisted Mickey Mantle, 1967 Triple Crown winner Carl Yastrzemski, umpire Emmett Ashford, and AL president Joe Cronin to promulgate one virtue or another related to the ballpark. Because the stadium was intended for use by pro football and other large-scale events, the NFL and preacher Billy Graham also gave their support. The effort was not in vain, as a huge turnout approved seven of the thirteen

The Seattle Pilots, recipients of a lukewarm reception in their hometown, whose tenure in the Pacific Northwest lasted but a single season. *National Baseball Hall of Fame Library, Cooperstown, NY.*

measures by the required 60 percent, including the new stadium. (Those that fell short, including the railway, still received over one-half favorable votes.)

Having cleared a major stumbling block—at least for the time being—the Sorianos began to staff their front office. Marvin Milkes, late of the California Angels, was brought in as general manager, and Gabe Paul Jr., who had just been honored as the *Sporting News* Triple-A Executive of the Year, was tapped as the traveling secretary. Scouting director Ray Swallow, whose services had benefited the Athletics as they cultivated a significant farm system in the mid-1960s prior to the emergence of the powerful Oakland teams of the early 1970s, came aboard, as did Bobby Mattick, who would later help build the great Toronto Blue Jay teams of the early 1990s. Former Indians ace Bob Lemon was recruited to manage Seattle's Triple-A farm team in Vancouver. Not least among the tasks at hand was the selection of a nickname for the club, and the choice of "Pilots" served as a dual tribute to those who flew aircraft—especially ones produced by Boeing—and those at the helm of vessels on the waters of the Pacific Northwest.

As 1968 progressed more names were added to Seattle's front office and field staff, including Harold Parrott as public relations director and Joe Schultz, the former third-base coach of the National League champion St. Louis Cardinals, as field manager. Schultz and Milkes had been acquaintances for more than a decade. When the expansion draft took place on October 15, Seattle decided to employ a strategy that stocked its roster with veteran players who were more likely to compete in the short run rather than embark on a long waiting game for the farm system to deliver prospects to the major-league level. Don Mincher, Rich Rollins, and Tommy Davis had been associated with teams that had played in the World Series, and management was willing to overlook age as well as the downturns and shortcomings that many of these veterans had recently experienced. A total of thirty players at a total cost of $5,250,000 were drafted by Seattle, while the new Kansas City franchise also spent as much but focused instead on more youthful players.[17]

The calendar turned to 1969, and in mid-February the Pilots embarked on their inaugural spring training in Tempe, Arizona. Suddenly a multitude of issues—some of which had been festering for quite a while—became more urgent. Bickering over the completion of new spring training facilities in Tempe affected the team just when it was trying to project a positive image in its earliest days of actually playing baseball. Contributing to the financial bind the team would find itself in was a contract the Pilots' parent company, Pacific Northwest Sports, Inc., signed with Sportservice, the company charged with providing concessions for the team. The terms of a $2 million loan from PNSI granted the concessionaire the right to provide services for the team for twenty-five years regardless of where the Pilots played. Although the club had ready cash, the fact that the new team was quickly in debt to its concessions provider created concern. Compounding its revenue stream complications was a minimal amount of television coverage, for which only three Seattle and Tacoma stations were contracted. Local outlets were fearful that Seattle-area residents would favor participating in the outdoor sports for which the region was known rather than sitting at home to watch the Pilots on television. Thus, the team did not air any local games except on radio, with KVI serving as the flagship station.

Harold Parrott, brought in at a hefty salary that supposedly justified his ability to promote the team—that is to say, generate revenue—was not living up to his advance billing. The effort with which he promoted the Pilots was not aggressive enough to suit the needs of a brand-new team, so Parrott was dismissed shortly after the season began. Sales of individual tickets and season packages prior to Opening Day fell far short of expectations, which may not have been completely Parrott's fault. To the consternation of many fans, they were being charged above-market prices for tickets to watch an expansion team that was playing its home games in a decrepit stadium.

The cost of game tickets and concessions were, by the standards of the day, outrageously high. At a cost of six dollars for a box seat, the Pilots' prices were on par with the San Francisco Giants, whose ticket prices were the highest in the National League, but Candlestick Park was decades newer than the ramshackle Sicks' Stadium, and the Giants' roster featured future Hall of Famers Willie Mays, Willie McCovey, and Juan Marichal. Some food items were priced at nearly double the cost of concessions at the nearby minor-league Tacoma Cubs stadium. This poor combination of price and value hardly sat well with the many working-class fans who did not vote in favor of the stadium referendum until the third attempt. Dewey Soriano overplayed his hand by thinking fans would be so enthralled with his major-league franchise that they would be willing to pay more than fair-market value for the privilege of attending Pilots games.

Meanwhile, the renovation and operation of Sicks' Stadium was plagued with problems. Disputes over whether the city or the team should pay for improvements—and how much money each party would contribute—caused interminable delays that threatened to extend completion of the work beyond the Opening Day 1969 deadline. Costs of repairs and renovations had not been accurately estimated, and as budgets were depleted, means were sought to finish work on the cheap, even at the risk of compromising the team's ability to play in a ballpark acceptable to the league. Three months before the first pitch was to be thrown, uncertainty remained over corrections to substandard field lighting, press box accommodations, plumbing and restroom reconfigurations, cramped clubhouses, and seating for fans. With much work remaining and a shrinking timeframe in which to complete it, there was even some concern that the league might revoke the franchise before the team had played its inaugural game.

When April 11 arrived, fifteen thousand fans turned out for the first major-league game in Seattle at a stadium that remained a work in progress, and workmen continued for weeks into the season to address outstanding items on the punch lists. To the embarrassment of both parties, fighting between the city and the Pilots' front office continued, not least of which included a possible eviction of the team from its own ballpark because of financial conflicts, and "[b]y the end of the season, any idea of the Pilots bringing credibility to a city on the rise was turning to ashes."[18]

Despite the difficulties among the politicians, the front office, and the fans, the baseball product itself was in some ways pleasantly surprising and in other ways typical of the expansion franchise experience. The team and area businesses traded on the theme of "pilot" in clever ways, such as labeling the table of contents of Seattle's inaugural yearbook—as it turned out, the only such publication—"The Flight Plan," and a welcoming advertisement by United Airlines in the *Seattle Post-Intelligencer* showed a hint of bias by noting, "We fly a lot of major league teams so we try to be impartial, but pilots are a little special with us."[19] Washington governor Daniel Evans declared the first full week of April "Baseball Week" and exuded optimism in his belief that the new club would be a boon to the local and state economy. The *Post-Intelligencer* also printed a supplemental section in its April 11 edition, not only promoting the Pilots but also capturing all aspects of the franchise's emerging history. On the field, manager Joe Schultz sized up his club and thought that his veteran-laden roster had a legitimate chance to reach third place in the new American League West division. Veteran pitcher Jim Bouton agreed with this assessment, given that Sicks' Stadium provided a favorable venue for the club's hitters. The Pilots did contend for that lofty position in the standings, but a brutal month of August saw the team tumble from its tenuous hold on third place to the basement of the AL West. Fans who had been dismayed by high ticket and concession prices were kept further at bay by a team policy that fined players fifty dollars for providing autographs, and special events such as a night to honor Tommy Harper, who was pursuing an American League stolen base record, drew fewer than seven thousand fans.

As a general manager with very limited patience, Milkes constantly tinkered with the roster in the hope of hitting on the right combination of players that would benefit his team. Milkes's petulance got the better of him as the season progressed, and the Pilots ended up placing fifty-three different players on the field during the 1969 campaign, the third-highest total for any single season in baseball history. Expansion teams have little foundation to stand on, and Milkes took his manager's expectations too literally, which in turn fostered a growing sense of disappointment as losses piled up during the summer. "Marvin Milkes is not a guy who will sit around in a situation that calls for panic," noted Bouton of the general manager's tendency toward impatience.[20]

If being forced to use Sicks' Stadium were not bad enough, more angst and drama were generated by the controversy over the new facility—including two proposals that introduced the intriguing idea of building a domed stadium using wood—that King County voters had sanctioned to be built. The struggle to obtain approval was hardly over when a subsequent battle erupted over selection of the building site. The American League office, which had been willing to be flexible with the Pilots in their use of Sicks' as a temporary home, became increasingly concerned as debates regarding their new permanent home dragged on seemingly without end. The league insisted that construction commence no later than December 1970, but as the 1969 season passed, disputes over five proposed building sites led to internecine battles among King County officials, Seattle politicians, several property owners, and real estate developers. Forty million dollars had been appropriated for the construction of a multipurpose domed stadium, and with the clock running, planners began to see that the construction budget was inadequate to keep pace with inevitably rising costs that were exacerbated by the delays. There was speculation in the press that the Pilots would move from Seattle between October 1969 and April 1970, and the irony was not lost on many that the new stadium, which was supposed to be the anchor that secured the franchise to Seattle, had turned into an intractable problem all its own. The sports editor of the *Post-Intelligencer* defended the way in which the Pilots conducted business in their first big-league season by drawing comparisons to the new National League franchise in Montreal, whose "mayor pledged the Canadian city would erect a permanent domed home for the Expos, [but] a year later, there is no such project on the books."[21]

As the Pilots came down the stretch of the regular season, Lamar Hunt and Tommy Mercer, both established Texans with strong sporting ties, offered use of Turnpike Stadium in Arlington, Texas, to the struggling team. This temporary move did not occur, but the Pilots were obviously in peril, and a group of fans at the final home game at Sicks' Stadium displayed a homemade banner exuding optimism that would not come to pass: SO LONG PILOTS. SEE YOU NEXT YEAR IN SEATTLE.[22] William Daley, the closefisted Cleveland financier, was still willing to give Seattle another try in 1970, but closely observing the deteriorating situation was an automobile dealer from Milwaukee, Allan "Bud" Selig. A crucial stage of the Pilots' tenure arrived at the time of the first game of the 1969 World Series, when Dewey Soriano and Selig met in Baltimore and reached a verbal agreement to transfer ownership for $10.8 million. But the American League remained committed to keeping the team in Seattle, and the necessary approval of the sale by 75 percent of AL owners was not forthcoming. The league reiterated its demands for improvements to Sicks' Stadium as well as selection of a site and start date of construction for the new stadium before December 1970, and also stated its desire to have Daley and Soriano sell to a local Seattle party rather than have the club relocate.

As 1969 drew to a close and with the Pilots' attendance total near the bottom of the American League, various banks and Seattle-area businessmen were enlisted to put up enough funds to purchase the team, but these efforts came to grief, as did a drive to entice local fans to purchase tickets on a single-game, season, or multiple-season basis for the sake of quickly raising cash to buy out Daley and the Sorianos. Given the state of the Pilots at that time, it defies logic why any fan would buy tickets to see games played by a team whose future was in so much doubt. Banks that had earlier expressed a willingness to loan money to Seattle interests—the Bank of California and the National Bank of Commerce among them—balked. Another civic leader, Ed Carlson, made the radical proposal of reorganizing the Pilots as a public trust that would operate as a nonprofit entity, an idea that was rebuffed by several AL owners who said they did not run their teams for charitable purposes.

Carlson's plan fell short by one vote in early February 1970 when AL moguls met, and with the beginning of spring training just two weeks away, the American League held its nose and returned control of the team to those responsible for its perilous circumstances. There was a palpable suspicion that the league was intentionally setting up the Soriano group for a failure at least as dismal as that experienced in 1969, the better to foster the excuse that the team would have to move in order to survive. Indeed, this was exactly the opinion of *Post-Intelligencer* sports editor John Owen, who presciently observed at the close of the Pilots' 1969 season, "If the American League makes the slightest move toward approving a transfer of the Seattle franchise this year or next, it will not be because of inadequate facilities here. . . . It will be because the owners of other American League teams think they might make an extra buck elsewhere."[23]

The torment dragged on for several more weeks, punctuated by disputes over bankruptcy proceedings and William Daley's reneging on his offer to infuse the struggling club with $8 million. Finally on April 2—with Opening Day of the 1970 season nearly at hand—the sale of the Pilots was completed and the team officially became the Milwaukee Brewers, now under the control of a consortium headed by Selig. "The $10.8 million Selig and his partners paid for the Pilots was comparable to other sales that took place around the same time," observed Pilots historian Bill Mullins, citing the costs of the new National League expansion teams and the recent sale price of the Yankees ($10 million each) as well as that of the Washington Senators to Bob Short ($11 million).[24]

Trapped in the miasma of the political, financial, and bureaucratic battles were the Pilots players and coaches. Their home field was an inadequate facility that became the epicenter of controversy over the futile effort to make Sicks'

Stadium fit for major-league baseball. The greater Seattle region, already proven to be only mildly enthusiastic about an American League franchise, held the team at arm's length because of the high prices charged to see an inferior product on the diamond. These factors were not the fault of the players or their staff, but an argument can be made that they ignored the off-field turmoil and overachieved for a good part of the year by flirting with Joe Schultz's goal of a third-place finish. Notwithstanding the angst normally experienced by an expansion club, the Pilots' cause could have been helped had Marvin Milkes counseled patience rather than reaction every time he observed a failure of performance of one of the players. Seattle's uniformed personnel may have been able to extricate themselves from their predicament only by somehow vaulting into contention in the AL West—a most unlikely possibility—and thus were the victims of forces well beyond their control.

Fraught with peril as the Pilots' voyage was, it nonetheless staked a claim in the Pacific Northwest for the American League and set the stage for major-league baseball to make good on its second opportunity when the Junior Circuit returned eight years later.

—⚏—

Two interesting parallels eventually emerged from the pair of American League expansion franchises of 1969. Ewing Kauffman gave the Kansas City Royals stability from their very beginning, a tangible factor the Soriano brothers could only have hoped for in Seattle. However, once Bud Selig arrived to rescue the Pilots in time for the 1970 season, he placed the team on firm ground that allowed it to escape the opprobrium of its first-year debacle. The Pilots' brief existence seems nearly lost to history, yet it is unquestionably a part of the Milwaukee Brewers' legacy. And by chronicling the team in his renowned book *Ball Four*, Jim Bouton unwittingly still breathes life into the Pilots, that most ephemeral of modern baseball franchises. Kauffman and Selig remained respected among American League owners for many years, with the latter assuming the role of acting baseball commissioner in 1992.

The creation of the Royals and the Pilots in 1969 set the American League on the path to divisional modernity. Trials and tribulations notwithstanding, they contributed to the landscape of the national pastime as founding members of the new AL West. Kauffman proved to be better prepared for the long term and quickly rejuvenated baseball in Kansas City, while the Sorianos unintentionally provided a team that facilitated the rebirth of major-league baseball in Milwaukee.

CHAPTER 4

National League Expansion

ONE UP, ONE ALMOST DOWN

To a certain degree the early existence of the expansion clubs in the National League mirrored that of their American League counterparts. The San Diego franchise was delivered to an ownership that, as was the case with Ewing Kauffman, appeared on solid footing, to say nothing of the fact that it had a brand-new stadium at its disposal. In Montreal, issues over who would constitute the team's ownership combined with the high drama regarding the club's ballpark to cause a near revocation of the franchise before it played its first major-league game. The stadium dilemma was a source of controversy not unlike that experienced in Seattle, but Montreal's entry into the NL gained traction and found favor with local fans, a circumstance lacking in the Pacific Northwest. San Diego would later experience turbulence that almost forced the team to relocate in 1974, but unlike the Pilots, the team was rescued from possible failure by a new owner with deep pockets. Montreal, on the other hand, endured for decades before finally falling victim to circumstances that placed the team in a new city in a different country.

More Major League Baseball Comes to Southern California

Nicknamed "America's Favorite City," San Diego had long enjoyed a rich baseball tradition prior to its membership in the Senior Circuit. A minor-league outpost dating back to the 1930s, San Diego had a mild, comfortable climate that made it very attractive for visitors wishing to partake of vacations and recreational activities. The former Hollywood Stars of the Pacific Coast League (PCL) moved south after 1935 and were recast as the San Diego Padres. Hometown star and future Red Sox Hall of Famer Ted Williams, who would become the PCL team's most famous alumnus, joined the Padres shortly thereafter, and two decades later the team came under the ownership of a local banker and real estate magnate named Conrad Arnholt Smith, whose business interests also included the Westgate Tuna Packing Company. Despite his vast wealth—Smith was the head of United States National Bank, worth an estimated $450 million—the new expansion club owner was called a "mystery man . . . [who] has escaped the glare of the spotlight" of public life.[1]

By the early 1960s the Padres had become a Pacific Coast League power-house, but movement was afoot on the part of San Diego ownership to attempt to land an American League team in 1961. Although this effort failed, Eddie Leishman came aboard as the new general manager in November 1960 and helped assemble a cast of players that achieved a huge measure of success through the 1960s. When San Diego was later awarded a new NL franchise, much regret was expressed by some fans, who were loath to swap their minor-league heroes—including, in the recent past, Bo Belinski, Tommy Harper, Tommy Helms, Lee May, and Tony Perez—for a big-league roster sure to be replete with expansion players of questionable quality.

The PCL Padres drew well at the gate, and in 1965 the city was thought to be on the verge of playing host to the Milwaukee Braves, who at the time were trying to find a new location. In November 1965, San Diego voters approved a measure that facilitated the construction of a multipurpose stadium that would become home to both the Chargers of the American Football League and the Triple-A Padres. Jack Murphy, a sportswriter for the *San Diego Union*, was instrumental as a proponent for building San Diego Stadium, which served as a fifty-thousand-seat lure for any future major-league franchise. The lobbying and arm-twisting that occurred during early 1968 finally yielded the intended result when Major League Baseball granted one of its expansion clubs to San Diego.

C. Arnholt Smith had a distinct advantage over the other three expansion clubs: namely, the ability to establish his team from the very outset in a brand-new facility. Free of the distraction of stadium issues, Smith devoted his attention to enlisting the best front office help he could find. Casting his gaze just to the north of San Diego, Smith found his man in Emil Joseph "Buzzie" Bavasi, the longtime general manager of the Los Angeles Dodgers. Bavasi had been groomed by Dodgers owner Walter O'Malley as well as a pair of stalwart baseball executives, Larry MacPhail and Branch Rickey, dating back to the team's glory days in Brooklyn. Bavasi had become ensconced in the Dodgers organization, but by early 1968 he was offered the opportunity to become Smith's partner in taking charge of a National League expansion team.

When the price tag of the new NL entries was disclosed—nearly twice the cost of those in the American League—Bavasi almost reneged. However, Smith was backed by an immense fortune and convinced his now-reluctant recruit that the team's finances would not be a problem. Tethered to the Dodgers yet longing for an ownership opportunity that he knew would never happen while working for O'Malley, Bavasi became increasingly uncomfortable with the glass ceiling he had reached. At this time, he also grew more candid about his desire to assume an ownership role with either a new team or another existing one. Bavasi's restlessness caused a strain in his relationship with O'Malley, and by June 1968 the two achieved a seemingly amicable separation that allowed Bavasi to leave the Dodgers and unite with Smith. "O'Malley has helped Bavasi with the San Diego deal," the *Sporting News* observed, but noted further, "They applaud each other publicly. But neither will wipe moisture from his eyes at the parting." Following Bavasi to his new employer was "the esteem in which [he] is held by baseball people [and] the respect [shown to him] from batboys to presidents."[2]

With Bavasi now in the employ of San Diego, the front office's responsibilities were clearly delineated. Smith was the chairman of the board and financier while Bavasi, also a "controlling stockholder," was the team president, charged with running baseball operations.[3] The task before Bavasi was unquestionably daunting, and he ranked acquiring scouts for his new club as the top priority. In the meantime, he would team with Eddie Leishman to find the players who would be among the first to take the field for the expansion club.

Upholding the tradition of San Diego's Triple-A affiliation, the new National League team retained the name "Padres" and adopted colors that catered to Smith's proclivity for shades of brown. Team uniforms were to be embellished with trim of capuchin brown and gold, which some snidely referred to as "monkey suits."[4] The Padres also appropriated the "swinging Padre" cartoon mascot formerly of minor-league fame. Although the color scheme was Smith's idea, so too was his inclination to maintain a low profile. Smith kept his post on the team's board of directors—the Padres' first media guide listed Smith's daughter, Carol Shannon, as the chairman—but in the press he was referred to as co-owner.

Bavasi began creating the club's management structure by reaching back to his erstwhile organization to hire Preston Gomez as field manager in late August 1968. Already committed to cultivating younger players who would work their way onto the San Diego roster, Bavasi believed that Gomez was the right man to handle the youth movement during the formative years of the franchise. One month later future Hall of Fame manager George "Sparky" Anderson, fresh off four consecutive years of success managing mostly in the lower minor leagues, was selected as the third-base coach. Former Dodger hurler Roger Craig became pitching coach, and Wally Moon, another ex-Dodger, and Whitey Wietelmann, who served as a coach for the Triple-A Padres, rounded out the coaching staff.

The initial roster was stocked by way of the expansion draft in mid-October, with the existing ten National League clubs obligated to lose three players each to San Diego and Montreal. Even before the first selection was made, Buzzie Bavasi had been backed into a corner of sorts. Fresco Thompson, a longtime friend of Bavasi's, had assumed Buzzie's role as Dodgers general manager after his departure from Los Angeles. While performing his new duties with the Dodgers, Thompson was diagnosed with late-stage cancer and his condition was very poor. When Bavasi visited him at a hospital in Fullerton, California, Thompson offered some advice regarding possible draft selections: "Fresco asked me to do him a favor. He named three players he wanted me to take—outfielders Al Ferrara and Jimmy Williams, and shortstop Zoilo Versalles. As ill as he was, I couldn't say no, but I thought he would get better and that I could talk him out of the agreement."[5]

Draft day arrived, and with Thompson still hospitalized and just weeks from passing away, Bavasi complied with the wishes of his dying friend, taking Versalles with the tenth pick, Ferrara with the fifteenth pick, and Williams as the twenty-second. Bavasi likely grimaced as he made each choice, knowing full well that players who should have been his primary targets among those in the Dodger system—those he believed had a bright future in the major leagues— were players he felt obligated to ignore. Four players in particular had drawn Bavasi's attention: Jeff Torborg, a twenty-seven-year-old backstop who caught Sandy Koufax's perfect game in 1965; shortstop Bill Russell, who would go on to anchor the Dodgers infield during his eighteen years in a Los Angeles uni- form; Ted Sizemore, a second baseman who would soon earn honors as the 1969 Baseball Writers' Association of America's National League Rookie of the Year and played for more than a decade in the NL; and outfielder Von Joshua, who enjoyed a modicum of success during ten years of major-league service spent mostly in the National League. It can only be left to speculation how well any three of these Dodgers might have performed for San Diego had they been se- lected rather than the trio of Ferrara, Williams, and Versalles. Ferrara did well in his first year with the Padres (.260 batting average, 14 home runs, and 56 RBIs), but Williams played in only two dozen games for San Diego in 1969 and 1970. And just days after the expansion draft, Bavasi traded Versalles to the Cleveland Indians for first baseman Bill Davis, who went on to play in only thirty-one games for San Diego before leaving baseball. By honoring Thompson's wishes, Bavasi certainly stilted the progress of the Padres right from the start.

Two curiosities about draft day are notable. Missing from San Diego's selec- tions was anyone capable of playing third base, although Bavasi corrected this omission during the December winter meetings by trading relief pitcher Dave Giusti to St. Louis for Ed Spezio and three other players.

The second oddity occurred as the draft session was winding down. After eight hours of poring over data and reports of eligible players as well as handling all the decisions made, Bavasi was clearly fatigued. Rather than forge ahead with the thirtieth pick himself, Bavasi sought the opinion of San Diego baseball writer Phil Collier and other members of the local sports media, letting them nominate the last player. The final pick was an outfielder from the Atlanta Braves named Clarence "Cito" Gaston, whose relatively decent playing career would later be eclipsed by his time spent managing the Toronto Blue Jays to consecutive World Series titles in the early 1990s.

Major-league baseball took more than three decades to arrive in San Diego, but when it did, expectations ran high among club ownership to reach the one million mark for attendance. On Opening Night, April 8, 1969, more than twenty-three thousand fans showed up to witness the big-league debut of the new Padres, who defeated the Astros 2–1 behind a sterling, twelve-strikeout performance by Dick Selma. But the front office had hoped to see a crowd of thirty-five thousand for the opener, and the following night only forty-two hundred enthusiasts took in the game, with just five thousand on hand for the third contest. Thus was established a pattern of low attendance, which hampered the team's bottom line and presaged the financial woes that plagued the Padres for the next several seasons.

The performance of San Diego's pitching staff was close to that of its expansion partner in Montreal, both finishing at the bottom of the National League in team earned run average and near the bottom in runs allowed. The anemic offense, however, was a greater source of concern, as demonstrated in the Padres' first eight games. During this opening stretch, they scored a grand total of nine runs—and amazingly won three contests. But the die had been cast, and for the entire 1969 campaign, San Diego scored a meager 468 runs, which amounted to 114 fewer runs than its next closest competitor, Montreal. The team batting average, not surprisingly, was also at the bottom of the NL, a woeful fifteen points worse than the Astros and the Expos (.225 to .240). Buzzie Bavasi likely shuddered to think what the Padres may have done had the names Jeff Torborg, Bill Russell, Ted Sizemore, or Von Joshua appeared on Preston Gomez's lineup card.

Lackluster pitching and meager hitting doomed Gomez's hope to win at least 60 games and consigned the Padres to 52 wins against 110 losses, a season consistent with the experience of most expansion clubs. For the 1969 season, San Diego counted just under 513,000 in attendance—last in the National League and a far cry from the anticipated million fans who were counted on to help keep the team solvent. A disturbing trend quickly emerged as the Padres consistently remained in the basement of the NL West, and although the number of fans going to San Diego Stadium broke the 600,000 mark during three of the next four years, the fiscal stability of the Padres remained tenuous. Fans appeared to make a statement that their heroes of the team's heyday in the PCL were preferable to the inferior big-league team that had assumed the place of the Triple-A franchise. The club's Waterloo soon followed in the spring of 1973

The advantage of debuting in a virtually brand-new stadium did not guarantee success for the San Diego Padres. *National Baseball Hall of Fame Library, Cooperstown, NY.*

when owner C. Arnholt Smith, "his reputation and financial empire in collapse," began to sell off Padres players in order to pay some of the team's debts.[6] Only the intervention of Ray Kroc, the McDonald's fast-food magnate, ultimately saved the team and prevented it from moving to Washington, DC.

Most dismaying about the predicament of the Padres was that among the four expansion clubs of 1969, they had the fewest problems regarding their home stadium, which was practically brand new. As previously shown, the Seattle Pilots were in shambles after one season, thanks in large part to the intractable debate over a new stadium, and although the Kansas City Royals had a plan in place to move to their new ballpark in 1973, they nonetheless had to endure several seasons at old Municipal Stadium prior to making their transition. That San Diego was on the firmest ground regarding an issue so central to its existence made its near demise within five years incredible. And, as will be demonstrated below, the other new club in the National League had to surmount the greatest difficulties in order to host its inaugural game of the 1969 season.

Les Expos Sont Là!

Another former Triple-A outpost accompanied San Diego in its move to the major-league stage. The city of Montreal was home to several minor-league affiliates dating back to the waning days of the late 1890s, but most recently had been the top farm club of the Brooklyn (and later, Los Angeles) Dodgers from 1939 until 1960. Alumni of the International League's Montreal Royals included Roberto Clemente, originally a Dodger farmhand, and, most famously, Jackie Robinson.

Those in Royals uniforms plied their trade at Delorimier Stadium, which seated twenty thousand fans, but at the conclusion of the 1960 season, the team transferred to Syracuse, New York. Portions of the old ballpark were dismantled and others repurposed to accommodate temporary classrooms for the Montreal school system. At the time Delorimier was being refitted, few would have envisioned a pressing need in a few short years for a stadium to play host for a major-league team. While enthusiastic at being awarded a National League expansion franchise to begin play in 1969, interests overseeing the creation of a new team in Montreal fell immediately into a morass of stadium problems and omnipresent financial difficulties of team ownership that needed to be addressed.

The euphoria in Montreal that accompanied the unexpected tapping of that city as an expansion site was explained by National League president Warren Giles. Some cities seeking to obtain an NL team were in close proximity to existing NL cities, Giles noted, meaning venues such as Milwaukee were certain to infringe on both major-league teams in Chicago, just 90 miles to the south.[7] In like fashion, Giles claimed that Dallas–Fort Worth would encroach on Houston's territory, but in reality, Astros owner Judge Roy Hofheinz undermined the efforts of the Dallas group so as to retain his team's exclusive hold on the Lone Star State. However, Walter O'Malley did not object to a new team in San Diego, a mere 125 miles away, and Montreal's location north of the United States border provided a cushion acceptable to the ten existing NL owners, even if harsh winters and cold spring weather brought the chance that games played in April could be subject to inclement conditions.

The World's Fair of 1967, which was hosted by the city of Montreal and dubbed "Expo 67," was the catalytic event spurring renewed interest in baseball. The fair "raised our sights and nourished our dreams . . . and inspired vision," a tribute reminiscent of the effect that the 1962 World's Fair had on Seattleites. Counter to this sanguine view, however, was the report of a Montreal baseball beat writer who explained that Expo 67 was drawing only about 50 percent of the expected four million monthly guests, thus forcing "concessionaires [to ask] for a delay of their rent payments."[8] Civic pride was one matter, but paying the bills to maintain the fair's solvency was quite another.

Nonetheless, credit needs to be given to city hall in Montreal for the effort put forward by Gerry Snyder, the vice-chairman of the city's executive committee, and Mayor Jean Drapeau, who persevered to ensure that Montreal would retain its franchise. In 1961 Snyder had lobbied baseball commissioner Ford Frick for a National League club during the first round of expansion in the Senior Circuit, but the request was summarily rejected because Frick's demand that a suitable ballpark be immediately available could not be met. By late 1967, fortified by the early success of Expo 67, Montreal's second attempt at securing a major-league team was better received. Snyder claimed that his favorable relationship with Dodgers owner Walter O'Malley was a factor in casting Montreal in a positive light for baseball's expansion committee.[9]

Several critical pieces of infrastructure had been created to support Expo 67, and these were in turn promoted as selling points for bringing baseball to Montreal. A modern subway system had been built to support mass transit, and an arena called the Autostade had been constructed as a sporting venue with an emphasis on track and field events as well as Canadian football. The Autostade would be used only for as long as it took the city of Montreal to build a new permanent stadium for the baseball club. With Drapeau's support, Snyder was confident that the Autostade's configuration, comprising nineteen separate grandstand sections, could be altered to accommodate a baseball field. The construction of a roof to cover the Autostade was proposed to help reduce the impact of inclement weather. Drapeau had a reputation as a man who not only set goals but also proved he could attain them, and the remodeling of the Autostade was viewed as yet another task he would confidently see to completion.

But an inspection by National League officials during the summer of 1968 failed to convince them that the site was appropriate for baseball. The Autostade was seen as *froid et peu invitant* (cold and uninviting) according to a historical Expos team publication. A chance visit to the old Montreal Royals ballpark, Delorimier Stadium, only revealed the sad condition into which it had fallen, and this site was quickly removed from consideration. Lest all options to find a venue fail, resulting in a revocation of the Montreal franchise by Major League Baseball, one final location was scouted. Jarry Park, "pretty and geographically well-situated," was a multisport complex that included facilities for swimming, tennis, and ice hockey as well as grass fields for soccer and a three-thousand-seat ballpark.[10] Enhancing the park's resources was access to nearby major highways as well as rail and subway routes. The site was well received by all parties, including National League attorney Bowie Kuhn and league president Warren Giles, and agreement was reached in August to expand this field to roughly thirty thousand seats. While the selection of Jarry Park evoked a huge sigh of relief, a massive amount of work needed to be done if it was to be ready for the opening of the 1969 season.

In addition to the funds necessary to rebuild Jarry Park, still more money was required to construct the permanent home. The mounting debt of Expo 67, Snyder contended, would not interfere with construction of a brand-new stadium for the benefit of the baseball team. The funding problem was what squelched the proposed Autostade roof, which came with a $7 million price tag and was determined to be too costly an appendage for a temporary site. A new ballpark holding fifty-five thousand seats was conservatively estimated to cost at least $40 million, and "a ringing editorial in the *Montreal Star* reminded [Drapeau] that welfare and slum-clearance should come first" in setting priorities for municipal spending.[11]

At the same time the stadium issues were creating anxiety, difficulties also surfaced in forming an ownership group, which was inchoate at best as the summer of 1968 proceeded. Gerry Snyder attempted to bring together ten investors who would contribute $1 million each toward the cost of the franchise, but instead a consortium of eight men stepped forward to offer assistance. The impressive list of initial shareholders was fronted by Jean-Louis Lévesque, a man whose immense personal fortune made him "the John Paul Getty of Canada."[12] Joining Lévesque were Lorne Webster, an oil executive, and Seagram's liquor magnate Charles Bronfman, who agreed to chair the board of investors.

Some of the financiers proffered aid as a token gesture, believing Montreal had little hope of actually being awarded a team. Yet when the National League surprised many observers by selecting the Canadian city, several became wary of actually making good on their pledge. The investors also committed their support under the assumption that a new domed stadium was to be built and ready for occupancy in 1972, a key factor which had been promised by Drapeau. As the stadium situation dragged on, the richest of the group—who likely could have bought the team on his own—was one of the first stakeholders to depart. Lévesque and Marcel Bourgie, another minority partner, withdrew their support, touching off a scramble to find investors willing and able to make the substantial payment to the NL required to secure the rights to the team, which was due by August 15. Further complicating the monetary issue was the fact that the value of the Canadian dollar was about 8 percent below that of the American dollar, and since the franchise cost was payable in US currency, the difference had to be made up by the investors.

The month of July was drawing to a chaotic close: The Montreal investment group and the city were engaged in their own standoff and the Lévesque consortium had backed out over the new stadium issue; these disputes were taking place while the city waited for the baseball interest to make its down payment to the league with money that supposedly had been available weeks earlier and which had made the group favorable in the eyes of the National League in the first place. The looming deadline nearly forced the league's hand in revoking the franchise, but fortunately, Bronfman filled the void created by the departure of Lévesque and underwrote a 70 percent share in the club. Finally on August 14, the hand-wringing ceased when Montreal remitted its deposit and officially joined the National League. NL president Warren Giles was delighted to display for the benefit of the press "a check that symbolized the initial franchise payment of $1,120,000," and the nascent team was saved from near death.[13]

As the stadium and funding issues yielded mounting frustration through early August, a third problem was playing out. John McHale, a former pitcher for the Detroit Tigers who went on to serve as an executive with the Braves in Milwaukee and Atlanta, was in the employ of baseball commissioner William Eckert in 1968. Several weeks after Montreal was invited to join the National League, McHale was interviewed for the position of Montreal's general manager. However, his hiring was contingent on resolutions to the ballpark problem and the club's financial backing. Even though Lévesque was still part of the ownership team in early June, no down payment had yet been made to the NL to fulfill the financial obligation toward acquiring the franchise, meaning the club technically did not exist in the eyes of the league. Alluding to the quandary the team faced, Lévesque said, "We have no company now. Who is going to employ anyone?"[14] In mid-June, McHale was the favorite to fill the opening, but an offer of employment was on hold until the stadium and financing problems could be resolved.

Once Bronfman increased his stake in the enterprise and Jarry Park was tabbed as the site of the team's ballpark, the deposit check was written and the front office quickly fell into place. McHale resigned from his position with the baseball commissioner's office to become an investor in the team, and rather than assuming the post of general manager, he instead was named chief executive officer and team president. He then immediately named Jim Fanning to be the general manager, and the team at last set up temporary headquarters in Montreal at the Windsor Hotel.

Several major items needed attention to market the club, not least of which was choosing a team name. The proposed moniker "Voyageurs" was a nod to the Canadian fur traders of the 1700s, but playing to the theme of the recent World's Fair, the name "Expos" was selected. The front office fielded queries from potential season ticket buyers anxious to secure seats for the upcoming season, and former Philadelphia skipper Gene Mauch was announced as the field manager. Mauch had been released by the Phillies in June in their effort to placate cantankerous slugger Dick Allen, who was often at odds with Mauch. Moving apace to prepare for the expansion draft in October to stock the team's roster, McHale and Fanning sought Mauch's opinions regarding player selections, and they officially brought aboard Bobby Bragan, Eddie Lopat, and Johnny Moore as scouts.

On draft day the Expos opted for players with big-league experience, and they hoped that favoring veterans would give them a quicker chance to be competitive rather than waiting to build a team that relied on youthful faces wending their way through the minor-league system. Even though their better days were behind them, hurler Jim "Mudcat" Grant, shortstop Maury Wills, and outfielders Jesus Alou, Mack Jones, and Manny Mota were among those chosen for their proven major-league ability.

The Expos' first pick in the second round of the draft, Donn Clendenon, instigated a complex and controversial episode in the new team's history. A power-hitting first baseman, Clendenon spent eight years with Pittsburgh, but the Pirates were willing to hand his position to Al Oliver, an untested yet promising twenty-two-year-old rookie. Montreal wasted little time making Clendenon a solid addition to their infield, and the Expos appeared content with the selection. But Clendenon was packaged with Alou in the first trade ever executed by the Expos, a deal with the Houston Astros for first baseman Rusty Staub, who was nine years younger than Clendenon and was twice named to the National League All-Star team. The transaction, which was completed on January 22, 1969, seemed to be nothing more than baseball business as usual: Montreal offering an attractive two-for-one swap in an effort to improve their club with the acquisition of a rising star. At the time, Clendenon denied rumors of his pending retirement—he was thirty-three and not thrilled to find himself with a Canadian expansion team—and stated that he was "here to help Houston win ball games."[15]

Clendenon, however, had second thoughts about continuing his career in the Astrodome, and shortly before spring training commenced, he advised

Houston's general manager, Spec Richardson, that he was retiring. When the Astros GM filed the appropriate paperwork with the commissioner's office, he also notified Staub to report to Houston's spring training camp because Clendenon's retirement had voided the trade. Clendenon "had envisioned a fat $50,000 contract with the Expos," but as he was traded to Houston before such a contract could be agreed upon, the first baseman found that Richardson was not going to pay him a salary that high.[16] In the meantime, Staub was instructed by new commissioner Bowie Kuhn to report to the Expos' camp and Alou to the Astros' facility. Montreal began using the former Astro as a marketing tool to attract fans and enhance ticket sales for the upcoming season, and, should Clendenon decide to truly stay retired, it was believed that Montreal would be able to find another player to send to Houston as a replacement for Clendenon.

However, Clendenon privately expressed a desire to play when he met with Kuhn on March 8, thereby prompting the commissioner to declare that Clendenon still belonged to the Expos. Kuhn also urged the Expos to find another player to send to the Astros. Enraged over this ruling, Richardson openly questioned Kuhn's refusal to accept Clendenon's retirement and also asked, "If Clendenon has expressed a willingness to play, then why isn't he here working out with us?"[17] Kuhn claimed an inability to rule on the matter of a retired player who was involved in a three-player trade, but two weeks later, Houston player personnel director Tal Smith told him that commissioner Ford Frick had voided a trade in 1960 by ordering a player to be placed on the voluntarily retired list when he refused to report to the team to which he had been traded. Smith appealed to the lawyerly Kuhn to use this case as a precedent, but Kuhn never responded.

As the affair dragged on through the month of March, Montreal GM Jim Fanning theorized that the Expos could meet Clendenon's asking price—to keep the trade valid—and then dump Clendenon along with his bloated contract on the Astros. On April 3 Fanning and Clendenon agreed to a two-year deal at $50,000 annually, and, now financially fortified, Clendenon announced, "In the best interests of the game, I feel I should come back."[18] But Richardson was having none of it and refused to accept the so-called retirement maneuver as anything more than a ploy for an increase in pay. With Clendenon persona non grata in Houston, the Expos brokered a repair to the mangled trade by sending pitchers Jack Billingham and Skip Guinn—along with some cash—to the Astros on April 8. The episode took a further strange turn two months later when Montreal shipped Clendenon to the New York Mets in exchange for pitcher Steve Renko, infielder Kevin Collins, and two minor leaguers. Clendenon saw action in only thirty-eight games for the Expos, but once he arrived at Shea Stadium, he became an instrumental player in the Mets' astounding charge to the World Series title.

A small entry in the 1969 Montreal Expos media guide informs readers that in mid-September 1968, the playing field at Jarry Park was being fitted out with new turf. But the brevity of this item belies the difficulty of stadium construction and field preparation in a harsh northern climate. Delays in beginning work at the site were the result of the protracted difficulties in securing the franchise that were not resolved until the middle of August, but the field was tended to first so that the Merion bluegrass had a chance to establish itself before frost set in. It was fortunate that the new turf had wisely been installed first, because the groundbreaking for construction of the stands came after two storms had already covered the site with a thick mantle of snow.

By early November, construction of spectator seating on the first-base side commenced, followed by erection of stands along the third-base side, and lastly seating in the outfield was put up. The can-do spirit of the region held that "[d]espite sub-zero temperatures, the construction industry continues through the winter in Montreal," and the Expos already had bought some time for themselves by scheduling their home opener on April 14, nearly one week after they were to play their inaugural game on April 8 in New York.[19]

As winter progressed, the Expos front office confronted their own unique logistical issues in building the team's administrative infrastructure. The accounting department was challenged in ensuring that allowances were made for the 8 percent difference in value between Canadian and US currencies. Communication of game broadcasts as well as team publications, advertising, and signage had to be handled bilingually, since 80 percent of those living in the province of Quebec spoke French, and Canada's Official Languages Act of 1969 required an accommodation of English and French. In terminology describing players, for example, pitchers became *lanceurs*, catchers were called *receveurs*, infielders were referred to as *intérieurs*, and those patrolling the outfield were *voltigeurs*.

Another bewildering event took place shortly before Christmas 1968 that could have crippled the Expos in the team's most formative stages. With William Eckert deposed as baseball commissioner during the most recent winter meetings, John McHale's name surfaced as Eckert's possible successor because of his experience working as deputy commissioner before he was named president of the Expos. At a special meeting convened to find a replacement, McHale was nominated by Detroit Tigers owner John Fetzer and was approved almost unanimously by American League magnates, but those in the National League were far less enthusiastic. After eleven ballots had been taken among all owners and with no approval in sight, McHale removed himself from further consideration for the post. McHale was burdened by "both a moral and legal obligation" to continue in his role with Montreal.[20] It is hard to imagine the fate of the franchise had McHale left the Expos, whose brief existence already had been nearly wrecked by overwhelming difficulties with financial and stadium exigencies.

McHale's departure would have put the club in an impossible situation. The team would have been tasked with finding his replacement at the same time as a substantial franchise fee of $6 million was due to be paid to the National League, and as work on Jarry Park was enduring a lengthy delay in the delivery of building materials—to say nothing of other ongoing preparations such as arranging television and radio broadcasts; creating a minor-league system; opening the team's spring training facility in West Palm Beach, Florida; and processing thousands of season ticket requests. Taken together with the festering problem of the Clendenon trade, the newborn Expos seemed to have suffered enough woes to qualify as a long-term franchise.

Persistence paid off at last, however. As work crews in February 1969 toiled nearly around the clock at Jarry Park, clearing five feet of snow from the field and fashioning stands from steelwork, the Expos opened spring training by greeting supporters with a hearty *bienvenue aux visiteurs*. The red-headed Rusty Staub quickly assumed the role of fan favorite with the nickname "Le Grand Orange," and in early April the Expos were accorded a hero's welcome by fans stationed along a parade route ten miles in length when the club stopped in Montreal prior to embarking on a trip to New York for their season-opening game against the Mets. When they returned to Montreal for their first contest at the new Jarry Park, the Expos sported a fair record of two wins and four losses, then proceeded to defeat the defending National League champion St. Louis Cardinals before an enthusiastic crowd of more than twenty-nine thousand fans. The condition of the playing field left much to be desired; one team history indicates that "the grounds crew could barely fashion a playing surface that had become a swamp."[21] Yet players sheltered in new, oversized dugouts that were one hundred feet in length, and the partisan gathering was entertained with cartoons—bilingual, of course—displayed on the ballpark's gigantic new scoreboard. The come-from-behind 8–7 victory was a feather in the red-white-and-blue cap of the Expos. *Les Expos sont là!*—Here come the Expos, indeed.

Trials and tribulations still lay ahead as early growing pains became evident with the struggling team, including a pair of games in which Montreal committed five errors and a losing streak of twenty consecutive games. During the course of the 1969 season, Montreal's offense was blanked on eighteen occasions, the Expos lost eleven times in their opponents' final at-bat, and they ended the season with a dismal 52–110 record. Shortstop Maury Wills slapped a Montreal beat reporter in mid-May, announced his retirement in early June, rescinded his retirement two days later, then was finally traded to the Dodgers on June 11. Through it all, Expos fans exuberantly clicked the turnstiles at Jarry Park, far outpacing the other three expansion franchises with attendance of 1,212,608, a total that put Montreal in a respectable seventh place in the National League.

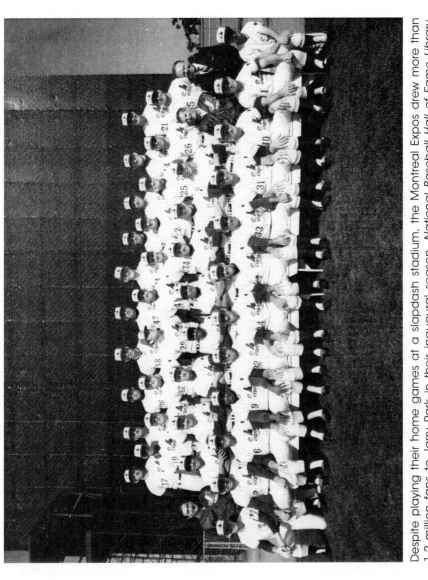

Despite playing their home games at a slapdash stadium, the Montreal Expos drew more than 1.2 million fans to Jarry Park in their inaugural season. *National Baseball Hall of Fame Library, Cooperstown, NY.*

Although the Expos faltered frequently, the ownership of Charles Bronfman and the baseball acumen of John McHale together provided a compass that the team followed to its glory days of the late 1970s and early 1980s.

It speaks well—in either English or French—that the Montreal Expos persevered through the dark days that lasted practically from the date of the franchise's birth, and the fledgling team gained a real foothold within a decade after its debut. Even though they eventually spent many years playing in Olympic Stadium—a ballpark so bleak that even the air seemed artificial—the roots they set down at Jarry Park embodied the real, if to a degree quotidian, baseball experience. The franchise's *bleu, blanc, et rouge* color scheme was imitative of its in-town hockey rival, yet the Expos placed their own indelible stamp on the national—or perhaps *international*—pastime.

The major-league baseball forays the National League took into southernmost California and the province of Quebec were certainly noteworthy if not entirely longstanding. The shortcomings endured by the Padres in their very early years nearly caused them to relocate to Washington, DC—the same city, ironically, to which the Expos would retreat after the 2004 season.

In the case of the Expos, the argument can be made that attendance of more than one million fans in each of the team's first six seasons proved that baseball could be sold beyond the borders of the United States. Bolstered by such encouragement, baseball's moguls granted the Toronto franchise as a partner with the Seattle Mariners, and the Blue Jays have held their ground since the mid-1970s. Shortly after the Expos opened their 1969 campaign, Mayor Jean Drapeau helped convince the International Olympic Committee that his city was worthy of an encore performance on the global stage and managed to secure Montreal as the site of the 1976 Summer Olympics. This event delivered the stadium that became the Expos' new home, the cost of which, less happily, was part of a massive $1 billion debt incurred in hosting the Games and earned *Stade olympique* the pejorative of the "Big Owe." Jarry Park, humble in its existence, had more than served its purpose as a short-term facility.

The Padres remain very much ensconced in the National League's West Division, although the legacy of their founding father, C. Arnholt Smith, serves as a mere footnote in the club's history. Buzzie Bavasi brought his baseball insight with him from Los Angeles, but this asset did not translate into any positive results on the field. Attendance at San Diego Stadium was last in the National League for four of the Padres' first five seasons and confirmed the fear that fans really would have preferred to see their Triple-A heroes rather than the brand of major-league ball that had been foisted upon them. Ray Kroc's arrival on the

San Diego scene was just in time to salvage the team from ruin and a likely move to the East Coast.

Through thick and thin, the Expos and the Padres nonetheless brought major-league baseball to new cities, and these additions helped the sport to shed some of the lethargy into which it had fallen and caused it to lose popularity to professional football. The national pastime needed to expand in order to keep up with the times, no matter how hurtful the growing pains may have been.

CHAPTER 5

The Commissioners

AN UNKNOWN SOLDIER AND AN UNKNOWN LAWYER

Only a handful of men have occupied the seat of baseball commissioner, none more powerful than the first and none weaker than the fourth man chosen for the office. As baseball moved through the latter half of the 1960s, the glaring deficiencies of William Eckert forced the hand of club owners, who brought in a new man to turn around a game that, while hardly facing extinction, had moved dangerously close to being relegated to second-class status among major spectator sports. The departure of Eckert in 1968 and the arrival of Bowie Kuhn in 1969 provide a vivid contrast of leadership style and an ability to move the game forward. This transition became a critical turning point in baseball history.

Created shortly after the 1919 Black Sox scandal, the position of commissioner was in the hands of Judge Kenesaw Mountain Landis for more than twenty years. Landis's reign was marked by his intimidating personality and, as one noted historian put it, a penchant to rule "in the interest of what he conceived to be justice."[1] He came to the commissionership by insisting that his underlings—namely, the sixteen club owners—grant him incontrovertible power, the team magnates bowing to Landis by acquiescing to an oath of fealty. When Landis died in November 1944, he left a legacy marked by his presumed prejudice against black players and a lust to ferret out any player whom he believed compromised the integrity of the game.

Following more than two decades of Landis's autocracy, the magnates sought to diminish some of the power that had been bestowed upon the first commissioner. When former Kentucky governor and United States senator Albert Benjamin "Happy" Chandler was selected to succeed Landis, he insisted on the same loyalty enjoyed by his predecessor. Chandler had a powerful ally among the ownership group, New York Yankees president Larry MacPhail, who had aided in Chandler's election. The new commissioner faced the defection of major-league players to the Mexican League in 1946, sought to uphold the integrity of the game by suspending Brooklyn Dodgers manager Leo Durocher for conduct deemed not in baseball's best interest, and launched investigations of baseball personnel who were rumored to have ties to gambling concerns. While Chandler held no sway over major-league rosters, the defining moment of his tenure was the 1947 debut of Jackie Robinson, which integrated the national pastime.

Owner opposition to Chandler began to mount after he probed violations pertaining to the signing of amateur players by big-league clubs and facilitated the creation of a pension plan for major-league players. Chandler requested a renewal of his seven-year contract in December 1949, well before its expiration, but formal discussion of his inquiry by the sixteen team owners in late 1950 revealed that seven of them did not want to see Chandler continue. The owners had included in the commissioner's contract a proviso requiring stricter guidelines for reelecting a commissioner, moving from simple majority approval to recognition by three-quarters of club ownership. Facing nearly 50 percent opposition from those who held the key to his fate, Chandler tendered his resignation and was gone in the early summer of 1951.

Turning their attention to a longtime baseball man, the owners tapped Ford Frick as baseball's third commissioner. A former writer and broadcaster, Frick had most recently served seventeen years as president of the National League. The owners insisted they wanted "a tough commissioner" willing to "make decisions without regard for whom they hurt," but in reality they actually sought a man who would cater to their needs.[2]

It can be argued that Frick presided over the first modernization of Major League Baseball. Less than two years after Frick's ascension to commissioner in September 1951, the shifting of major-league franchises commenced, mostly from cities in the greater Northeast to those in the Midwest and beyond. By the dawning of the 1960s, baseball was ready to add expansion teams; this occurred in 1961 and 1962 after the looming threat of the creation of a third major league fell flat. Despite presiding over these sea changes in the game's structure, Frick was viewed as "a spectator who went along for the ride," and was thought by a well-respected baseball columnist to be "a reluctant leader" whose handling of his job was tinged by a "low-keyed tone."[3] Nonetheless, Frick was rewarded for his service with a second term and served as commissioner until November 1965.

In addressing competition from the expansion of pro football and the general rise in football's popularity in America, baseball would have to rely less on its longstanding reputation as the nation's preeminent sport and more on meeting the increasing demands related to the business side of its operations. By the end of Frick's tenure, newer ballparks such as Dodger Stadium, Anaheim Stadium,

Shea Stadium, D.C. Stadium, and Atlanta Stadium had opened or were soon to open, enticing fans to attend games at comfortable and modern venues. Television revenues for the clubs were on the rise, and with Marvin Miller not yet in command of the players' association, the owners still held a decidedly upper hand at the bargaining table.

Enter Eckert

To better face the changing milieu into which baseball was increasingly drawn, club owners made a curious choice to replace Ford Frick. The ownership tabbed a military man who was completely outside the realm of baseball yet nonetheless seemed qualified to handle the business logistics the game demanded. William Dole "Spike" Eckert was a fifty-six-year-old retired lieutenant general who had served in the United States Air Force, a member of the West Point Class of 1930 whose service with the Army Air Forces during World War II earned him honors including Legions of Merit, Distinguished Service Medals, and a pair of Croix de Guerre. Upon entering the field of business management with the air force following the war, he earned his MBA at Harvard and ascended to the position of comptroller of the air force before his retirement in the spring of 1961 due to health reasons. Eckert then worked as an aviation consultant and director of a Defense Department advisory group.

When the baseball owners began the search for Frick's replacement, their list of candidates contained the names of more than 150 men and was pared to fifteen; Eckert's name was not among those on the short list. But Eckert reemerged and quickly became a finalist for the commissioner's job. Detroit Tigers owner John Fetzer was a member of the committee in charge of screening candidates and the first person to interview Eckert. Working in Eckert's favor were his expertise—albeit militarily related—in business, and his reputation as man who could "analyze problems and come up with proposed solutions" and who was "no stranger to tough assignments."[4] The contacts he had made in Washington, DC, as a result of his many years working with the government seemed to underscore his credentials.

The evidence to support Eckert's business acumen in the military world, however, was offset by his dearth of insight about the game he would be charged with leading. In the world of sports, his interest was skewed toward squash, golf, and polo, and his knowledge of baseball was so poor that he appeared not to realize that the Los Angeles Dodgers had once played in Brooklyn. Eckert may have had connections in the nation's capital, but these "contacts were in the Pentagon, not on Capitol Hill," and as far as the owners were concerned—especially in the area of antitrust issues—"when the General couldn't give [them] any political pull, he

Quickly shown to be out of his depth as a baseball executive, William Eckert was relieved of his command well before the end of his seven-year term. *National Baseball Hall of Fame Library, Cooperstown, NY.*

couldn't give them anything."[5] Certainly those vetting Eckert's qualifications, such as they were, had to be aware of his shortcomings, but they demonstrated their faith by unanimously recommending him to the ownership of all teams, who in turn stood firmly with the committee and handed the reins, plus a $65,000 annual salary, to Eckert.

To prop up the poorly credentialed Eckert, a small team of aides—any of whom would have been a better choice for commissioner—was created to guide the head of baseball's executive branch. The most prominent of this group were former New York baseball writer Joseph Reichler, who acted as Eckert's personal assistant, and Lee MacPhail, late of the Baltimore Orioles front office, who was appointed to aid the new commissioner's understanding of baseball's administrative functioning. Had the owners not been so steadfast in their desire for an outsider such as Eckert, an argument can be made that as a sound baseball official, MacPhail would have been a fine choice for the commissionership.

Embarking on his seven-year term as commissioner in mid-November 1965, Eckert intended to draw on his vast military experience and ostensibly took charge from his first day in office. "I'm no czar, . . . [but] I'll call the signals as I see fit," Eckert told the *Sporting News.* "I'm going to make decisions that I'm authorized to make under the Major League Agreement."[6] He stated his objective not to be a yes-man for the team owners and also expressed his appreciation for MacPhail's willingness to ease the transition to his new post.

To better acquaint himself with the overall landscape of baseball, Eckert wanted to visit minor-league facilities to gain a sense of what happened in the game's lower ranks. The topic of possible expansion was raised shortly after the December winter meetings, but Eckert said that broadening the reach of the major leagues to new cities was not on the immediate horizon because time was needed to deal with the logistics of laying groundwork for any new franchises. This statement prompted a quick rebuttal from one sportswriter, who noted the swiftness employed by the American League to catch up with the National League when the Junior Circuit acted to add clubs in Washington and Los Angeles for the 1961 season.[7] If the AL could jump to add two teams ahead of the NL's intended 1962 expansion in New York and Houston, then maybe long lead times were not all they seemed to be, and it *was* possible for baseball to move more quickly than Eckert believed.

In early June of 1966, Eckert tried to clarify his position by saying that there was no firm timetable for expansion, which he viewed as taking perhaps eight to ten years to accomplish. But in stating the obvious, he insisted that whenever expansion was to occur, "it should be done in an orderly and proper manner."[8] However, this was becoming a critical time for baseball, as pressure from other groups was growing not only to meet the demands of the sporting public but also to compete for the discretionary dollars fans would spend on games. Competing interests were emerging from the National Basketball Association, which was adding new teams; the American Basketball Association, already in the process of getting organized to open its first season in 1967; the National Hockey League, which planned to double its number of teams from six to twelve in 1967; and the National and American Football leagues, both of which were adding new franchises, albeit at a slower pace than basketball and hockey. Baseball cities such as Pittsburgh, Los Angeles, Minneapolis, St. Louis, Philadelphia, New York, and Atlanta were now hosting or were about to become the new homes of non-baseball sporting enterprises. Major-league baseball would still hold a monopoly on fans' attention during the peak summer months, but in the spring and autumn, many fans would have an increased number of choices conflicting with their patronage of—and money spent on—the national pastime. As discussed earlier, baseball was spurred to expand only when Senator Stuart Symington decried the shift of the Athletics from Kansas City to Oakland following the 1967 season, not as a result of any plan initiated by Commissioner Eckert.

Because the heretofore anonymous Eckert was suddenly thrust into baseball's forefront, patience was counseled by a host of sources willing to allow him time to adjust, including the publisher of the *Sporting News* and baseball writers from across the country. The most prescient of the remarks, however, came from Leonard Koppett, the astute baseball maven of the *New York Times*. Aware of the rough road faced by Major League Baseball in warding off threats to its supremacy in the world of American sports, Koppett observed of Eckert, "If he can't come across as forceful . . . or informed . . . in face-to-face meetings, his capacity to sell baseball in the bitterly competitive battle for attention is not promising."[9]

The business side of affairs proved to be only slightly less challenging for Eckert, and he desired a bigger presence for baseball on the world stage, including a vision of "major league baseball as a means of contributing to international friendship." But the manner in which Eckert was viewed evolved into a ratification of Koppett's opinion. Reichler gave Eckert notes on index cards to use when he spoke at various gatherings, but sometimes he accidentally used the wrong set of notes without realizing who he was addressing. Reichler, who tried to ensure that the commissioner was putting his best foot forward when in public, was often at odds with him because Eckert's "streak of vanity" made it difficult for him to accept the orders of those with inferior rank. Another source of embarrassment was his comparisons of various aspects of baseball to those he found analogous in the air force, remarks which caused "baseball insiders to wince." Whether it was his use of incorrect index cards or a reference to a team like the Cincinnati Cardinals, which had to exist only in his mind, Eckert was perhaps the most uncomfortable man ever appointed as baseball commissioner, despite his efforts to learn about the game and its history while partaking in on-the-job training.[10]

Such training, in John Fetzer's mind, included tackling the biggest issues baseball had to face. Under consideration was an amended regular-season schedule that strove to improve the lot of teams in the northern part of the country, which had problems with inclement weather earlier and later in the year. Also drawing notice was an initiative to reduce the length of time it took to play an average game, and innovative ideas like interleague play—first discussed in the 1930s—were being mulled over in some front offices. For his part, the commissioner wanted "to bring more highly-qualified players to the major leagues" by a process of improved player selection and training at the minor-league level, an incredible statement given that the function of the minors to do just that had been in place for decades.[11]

As the opening of the 1966 season approached, *Sports Illustrated* weighed in with a review of Eckert's first full quarter in office, noting that "Spike Eckert is proving that he is a man who came to play," and that he was not "the totally unimpressive man he might have seemed" at the time he was chosen as baseball's fourth commissioner.[12] The calm and collected Eckert impressed as being omnipresent in carrying out his duties—meeting with players, owners, collegiate officials, and Little League interests—as he endeavored to grasp all he could about the game.

The magazine also noted Eckert's important decision regarding a collegiate player who had been drafted by the Atlanta Braves and signed to their Triple-A team but had commenced his third year of play with his school. By voiding the contract and precluding the Braves organization from signing him again for another three years, Eckert hoped to put the player back in the good graces of the NCAA. Because he had signed a professional contract with the Braves—even though the team had made no payment to the player—he was barred by the NCAA from playing for his school, so Eckert announced that any club willing to match the Braves' offer could participate in a special draft to negotiate with the player now in limbo. The player drew the interest of three teams—the Cleveland Indians, the New York Mets, and the Philadelphia Phillies—who elected to take their chance in the lottery, with the Mets randomly chosen by the commissioner as the winner. Thus was the active hand Eckert had in launching the Hall of Fame career of pitcher Tom Seaver.

Eckert's handling of another matter at the time of the Seaver imbroglio showed his resolve to take charge. When the National League teams voted unanimously to raise Triple-A roster limits from twenty to twenty-one players, the American League failed to do so, with seven clubs dissenting while only three agreed. Seeing that well over half of all teams wanted the increase, Eckert decreed that larger rosters would be in effect so that all Triple-A franchises would be on equal footing. Even Leonard Koppett was coming around to the opinion that Eckert was shedding the "puppet rap" bestowed on him in expectation that he would be nothing more than a figurehead serving at the beck and call of major-league ownership. Controversy lingered over the recent transfer of the Braves from Milwaukee to Atlanta, but when questioned about it, Eckert struck a diplomatic pose by stating that if a franchise shift was conducted in a legal way, then he was not in a position to prevent it from happening. This reply catered to the laissez-faire handling owners desired for their franchises, but Reichler insisted the commissioner correctly gave "the only answer."[13]

In the summer of 1966, the commissioner was on hand to chair two important meetings: a groundbreaking session of all owners and player representatives, and the annual meeting of team owners, during which the decision was made to increase their contribution to the players' pension fund to a flat $4 million in both 1967 and 1968, a significant amount at that time. The latter issue was urgent because the existing pension agreement, set to expire in March 1967, quickly evolved into Marvin Miller's first tussle with club owners and other baseball executives after his appointment as the director of the Major League Baseball Players Association. Once Miller was officially installed as the director of the players' union, he set to work claiming what he believed was the rightful share to which the players were entitled, thus ending a period of general player obsequiousness to team ownership and beginning an era of labor relations that often resembled trench warfare between players and owners.

This multimillion-dollar "unprecedented windfall" meant that trainers and uniformed field personnel would no longer be required to contribute two dollars per day from their salary during the season to the pension fund. Instead that money was to go—if the players so chose—toward funding the Major League Baseball Players Association, although this point stirred controversy as a possible breach of the Taft-Hartley Act, which the owners viewed as precluding the use of pension money to pay the head of a union. Eckert stated that a new television contract in place for networks to secure rights to broadcast All-Star and World Series games was the source of the "substantial and generous" sum now earmarked for the players, but Miller was quick to observe that the fixed amount set for 1967 and 1968 was a change from the 60/40 percent revenue split used previously and could work against the players in the future should media payments to the owners increase.[14]

Marvin Miller was sharpening his claws in his early duels against baseball's hierarchy, and Eckert was fodder for the shrewd union leader. The baseball owners realized Eckert was no match for Miller, who pointed out that since the MLBPA was the players' bargaining entity, any unilateral action on ownership's part would be illegal. To counter Eckert's obvious shortcomings, the owners formed a Player Relations Committee to bargain with the players' association and in August 1967 brought in John Gaherin, formerly a management representative and lead negotiator for the New York Newspaper Publishers Association, as the PRC's director. Miller praised Gaherin's appointment and commended him as a negotiator who "acted in good faith," but the move also pushed Eckert further away from having a hand in labor affairs.[15]

A milestone was reached in early 1968 when the players' association and the owners negotiated a collective bargaining agreement, a two-year pact believed to be the first such contract in sports. However, Eckert's role in the matter was relegated to that of a spectator as the club owners sought more direct control in their dealings with Miller and the union. During this time, Bowie Kuhn, a counselor for the National League, was becoming more actively engaged on the owners' side of the labor front, a foreshadowing that would have further consequences just one year later when Kuhn was named commissioner and became more frequently engaged in disputes with Miller.

As Eckert drifted further from work issues with the players, he was not endearing himself to owners in either league as expansion grew into a pressing topic in the autumn of 1967. When the Athletics were relocated from Kansas City to Oakland, paving the way for the creation of the Kansas City Royals and the Seattle Pilots, some magnates were critical of Eckert for allowing Charlie Finley to infringe on market territory already occupied by the San Francisco Giants.

Other National League owners insisted that Eckert should have prohibited the American League from creating two divisions to accommodate the new twelve-team circuit—recall that the NL favored maintaining a single league following its own expansion—and the Senior Circuit felt harried by the need to add Montreal and San Diego in order to keep pace with the new Kansas City and Seattle teams. Nonetheless, Eckert's summary of baseball for 1967 trumpeted the "unabated rise" in "fan enthusiasm," and he anticipated "continued progress in all areas."[16]

The collective bargaining dispute now behind him as spring training of 1968 began, the commissioner told the *Sporting News* that he was looking forward to addressing "dead spots" in order to make the game more attractive to its paying customers. But the interview, as portrayed in print, still conveys the impression of a man trying to learn about the national pastime by traveling "here, there, and everywhere on his baseball beat" while answering some interviewers' questions from "long, handwritten notes."[17]

Eckert's business acumen indicated that he was well aware of attendance figures and television ratings—as well he should have been, since these assets translate into the revenue which is the lifeblood of any sports enterprise. But in an attempt to present Eckert in a good light, those notes may have been the work of Lee MacPhail or Joe Reichler, both of whom better understood how baseball functioned. The addition of four major-league franchises also meant that minor-league systems had to grow in order to meet the demands of an expanding pool of talent the new clubs would require, a situation Eckert acknowledged numerous times in the media.

Eckert expressed a desire to keep the World Series played only during the daytime—night baseball for the Fall Classic would not be experimented with for another few years—but the 1967 All-Star Game was switched to an evening affair and has been played under the lights ever since. During Eckert's tenure there was a continuing effort to combat the cheating perpetrated by pitchers throwing spitballs, his office worked to enhance summer leagues in Mexico and Latin America, and the Major League Baseball Promotions Corporation was formed to advance baseball's stature and prepare the national pastime for its centennial season in 1969. This variety of issues demonstrates that although Eckert himself proved to be far short of fully qualified for the job of commissioner, the office of his position—with assistance from MacPhail and Reichler—tried to keep baseball moving forward to meet the demands of the day.

As the curtain was about to rise on the 1968 campaign, the commissioner was optimistic about baseball's improved exposure as a result of the new teams soon to join the Major League Baseball fold. Eckert informed a meeting of baseball's Executive Council that "much progress had been made through *joint* efforts of the Leagues and the Commissioner's office, such as the national TV contract, the college program, player relations, the promotion program, the free agent draft and public relations activities."[18] Baseball also answered the call from Vice President Hubert Humphrey to support the President's Council on Youth Opportunity, which distributed game tickets at no charge to "underprivileged children from slum areas" during 1968, while individual teams enticed students to excel at school by furnishing passes to those with good grades, sponsored youth clinics, and hired youngsters for summer jobs at stadiums and in team front offices.[19]

Yet a number of forces came together against William Eckert in 1968, shortly after a rumor surfaced that the youthful Michael Burke, president of the New York Yankees, was in the running to succeed Eckert as baseball commissioner. That such a story would circulate as spring training was ending, despite the more than four years remaining on Eckert's contract, gives reason for pause. Of far greater import to baseball, however, was the pair of tragedies that shook the nation to its core when Dr. Martin Luther King Jr. was assassinated on the eve of the opening of the season and Senator Robert Kennedy was assassinated on the presidential campaign trail in early June. The reaction of Major League Baseball to these events was inchoate and awkward, and Eckert, looked upon as the spokesman for all of baseball, found few friends—especially in the media— when he failed to establish a set policy to postpone or cancel games in honor of the slain civil rights leader and the popular politician. Roundly criticized for baseball's clumsy response, Eckert did have one ally: the editor and publisher of the *Sporting News*. C. C. Johnson Spink came to Eckert's defense by pointing out that baseball did more out of respect for Kennedy than did the New York State Racing Commission, which "forced Belmont [Race Track] to run its program of horse races . . . on a day when baseball called off or delayed all its activities in deference to the Kennedy funeral." Another New York scribe noted baseball's "loss of stature" due to Eckert's indecisiveness in the matter, but he also blamed the club owners for having put the underqualified Eckert in the commissioner's office in the first place.[20]

Another alleged fault of Eckert's—although such claims were made well after the fact and only with historical hindsight—was his failure to address the problem of performance-enhancing substances used by players. While steroid use would become a notorious problem later in the twentieth century and continues to receive scrutiny, the use of amphetamines by players in the post–World War II era has received much attention. Throughout the 1960s, players discovered that the use of "greenies" could alleviate the unwelcome effects of a hangover or otherwise make them more alert come game time. In the face of this growing phenomenon, there is little evidence to suggest that Eckert was inclined to take action against those using pep pills. Given his overall lack of knowledge of the game, Eckert may have been oblivious to an undercurrent of amphetamines in baseball; it's also possible he may have been shielded from their presence.

The timing of Eckert's tenure as commissioner coincidentally placed him in office during one of the most exciting pennant races ever, the great American League scramble of 1967. Although increases and decreases in attendance at major-league games cannot be ascribed directly to Eckert, a falloff in the number of fans coming to the ballpark over the three years of his tenure was unmistakable. Total big-league attendance in 1966 was 25.1 million, but the following year it slipped to 24.3 million, and in 1968 a further decrease put the figure at 23.1 million. To be sure, some teams enjoyed strong growth over these years—Boston more than doubled its figure at the gate, from 811,172 in 1966 to more than 1.9 million two years later—but others experienced sharp declines, such as the Los Angeles Dodgers' plummet from 2.6 million to 1.5 million. If the overall figures were an indicator of the general financial health of baseball, there was cause for concern when viewed from the standpoint of a collective loss of more than 2 million fans between 1966 and 1968. With pitching becoming dominant by 1968, some decreases in attendance can be attributed to fans' reluctance to go to low-scoring—which is to say, dull—contests. A spark was lacking to sustain interest or encourage more people to visit a major-league stadium, and as baseball was a for-profit enterprise, many club owners could easily perceive a dearth of leadership from baseball's highest office as another reason for the ailing state of the game.

Through the summer of 1968, Eckert busied himself with appearances at the College World Series, meetings of minor-league executives, and the American Legion tournament. Eckert was mindful of ensuring that the USO had a contingent of past and present major-league players available to visit troops serving in Vietnam, and he earned praise for adding Monte Irvin, a former Negro League standout and future Hall of Fame inductee, to his staff as a public relations liaison.

For all this work as a goodwill ambassador and his ongoing remedial education on the history of baseball, Eckert was still dogged by his own ineptness. Columnist Jim Murray's acerbic pen lampooned a fictional baseball commissioner named William I. Egghead, but the real target was obviously Eckert. Not standing by idly, Eckert's son, William Douglas Eckert, a second lieutenant in the air force, wrote a letter rebuking Murray for the "ridiculous and irresponsible insults" directed at his father. But the younger Eckert's defense could not rescue the elder, who "once again sat by as events unfolded" during a dispute with major-league umpires, who threatened to strike the 1968 World Series after American League president Joe Cronin dismissed two arbiters who had encouraged their fellow AL umpires to join an existing union organized by their colleagues in the National League.[21]

When baseball's winter meetings convened in early December at the Sheraton-Palace Hotel in San Francisco, change was in the air, and it produced a gust that swept William Eckert out of office. Eckert fell victim to a cabal of owners who found the commissioner "[reluctant] to take strong action on any issue." From the outset of the meetings, rumors of displeasure over Eckert's shortcomings were openly discussed among owners, and the commissioner arrived at the gathering "with apprehension and with the wish to survive." Credited with leading the charge against Eckert was Baltimore Orioles owner Jerry Hoffberger, and the stage had been set for the jettisoning of Eckert for quite some time. Whether by accident or design, Hoffberger tipped his hand at an Executive Council meeting on December 3—with Eckert in attendance—when he stated, "A study by competent outside agencies of all facets of the business is needed," and that a Survey Committee report recommended a "broad-based study of the entire baseball business."[22]

On the second day of the convention, Eckert chaired a joint gathering of executives from both leagues, and when he was still standing at the conclusion of that meeting, Eckert "thought he had it made" and went to a press conference to review the day's business with the media.[23] But Hoffberger reconvened an owners-only session, the gripes against Eckert were discussed, and, by a vote of 22–2, the club magnates quickly decided to oust the commissioner. Eckert was summoned from his press conference to rejoin the owners, and it was then that the bad news was delivered.

One frequently stated reason for the dismissal was Eckert's inability to take a firm stand on important topics—for example, a coordinated expansion strategy—even if his position may have upset those who disagreed with him. Eckert's failure to achieve consensus between the National and American leagues "by persuasion or force" affirmed his incompetence in the world of baseball. Eckert's tenure was a debacle from the very beginning, but several baseball writers fingered the real culprits in this caper: the team owners, who wanted a figurehead to represent the game but at the same time desired to run their businesses as they individually saw fit, all to the exclusion of what may have been best for baseball as a whole. To have left the commissioner's office vacant upon the departure of Ford Frick would have been "a public relations disaster" for the game, in the opinion of one learned sportswriter, while another scribe noted, "What baseball needs—and has needed—is a visionary who can see beyond the greed of today's owners . . . who can fight off this challenge of pro football."[24]

Determined to right baseball's listing ship, the owners were determined to bring in a man familiar with the game and its inner business domain. One trait the new commissioner would need to possess was physical youth, or at least a youthful approach to recasting the image of baseball. "Baseball has lived for too many years in an old-fashioned house that has become weather-beaten and unfit for modern occupancy," noted the *Sporting News* in a soul-searching editorial. Equally as important as modernity, the honor of the game was also at stake. The same owners who forswore direction or advice with regard to how to run their teams—so long as they could make a profit—wanted only a puppet for a commissioner yet "could not face the public relations consequences of abolishing the office that stood for baseball's integrity."[25]

William Eckert was pilloried as "a man whose most significant achievement in three years of office may have been to declare a Baltimore hotel 'substandard housing' for ballplayers and to order the Chicago White Sox front office to find flossier lodgings for its team."[26] Having divested themselves of the most incompetent man who ever served as commissioner, club owners now countenanced an uncertain future. Aware that Eckert had been mocked as the "unknown soldier" from the time of his appointment, the moguls had to act swiftly and decisively to fill the vacancy. This new search would yield a candidate who was far more in step with baseball, not only in knowledge of the game itself but in understanding how the business and legal side of the sport functioned.

Passing the Torch

In the immediate aftermath of Eckert's dismissal, Leonard Koppett of the *New York Times* identified five key areas he felt needed to be addressed by a new baseball commissioner: Handling of the World Series and the financial package associated with the television rights to broadcast it; the wider issue of "policy-making power" regarding radio and television broadcast revenue for all teams; recognition of the rapidly rising influence of the Major League Baseball Players Association, now under the direction of Marvin Miller; the matters of baseball's exemption from antitrust laws and the "legal attack" to which the reserve clause might well be subject; and a meaningful restructuring of the league offices so that the commissioner—rather than the owners within the American and National leagues—would have authority to adjudicate issues on which the circuits may not be in complete agreement.[27]

Baseball team owners were in an increasingly uncomfortable position requiring them to relinquish at least some control to a commissioner modeled after Pete Rozelle of the NFL. "The owners must not only pick the right man for the job," advised the *Sporting News*, "they must let him call the tune."[28] Early speculation regarding Eckert's replacement focused on several men with firsthand knowledge of the game, and this short list included New York Yankees president Michael Burke, American League president Joe Cronin, and St. Louis Cardinals executive vice president Bing Devine.

However, the most notable name mentioned in the early running was Robert Cannon, who in late 1968 was serving as a judge in a Milwaukee circuit court but before that had been Marvin Miller's predecessor as an adviser to the players' association. Cannon, who was on the baseball scene during the administrations of Ford Frick and William Eckert, was deemed a worthy candidate whose credentials were burnished by his judicial title. "The idea of having a judge in office has a good ring to it," said one national magazine, but the scrum to select the new commissioner devolved into a familiar internecine struggle between the American and National leagues.[29]

Just before Christmas, an owners' meeting was convened in Chicago in the hope of filling the vacancy. The slate of contenders for the post included Charles "Chub" Feeney, vice president of the San Francisco Giants; Lee MacPhail, who was now serving the Yankees as general manager; and John McHale, president of the expansion Montreal Expos. Because a candidate needed approval of three-fourths of the members of each league, it came as no surprise that ballots split along league lines. Burke, MacPhail, and especially Feeney drew support from their respective circuits but found little advocacy in the other league.

McHale was "flattered" by the consideration he was being given, but he was understandably conflicted over the choice now before him—remain with the fledgling Expos or pursue becoming commissioner. When he sought the advice of a lawyer for the National League, he was counseled not to leave the Expos and so chose to honor his commitment. The attorney who furnished that recommendation was Bowie Kuhn, and McHale later "wonder[ed] if [he] had been duped" by Kuhn's opinion.[30]

The Chicago gathering failed to produce the intended result due in part to the fact that members of one league at times felt pressured by the other league to sanction a nominee against their better judgment. Genuine concern arose that if a candidate from the greater baseball community could not be agreed upon, a search outside the sport would be necessary. But with the most recent experience of the ill-fated Eckert still fresh in their minds, the owners realized a bold step had to be taken.

On February 4, 1969, the magnates reconvened near Miami, Florida, to resolve the dispute and again found themselves at loggerheads over Feeney and Burke, each receiving support from his own league but not the other. While the owners continued the debate over the commissioner's position, Bowie Kuhn was on site working with Sandy Hadden, a lawyer for the American League, on upcoming negotiations between the collective ownership and the players' association. At an owners' meeting recess, Kuhn's name was raised and subsequently placed in nomination as a temporary commissioner to manage a handful of key tasks: standardization of procedures affecting both the American and National leagues, the unification and reorganization of the bureaucratic structures of both circuits, and updating baseball's image. Given the rancor that surrounded the deliberations over electing a more permanent commissioner with a seven-year term, the leagues opted for a short-term solution that allowed them to evaluate the commissioner pro tem and replace him should he fall short of expectations the way William Eckert had.

Quite astoundingly, Kuhn drew the unanimous support of both leagues on the very first ballot following the break, but he evinced a large degree of suspicion at his unexpected appointment. Realizing that he would have to resign from Willkie, Farr and Gallagher, his Wall Street–based law firm—perhaps for only one year should the owners drop him after his term—Kuhn "was not thrilled" about a job offer that "reeked of compromise." Understandably, Kuhn was loath to resign from his firm only to find himself one year hence in the same position as the banished Eckert. But after conferring with Lou Carroll, a senior partner at his office, Kuhn accepted the commissionership—and the interim position's salary of $100,000—as well as all its attendant challenges. One of the nation's leading sportswriters reserved judgment as to how he thought Kuhn would handle his new role, but he was impressed by "the way he rolls up his sleeves and gets right to work."[31]

With baseball in need of a knowledgeable leader at the commissioner's post, Bowie Kuhn was the right man in the right place when he was named as the replacement for William Eckert in February 1969. *National Baseball Hall of Fame Library, Cooperstown, NY.*

Towering at six feet five inches in height, the resident of Ridgewood, New Jersey, quickly earned the respect of those who may have been suspicious of his credentials. Giving himself the title "The Unknown Lawyer," Kuhn was hopelessly romantic about the old Washington Senators, for whom he once served as a scoreboard operator. Kuhn was a Princeton graduate with a law degree from the University of Virginia, and his previous work with some of the National League's legal matters as well as his own passion for the game put him on solid footing that the forlorn William Eckert could only have imagined. "[H]is knowledge of the complicated details, the paperwork, and the playing of the game is boundless," was how Kuhn was portrayed in a news article that introduced him to the sporting community.[32]

The new commissioner was aware of the unkind remarks made about Eckert by members of the press, as well as the manner in which he was treated by the owners. So it was with a fair degree of discomfort that Kuhn had to tell Eckert directly that he need not come into the office to ostensibly serve in an advisory capacity. Although this compounded the humiliation Eckert already had endured, Kuhn realized that he had to establish himself in the commissioner's seat as he saw fit, and with the reins officially handed over to him, it was up to Kuhn to decide his own course of action. A headline in the *Miami Herald* on February 6—CHEF BOWIE KUHN JUMPS INTO FRYING PAN—served as an apt metaphor for the commissioner's milieu.

Kuhn's maiden voyage began in February 1969 and was marked by a rocky beginning when the players, en masse, elected to boycott spring training until a favorable settlement was reached with the owners in their pension plan dispute. Before he even warmed the chair in his new office, Kuhn was already viewed by the players as a yes-man for the owners because he had spent nearly two decades as a National League attorney. Wisely, Kuhn recused himself from direct intervention in the struggle, instead choosing to maneuver in the background between the two sides, "acting as a mediator and advocating a compromise settlement."[33]

The pension issue had hardly been calmed before a battle erupted over the trade of Rusty Staub from the Houston Astros to the expansion Montreal Expos in exchange for Donn Clendenon. As described in chapter 4, the Clendenon retirement affair played out for several weeks before at last being resolved, providing an unwelcome distraction while Kuhn was tending to more pleasant duties such as visiting spring training camps and then attending seven home openers in April when the regular season commenced. In the midst of those debuts, however, another trade imbroglio came to the fore, this one involving one of baseball's chicest players.

After falling out of favor with Kansas City owner Charlie Finley, Ken "The Hawk" Harrelson was released by the Athletics on August 25, 1967, and signed days later as a free agent by the Boston Red Sox to fill a huge void in the BoSox lineup due to a devastating eye injury suffered by right fielder Tony Conigliaro. With only a few weeks left in the regular season and the Red Sox caught in a frantic scramble with the Twins, Tigers, and White Sox for the American League pennant, Harrelson batted only .200 in twenty-three games for his new team. But the twenty-six-year-old drove in fourteen runs and contributed some timely hits during the stretch run, becoming a major influence in the clubhouse for his demeanor in easing the pressure of the pennant race and also winning over a legion of fans with his long, stylish hair augmented by a mod wardrobe that included turtleneck sweaters and Nehru jackets. The Hawk basked in the limelight, spent lavishly, and helped deliver the AL title to the Red Sox, but no one was more disappointed than Harrelson himself by his performance in the 1967 World Series, getting just one hit in thirteen trips to the plate against the Cardinals.

Fearing a trade as the 1968 season approached, Harrelson honed his already excellent golfing skills over the winter and then diligently took to the task at hand on the diamond, performing so well that by the end of the campaign he batted .275—which placed him eighth among AL hitters—slugged thirty-five home runs, led the American League with 109 RBIs, and finished third in the balloting for the Most Valuable Player Award. Now also involved in several business ventures and an array of personal endorsement deals, The Hawk was thought to be more firmly entrenched with the team than ever, but right field was becoming a crowded position on the Boston roster.

In the spring of 1969 Conigliaro was gamely attempting a comeback, rookie Joe Lahoud was pushing to land a spot in the outfield, and Harrelson's alternate spot at first base was already occupied by the slick-fielding George Scott, who was trying to reassert himself at the plate after a dismal year in which hit .171 in 124 games. The Red Sox were also hampered by the need for a catcher and sought improvement of their pitching staff, so they took a bold step in mid-April to correct the deficiencies by swapping The Hawk and spare pitchers Dick Ellsworth and Juan Pizarro to Cleveland for catcher Joe Azcue, reliever Vicente Romo, and starter Sonny Siebert, a former All-Star. Harrelson was "inconsolable" upon hearing the news that he would be forced to leave behind those who idolized him, and his fans in Boston and other cities were outraged.[34]

Harrelson elected not to abandon the business enterprises he had engaged in during his brief time in Boston, which included a sandwich shop, a nightclub, real estate investments, and a proposed Harrelson's of Boston haberdashery. Noted as "a ball-playing hipster with an uncanny sense of public relations," Harrelson chose to retire rather than lose out on the business portfolio he had accumulated.[35] His announcement to quit unleashed a series of complications, not the least of which was caused by the advice of his attorney, Robert Woolf, who suggested that a new baseball contract to compensate for some of the financial damage resulting from a move to Cleveland might persuade the baseball idol to reconsider his decision to walk away from the game. Quite simply, the affair was rife with the same pecuniary odor as the Clendenon tussle. Adding more friction to the debacle was the refusal of former Indians Azcue, Romo, and Siebert to return to Cleveland, while Boston general manager Dick O'Connell, who saw Harrelson's salary nearly triple from $12,000 in 1967 to $35,000 in 1968, dug in his heels by vowing to prevent The Hawk from again donning a Red Sox uniform.

Stepping into the breach was the new commissioner, who, according to Harrelson, "made me see some things I had not considered," but whether Bowie Kuhn had any direct bearing on the resolution is debatable. In an April 22 meeting called by Kuhn in New York, to which he summoned AL president Joe Cronin, Cleveland president Gabe Paul, O'Connell, Harrelson, and Woolf, the commissioner was anxious to close the matter as quickly as possible. Kuhn asked that Harrelson and his attorney confer in private with Paul—the owner of Harrelson's intended team—and the closed session yielded a new two-year contract for The Hawk calling for $50,000 per season. Kuhn made light of his intervention, noting that he had brought all the interested parties together to let them arrive at their own solution rather than dictating the terms himself. The following day, Harrelson landed in Cleveland to join the Tribe, his welcoming reception featuring "a voluptuous model [who] presented him with a bouquet of flowers, then a kiss." After his participation in settling the Clendenon/Staub and Harrelson disputes, Kuhn fretted over having impressed baseball owners as being a "players' commissioner," but he defended his actions by observing, "The commissioner had more clout than anybody and ought to use it."[36]

Kuhn called upon some of that clout when he demanded that two team owners, Oakland's Charlie Finley and Atlanta's Bill Bartholomay, divest themselves of interests they both held in a consortium that included three casinos in its holdings. Cognizant of any unsavory influence trying to find its way into the national pastime, Kuhn sought to forestall any possible taint that even an indirect connection with gambling would bring to the game.

Interleague play, a subject raised during the Eckert administration, was brought to Kuhn's attention in the summer of 1969.[37] A carefully constructed proposal was devised in which the extant twenty-four big-league teams were aligned into a trio of eight-team divisions (or "leagues," as cited in the memo) which, by and large, lived up to their geographically oriented titles. Even though this idea was advanced barely two months into the season, conspicuous by its absence was the Seattle Pilots, a team which had already been recast simply as "Milwaukee" (see table 5.1).

Table 5.1.   Proposed Major League Divisional Realignment

Western	Midland	Eastern
California Angels	Atlanta Braves	Baltimore Orioles
Houston Astros	Chicago Cubs	Boston Red Sox
Kansas City Royals	Chicago White Sox	Cleveland Indians
Los Angeles Dodgers	Cincinnati Reds	Montreal Expos
Milwaukee	Detroit Tigers	New York Mets
Oakland Athletics	Minnesota Twins	New York Yankees
San Diego Padres	Pittsburgh Pirates	Philadelphia Phillies
San Francisco Giants	St. Louis Cardinals	Washington Senators

Source: Papers of Bowie Kuhn, National Baseball Hall of Fame.

Referred to as an "inter-locking schedule," a slate of 150 regular-season games would consist of 75 home and 75 away contests, comprising eighteen games against each of the seven rivals in a team's own division and twenty-four contests against four select clubs from the other two divisions. The proposal suggested that instead of facing a variety of opponents, the select interleague contests would be skewed to allow teams to "come into cities where they have long-established associations."[38] A pair of two-week stretches, one each in June and August, would feature the interleague series, which could have been adjusted to include three-game series against all eight opponents of the other two leagues rather than six-game series against only four from each. Another generation would pass before an interleague schedule was adopted, but at least baseball was aware that it needed to be forward-thinking in its competition against the National Football League, which was about to merge with the old American Football League and implement an interleague schedule of its own formulation.

Kuhn had much working in his favor that cast his early regime in a good light. Professional baseball commemorated its one-hundredth anniversary, the expansion teams—whose varying degrees of success have been noted—opened in new venues, and rule changes meant to reignite offenses gone sluggish were successful in making 1968's Year of the Pitcher a thing of the past. To the delight of fans, home run production was on the rise to such a degree that one prediction had it that sixteen sluggers would eclipse the forty home-run mark. In an effort to draw fans closer to the game, a series of "All-Time All-Star" teams from each major-league city were named based on fan selections, and the 1969 All-Star Game festivities in Washington, DC, were highlighted by a gala hosted at the White House by Kuhn and President Richard Nixon, who greeted two thousand guests, including players, club owners, baseball executives, writers, and, of course, politicians. Major League Baseball's financial contribution for the soirée ran to $60,000, and despite torrential rain that plagued the occasion, Kuhn beamed, "There were U.S. Senators standing there in two inches of rain talking about baseball. How could I get depressed?"[39] When the rain-delayed All-Star Game was played the afternoon following the originally scheduled date, both teams were clad in their traditional home and away uniforms, although a proposal for players and coaches to wear special old-timer uniforms had been taken under consideration.

By early August, Kuhn was strongly alluding to a shift in the starting times of weekday World Series games from the afternoon, a time when the majority of men were engaged in their employment, to prime time in the early evening. "What's wrong with night games?" demanded Kuhn. "The TV audience has doubled since the All-Star Game was shifted under the lights [in 1967]."[40] Television contracts already projected to bring increasing revenues to Major League Baseball's coffers could only be made more attractive by moving an increasing number of league championship series contests and World Series games to a start time when a male-dominated audience could best be reached. While the viewer reaction to the NFL's venture into prime time with ABC Sports' upcoming *Monday Night Football* was still an unknown quantity, the maximization of profits dictated catering to the largest audience possible, which entailed the inevitable migration of games from afternoons to evenings. The period of the late 1960s and early 1970s saw networks and major sports leagues becoming ever more closely linked in a symbiotic relationship whose accompanying soundtrack was the siren song of television money.

The owners were so enamored with Kuhn's performance that when they convened for a meeting in Seattle, they rewarded him with a "unanimous declaration . . . that Bowie K. Kuhn is hereby elected Commissioner of Baseball for a seven-year term commencing August 13, 1969, at a salary of $150,000 per year."[41] And the stunning deeds of the New York Mets in capturing the World Series culminated a baseball season that helped rescue the game from losing more ground to other major American sports.

Certainly Bowie Kuhn had many good reasons to be proud of the upswing the sport experienced in his first summer as commissioner. There was a fortuitous increase in offensive production that led one major publication to enthuse that "there is nothing wrong with the sport that a vigorous new commissioner and a livelier ball can't cure."[42] However, it must be noted that revisions to the rules, expansion, the splitting of each league into two divisions, and the introduction of the playoff system all were in place when Kuhn arrived as commissioner in February 1969.

Some of the fervor was also premature because the hard numbers found on the bottom line indicated that baseball still had much work to do in order to hold the attention of its fans. Throughout Kuhn's first months in office, he received a mixture of bad news and suggestions for enhancements to give baseball more appeal, particularly with regard to television coverage. The vice president of sports for NBC voiced concern over his network's still sagging ratings for the Saturday Game of the Week, and wrote to Kuhn asking "why we can't get into the dugout and why we can't talk to the players, managers, and coaches during the game." Noting that such conversations were already being initiated during football broadcasts, he further suggested that adding appearances by "guest personalities like [comedian] Flip Wilson and [football star] Sonny Jurgensen" would make the game more attractive for TV viewers, one of whom claimed that the networks "take the game too seriously." Adjusting the starting time of some night games shown on NBC from 7:00 p.m. to 8:00 p.m. offered encouragement by way of a 23 percent increase in homes tuned in, but the network's ratings in general were "extremely disappointing."[43]

Kuhn also received a memo refuting the death of baseball—which rhetorically asked, "Is that why NBC recently agreed to pay for the next three years approximately $50 million to baseball, . . . representing a sizable increase over the previous three-year figures?" but at the same time conceding, "We are in the midst of an age of jet propulsion, supersonic speed, violent uprising, and youth rebellion. . . . We must supply more action because the public demands it." As the 1969 season drew to a close, and with three of the four divisional races just about settled, ballpark attendance for all teams during the week ending September 21 barely topped one million, "one of the lowest figures we've had in weeks," read one report to Kuhn. Only eight National League teams and five in the American League were expected to cross the one million mark for the year.[44]

Yet baseball bested pro football in one area, thanks to the newly created league championship series. The extra postseason games—featuring the New York Mets, Minnesota Twins, and Baltimore Orioles, who shared Shea Stadium, Metropolitan Stadium, and Memorial Stadium, respectively, with the Jets, Vikings, and Colts—resulted in a small cascading effect that forced the NFL into changing the venue or starting time for eight football games. When the Mets exceeded expectations and captured the World Series, NFL commissioner Pete Rozelle sent a memo to Kuhn that included a summary of the forced changes in the football schedule as well as warm "[c]ongratulations on an outstanding season that had a climax which captivated the entire country."[45]

Shortly after the dismissal of William Eckert in December 1968, the Planning Committee of league owners adopted a resolution to restructure the highest offices of baseball, with Orioles magnate Jerry Hoffberger chairing the initiative. One year later, a special joint meeting of the major leagues was convened by Bowie Kuhn to review a report produced by Dr. Russell Ackoff of the Wharton School of Finance and Commerce at the University of Pennsylvania. While Kuhn was unimpressed with some of the report's recommended changes—"not new" was his marginalia regarding the entry that stated, "The Commissioner is given responsibility for coordinating the legislative, judicial, and administrative aspects of Baseball," as well as several others—he agreed most strongly with the very first proposed change.[46]

Salient among the bureaucratic modifications was one attempted—but that gained little traction—during the administration of Ford Frick. What caught Kuhn's attention now was the establishment of a base of operations in New York City not only for Major League Baseball but also for the National Association of Professional Baseball Leagues, which tended to the affairs of the minor leagues. "This consolidation," the report stated, "will permit greater *daily* cooperation among these offices, . . . remove redundancy of administrative services, . . . [and] also give credence to the importance attributed to the Minor leagues and amateur baseball."[47] Manhattan had a long-established reputation as a media hub and center of the advertising world, but with only the commissioner's office located in New York at that time, direct dealings with the headquarters of the American League (in Boston), National League (in Cincinnati and later in San Francisco), and National Association (in Columbus, Ohio) were awkward and cumbersome. The importance of a united front would speak well for the game, even though several years passed before the physical consolidation of the major-league offices in New York actually occurred.

The closing synopsis of the report indicated that the recommendations contained therein were not intended to reach down to the level of each team but rather to stimulate further improvements to the organizational structure of baseball that "can have a significant effect on the appeal of the game to fans, that can accelerate the development of young talent, and enhance the profitability of professional baseball." Kuhn later noted that "significant elements of [the Wharton Report] were adopted, . . . but not on the timetable I had in mind."[48]

After the owners and league officials had the opportunity to review the report, Kuhn found it necessary to deny that there would be changes in the power structure of the game's highest offices—in which the league presidents were "responsible" to the commissioner and would "report" to him—because there was no effort being made "to change the relationship between them and the commissioner." And because another segment of the report recommended a reduction in the majority of votes—from three-quarters to two-thirds—cast at joint major-league meetings on matters of changes to major-league policy as well as election of the commissioner, fear was expressed by some owners, according to Kuhn, that the report contained a veiled attempt "to achieve interleague play and a shortening of the major league season" if fewer votes were required in each league to approve such changes.[49]

The year 1969 concluded with Bowie Kuhn assuming the commissionership while attending to myriad issues that it is impossible to imagine his predecessor competently handling. Kuhn's legacy would years later become a subject for debate, not least of which was his induction into the Baseball Hall of Fame.

But given his work as an attorney for the National League, his inside knowledge of baseball's bureaucracy, and his genuine love of the game, one would be hard-pressed to name a better man to step into the milieu Kuhn entered in February 1969. Granted, some important building blocks—such as new expansion teams and rule changes—were already in place at the onset of his tenure as commissioner, but it was still up to Kuhn to execute the duties of his office to the best of his ability at a trying time. Marketing baseball in the face of stiff competition, especially from pro football, would be a key to putting the spring of popularity into baseball's step, yet Kuhn's legacy could have been burnished had he better grasped the implications of the rising power of the players' union and been able to broker the new realities of the labor situation with the club owners.

Despite the ridicule he endured at times for acting "in the best interests of baseball"—and ruffling the feathers of several owners in the process—Bowie Kuhn played host to a resurgence of the national pastime that not only survived but thrived following the prophesy of doom predicted when the Messersmith-McNally decision was handed down in the mid-1970s.

A curious incident took place in the immediate aftermath of Kuhn's naming as baseball commissioner. When he returned to New York from Florida following the meeting at which he was appointed, he wasted no time in going to his law office and conferring with his partners regarding the career change upon which he was about to embark. But then picking up the telephone, Kuhn placed a call to the head of the Major League Baseball Players Association, with whom he had worked on a variety of issues in recent years. The tone of Kuhn's recollection of the incident is lacking in any animosity, as indicated by the cordial manner in which he invited himself to Marvin Miller's office to show off the "new crown" of his position as baseball's top executive, and when they got together for an hour-long confab, the two, along with Miller's assistant, Dick Moss, "laughed a lot."[50]

The jocularity that infused this select gathering would be very short-lived. Indeed, there were gains to be fought for by the players' union, and there was turf to be defended by owners unwilling to part with money under terms not of their own making. The set piece battle between labor and management was still a few years away, but the first major skirmish took place just weeks after Kuhn and Miller socialized at the Seagram Building in Manhattan.

CHAPTER 6

Marvin Miller Comes to Play

The manifestation of what would become the strongest union of athletes in professional sports was cultivated mainly in an era when post–World War II attitudes in the United States were evolving on several fronts. It is important to note that the creation of such an entity for the benefit of major-league baseball players was not done in a vacuum but was greatly influenced by forces external to the game. That it took until the mid-1960s to gain significant traction can be ascribed to the prevailing control club owners traditionally held over their players for nearly a century. Not until the arrival of Marvin Miller, who, after much work, finally convinced his charges that they were getting shortchanged in numerous ways in their bargaining with club owners, was the inchoate and weak organization of subservient players at last transformed into a formidable body that acquired more gains for its members at the negotiating table than anyone could have ever imagined.

Paid for Playing a Game

Dating back to the late nineteenth and early twentieth centuries, attempts at unionization in general were undertaken with the goal of improving the lot of workers, many of whom endured poor working conditions and toiled for wages not necessarily commensurate with the reward they may have expected or to which they may have been entitled. With regard to professional baseball, player participation in the game was not a full-time endeavor, and at the conclusion of a baseball season, those players would return to their respective vocations until it was time to prepare for the next season. Barnstorming and exhibition games became sources of supplemental income for some players, notably stars like Babe Ruth and Lou Gehrig, with their Bustin' Babes and Larrupin' Lous. Through the Great Depression of the 1930s, when so many people were fortunate to have any job at all, being paid to play a game had to be viewed as a bonus. Relative to the time, only the very few superstars of the day could make a living comfortable enough to require no income from beyond the playing field.

Team rosters were filled with men whose upbringings were rural and whose educations included little or no college. Unsophisticated, naive, and on their own in negotiating with the owners, players were perennially disadvantaged as they were bound to their teams by contracts that included the reserve clause. With no avenue of escape to enable them to seek employment with another franchise, players were forced to accept the terms imposed upon them by owners. The system fed on itself because club magnates treated each round of incoming players, as well as holdovers, with a paternalistic attitude that left no doubt in the players' minds that the club was taking care of them in a most generous way. What could be better, so the line went, than to be paid for playing a game?

In the aftermath of World War II, the dynamics of a vastly changed United States shifted the country into a postwar culture influenced by various factors, not least among them being what sportswriter Leonard Koppett termed "a tremendous awakening of the reality of new relationships." In the early to mid-twentieth century, sea changes in America seemed to be delineated by decade, as the Roaring Twenties segued into the Great Depression and led into the Second World War. At the end of the war, a civil rights movement began to emerge—with Jackie Robinson in the vanguard—and African Americans strove for the racial equality they had long been denied. In addition, as untold thousands of members of the nation's armed forces left the military and returned home, these men, many only in their early twenties, had "found out what it is to have to follow orders blindly" when in uniform. Now back at the workplace, they now felt resentment when their bosses acted like "commanding officers," an attitude Koppett says contributed to an upsurge in the organization of labor unions "in every industry."[1]

An attempt to bring players together in a collective bargaining group was led by attorney Robert F. Murphy, who began a short-lived association called the American Baseball Guild just after the conclusion of World War II. Murphy was able to coax from the owners a $5,500 minimum salary and per diem expenses for the players during spring training—the latter referred to as "Murphy Money"—but ultimately Murphy was undermined in his effort by nefarious action from commissioner Happy Chandler's office and a general antiunion sentiment among players.

Although the idea of a man being a professional baseball player as well as a member of a union may have seemed incongruous, some players with recent war experience came to an important realization: If a soldier spent enough time in the service, "there's only one good thing about the army—you get a pension when you get out. So *pension* was the magic word of the 1950s, in all industries, in all unions, but something baseball players particularly could relate to."[2] By the early part of that decade, Ralph Kiner, one of baseball's biggest stars and the player representative for the National League, sounded the call for players to receive financial accommodation at the conclusion of their baseball careers. Formation of a players' union per se was not foremost in their minds, but a pension committee—loosely called a players' association—became a priority and was assembled to handle a share of money derived from All-Star Game and World Series revenue. Riled by the commissioner's complicity in this effort as well as his refusal to be simply the club owners' yes-man, the moguls jettisoned Chandler in July 1951 and named Ford Frick as his replacement.

J. Norman Lewis, an attorney experienced with labor issues, was approached by Kiner and New York Yankees ace Allie Reynolds in the summer of 1953 about assisting the players with pension issues whose funding had been at the mercy of the club owners. Working on a part-time basis for the players, Lewis was able to assemble an organization called the Major League Baseball Players Association, the forerunner of today's MLBPA. When Lewis suggested to the players that they were entitled to more benefits than simply a pension, he became a marked man in the eyes of the owners, who demanded his ouster. In early 1957 Lewis was denied in his attempt to exact an increase in the minimum major-league salary—a $1,500 raise to $7,500—but later that year an agreement was reached for $7,000.[3] The episode demonstrated the continuing subservience of the players in their relationship with the team magnates despite this latest effort to form a union to champion their cause for a better wage.

Frank Scott, formerly of the Yankees' front office before a career change to become a "promotional agent," became interim director of the nebulous players' association, but the vacancy was at last filled in earnest in December 1959.[4] The new director was an avid baseball fan with paternalistic ties to the national pastime. Raymond Cannon had been an attorney who counseled several members of the Chicago White Sox in the 1910s and attempted to form a players' union in the 1920s. In 1945 his son Robert became a civil court judge in Milwaukee and eight years later was appointed to the city's circuit court. By the end of the 1950s, the player representatives who had joined to bargain with the owners' pension committee needed someone to take over for Lewis. Robert Cannon came recommended by the owners and appeared to be a competent choice. Cannon did not relinquish his judicial duties, following in Lewis's footsteps by becoming another part-time adviser for the players. Pittsburgh Pirate hurler Bob Friend was now the player rep for the National League, and he strongly advocated on Cannon's behalf.

Unfortunately for players who were trying to organize in order to better their lot, Robert Cannon's appointment could not have been worse for them, nor better for the owners. Many years after Cannon's ascension to the director-ship, one pitcher offered his opinion that Cannon "wasn't as sharp as a lot of players thought he was," but in actuality, it was more a matter that Cannon was in the owners' corner more than that of the players. The director of the players' association led his membership using the same strategy that Booker T. Washing-ton did in seeking civil rights for African Americans, taking a passive approach in the expectation that conditions would improve over time and that obstreperous demands would only hurt the cause for which they were fighting. During tours of spring training camps, Cannon told players "to make no waves" in order to "foster a greater relationship with the *benevolent owners.*"[5]

Generations of men—so many of whom came to professional baseball with little more than a twelfth-grade education and had been shepherded along through the system thanks to the ostensible charity of the ball club—had heard propaganda from the owners themselves with regard to how fortunate the players were. Now the words were being delivered by an adviser supposedly speaking on their behalf; however, the status quo held fast. A certain degree of trust had been placed in Cannon, who some players believed would be able to get a better deal for them because he got along with many owners and officials of both leagues. To be sure, some improvements were realized by the players during Cannon's tenure, such as a greater share of pension fund money originating from the All-Star games and some minor clubhouse issues that were addressed. And although Cannon was serving in a part-time capacity, his position drew no compensation, so there was no cost to the players.

Yet by 1965 the players had grown weary of Cannon, whose attempts at helping the players were "disproved so many times," and led one player to ob-serve, "Even Jimmy Hoffa would have been better than what we had." The shift-ing mood of America also informed the players' sentiments about the treatment they received at the hands of their employers, and some of those players were in positions of authority within the ranks of their association. "Mature players [such as] Robin Roberts [and] Jim Bunning are now aware of what's going on around them in the outside world. And black players know all about who's tak-ing advantage of them. . . . People in all walks of life were changing their ideas of what they're entitled to."[6]

"Impervious to the Barbs of Management"

In late 1965 Marvin Miller was serving the United Steelworkers as their chief economist and was attending an industry-related conference in San Francisco to present findings that he had written for a committee. The chairman of that com-mittee, Dr. George W. Taylor, was an economist and the dean of the renowned

Wharton School who had been approached by pitcher Robin Roberts asking for suggestions to fill a full-time position as the leader for the baseball players' association. Taylor queried Miller as to his interest, and Miller indicated his willingness to learn more. Having been through a difficult summer—the leadership of United Steelworkers was in revolt and negotiations for a general contract in the industry had not gone well—Miller was caught at a weak moment and decided to pursue an interview with an ad hoc search committee made up of several notable players: Roberts, pitchers Friend and Bunning, and former Tigers All-Star Harvey Kuenn.

As most players transitioned out of baseball and into the working world after having devoted years of their lives trying to reach the major leagues, many had little to fall back on economically other than some sort of post-baseball retirement plan. While improved working conditions such as comfortable clubhouses—with modern amenities such as electrical outlets for hair dryers—and a better travel schedule would make life in the big leagues more palatable for players, Miller noted that "the players were *most* concerned about the pension plan . . . to the exclusion of everything else." Roberts stressed that by 1966 the situation with revenue earned by the teams from the sale of broadcasting rights was "getting more complicated," and it would work to the advantage of the players to solidify their union by bringing in someone who had a better understanding of labor negotiations so the players would be less likely to be hoodwinked by ownership as they sought their fair share of the broadcast package.[7]

Marvin Miller was the most dynamic force in reshaping the MLBPA into a formidable union. *Tamiment Library, New York University.*

During Miller's interview, the search committee also revealed their choice of legal consultant to assist the new players' association leader: former vice president Richard Nixon. With most players leery of unions to begin with, the notion of employing Nixon—a conservative Republican—as counsel for the players' association was offered as a way to create what Miller called "a balanced ticket" to present to the players.[8] In the eyes of the search committee, the pairing of Nixon with a liberal—as Miller was viewed in his unionist role—would assuage the concerns of those disinclined to support Miller.

The suggestion of Nixon hit Miller "like a ton of bricks," and Miller pointed out that the players' association office had a limited staff, and "in that kind of a small organization, you can't have two people who are as incompatible as Richard Nixon and me."[9] Miller was also aware that Nixon was laying the groundwork to seek the White House in 1968, so Nixon's presidential ambitions would take him away from his baseball role in just two years. Miller left the interview feeling certain that he had fallen out of favor with Roberts and his colleagues, and he may have rued passing on a chance earlier in 1965 to become a visiting professor at Harvard. The search committee was willing to rethink its position on hiring Nixon—Richard Moss was eventually selected as general counsel—and told Miller that they would place his name in nomination for the players' association directorship.

Yet Robert Cannon remained the association's man, as shown in balloting by team player representatives in early 1966, a bias that was informed by Friend's influence over those voting. The turning point that again brought Miller to the forefront, however, came shortly thereafter, when Cannon demanded a compensation and pension benefits package from the players' association, a mandate that rankled the search committee so badly that they rescinded the offer. Miller won on the second round of balloting by the committee.[10]

With Cannon now out of the running, Miller was afforded the opportunity to claim the position. To put himself before his potential constituency, he visited spring training camps in Arizona and California, but the players' antiunion sentiment was unmistakable. In polling taken to gauge reaction to his candidacy for the association director, Miller recalled that "the California Angels voted something like 32–1 against me. The Giants were unanimous with one abstention. Cleveland had . . . one vote for me, . . . the Cubs, maybe four or five." What turned the tide in Miller's favor was his appearance at the Florida training camps of the remaining sixteen teams, where he was able to bring players to his side by demonstrating to them that "[their] salaries are a far tinier proportion of what they take in than people who work in a factory. [Baseball] is what is known as a labor-intensive industry, where all the costs . . . should be [related to] labor."[11]

After initial confusion by the players as to whether Miller's name was simply being put into nomination or being brought before the union for official sanctioning as the director—to say nothing of another tussle over antiunion resentment evidenced by a small faction of player representatives remaining partial to Cannon—Marvin Miller was at last named as head of the Major League Baseball Players Association on April 12, 1966, just a few days short of his forty-ninth birthday. By Miller's own recollection, the players approved his appointment by a vote of 489 to 136, and assuming 120 management employees—managers and coaches—voted against him, only sixteen players were opposed.[12] Several disputes arose over Miller's contract, which was initially for thirty months beginning on July 1, 1966, and the source of funding for a permanent office for the association to be located in Manhattan. The establishment of such an office was not a minor point. Because Miller's part-time predecessors could be difficult to contact in years past, it was important to maintain a base of operations dedicated to the players' association to facilitate communication between the players and Miller.

A budget of $150,000 for the MLBPA bureau was to be derived from All-Star Game revenue, and although the owners were comfortable with this arrangement with Cannon at the helm of the players' association, they blanched at the thought of adhering to the same conditions with Miller. The moguls wanted to play both sides of the street, saying they could not provide funding because of the illegality of employers financing an employees' association—to say nothing of the $50,000 annual salary to be drawn by the director—when in fact they had done so under the administrations of both Cannon and his predecessor. Although Miller was not an attorney, he was very well versed in ferreting out double standards such as this, which continued to be perpetrated by the owners on the union.

Miller's road to astonishing future success with the MLBPA was fraught initially with the arduous chore of winning the players over to his side. But a man "who was impervious to the barbs of management" would bring to light uncomfortable truths regarding the state of affairs to which the players had been subjected for decades by the club owners. Miller realized quickly in face-to-face meetings with groups of players that "no one had ever encouraged [them] to think independently or critically about their situation."[13] He produced a vivid example by showing members of the California Angels that when the players' 1966 pension benefits were adjusted for inflation, their value had actually regressed and were worse than they had been in 1947.

Miller later admitted that he was confused as to why the players were so focused on the pension. "In the Steelworkers Union, there was interest in pensions, but only by the older, more senior workers, who were up there in their sixties. Young steelworkers couldn't care less," recalled Miller.[14] Relatively youthful ballplayers leaving the game while still in their thirties were decades away from taking a traditional retirement at the age of sixty-five, like many in the workforce, but Miller eventually came to understand that players were concerned about how they would be able to support themselves when their playing careers ended.

A man of great composure who lost his temper only on the rarest of occasions, Marvin Miller "wasn't charismatic in the conventional sense," yet he was gifted with an ability to communicate and lead.[15] The type of man Miller preferred to be a player representative was not so overly emotional that he might gather 80 percent support among his teammates on a given issue, but rather someone who was circumspect, reserved in his judgment, and able to garner unanimous support. For the players' association to be effective, the player representatives, who had the most direct contact with their teammates, also had to be possessed of means to communicate and lead. Many representatives in the past had been selected by owners with the intent of keeping them in abeyance as part of a feudal system. The new breed of player leadership required a departure from the traditional way business had been conducted with ownership, which is also to say that it turned the tables on control over the way players were to be treated.

Also handicapping Miller's effort was the reporting of media members who "simply parroted management's line" and fostered an antiunion attitude. Miller was burdened by his past association with an industry notorious for its history of violent upheavals between labor and management. "Players believed that the owners really had their best interests at heart," said pitcher Jim Bouton, who further explained that the players hated to think of their association as a "union" because of implied Bolshevik connotations as well as the perceived threat of violence on picket lines. Assumptions—incorrect, as the record would show—on the part of baseball players and owners alike held that Miller would carry the taint of steelworkers' malevolence to the directorship of the players' association. One industrial relations author claimed that by 1966 players had shown a "readiness for unionization," but they were warming up to Miller at a very slow pace and, as Miller himself admitted, "the players are basically conservative . . . and they are not unionists."[16] Reluctant to blindly offer their support, the players proceeded with caution until Miller earned their trust through carefully crafted persuasion and the definitive results he won on their behalf in early negotiations with the owners.

However, as Miller became acclimated to his new post, he discerned that gains could be won only with calm rationale and persistence. He understood and believed from his first day with the MLBPA that it was necessary to employ "the traditional union views of good faith, hard bargaining," coupled with a recognition that there would be player demands that must be granted by owners as well as concessions that must be made by the union in order for labor and management to reach an accord.[17]

On the eve of Miller's appointment to the players' association, the *Sporting News* commented on the dual holdout of Los Angeles Dodgers pitchers Don Drysdale and Sandy Koufax, applauding the high road the players and the Dodgers front office took in coming to a resolution of their pay dispute, yet ominously predicting that "ruinous results" awaited all parties if collective bargaining was improperly handled.[18] Perhaps more ominously, as Miller tried to ease his way into the MLBPA, his antithetical labor counterpart, Jimmy Hoffa, was lobbying to allow professional athletes join the fold of the International Brotherhood of Teamsters. If ever there was reason to fear unionization by the baseball players—even before Miller demonstrated his patented quiet tenacity—one could only imagine the angst among team owners at the prospect of seeing a labor boss with ties to organized crime sitting across the bargaining table from them.

Miller insisted players be on hand "to see what's going on" during all sessions with owners and their representatives, thus making clear that he would not bargain in isolation from his constituents. San Francisco catcher Tom Haller, the Giants' player representative whose father drew only $72 a month for his pension after working for U.S. Steel for thirty-one years, viewed Miller initially as "[coming] on pretty strong," yet was struck by the degree to which he was prepared for each meeting and thought him to be "the best negotiator on both sides of the table."[19]

Through 1965 the formula for dividing broadcast revenue for the players' pension fund was 60 percent for the players and 40 percent for the owners. Beginning in 1966 the owners consented to increase their pension funding by $2 million to a flat $4.1 million per year for the next three seasons, an amount that coincidentally came very close to what the 60/40 split would have provided anyway. But Baltimore relief pitcher Dick Hall, a certified public accountant who assumed the role of pension expert on the players' behalf, said that with World Series revenue "jumping like mad" due to new television contracts, the magnates were "getting a gold mine for nothing" and growing increasingly reluctant to share the resultant windfall.[20] Another episode in the contribution affair would dramatically appear in just a few short years, with Miller again leading the charge against ownership.

In the spring of 1966 the MLBPA proposed an increase in the annual minimum player salary from $7,000, a rate that had been static for eight years, to $12,000. Even the *Sporting News* endorsed Miller's suggestion for this raise in an editorial that criticized a "base [wage] that has not been raised since 1958 [and] does nothing for baseball's prestige."[21] The publication also favored another proposal, first suggested by Baltimore general manager Harry Dalton, that Miller would later make to the owners: A shorter regular-season schedule that would also establish a criteria for slating doubleheaders, along with other considerations such as precluding day games that required travel to a new city immediately following a night game.

Miller continued to establish himself in his new role and prepared to work out a renewal for the players' pension contract as well as the first basic agreement between players and owners. By midsummer of 1967 he had compiled a manifest of negotiating points—"described as a 'guide' but not an ultimatum," as one sportswriter noted.[22] After three sessions between players and owners from late October to late November—held in the offseason at the owners' request—proved fruitless, team magnates, represented by their Player Relations Committee, cancelled a fourth meeting with player representatives. These unsuccessful meetings had been slated by the players in the hope of establishing an agenda for a dialogue on wages during the upcoming winter meetings in Mexico City. At the end of November, Miller noted that one year had passed since the minimum salary issue was raised, and no resolution was in sight.

At the December 1967 winter gathering, Miller was accompanied by Jim Bunning, Bill Freehan, Joe Torre, and eighteen other player representatives, who had an understanding that they would be able to speak with a group of owners regarding minimum pay. But the player contingent was turned away, leading a frustrated Miller to inform the press, "We have come to the conclusion that the owners are just not paying attention to the players' legitimate interests." Adding to the tense atmosphere was Paul Richards, the union-loathing Atlanta Braves vice president who "was a company man to his bones" and who espoused the stereotypical management attitude with statements such as, "The ballplayers don't know when they're well off."[23] At the onset of what would become an enduring feud between the two, Richards rebuked Miller by hinting that the players' association director had lied about meeting with club owners and left no doubt regarding how he believed ownership should handle Miller: "If this guy continues these kinds of tactics, we'll just have to get in the gutter with him, I guess." Labeled by some as "militant" for their demands, players thus far were trusting Miller's judgment regarding the manner in which he was proceeding in the confrontation with management. Yankees pitcher Steve Hamilton felt that "the players have been very patient" in trying to reach a settlement with the owners, but the threat of a work stoppage to achieve bargaining leverage was not yet considered.[24]

Miller's disillusionment came as a surprise to National League attorney Bowie Kuhn, who had dined with the union leader the night before the player representatives were rebuffed and claimed that Miller never mentioned that such a meeting was imminent. An aide for Commissioner William Eckert blamed the problem on a schedule that erroneously indicated a forum would take place. The *Sporting News* commented that the mix-up was "only a molehill among mountains," but also expressed worry over the owners' reluctance to address the salary issue and cautioned both players and owners to "refrain from any further playground scrapping . . . and get down to adult business of drawing up an agreement."[25]

By mid-January 1968 a deal appeared to have been struck to increase the minimum salary to $10,000 for the upcoming campaign, although open questions persisted that gave owners reason for pause. Miller interpreted the delay in concluding a settlement as yet another untoward tactic by the owners, but John Gaherin, a consultant employed by the magnates, countered Miller's charge by claiming that the director of the players' union was "injecting new issues" such as "scheduling abuses and perhaps . . . a longer season" into the discussion.[26] His patience wearing thin, Miller sought remediation through Commissioner Eckert's office, but the Player Relations Committee denied the request, prompting Miller to threaten to reach out to federal mediators in an attempt to bring the matter to a conclusion.

The owners had consented to raise the minimum salary to $10,000 and hike per diem meal money allowances during spring training and the regular season. But they also viewed as anathema the pound of flesh Miller wanted to extract as a safeguard against the owners adding more games to the regular-season schedule as expansion in both leagues loomed. Players' association attorney Richard Moss stated that Miller was defending the union against a repeat of what happened during the 1961 and 1962 expansions, when schedules were increased by eight games—from 154 to 162—"without consulting or paying the players. . . . The players want to have their say on the schedule."[27]

At last, the acrimony subsided just as spring training was about to start. On February 21, 1968, representatives for the players and the owners met in New York and formalized an agreement covering the 1968 and 1969 seasons. The major points included the revised minimum salary and meal money adjustments but also covered moving expenses for players called up from or sent down to the minor leagues, as well as those costs incurred because of a trade to another franchise. The maximum pay cut a player could face when signing a new contract was reduced from 25 to 20 percent, and payment for time away from baseball during the season in order to fulfill military obligations was upheld. Only charity exhibition games would be allowed during the annual All-Star break, and there would be consultation between players and owners when the 1969 regular-season schedule was being formulated. One last item was addressed that drew a modicum of notice at the time: "A joint study involving 'possible alternatives to the reserve clause as now constituted' [was] to be completed prior to December 31, 1969." On the reserve clause, the *Sporting News* commented further that perhaps baseball should consider following the example of professional football, which allowed a player the option year to fulfill his obligation to his present team before moving on to a new club, although the original team would be due compensation of some sort for having lost that player.[28]

The instigator raising these issues on behalf of the players was, in retrospect, almost blasé about his accomplishments. In his autobiography, written many years after his landmark deal was brokered, Marvin Miller remarked, "It didn't seem earth-shattering at the time, but in many ways the 1968 basic agreement was the building block for major gains to come."[29]

Miller Continues to Fight

Separate from haggling with the team owners but nonetheless of small benefit to the players, Miller secured a better deal for the players' rights fees for use of their images on Topps baseball cards. An ostensibly innocent transaction, signing a contract with Topps entitled a player to a payment of either $125 or wares he could select from a catalog provided by the card company, and for many fringe players it was the realization of a dream to have their picture on a bubblegum card. However, Miller looked at the business side of what was happening: Topps founder Sy Berger was taking advantage of players by signing them to a five-year contract, then renewing the deal for five more years well in advance of the expiration of the current deal. In a twisted way, this was another version of the reserve clause to which players were subjected in the standard contracts with their clubs.

Negotiations with Topps were predictably slow, and in the spring of 1968 Miller suggested to the players that if they refused to sign with Topps, fewer and fewer players would be available to be photographed. By that summer Joel Shorin, president of Topps, fully recognized the ploy and finally gave Miller due attention. The result was a small but important victory: a doubling of the rights fee from $125 to $250 and a percentage of card sales that would put more than $300,000 in the coffers of the players' association. Significant about the Topps deal was the fact that, in addition to coming on the heels of the first basic agreement, it demonstrated Miller's concern for the welfare of the players despite the relatively nominal payment involved: "Baseball-card royalties . . . were like found money, and it reinforced the players' confidence in Miller."[30]

Next in the union director's sights—and carrying more weight than baseball card fees—was the contribution made by the owners to the players' pension fund. Miller believed strongly enough about the issue that in the early summer of 1968 he alluded to a possible player strike unless a resolution was reached. The point of contention was the amount of money added to the fund each year, traditionally a 60/40 split of television revenue derived from Major League Baseball's contract with radio and television networks for rights to a limited number of regular-season games, the All-Star Game, and World Series contests. Until 1966, rights to the Series had not been sold in conjunction with other regular-season games, but after that year the owners received $6 million for the weekly package and the same amount for the Series. Gifted with this generous revenue, ownership sought a way to abandon the 60/40 split and instead gain control of a larger portion of the broadcast income.

Because the existing three-year pension benefit agreement was due to run out in March 1969, Miller endeavored to begin negotiations on a new deal well ahead of the expiration date. In an era when a pension and insurance benefits held a greater proportional value to players, he believed that players were entitled to know what those benefits would be prior to signing their contracts for 1969. Following the All-Star Game in Houston in July 1968, Miller recommended that players not sign any contract for the following year until the pension debate was settled.

The players' association director wanted to meet during the summer, but owners sought to delay bargaining until after the World Series, so as not to disrupt the season or have bargaining sessions "take [the players'] minds off the game." As the nation was convulsed by assassinations and antiwar protests, Miller thought it was inane of the owners to expect that the players would concentrate only on baseball. Miller was further upset upon learning that the team magnates, whose number had grown to twenty-four thanks to the new expansion clubs, intended to put "a much *lower* share of the television revenue" into the pension fund.[31]

As the 1968 season drew to a close, Miller convened with the players on all twenty extant teams and informed them of the "regressive nature of the owners' demands," reiterating his advice to withhold signatures from any new contracts with their teams. In the meantime, as the year moved on, owners renegotiated the television contract beginning in 1969 to include the sale of rights to the weekly national game, All-Star Game, and the new league championship series as well as the World Series. The amended package was valued at $16.1 million, but the owners continued to hold the players at arm's length and claimed that their pension stipend would now come from myriad sources, including ticket sales, parking, and concessions. "Ownership tried to whittle away the 60–40 split," said Giants catcher Tom Haller, and the players took exception to the magnates' unilateral move by demanding the division by percentage continue to be honored.[32]

On December 3, 1968, in one of his last official acts as commissioner, William Eckert gave his approval for the payment of $4.1 million to the First National Bank of New York to fulfill the American and National leagues' requirement to contribute to the players' benefit plan. Two weeks later the owners made known their intention to add another $1 million to the existing contribution, but the players' union overwhelmingly rejected this ploy by a vote of

491–7. Miller cited the substantial increase in television money, from $12 million to $16 million, and insisted that a 60/40 split of the renegotiated contract should yield far more than an extra $1 million for the players' fund. For the upcoming 1969 season, the payment schedule to which NBC agreed included $8.06 million for All-Star Game and World Series rights, $7.44 million for the Game of the Week, and $500,000 for the new league championship series. Rates were also established for the next two seasons, a total of $16.75 million for 1970 and $18.75 million for 1971. Retention of the 60 percent split for the players would yield $9.6 million for the pension, far more than the $5.1 million offered by the owners.[33]

One bargaining chip Miller was ready to play concerned "the first mass holdout in baseball history," whereby players would refuse to report to spring training, scheduled to open in two months. Reliever Bob Locker, player representative of the Chicago White Sox, stated that such a job action figuratively offered the players "a chance to shoot back" at the owners in defending their position. For their own part, the team magnates of both leagues convened a meeting and made their position unequivocal through unanimous approval of a resolution supporting their "Player Relations Committee's present posture in the negotiations including its insistence that *there shall be no relationship between radio and television revenues and the clubs' pension contribution*."[34]

On February 3, 1969, a significant group of players met in New York on the heels of the New York baseball writers' annual dinner. Well over one hundred players—among them some of the game's biggest names—convened in what was at the time the "largest mass player meeting in history."[35] The fact that many star players were in attendance lent much credibility to the show of solidarity, demonstrating to all members of the players' association that the better players—which is to say, the more highly paid players—stood to lose more in the event of a work stoppage but were willing to do so in support of the cause. Strength among the players was evident when polling showed that more than four hundred of them expressed support for Miller's demands.

If the players impressed anyone as being radicalized by a figure formerly associated with the steelworkers, there was little evidence of it in the behavior or speech of those who were at the forefront of negotiations alongside Marvin Miller. The players' association director noted that Yankees player representative Steve Hamilton possessed a "soft and reasoned manner," and he was particularly rapt by the Phillies' Dick Allen, a controversial figure who was often criticized for marching to the beat of his own drummer. Allen, noted Miller, "spoke with quiet dignity" and was an "eloquent and forceful" presence at the meeting in New York.[36]

As expected, players refused to sign contracts with their teams, and Miller suggested that the players and owners submit to an arbitration board to rectify the matter. But John Gaehrin, a spokesman for the owners, declined, insisting that any resolution be a result of bargaining strictly between the players and owners, without any mediation by a third party.[37]

Shortly after the offer of arbitration and with training camps on the verge of their scheduled openings, the owners said they would put a total of $1.2 million more into the pension fund, bringing the contribution to $5.3 million. Player representatives for the major-league teams voted the proposal down unanimously. Atlanta GM Paul Richards, who could often be counted on "for an inflammatory quote," proposed that big-league baseball carry on with minor-league players if necessary. But NBC, the television network that had purchased the broadcasting rights for more than $16 million, was having none if it. NBC was averse to "paying major league prices for minor league games," and concern began to grow that as the conflict dragged on, commencement of spring training would be in jeopardy.[38]

Players refused to report to camp, but some chinks in the armor appeared when two future Hall of Famers, Carl Yastrzemski of the Red Sox and Ron Santo of the Cubs, pledged loyalty to Tom Yawkey and Phil Wrigley, their respective club owners, declaring they would break from the players' stand and arrive at camp by March 1, the latest date on which spring training technically began. Yastrzemski sought a remedy by trying to assemble a group of players who would negotiate apart from the Miller-led union, prompting one of his former teammates, pitcher Gary Bell, to rebuke him: "[He] is for himself first and second and the hell with everybody else." Mets catcher Jerry Grote enraged many of his colleagues by personally appearing at the players' meeting in New York but then endorsing his 1969 contract with no regard for his initial show of support for the union. And the Braves' Paul Richards, suffering no fools among his roster, was said to have pressured a "large number" of his players into breaking with the union and signing for 1969.[39]

On February 24 a marathon meeting of Miller and all the player representatives took place in New York to refine their demands and determine their course of action. The results of this session fueled a successful end to the imbroglio; within twenty-four hours the players' association and the owners reached consensus on a three-year pension and benefit agreement. Included with the deal were a contribution of $5.45 million to the pension fund by the owners, enhancements to retirement benefits for the players, a reduction of major-league service time necessary to qualify for a pension as well as a drop in the minimum age in order to begin receiving its benefits, adjustments to life and health insurance coverage, and, somewhat vaguely, "an understanding that [the players] were entitled to some stipulated percentage of national television income."[40]

In retrospect, Leonard Koppett astutely noted that Miller's scheme may actually have contained more bluff than substance. The holdout "was a conscience-raising exercise . . . [that] would give [the players] a sense of solidarity, would make a point, . . . and cost them nothing to do it."[41] Koppett opined that the players were not likely to stay away from training camps too long because they needed time to prepare for the upcoming season—preparation that was more crucial in an age when many baseball players devoted the late autumn and winter months to a secondary job rather than staying in top physical condition. And if money were any kind of motivation, striking players certainly were not going to receive any pay once the regular season started in April.

Salary was not the only incentive for some players to report to camp. Those whose job security was tentative also faced a difficult decision as to whether they should back the vast majority of their teammates in the holdout or report to camp to compete for a job. Signed out of high school as an amateur free agent in 1957, Red Sox catcher Russ Gibson toiled for a decade in the minor leagues before finally getting his chance in Boston. In 1968 Gibson was a part-time player, starting sixty-five games behind the plate, but at the time of the 1969 holdout, he was expected to be vying for a roster spot with fellow catchers Jerry Moses, who would be named to the American League All-Star team in 1970, and young future Hall of Famer Carlton Fisk. Gibson felt partial to Red Sox manager Dick Williams, who had encouraged Gibson to keep pursuing a baseball career when he was inclined to quit after spending so much time in the minors, and he also benefited from the generosity of owner Tom Yawkey—"a fine gentleman," according to Gibson—who gave the backstop a new contract. Gibson's experience corroborates why Yastrzemski, who enjoyed his relationship with Yawkey, was inclined to report to camp when the players' association was trying to remain firm in its display of solidarity during the holdout. Torn between showing loyalty to his owner or supporting the stand taken by hundreds of other major-league players by continuing to stay out of camp, Gibson sought the advice of Sox ace Jim Lonborg and coach Bobby Doerr as to what course he should follow. But his decision became a moot point when Miller brokered a settlement the day after Gibson conferred with Lonborg. Even from the point of view of a journeyman like Gibson, the players "were very fortunate to have Marvin Miller" as their labor leader.[42]

Having barely warmed his chair in the commissioner's office, Bowie Kuhn kept his distance from the fray, but he nonetheless played a role by actively encouraging both players and owners to keep open lines of communication so that negotiations could move forward. Even Miller, who would become an archenemy of Kuhn, confessed that the settlement was "amicable," and thought the new commissioner deserved "much of the credit . . . and I was happy to tell him so." Kuhn, already familiar with the battleground onto which he was delivered when he accepted his new post, bemoaned his baptism by fire—"This was no way for a new commissioner to start out," he later wrote—but the promise of a new season beckoned.[43] In March 1969 a truce prevailed, and the time had arrived for all parties to devote their energy and full attention to preparing for the long haul of another season.

The Reign of the Reserve System

Toward the end of Major League Baseball's reserve clause era, players continued to find themselves subject not only to the dictates of the team owners but, in many cases, duplicitous behavior from others in their club's front office. That teams took advantage of naive and less educated players was an extension of the plantation mentality inherent in ownership's treatment of its most important field personnel.

In his classic book *Ball Four*, Jim Bouton explained how Marvin Milkes, the general manager of the expansion Seattle Pilots, would tell a player on the disabled list not to worry because he would not lose any of his salary while he was inactive, or indicate that a player brought up from the minor leagues would have his rent paid by the team.[44] Such information was conveyed by Milkes in a paternalistic tone, as if he were doing the player a personal favor. In most cases, the player had little idea that the team was obligated to pay salary or rent as stipulated in the basic agreement with the players' association.

Bouton also observed that general managers could make disingenuous use of the waiver wire if they really wanted to trade a player after a trading deadline, and he was critical of such abuses that were perpetrated by "front office capriciousness."[45] When he was traded to the Houston Astros late in the 1969 season, Bouton noted another ploy used by the ownership of his new team to maintain a hold, of sorts, over its team members: Players had their paychecks deposited into a bank owned by Judge Roy Hofheinz, who also happened to own the Astros. While such an arrangement may not have been illegal, the situation could be viewed as tinged with a conflict of interest on the part of Hofheinz, who may have been trying to do his players a favor but was also restricting—to a degree—their freedom of choice about where to send their wages.

But the larger question related to the generations-old issue of player servitude concerns the reserve clause. Dating back to 1859, the roots of the reserve system imbued it with a significant dose of legitimacy. The clause was founded at an amateur level in an effort to "maintain the type of honest competition that would make baseball an honorable game" by discouraging a team from "stealing" players from another club.[46]

In the 1870s, when the game became a sporting profession, team owners took an entrepreneurial risk to establish their clubs and were entitled "to protect the investment [they] had made in the skills of their baseball players."[47] But the initial concept of contractually securing five players to a team quickly accelerated to securing every player, and within a few short years all contracts contained legal wording that bound a player to his employer for as long as the team saw fit. Such a stranglehold over the player meant he was unable to offer his services to another club, and this scheme also served as a rein on salaries, since the player had no choice but to accept the terms offered by his team.

Management and players had been exposed to this system for so long that it was accepted as a permanent fixture of baseball's business and economic landscape. Scolding his players in 1969 as Marvin Miller's rumblings about modifying the reserve clause were surfacing, Seattle Pilots skipper Joe Schultz intoned, "Boys, the reserve clause is the only thing you can't fool with. It's the foundation of this game. If you get rid of it, we're all out of business." Indeed, the cornerstone of management's reserve structure was anchored in paragraph 10A of the Uniform Player's Contract, which, when distilled to its core, meant that "if a player and [his] team could not come to terms, the team could unilaterally renew the player's contract for one year."[48]

A degree of innocuousness was couched in the clause: namely, the contract period of a single year. However, the annual renewal timeframe continued ad infinitum, and under these conditions the player would be forever the property of his team. In 1922 the United States Supreme Court ruled in *Federal Baseball Club v. National League* that baseball was exempt from antitrust laws, and subsequent challenges affirmed the national pastime's status as sport rather than interstate commerce that was subject to federal regulation. Yet in the aftermath of World War II, two players dared to challenge this sanction, a pair of Davids who ultimately became fodder for the Goliath of Major League Baseball.

New York Giants outfielder Danny Gardella jumped to the Mexican League in early 1946 but found himself blacklisted by Major League Baseball upon his return shortly thereafter. Suing for reinstatement, he settled out of court in October 1949 after failing to undo baseball's galvanized reserve system and its attendant antitrust privilege, although his effort prompted "a freshet of eight additional antitrust suits" in the 1950s.[49]

One of these was initiated by George Earl Toolson, a minor-league player in the Yankees organization who sought redress after being demoted from New York's Triple-A team to its Double-A club. Had the reserve clause not been in effect, Toolson argued, he would have been free to find a better situation with another team or organization. Bowie Kuhn, employed at that time as a young National League attorney who was actively involved with the *Toolson* case, later said that even though baseball's antitrust privilege—and so the reserve system—again prevailed before the U.S. Supreme Court, the spate of legal action was drawing the attention of congressmen in Washington.

Twenty months after Gardella's case concluded, Emanuel Celler, a congressman from Brooklyn who chaired the House Committee on Monopoly Power, convened hearings into the antitrust conundrum. However, grandstanding held sway more than scrutinizing the issue, and all that emerged was the status quo as "the committee had no desire to upset baseball's applecart."[50] So with its reserve system intact, baseball carried on until the telephone of a Cardinals outfielder rang on October 8, 1969.

The Case of Curt Flood

The phone call placed to Curt Flood of the St. Louis Cardinals was made to inform him that he was among several players involved in a trade with the Philadelphia Phillies. Flood was being packaged with catcher Tim McCarver, pitcher Joel Hoerner, and outfielder Byron Browne in exchange for second baseman Cookie Rojas, pitcher Jerry Johnson, and Dick Allen, the Phillies slugger and three-time All-Star whose personality frequently rubbed management the wrong way and whose "perceived obstinacy had become national news."[51]

As a youth signed out of McClymonds High School in Oakland, California, to a contract with the Cincinnati Reds, Flood was one of three noted alumni—Frank Robinson and Vada Pinson being the others—who played for legendary coach George Powles in the mid-1950s and went on to enjoy significant major-league careers. The eighteen-year-old Flood followed in Robinson's and Pinson's footsteps to Cincinnati, and he debuted in 1956 in a Reds uniform during a September call-up from the minors, where his salary was $700 per month.[52] His total time in Cincinnati during 1956 and 1957 consisted of a mere eight games, and the Reds, leery of placing Flood in the same lineup with Robinson and Pinson—thus forming an all-black outfield—at a time when major-league front offices were still sensitive to racial issues, dealt Flood to St. Louis in early December 1957 in a multiple-player trade.

Given a new opportunity with a different organization, Flood cracked the Cardinal lineup, although this endeavor was laden the ignominy of playing for a racist manager in the form of Solly Hemus. But Flood exhibited talent that put him on a par with his famous high school teammates, and beginning in 1961 he batted close to or well over .300 in seven of the next nine seasons, was named to the National League All-Star team three times, and won seven straight Gold Gloves from 1963 to 1969. During 1968, when pitching was dominant in both the American and National leagues, Flood was only one of five players to hit over .300 in the Senior Circuit.

The following season, the thirty-one-year-old Flood dipped to .285 while playing in 153 games, but several factors conspired against one of the best center

Although Curt Flood was not the first player to challenge the reserve clause, his pairing up with Marvin Miller helped to create a symbiosis that eventually led to a truly open labor market for players. *National Baseball Hall of Fame Library, Cooperstown, NY.*

fielders of his era, ensuring his days in St. Louis were numbered. Advancing age was evident in his batting average, but more alarming was the blunder Flood committed in the final game of the 1968 World Series, when a two-out fly ball off the bat of Detroit's Jim Northrup went over his head for a triple that plated two runs and gave the Tigers a lead they would not relinquish. Prior to the 1969 campaign, Flood openly hinted at retirement if he could not crack the $100,000 salary plateau—he ended up signing for $90,000—and when the Cardinals were struggling to catch the Chicago Cubs and upstart New York Mets for supremacy in the new National League East division, late-season anonymous statements in the local press—attributed to Flood—regarding some decisions pertaining to the St. Louis lineup irked the Cardinal front office.

General manager Bing Devine felt the quality of his center fielder's play was good enough to see him through a few more years, but, upset with Flood's attitude, the GM targeted him for the trade market. Already the subject of early-season rumors that had Flood being traded back to the Reds, Devine found a new home for him in Philadelphia in a swap featuring a notable malcontent from each club. However, after investing more than a decade in St. Louis, during which time he established his residence and a personal business, Flood took exception to the brusque dismissal handed him by Devine.

In his important biography of Flood, Brad Snyder noted that the transaction intended to put Flood in a Phillies uniform "reawakened latent feelings of unfairness about the reserve system."[53] As a black American exposed to the ugly racial currents that coursed through the United States, Flood had grown up in an Oakland ghetto and had endured abuses at the hands of whites when he played two seasons of minor-league baseball in the Carolina and South Atlantic leagues, as well as during his successful but uneasy attempt to move into a home in a white neighborhood near Oakland. In his role as an activist who drew inspiration from Jackie Robinson's feat of integrating major-league baseball in 1947, Flood spoke in defense of civil rights and participated in charitable causes to help those less fortunate.

Disinclined to acquiesce to his trade from St. Louis, Flood believed the time had come to take a stand against the reserve clause. Richard Moss, no longer counsel for the players' association but now acting as Flood's attorney, met with his client and Marvin Miller. Flood was adamant in his refusal to report to the Phillies for the 1970 season, and as he insisted on proceeding with an antitrust suit against Major League Baseball, "all he wanted from [Miller] was an indication that the union would back him" despite the belief that there was only "a million-to-one shot of winning this case."[54]

Rather than encourage Flood, Miller took a contrarian view to emphasize that the outfielder's stance against the baseball establishment would for all intents and purposes end his playing career and preclude him from ever working in any baseball capacity—as a scout, coach, or manager—to say nothing of the fact that a trial would entail dragging before the public "anything in [his] personal life that [he didn't] want to see on the front page of the newspaper." Despite the earlier failures of suits against baseball, Flood remained undaunted and told Miller, "If we win, it would benefit all the players in the future."[55] Important to the context of the time, Flood denied any underlying racial motivation to his challenge to the system. And should Flood win his case and, in essence, become a free agent, he likely would have been hard-pressed to find a new employer after dealing a blow against the reserve system that had bound Major League Baseball for nearly a century.

As 1969 drew to a close, Flood spoke to the player representatives of all the major-league teams and asked for their financial support to foot his legal expenses. Buoyed by their unanimous approval, Flood acceded to the only stipulation the reps imposed: that he use an attorney selected by the players' association, not one of his own choosing. At this time, Flood petitioned commissioner Bowie Kuhn to allow him to offer his services to any teams besides the Phillies who might be interested in him, thus proving Flood's wish to continue playing baseball rather than pretend to retire from the game for the sake of trying to obtain a more favorable contract. Not surprisingly, Kuhn denied Flood's request, so Flood moved forward with his legal action despite being the only man in uniform fighting for the cause. "The players were not unified enough in December 1969 to strike over the reserve clause," wrote Snyder. "They chose to let Flood do the striking for them."[56]

A procedure was available at the time whereby players could bring grievances, such as Flood's trade, before the commissioner, but realizing that Kuhn was an employee of the owners, Miller said it would be futile to expect a fair hearing. Not until "the first basic agreement *after* the Flood case was filed" would an impartial arbiter adjudicate such issues.[57]

There was never a shortage of jeremiads against striking down the reserve clause. Whether ownership's defense of it was simply the fact that baseball contracts had included it for generations, or declarations imbued with the sentiment of Clark Griffith, the late owner of the old Washington Senators, that "freedom of contract would be fatal to baseball," Flood was unquestionably playing the role of another David in his battle against the Goliath of the baseball establishment.[58]

As the wheels of the court system began their first movement, Flood took his case to the public. Appearing with Howard Cosell on *ABC's Wide World of Sports*, Flood addressed the comment that his $90,000 salary—among the better wages in its day—should imply willing subjection to the more inconvenient terms of his contract. "A well-paid slave is nonetheless a slave," the outfielder calmly stated. He also nixed the possibility of settling out of court by declaring, "I cannot be bought." Flood's suit of 1970 was "an action . . . to enjoin the defendants—several major league baseball clubs, the American and National Leagues of Professional Baseball Clubs, the Commissioner of Baseball, and certain named individuals—from enforcing organized baseball's reserve system against him."[59]

In his early years as the director of the players' association, Miller was wise to pick and choose his battles against ownership, because he had to build a track record of modest but important victories—such as those related to pension issues—while at once trying to gain favor among players skeptical of both Miller and unionism. Recognizing the impracticality of "set[ting] a target that was too high to reach fast," he sought to move carefully on the issue of the reserve clause. By the summer of 1969, the MLBPA was arguing about "the inability of [a] player to choose freely his employer . . . never having a voice in the bartering of his contract to other employers," which was "a right available in other walks of life."[60] The system affected all players, and the freedom of movement they sought was reasonable in terms of what workers in other occupations already enjoyed. Curt Flood decided that the time had come to act, and Miller, having forewarned him about the longs odds of overturning the reserve system, let events run their course.

Flood paid a dear price in the process. He stayed away from the game, having fled to a self-imposed exile in Denmark, and lost out on Philadelphia's $100,000 offer to join the Phillies. In the spring of 1970 Monte Irvin, the former New York Giant who served as a special assistant to Kuhn, reached out to Flood in an effort to arrange a meeting between Kuhn and Flood, but to no avail. Despite Flood's rejection, Irvin "assured [Flood] that the Commissioner's door would always be open to him should he ever change his mind."[61]

When Flood was traded to the Washington Senators in November 1970, he relented and signed a $110,000 contract for the 1971 season. By this time, however, Flood was now possessed of what the baseball team's physician called "the oldest 33-year-old body I've ever examined," and he stumbled at the plate and in the outfield during spring training.[62] Flood's consumption of alcohol, an old habit that died hard, did nothing to improve his chances of regaining his playing ability. He distanced himself from his teammates, some of whom, like a young Elliott Maddox, genuinely cared for him and sought his advice on how to improve their playing ability. But Flood had fallen into a downward spiral from which there was no recovery, and less than a month into the 1971 season, he quit the game for good after playing in only thirteen games and batting an uninspiring .200.

He fared no better in the courtroom than on the field. The district court in New York that heard the case initially rendered its verdict in March 1970. Although recognizing that "for years professional ballplayers have chafed under the restrictions of baseball's reserve system," the court denied the plaintiff's motion due to the "well-established and controlling precedents against his position." Even Kuhn testified that the "'renewal option' clause . . . in effect gives the club the perpetual right to renew [a player's] contract," although he immediately followed this with a patronizing qualifier: "It does not, of course, require the player to play baseball." When Flood sought redress through an appeal in early 1971, the United States Court of Appeals for the Second Circuit was "compelled to affirm the district court's decision," citing the 1922 *Federal Baseball* decision and the *Toolson* verdict as primary reasons for ruling against Flood.[63]

Flood's last attempt, in 1972, to unseat the reserve clause came in an appeal to the United States Supreme Court, and as had happened in the previous two court battles, he again failed as the *Federal Baseball* and *Toolson* rulings continued to set the tone in the view of the justices. In the last instance, however, the Supreme Court overtly acknowledged, "1. Professional baseball is a business and it is engaged in interstate commerce [and] 2. With its reserve system enjoying exemption from the federal antitrust laws, baseball is, in a very distinct sense, an exception and an anomaly. *Federal Baseball* and *Toolson* have become an aberration confined to baseball."[64] This antitrust exemption was an issue for Congress to deal with, said the Supreme Court, and players and the teams were welcome to solve the enigma through the collective bargaining process. Thanks in part to poor performances before the Supreme Court by his attorney, Arthur Goldberg, Curt Flood was 0-for-3 in his ostensibly quixotic jousts against Major League Baseball. However, a more appropriate retrospective is in order.

If Flood had not been obstinate enough to persevere in the face of adversity from the courts—who simply relied on the doctrine of stare decisis to retain the status quo of the reserve clause—and from the public and the press—who reviled him for his "well-paid slave" comment—we have to ask one question: What other player would have been in a position to challenge it and make the sacrifice that he did? Several players of note—veterans such as Al Downing, Ted Simmons, Sparky Lyle, and Bobby Tolan—refused to sign contracts but reported to their teams ready to play while making the argument that the reserve clause, which automatically renewed the contract for one more year, implied that the player's signature was not necessary to validate the contract. Downing was with the New York Yankees in February of 1969—eight months before Flood was dealt to the Phillies—when he elected to report unsigned to spring training. When management contended that he could not suit up until he inked his contract, Downing pointed out—in *his* interpretation of the reserve clause—that not only was he already under contract, but that should the Yankees turn him away, he would become an unrestricted free agent because the team elected to ignore the terms of a valid contract. Miller termed the affair "illuminating," and it certainly was a groundbreaking episode that, for once, turned the reserve clause to the favor of the player.[65]

Simmons (in 1972), Lyle (in 1973), and Tolan (in 1974) presented variations on Downing's theme by signing at different points during the season *but before the season ended*. The final salvo against the reserve clause was unleashed when Dodgers pitcher Andy Messersmith played the entire 1975 season unsigned, thus providing Marvin Miller with a case that could be brought to an arbitrator, Peter Seitz. Ruling that Messersmith had fulfilled the obligation to play one year under the reserve clause's renewal, Seitz declared Messersmith now free to make a deal with any team of his choosing. Montreal pitcher Dave McNally was also unsigned but had retired due to injury partway through the same season. He allowed Miller to use his circumstances as a backup test case because of uncertainty as to whether he would remain the property of the Expos or be permitted to sign with another team should he decide to return to baseball. The Seitz decision in December 1975 created the era of true free agency, and baseball has never looked back.

Curt Flood, however, reaped the fewest rewards of anyone who fought the reserve system after Marvin Miller's arrival with the players' association. He sacrificed what was left of his baseball career after 1969 and collected one-half of his $110,000 salary in early 1971 when it was clear that he was no longer fit to play major-league baseball. In late April, before boarding a jet for Barcelona, Spain, he sent a telegram to Senators owner Robert Short indicating that "serious personal problems" were overtaking him.[66] Departing, Flood never looked back, either.

Historian David Bohmer labeled 1969 as the "pivotal year" in the history of free agency, and it is difficult to dispute this claim.[67] The concessions wrung by Marvin Miller from the club owners beginning in 1966 served to prove to the players that he was truly on *their* side, and by taking slow but methodical steps Miller was able to have an increasingly tangible impact on the manner in which the magnates handled and compensated their most valuable commodity—the players. Generations of players had been treated disingenuously by ownership and held at bay unilaterally by a contract stipulation upheld even by the Supreme Court of the United States. Although Curt Flood's venture came to grief, he began to substantively loosen the linchpin of the reserve clause—at his own peril—and in this sense he did serve to the benefit of multitudes of players who came after him.

Two Umpires Called Out

As the 1968 regular season was winding down, another labor issue arose, this one affecting a noticeably smaller segment of baseball's workforce yet nonetheless important in its own right. A pair of youthful but veteran American League umpires working on the same crew were rudely awakened in mid-September by the news that they "were being released for incompetence and that their contracts would not be renewed for the 1969 season." A terse statement from American League president Joe Cronin—"They're just bad umpires, that's all," said the AL prexy—defended the dismissals of Al Salerno and Bill Valentine, who had major-league experience of eight years and seven years, respectively.[68] From the time of their hiring until the day of their release, no apparent indication of substandard performance on the job had been attributed to either arbiter, but Cronin perfunctorily fired Salerno and Valentine with two weeks left in the campaign.

An underlying factor in the dismissals, which Cronin denied, was Salerno's attendance at a meeting of National League umpires just two days prior to Cronin's decision. Senior Circuit umpires had formed a union in 1963, and Salerno went to a session of NL arbiters in Chicago to express an interest on behalf of his American League counterparts to join the extant union. AL umpires would be allowed to do so, according to union officials, if they were unanimous in their support. Not all of them embraced the idea of a union, but "the Salerno and Valentine firings fused the umpires together as never before."[69]

Umpires from both leagues—including eighteen of twenty from the American League—gathered, again in Chicago, to discuss a course of action. Furious in the belief that Salerno and Valentine were fired strictly because of their attempt to persuade other AL umpires to fall in with the NL, the umpires considered the issue on the eve of the 1968 World Series, which seemed a most fitting action, given the strife the rest of the country had endured during that most turbulent of years.

Collectively, the umpires sought the reinstatement of their colleagues, and calling a strike during the national pastime's signature event was thought to be the most expedient step to force Cronin's hand. The two ousted arbiters appealed to the other umpires not to take such a drastic measure. Indeed, fearing that any job action during the World Series would inflict more harm on the cause prompted the attorney for the NL umpires, Jack Reynolds, to implore them to not use it as a bargaining chip. "If he hadn't been so persuasive," said one unnamed umpire, "there would have been a strike."[70]

Reluctant to unionize until the twin firings in September, the incited American League arbiters now sought to gain equal footing with those in the NL. Since forming their union in 1963, the National League umpires had enjoyed better wages and pension benefits, and commensurate compensation for the same kind of work performed by AL umpires was hardly an unreasonable demand. The newly renamed Major League Umpires Association was formed when the National League arbiters unanimously voted to allow the AL to close ranks with them. By early January 1969, Reynolds and the revamped union reached an accord with the American League, and Reynolds advised all umpires to come to terms with their respective leagues in preparation for the new season. Marvin Miller had been approached by the umpires regarding the creation of a single players'/umpires' union, but Miller declined, citing the "disciplinarian authority" that umpires held over the players as leading to a conflict of interest should the two groups be conjoined in the same labor organization.[71]

The two umpires at the center of the fracas, however, were still on the outside looking in. Salerno and Valentine were not reinstated by Cronin, and the umpires' union came to their defense as it filed an unfair labor practice charge with the National Labor Relations Board (NLRB) days after Reynolds gave the union membership approval to sign their individual contracts. While the case waited in the NLRB queue as autumn of 1969 approached, Salerno and Valentine filed suit, for good measure, against the American League, Major League Baseball, Joe Cronin, and Bowie Kuhn. The suit in Manhattan's federal court was thrown out as being another iteration of the *Toolson* case and baseball's antitrust exemption, and a plea by Salerno in May 1970 met the same fate in the United States Court of Appeals for the Second Circuit.

In the meantime, the American League brokered "a confidential settlement" with the umpires' association in early 1970 whereby Salerno and Valentine would be reinstated upon meeting two conditions: The halting of both the complaint with the NLRB as well as the lawsuit, and the successful completion of "a brief probationary period in the minor leagues" intended to show the umpires as worthy of a return to the major leagues.[72] Valentine was amenable to the terms but Salerno was determined to press on, much to Valentine's chagrin, as the proposed settlement was to be applied to both umpires. Unless they both agreed, there would be no deal.

When the NLRB hearing took place in the summer of 1970, several current big-league managers and some colleagues in the umpiring profession spoke in support of Salerno and Valentine, but in November the verdict handed down by the board was against the umpires. The only evidence offered by the umpires, said the board, was speculation that Cronin fired them because of their unionization activities, and the lack of a direct connection to Cronin, in the eyes of the NLRB, absolved the AL president. The involvement of the NLRB in this dispute proved that "the government was paying attention to labor issues in baseball and could readily take jurisdiction over an issue."[73]

More gains for the players' association were still on a horizon that extended beyond 1969. From the time of Marvin Miller's naming to the MLBPA in 1966 until the end of the decade, he diligently coalesced hundreds of players cynical of union involvement into an organization that went on to strike down the entrenched reserve clause. Systematically eroding the bedrock that allegedly buttressed Major League Baseball, Miller did what he was being paid to do—fight for the players and earn for them those benefits to which they were entitled. In his struggle to get a "fairer slice of the pie" for the players, Miller insisted in his autobiography, "that pie became much bigger *because* of the players' unionizing efforts."[74]

In the current debate regarding whether Marvin Miller should be elected to the Baseball Hall of Fame, the impact he had on the game is beyond dispute. In the post-Messersmith era, the game was not doomed to economic catastrophe, and despite the untold millions of dollars spent on admittedly exorbitant player salaries, ball clubs with deep pockets have not cornered the market on the best talent nor have rich teams created unending dynasties. The groundwork carefully cultivated by Miller in the late 1960s eventually yielded unimagined riches for players and—though they themselves may be loath to admit it—the club owners, whose franchises in some cases are now worth billions of dollars.

A closing anecdote provides a thoughtful perspective. In an interview he gave in 1992, former Yankee Jim Bouton opined that players in the early part of the 1960s would not have cared about the pension plan as much as they did had the owners been willing to provide a better minimum wage.[75] Bouton suggested that an extra $1,000 per year over twenty years may have been enough to get players to not become so firmly attached to the pension that seemed to always be in dispute. Whether Bouton's dollar figure was rooted in economic fact or simply a round figure that happened to come to mind cannot be determined. However, if there is any veracity to Bouton's speculation, one can only wonder how the script would have been written had those few extra thousand dollars been given to the handful of players on each team who would have been entitled to receive it. This modest display of generosity on the part of the owners might have endeared them to the players and allowed them to hold on to the reserve system longer than they did.

Not subject to conjecture is a statement made by pitcher Jim Bunning in December 1967. "I have news for [the owners]," said Bunning, who was inducted into the Baseball Hall of Fame thirty years after the fledgling Major League Baseball Players Association named its new director. "Marvin Miller will be around in his present job for a long time."[76] Miller was the ideal man to lead baseball's labor force into a new modern era.

CHAPTER 7

Race, War, Politics, and Cultural Zeitgeist

With very good reason, much scholarship has been devoted to the tumultuous 1960s. While many of that decade's events—political, cultural, and societal—had formative roots in the 1950s or even earlier, the ten years beginning in 1960 took on an increasingly conflicted tone, at once more free-spirited and more confrontational. As the decade progressed the burgeoning civil rights movement and the escalating war in Vietnam spawned demonstrations in support of the former and against the latter. In each case the voices for both causes grew louder as the years passed and as expectations of equality for one issue and peace for the other went unfulfilled. Finally, over the course of the first half of 1968, several significant incidents occurred that shook the nation to its core.

At the end of January the Tet Offensive erupted across South Vietnam, sounding a Klaxon call of alarm and putting the lie to what US officials had been promulgating for many months—namely, that "a light at the end of the tunnel" could be seen in bringing the conflict to a victorious conclusion. On the home front, and running concurrent with developments in Southeast Asia, the civil rights movement was in the throes of struggle during the 1960s. Race riots in several major urban areas of the country were sparked by African American anger over police brutality, disenfranchisement, and lingering racial discrimination. The passive resistance attempts by Martin Luther King Jr. to bring about change were shattered when he was assassinated in April. Barely two months later the presidential aspirations of Senator Robert Kennedy—whose ambitions included an end to the war in Vietnam—were extinguished by another assassin at the close of the California Democratic primary. Antiwar protesters vented their spleen in late August at the Democratic National Convention, and it seemed painfully ironic that two of the top songs on the pop charts at the time were the Beatles' "Revolution" and "Fire," recorded by the Crazy World of Arthur

Brown. In 1968 alone more than 16,500 American servicemen died in Vietnam, and there was no end to the war in sight.

In January 1969 a new president was inaugurated, and hopes prevailed that the next commander-in-chief, Richard Nixon, would be able to deliver on his campaign pledge to end the Vietnam War. But the conflict persisted, and unsavory events—Ted Kennedy's automobile mishap, which claimed the life of a young woman, and the notorious Tate–La Bianca murders—found their way into news headlines. A boost in the country's morale came in July when Apollo 11 completed the first manned lunar landing, and just weeks later a dairy farm in upstate New York became the site of a musical lovefest known as Woodstock, which delighted the youthful crowd of more than four hundred thousand. However, Americans expressed shock and dismay upon the revelation in November that twenty months earlier a group of American troops had perpetrated the massacre at My Lai, in which 567 South Vietnamese—mostly women and children—had been murdered. A modicum of good news as far as protesters were concerned arrived in late December when President Nixon announced that the number of American troops in Vietnam would be cut to 434,000 by the spring of 1970. By and large, racial violence had settled down because riots earlier in the decade had forced local governments to address more forthrightly problems concerning minorities. A rise in black voter registration also encouraged some African Americans in more heavily populated areas to run for office, but blacks continued to feel the sting of discrimination.[1]

The United States was hardly at peace by the end of 1969, but the country was in a less frenetic condition compared to 1968. A long, slow turning of the corner in race relations was in progress, yet a new decade would still require the shouldering of burdens acquired in the old decade, primarily prosecution of an unpopular war and the fallout of the protests against it. Hardly impervious to the forces of politics and culture, baseball in these two years was enduring its own transformation, affected by both contemporaneous issues in America as well as demands that forced it to confront the modern age into which it was inexorably moving.

Issues of Race

To many people unfamiliar with the topic of race as it pertains to baseball, the inclusion of African Americans in Major League Baseball may impress as commencing with the breaking of the color barrier by Jackie Robinson on April 15, 1947. Participation in baseball by African Americans can actually be traced back to the 1800s, but in 1867 sanctioned discrimination was established by the National Association of Amateur Base Ball Players. African American players endured only through the creation of all-black teams and leagues in the twentieth century, notably through the efforts of Rube Foster.[2]

By the mid-1940s and in the aftermath of World War II, Brooklyn Dodgers general manager Branch Rickey had decided to cultivate one particular black player capable of withstanding the pressure he knew would be brought to bear on any African American chosen to force the integration of Major League Baseball. With Jackie Robinson so selected and having surmounted the attendant trials associated with his ascension to the big leagues, the new Dodgers star paved the way for other black players who would follow in his footsteps. The integration of Major League Baseball in 1947 did not mean that each of the sixteen teams joined a stampede to sign minority talent.

To be sure, Brooklyn was quick to exploit the advantage demonstrated by Robinson and followed up by bringing Don Newcombe and Roy Campanella into their organization. Other clubs in the Senior Circuit moved to improve their lineups with the likes of Willie Mays, Ernie Banks, and Hank Aaron. However, the Cleveland Indians under owner Bill Veeck were among the few teams in the American League to enthusiastically embrace black players, with Larry Doby being the first to integrate the Junior Circuit. Yet the attainment of a spot on a major-league roster had little bearing on the manner in which minority players were treated, especially for those participating in Florida spring training camps. Only in 1965 did the last of the major-league clubs—the Minnesota Twins—finally integrate their hotel accommodations; until that time black players were forced to seek lodging and other services such as barbers and laundries in African American sections of town. Their status as ballplayers did not carry much weight for these men in the everyday world away from the ballpark.

Integration at other levels of Major League Baseball, however, proceeded at a snail's pace. Not until 1962 was there an African American coach, when Buck O'Neil joined the Cubs. Yet in the spring of 1966 the *Sporting News* trumpeted in an editorial that there were "new horizons for the Negro" not just on the playing field but also in management ranks, and the notion of a black baseball manager was "not as far-fetched" as one might believe.[3] In the vocation of umpiring, Emmett Ashford debuted as the first black arbiter that same year after an apprenticeship in the minor leagues that lasted well over a decade. The ebullient Ashford harbored no animosity at having been kept from reaching the majors sooner than he did and was optimistic that harmony between African Americans and whites would be achieved, telling the *Kansas City Star*, "If people are willing to work at it and exercise some patience, our racial problems can be worked out."[4]

Ashford's approach to his profession drew criticism from some corners that he was caught up in his own theatrics on the diamond, but his enthusiasm was genuine and curried favor with many fans. A countervailing demeanor was espoused by Dick Allen, the Phillies slugger and winner of the 1964 National League Rookie of the Year Award. Allen's first-year exploits, especially at the plate, helped drive the Phillies to the top of the Senior Circuit—until the club faltered in the stretch run for the pennant—but by 1969 he had worn out his welcome through a display of rebellious attitude and had turned into the Peck's bad boy of the franchise. One baseball scholar, who analogized Allen to Herman Melville's "Bartleby, the Scrivener," opined that Allen's overall resentment was fueled by his belief that players were chattel who served at the pleasure of their team's owner, "with [the player's] value tied solely to his ability to produce for the organization."[5] Allen sought relief through acts of defiance and protest against the establishment, which in this case was Phillies management. Disassociating himself from his teammates by using a closet instead of his assigned locker, Allen grew reluctant to attend team meetings, and he resented small favors bestowed on him by management, gestures he interpreted as indulgences meant to humor the hired help. Unwilling to accept his station in the caste of the Phillies' system, the brooding Allen led a one-man crusade against the slights—real or perceived—inflicted on him.

At last fed up with trying to placate their petulant outfielder/first baseman, Philadelphia traded Allen to St. Louis at the end of the 1969 season for, among others, Curt Flood, who would go on to champion the cause of free agency. That the principals in the deal were both black men who expressed discomfiture with the treatment they received from their respective team ownerships may be more than a coincidence. What Allen and Flood saw as taking a stand for better treatment was seen by others—whites, for example—as pretentiousness imbued with racial overtones.

The late 1960s also exhibited a compelling variation of the race issue. As a growing number of Latin American players reached the major-league level, some of them also found tension in their relations with black teammates. Manifestation of this friction existed on the roster of the Pittsburgh Pirates, a contending team whose roster was replete with black and Latino stars such as Roberto Clemente, Willie Stargell, Maury Wills, Matty Alou, and Bob Veale. Clemente, seen by many as possessed of a large streak of vanity, sought nothing more than fair treatment inside and outside of baseball, and his multidimensional talents earned him glowing recognition among his peers, if not necessarily those in the press.

When the Pirates acquired Maury Wills in a December 1966 trade with Los Angeles, the infielder was accustomed to the fame he had garnered with the Dodgers. Already an established star himself, Clemente now faced competition in a sort of popularity contest as Wills "was beginning to outshine Clemente in the public sphere" off the field. Adding to the volatile mix of personalities were manager Harry "The Hat" Walker's racist tendencies, although Walker cultivated positive relationships with many black Latino players—including several after he retired from managing—due in large part to his excellent tutelage as a batting instructor. The Pirates had problems between factions of black, white, and Latino players, but the situation was exacerbated by what one historian cited as a pronounced fissure "between African Americans and Caribbean blacks in the United States—in baseball, and in society in general."[6]

Another example can be found in a notorious incident from the summer of 1967 after the Atlanta Braves suffered a no-hit loss to Don Wilson and the Houston Astros. On the Braves' flight to Los Angeles after the game, Hank Aaron heard teammate Rico Carty refer to him as a "black slick," precipitating a brief but spirited melee. Prodigious with the bat but wanting on defense, Carty was characterized as a "lightning rod" because of his swagger, and in his autobiography, Aaron noted that Carty "was as dark-skinned as any of [the other black players], but he didn't consider himself black."[7] The future home run king later feuded with his team's television announcer, Milo Hamilton, over remarks Hamilton made regarding his belief that Clemente was the best right fielder in the National League. Because Aaron—also a right fielder—and Clemente were named to that year's All-Star team, Aaron accommodated the NL's lineup by shifting to left field, but the Atlanta slugger felt that in ordinary circumstances, right field "was my turf" and confronted Hamilton over his bias toward the Pittsburgh star.

Not immune to the social turmoil of the day—not least of which included several horrific race riots in over a dozen cities, large and small, during 1967—notable baseball personalities weighed in, and their opinions were not necessarily in harmony. The man who integrated baseball in the modern era, Jackie Robinson, supported the Black Panther movement's goals of "self-determination, protection of the Black community, decent housing and employment, and [the right to] express opposition to police abuse."[8] Robinson was on record as supporting African American business and marketing opportunities that could lift African Americans from economic oppression, and wrote to President Lyndon Johnson to thank him for his willingness to fight for civil rights.

But the Brooklyn Dodgers star also chided Giants outfielder Willie Mays for not lending his voice to the cause of civil rights, prompting Mays to rebuke Robinson. Admitting that he appreciated what Robinson had faced in his quest to integrate baseball—to say nothing of what Mays himself endured—Mays countered by stating that Robinson "didn't speak for [all black athletes]," and that those in the vanguard of the civil rights movement, such as Martin Luther King and Roy Wilkins, "are better equipped than I" to use their position of nonviolent leadership in bringing about desired change. According to Mays, two of his black teammates, Willie McCovey and Jim Ray Hart, "have been treated like kings" during their time in the big leagues, and Mays cited the comfort of his "big, fancy house" and his various memberships in social clubs as proof that Jackie Robinson did not have to speak out for him.[9]

Indeed, as Mays's biographer pointed out, the future Hall of Famer—esteemed as "the most popular player in the league" in 1968—was "subject to a double standard" because few complained that other black baseball stars . . . rarely voiced their opinions [on civil rights]." To wit, Chicago Cubs first baseman Ernie Banks declined to be vocal about the plight of African Americans, disagreeing with those who believed they should be "militant" about their views. "I don't think it's up to black athletes to get involved in political or racial issues," he opined as he distanced himself from the fray.[10]

However, Mays missed the point of Robinson's argument: Although black stars like Mays employed their talent to overcome disadvantages and rise out of poverty to earn fantastic amounts of money, the same was not true for the vast majority of African Americans for whom improved civil rights could become a stepping-stone to better economic opportunity and a higher social station.

Jackie Robinson also took issue with another luminary of the day, Frank Robinson of the Orioles, who, rather than speaking out to champion the cause of civil rights, was cutting his teeth as a manager with a Puerto Rican winter league club in the hope of one day becoming the first black skipper in the majors. "I suppose, Frank, you feel your attitude will get you a manager's job and that some white people may like you better, but respect you is another thing," wrote Jackie in a note to the Baltimore star.[11] Jackie believed that the managerial apprentice should have been advocating for African Americans at home—and to more immediate benefit for other African Americans—rather than working to achieve a long-term goal for himself, however important that aim may have been.

However, one player, Willie Horton of the Detroit Tigers, plunged head-first into harm's way in an attempt to save his city in the conflagration of the summer of 1967. Removing his baseball shoes but otherwise staying in uniform after a home game played during the worst of the rioting, Horton went to one section of his adopted hometown to implore those participating in the mayhem to stop. Horton's active approach to quelling a disruption was a rare occurrence, to say nothing of its potentially injurious results, but his teammate, pitcher Mickey Lolich, soon found his National Guard unit placed on active duty near the site where the riot began in an effort to restore order. St. Louis ace Bob Gibson noted that, like Ernie Banks, ballplayers had the luxury of turning away from many ills of society, but as 1968 devolved into a series of unfortunate circumstances, the Cardinals "were more socially conscious than most clubs, . . . were deeply affected by what went down [that year], . . . [and] were angrier than usual."[12]

As training camps were in progress in the spring of 1968, Baltimore out-fielder Frank Robinson was openly critical of the lack of African American representation in baseball's managerial ranks—later that year he began his own apprenticeship as a pilot in the winter league—but former Olympic gold medalist Jesse Owens, on hand for the groundbreaking ceremony to begin construction on Three Rivers Stadium in Pittsburgh, struck a more conciliatory tone with his plea for a union of "men of all colors and creeds" who would play baseball and football at the new facility. Several months later, as if to apply a salve to the wounds of racism, the office of Commissioner William Eckert named former Negro League star Monte Irvin as a public relations aide, a move that won the approval of the *Sporting News*. Praising the appointment of baseball's first black executive, the paper conceded, "With more and more educated Negroes making their mark as standout players, some are surely equipped to handle teaching, managerial and other leadership duties."[13]

As the expansion season of 1969 unfolded, the *Seattle Post-Intelligencer* chirpily informed its readers that the indignities suffered by African American players were "all behind now," and the Pilots were counting on black players such as Tommy Davis and Tommy Harper to figure prominently in the new club's success. By 1969 a tentative peace becalmed the tempest over race. Proving the point made by the *Sporting News* one year earlier, the New York Yankees tabbed longtime catcher/outfielder Elston Howard to be their first-base coach, and former Oriole Curt Blefary broke new ground upon his trade to Houston, where he became the road roommate of African American pitcher Don Wilson, thus forming the first such interracial tandem. And after spending several formative seasons together in Baltimore, teammates Brooks Robinson and Frank Robinson had formed a curious couple as they approached the twilight of their respective Hall of Fame careers.[14]

Brooks, the stellar third baseman and 1964 American League Most Valuable Player, was prematurely balding, white, and a native of Arkansas. Frank, a two-time MVP with the Reds in 1961 and again five years later with the Orioles, was born in Beaumont, Texas, but grew up in Oakland, California, and he was one of a trio of African American stars—Curt Flood and Vada Pinson being the other two—who excelled at McClymonds High School under the tutelage of George Powles and went on to superb major-league careers. Carrying more baggage than Brooks, Frank arrived in Baltimore via a trade with Cincinnati and was saddled with a reputation as a malcontent. But the change of venue worked wonders for Frank in 1966, as he fit well in both the Orioles lineup and, just as importantly, the Baltimore clubhouse. "He had a strong personality," said Brooks of the newcomer, "and it took a little while for everyone to get used to one another. But it all worked out."[15]

Frank and Brooks cultivated a symbiosis that went far beyond the surname they shared. In some circles they were jokingly referred to as "the Robinson brothers," and despite the years they spent in major-league ball—heading into 1969 each had more than a decade of experience—they were still performing at a level that ensured selection to the American League All-Star team. Their regular appearance in the Baltimore lineup was key to the success of the 1966 squad as well as the dominant teams fielded under manager Earl Weaver from 1969 to 1971. "The Robinsons emerged as more compatible than they could ever realize," noted *Sports Illustrated* in a feature story that juxtaposed the pair's differences in personality and racial background as they "struck a delicate, winning balance" for the Orioles.[16]

As more African Americans entered Major League Baseball on the heels of Jackie Robinson's inroad—and as they gained greater acceptance among fans, front offices, and especially their teammates, with whom they interacted the most—a detente among races slowly enveloped the game. Moving on after the riots of Watts, Newark, Detroit, and many other cities, the close of the 1960s saw subtle but tangible changes emerging in American culture and society. "It's not 'colored' now," intoned Tommy Davis of the Seattle Pilots. "It's 'black.'"[17] Whether intended or not, Davis's comment certainly echoed singer James Brown's sentiment in his August 1968 hit song "Say It Loud—I'm Black and I'm Proud," and surely African Americans were just as entitled to dignity of ethnic heritage as anyone else.

In *Ball Four*, author Jim Bouton wrote that in his time with the Pilots, teammates of different races got along well, but not to the degree that he saw with his new teammates following his trade to the Houston Astros. Not only were Curt Blefary and Don Wilson rooming on road trips, but Bouton noted that the cordial relationships among other black and white players appeared not to be "forced," as "blacks go out of their way to join with whites and the whites try extra hard to join in with the blacks."[18] To be sure, some players paid a price for this intermingling—third baseman Doug Rader was called a "nigger lover" by some disapproving white players—but a corner was slowly being turned, and for the better. Whereas the 1967 Kerner Commission foretold of the United States on a path to distinct and unequal societies, the atmosphere in the Astros clubhouse seemed to embody the vision of Martin Luther King's most famous oration: a world in which the content of one's character trumped the color of one's skin.

A generation following his debut in Brooklyn, Jackie Robinson refused to give up carrying the torch for equality. He boycotted the 1969 Old Timers' Game at Yankee Stadium to protest the lack of African Americans in major-league front offices and in managerial roles on the field. Had he lived until 1975, however, he would have seen Frank Robinson, one of the catalysts on the great Baltimore teams, finally assume his place at the helm of the Cleveland Indians.

By the mid-1970s participation by African Americans would reach a high of 17 percent of big-league players, but that number has been in decline ever since. One scholar noted that this trend has been spurred by increased interest among black players in football and basketball, a trend that "contributed to the reduced pool of baseball talent from that sector of the American population" and in turn cleared the way for growing numbers of Latino players to enter the game. "The anger that characterized the 1960s began to seep out of public discourse," and baseball was helped in its own way as the great African American players whose careers spanned the 1950s and 1960s—Hank Aaron, Frank Robinson, Ernie Banks, Willie Mays—ceded their places to those who carried on from the 1960s into the 1970s—Lou Brock, Bob Gibson, Reggie Jackson, Willie McCovey, and Dick Allen.[19] These lists, though brief, are indicative of the excellent skills that black players brought to the major leagues once given their rightful opportunity.

Aaron wrote in his autobiography that Jackie Robinson had implored him "never to be satisfied with the way things are," and the slugger noted that Robinson "gave us our dreams." Those dreams of donning a big-league uniform evolved over time, becoming gradually easier for minorities to realize, and the game has been the better for it. Looking at the broader picture, though, a frustrated Robinson believed the struggle for racial equality had far to go. "There are not enough people around," he said in the summer of 1968, "who give a damn about what is going on as far as the Black man is concerned."[20]

Although the total percentage of black major-league players—African American *and* black Latinos—nearing the close of the 1960s was around 22 percent, the pace at which baseball was moving to open opportunities in management positions for African Americans was at a virtual standstill, and a lingering suspicion implied use of a quota system to purposely cap the number of black players on rosters. This last point was substantiated by evidence that the reserve roles were occupied mainly by white players, leading former Yankees southpaw Al Downing—an African American—to observe, "You don't see too many black ball players in the role of utility infielder, or the fifth or sixth outfielder. Or even, say, a relief pitcher." Indeed, a study by the RAND Corporation concluded that among all players at the major-league level in 1968, "blacks are underrepresented as pitchers and catchers, and overrepresented as outfielders and first basemen."[21]

When Curt Flood became enmeshed in the fight against the reserve clause, he invoked the memory of Martin Luther King Jr. to interesting effect. Featured in a *New York Times* article as his lawsuit took root, Flood was pictured next to a portrait of King that he was believed to have painted and later presented to King's widow, with the image of Flood and King portrayed as if to conflate their respective struggles for freedom.[22] This type of activism differed from that exhibited by some other black players such as Hank Aaron, who were less vocal in taking a stand for racial equality and chose to contribute to the cause "in the little ways that [they] could" by "endorsing sympathetic [political] candidates" who ran for office.

Atlanta mayor Ivan Allen credited Aaron with helping the cause of integration "through his thoughtful consideration and exemplary conduct," yet the Braves outfielder was frustrated by continuing prejudice evidenced in financial opportunities offered to black players. Aaron noted that when Carl Yastrzemski won the Triple Crown in 1967, the Boston star "got rich on endorsements," but when Bob Gibson won both the National League Cy Young and Most Valuable Player awards, he "made enough extra money for about three loads of laundry."[23]

While Aaron's observation has much merit, Gibson's demeanor had more to do with his inability to cash in on his success than the fact that he was black. The highly competitive St. Louis star thought of himself as "a ballplayer with a personal point of view, not an activist with a fastball," and his attitude was clearly manifested in a slogan he displayed on his locker prior to the 1968 World Series, which read, "I'm not prejudiced. I hate everybody." Nonetheless, the RAND study also compared signing bonuses for high school and college players and found that the skewing of payments in favor of whites "was almost totally eliminated" by 1967. In fact it determined that black players "receive compensation commensurate with their demonstrated abilities in the same way that white players do."[24]

And the 1967 American League Rookie of the Year, Rod Carew, soon faced his own challenges, not only as a black player in white America, but also as a partner in an interracial marriage to a Jewish woman. Although Carew suffered his share of prejudice and indignities, he noted that the racial jokes he shared with some teammates "never bothered me," and Carew was accepting of the "locker-room mentality" that imbued such exchanges, except on occasions when "guys go too far."[25]

Floyd McKissick, the leader of the Congress for Racial Equality and adviser for the Olympic Project for Human Rights, wrote in December 1969 of the prevailing struggles still confronting African Americans. His article, which originally appeared in the *Amsterdam News*, offered the opinion that "a Black athlete is expected to play ball like a white man, but live like a Black man in a white world."[26] In the aftermath of the many riots that took place from 1965 to 1968, a trying and lengthy rapprochement between white and black America slowly emerged, and prominent athlete-activists who were drawn into the movement— notably, Muhammad Ali, Jim Brown, and Arthur Ashe, all of whom followed Jackie Robinson—broke their own ground in staking a claim.

Frank Robinson joined this vanguard in the winter of 1968 when he piloted the Santurce Crabbers of the Puerto Rican Winter League and earned Manager of the Year accolades in his first season on the strength of a 49–21 record. Robinson would be subjected to scrutiny regarding any favoritism shown toward black players on his roster, but he later claimed that black players told him he "was harder on them than on anybody," thus dispelling any notion of preferential treatment he may have been perceived to lavish on minorities.[27] To be sure, Frank Robinson became a trailblazer for major-league managers in 1975, and although the front offices of teams continued to be preserved as a whites-only domain, that barrier was soon broken as well. Seventeen months after Robinson took the helm of the Cleveland Indians, Bill Lucas—the former brother-in-law of Hank Aaron—became the general manager of the Atlanta Braves after having worked in the franchise's player development department.

The issue of race vis-à-vis baseball has no definitive end point or closure in either 1968 or 1969. Rather, the late 1960s were a continuum through which the game passed, and barely one decade after the last major-league team was integrated, the national pastime continued to put minority talent on the field and was at last allowing African Americans to assume positions of leadership.

Vietnam—"9875 Miles to Shea Stadium"

The struggle for civil rights had taken hold well before the end of the 1960s, but drawing increasing attention across the country—and affecting arguably as many households as were racial issues—was the protracted and complicated misfortune of American involvement in the war in Vietnam. In March 1965 President Lyndon Johnson's decision to widen the conflict ultimately "spurred the polarization that characterized the Sixties in the United States."[28]

While not drawn into the fray in the same manner as during the declared wars against Germany in 1917 and against Germany and Japan in 1941, the might of American military power nonetheless depended on enlistees and draftees to fortify its ranks with men in their late teens and twenties. These vast legions included baseball players, many of whom fulfilled their military obligations by serving in reserve units stateside while others performed active duty in Vietnam.

Attitudes among players about service in the armed forces varied in the years before Southeast Asia became a flashpoint in American current events. Hank Aaron remarked on registering for the draft in the 1950s, "[W]hen you grow up as a black kid in a Jim Crow city, you somehow don't feel a great urgency to serve your country,"[29] and when twenty-one-year-old Willie Mays was called to the colors following the 1951 season—just when his baseball career was taking form—his appeals to the draft board were denied, forcing him to join the army in late May 1952 and miss nearly two full years with the New York Giants.

Future stars who made their mark in a major-league uniform by the end of the 1960s found that becoming part of the reserves had the advantage of discharging their military duty while minimizing the impact to their time playing baseball. After his graduation from Fresno High School in California, Tom Seaver worked at a raisin-packing plant for six months as he awaited his entrance into a six-month stint with the Marine Corps Reserve. After serving in early 1963 he built a notable collegiate baseball résumé that eventually placed him with the New York Mets. Rod Carew, who, like Seaver, would win major-league Rookie of the Year honors in 1967, opted for the Marines because he was a native of Panama and thereby eligible for service as a permanent US resident. Six months of active duty were followed by more than five years of reserve meetings, a choice Carew found more palatable than "tak[ing] the chance of being drafted for two years."[30] To honor his service as well as his baseball career, in 2002 Carew was inducted into the United States Marine Corps Sports Hall of Fame.

As players suffered their own private angst about being in the military, so too did personnel in the front offices of baseball teams endure trepidations over the rosters in their organizations. Players had to look out for their individual fates, but general managers were forced to keep vigil over scores of prospects scattered throughout several layers of their minor-league system. During spring training, one prospect with the Tigers, who was "taking correspondence courses . . . in order to keep [his] student deferment draft status," found a tally sheet containing "the names of every ballplayer in the Detroit organization listed on the wall followed by a colored star indicating his military draft status."[31]

Whether a player was classified as 1-A, beholden to the National Guard or a reserve unit, or otherwise potentially within the grasp of the Selective Service System, the composition of a franchise's roster could be altered quickly should the call arrive from the draft board. Enlisting with the National Guard or reserves at least offered hope to avoid a full-time commitment, and as the war in Vietnam intensified and required more men in uniform, picking the lesser of evils took on heightened urgency. However, each team had to prepare itself for the possibility that a player might have to change his baseball uniform for fatigues, and quite often there was no set timetable indicating when a player might be called up, nor was there a definitive length of time when he might be away from his club. "On some of the teams at least 40% of the talent will have to perform some sort of service duty [in 1968]," reported *Sports Illustrated* in early March, this coming at a relatively calmer time prior to the King assassination and the disturbances that marred the Democratic National Convention in Chicago.[32]

During the second month of the 1967 season, a young Ken Holtzman of the Cubs was whisked away after running his record to 5–0, missing nearly three full months while serving in the National Guard. His manager, Leo Durocher, expressed resignation in losing his promising southpaw by patriotically noting the priorities involved. "His country comes first, baseball second," said the Lip.[33] And just when the St. Louis Cardinals were beginning to hit their stride that same season, they lost Tim McCarver, Bobby Tolan, and Alex Johnson to mili-

Although this particular antiwar protest was calm, many others in the 1960s were more vociferous and, in some instances, violent. *Courtesy of the Library of Congress, LC-U9-18528.*

tary obligations all at the same time in late June, a circumstance that challenged the ability of manager Red Schoendienst to field a competitive squad. Ironically, the Cardinals had recently sponsored a very public display of duty to country when they hosted an on-field event prior to their June 13 contest in which a fresh contingent of one hundred naval recruits was sworn in. The timing of this ceremony came weeks after heavyweight boxer Muhammad Ali refused to be inducted into the armed forces, thereby allowing baseball to showcase its capture of the moral high ground in terms of patriotism and service to country.

At the peak of American bloodshed in Vietnam from 1968 to 1969, another future Rookie of the Year was commanding his platoon and earning a Bronze Star. Lieutenant Al Bumbry was plucked from the Orioles in circumstances similar to those of Willie Mays, at the outset of his professional baseball career and for a two-year hitch. Outfielder Garry Maddox of the San Francisco Giants likewise lost a pair of seasons to service in the army, during which time he suffered the effects of contact with toxic substances while in Vietnam and eased the subsequent discomfort of shaving by growing his signature closely trimmed beard.

Over the course of the Vietnam conflict, more than 58,200 men—as well as 8 women—in uniform would perish in service to the United States. No baseball players died of their wounds, which is not to trivialize the suffering of those who were afflicted physically or psychologically, yet two of them did sustain injuries of note. A strapping six-foot-five prospect in the Los Angeles Dodgers system, outfielder Roy Gleason, received a promotion from the minors in 1963 at the tender age of twenty, appearing mostly as a pinch runner. When his draft status was reclassified from 3-A to 1-A in 1967, PFC Gleason was bundled off to Vietnam, where he was wounded by a mortar round in the summer of 1968. Attempting to rehabilitate from injuries he sustained to his left arm and leg, he conceded that he "was simply going through the motions" in a vain attempt to find his way back to Dodger Stadium. Gleason remained the only major leaguer who was wounded in action in the Vietnam War. Sadly, twelve minor-league, college, and amateur players lost their lives in Vietnam, as did one minor-league umpire.[34]

Another player who was injured but was able to continue playing baseball was Carlos May of the Chicago White Sox. While serving with the US Marines at Camp Pendleton, May was injured in August 1969 when a mortar he was cleaning discharged, severing a portion of his right thumb. Posting impressive numbers until the time of the mishap and having made the American League All-Star team, May was on his way to claiming a stake as AL Rookie of the Year and finished third in the balloting. His successful recovery allowed him to play more than one hundred games each year from 1970 to 1976.

That baseball contributed players to the war effort has been well noted, but it also performed duties that helped to raise the morale of those men serving on the front lines and in foreign lands. It was becoming increasingly obvious that the United States' commitment to the conflict was evolving into a long-term obligation, and baseball offered support through the visits of notable players—active and retired—who joined various USO junkets to Vietnam. During a 1966 tour Hank Aaron roomed with Stan Musial, and the pair of National League stalwarts were joined by Joe Torre, Brooks Robinson, Harmon Killebrew, and Yankees announcer Mel Allen. However flawed William Eckert may have been as baseball commissioner, he nonetheless drew praise from some of his former military peers—including the air force chief of staff and General William Westmoreland—for his role in facilitating the participation of baseball personalities in trips to Southeast Asia in 1966 and 1967.

As he visited military hospitals in the Far East in late 1967, California Angels shortstop Jim Fregosi was humbled by his encounters with men wounded in action. Insulated from direct exposure to combat, the twenty-five-year-old Fregosi faced the harsh fallout of a war to which he had given little regard. "We visited the casualty lines of guys coming right in from Vietnam," Fregosi said. "[An eighteen-year-old soldier] looked at me and said, 'Jim, how can I go back to the States and not be able to drink or vote?' What could I say? It really hit me."[35]

Following the 1968 season Eckert announced that another tour had been arranged, this one to last sixteen days and include stops at positions very much in harm's way. St. Louis Cardinals public relations counselor Al Fleishman cited a call paid on troops near Da Nang who had been under fire a day earlier. Although headliners Joe DiMaggio and Ken Harrelson had to cancel, the troupe was joined by Orioles hurler and National Guardsman Pete Richert; Ron Kline of the Pirates, who reported that the wounded men "seemed to ask more about Roberto Clemente than any other player"; and Ernie Banks, who, with eternal optimism, promised soldiers that "the Cubs will shine in '69."[36]

The baseball group sometimes stopped at six or seven venues a day to maximize their exposure and spread good cheer through the screening of World Series films and distributing autographed pictures and baseballs. Many were impressed by the depth of baseball knowledge displayed by the soldiers despite the inconsistent availability of sports news. Mets outfielder Ron Swoboda, who "didn't have any political convictions" and "just wanted to see what [soldiers] were going through," looked back on the tour by expressing conflicted views. While heartened by the genuine care he saw provided by some Americans to the Vietnamese people, he also voiced concern about the viability of US forces trying to perform a job that could be undone by the Vietcong. Thus was Swoboda pointing out the conundrum faced by American military and political leaders who sought to instill democratic values in Vietnam: "I kept thinking maybe we could help that country if we didn't burn it down first."[37]

The 1969 World Series was a focal point of controversy due to the coincidental scheduling of Game 4 on the same day as the Vietnam Moratorium of October 15. America was still divided over the war, and the moratorium had been called as another major protest against it. In New York City, Mayor John Lindsay requested that flags be flown at half-staff in support of the protestors, some of whom called themselves Mets Fans for Peace—BOMB THE ORIOLES, NOT THE PEASANTS, read one of their placards—and distributed antiwar handbills at Shea Stadium. Also at Shea were more than two hundred military patients from St. Albans Naval Hospital, calling for the Stars and Stripes to be flown at full staff in favor of continued US involvement, a predicament that put first-year commissioner Bowie Kuhn in the uncomfortable position of having to choose how to fly the flag at the ballpark. The commissioner ruled in favor of the wounded veterans—and, by extension, the war—when he ensured that the flag would be at full staff, or as he put it, "[taking] whatever step would promote the greatest amount of respect and quiet in the stadium."[38] Knowing that Major League Baseball was just a few weeks away from sending a quartet of players to Southeast Asia to tour military installations and medical facilities, Kuhn certainly was not going to poison the atmosphere by ruling against those in uniform and those rehabilitating from war wounds.

In contrast to the attention the *Sporting News* gave to earlier tours to Vietnam, the publication unfortunately all but ignored the November 1969 intercontinental trek led by the commissioner. Accompanied by Swoboda of the world champion Mets, Yankees great Joe DiMaggio, and pitchers Mudcat Grant and Milt Pappas—but absent Reggie Jackson, who had canceled—Kuhn in his autobiography distilled the venture to less than two pages, which included a recounting of a harrowing episode in which the helicopter ferrying his contingent was shot at while flying in an area northwest of Saigon. However, Kuhn told a different and more detailed story to his diary, which he kept to record many aspects of the goodwill tour.[39] Kuhn's notes furnish extensive, candid glimpses that span the emotional spectrum of his experience, although the peril of which Kuhn wrote in his memoir does not appear in the journal of his trip.

Departing on November 7 from Travis Air Force Base near San Francisco and hop-scotching to Honolulu, Manila, and finally Tan Son Nhut Air Base in Saigon, Kuhn spent "the endless flight reading and re-reading Honolulu and Los Angeles newspapers and trying to ignore stepped-up [Vietcong] activity in Vietnam." Upon arrival in Saigon—"9875 miles to Shea Stadium"—he was taken to the Meyerkord Hotel for a three-hour respite and then off to cocktails and dinner with General Creighton Abrams, who had been named as the successor to William Westmoreland in June 1968. Discussions included the most recent All-Star selections such as "Kess," "Killer," and "Petro," which Kuhn shorthanded for Don Kessinger, Harmon Killebrew, and Rico Petrocelli. At this time, Kuhn requested that Abrams "put us to work beyond the customary safe zones" so the commissioner could bring his entourage to troops who otherwise would not have had the chance to meet them.[40] DiMaggio was in agreement with Kuhn in wanting to travel afield.

The hectic schedule of the commissioner's visit offered few breaks. While moving about the southern reaches of the country, Kuhn jotted down the names of many uniformed personnel with whom he came in contact, the types of aircraft used to transport him, and pertinent armament employed to safeguard his travel. Radio station AFVN, which had provided fertile ground for disk jockey Adrian Cronauer a few years prior to Kuhn's visit, used its loudspeaker to invite station personnel to meet the ensemble: "Got some ballplayers here if you want to meet them. Joe D[iMaggio] is one of them." Kuhn caught a wry comment regarding the tour's baseball focus that came as a disappointment to at least one member of the military: "What no girls?"

Kuhn spoke at isolated fire support bases, artillery headquarters, dock unloading areas, aircraft maintenance hangars, construction facilities, and, most compellingly, medical facilities. During a ninety-minute visit to the 3rd Surgical Hospital in Binh Thuy, southwest of Saigon, Kuhn observed the cases of various patients—"civilian, US, ARVN, couple VC"—recovering from surgery or afflicted with malaria or hepatitis. Although equipped with 166 beds, the "wards [were] sparsely populated—thank God," a relief that was short-lived as Kuhn became emotionally wracked by another encounter. "Very sick kid with tubes whispering thanks to me for what I did for [baseball]—had to turn away." Overall, the visitation was "most successful," according to a post-tour report, but as might be expected, there were a variety of difficulties.[41]

With the proceedings in Vietnam barely begun, DiMaggio expressed irritation at a question posed by a reporter from ABC News, who queried the former Yankee regarding his opinions on the war. DiMaggio "commented that he was on a handshake tour and not here to gather or make conclusions about the conduct of the war," and the mood for some troops was soured at several stops when the expected screening of World Series highlights did not occur because the films were not ready in time for the players to bring. At the conclusion of one particularly busy day, a dinner hosted by General Abrams "was enjoyed by all, but due to fatigue, the ball players were not the most congenial guests." A visit to Cam Ranh Bay proved extremely irksome, as Pappas noted in a report he filed for the military: "Mr. [Don] Chandler was [the] worst representative on tour—made all kinds of excuses for bad billets. Our plane was 7 hours late. . . . Guys were dead tired. No hot water in trailers—no hot water or soap. No bathroom on trailer. . . ."[42]

In some cases, attendance at various sites was hampered by combat operations or snafus with pre-visit publicity, but the biggest letdown was the result of an early exit by "baseball's greatest living player" and the commissioner. "Mr. Kuhn and Mr. DiMaggio had to depart [Republic of Vietnam] after only 3 days for tour. *Many troops disappointed,*" the military's official summation of the trip stated; the former headed back to the States while the latter made a stop to see military personnel in Japan. Yet the goodwill spread by the active players who remained in Vietnam and endured more trials and tribulations was greatly appreciated. Willing to risk the potential danger of traveling to outlying regions, "the ball players enjoyed these [visits] more, because the area was right where the bulk of fighting in Vietnam takes place" and honored the request to allow them to see soldiers who had few entertainment options. While Pappas was exhibiting signs of fatigue and "required a little coaxing to keep him going," Swoboda wanted to journey to Da Nang—on an off day, no less—and was so captivated by the setting there that an escort officer had to dissuade him from going on a combat mission.[43]

Hardships notwithstanding, Grant, Pappas, and Swoboda carried on in what ultimately was an endeavor greatly appreciated by the approximately seven thousand armed forces personnel they encountered. Despite the premature departure of Kuhn and DiMaggio, the troops enjoyed receiving handshakes, autographs, caps, and baseballs, to say nothing of the boost in morale just from seeing major leaguers.

Baseball's executive suite helped to ameliorate the woes of soldiers in Vietnam, as did another group of players led by 1969 Cy Young co-winner Denny McLain, Tug McGraw, Pete Ward, Ron Taylor, and Padres third-base coach Bob Skinner. On a tour one month after Kuhn's, McLain noted that "the smell of marijuana was pervasive" nearer the front lines, and despite the goodwill he dispensed on the trip, the Detroit pitcher was "left with an overwhelming distaste for U.S. involvement" in the war.[44]

Meanwhile, ordinary citizens offered assistance in seeing that baseball news reached those under arms. The *Sporting News* published the names of individuals and organizations, including some big-league clubs, who paid for discounted subscriptions—six dollars for fifty-two weeks, or half off the regular price—that were forwarded to men in the war zone. Years later a military veteran, whose duties included distribution of weapons and supplies, said that on occasion his depot would receive a supply of books, and soldiers seemed to ask for those related to the national pastime more than any others. "Baseball books, we concluded, were not just entertainment but an essential temporary escape from the stress of war and the angst of homesickness."[45] Ultimately, the complete disengagement of participation in an increasingly unpopular war would force the return of troops to the United States, but until that time arrived, baseball provided a boost in morale and, in some ways, a spiritual lift to the men who needed it most.

Honoring Two Slain Leaders

Baseball's role as a salve to the wounds imparted by untoward current events was always well intended, but there were occasions when the sport's reaction impressed as less than commendable. During the spring of 1968, baseball's response to the assassinations of Martin Luther King Jr. and Robert Kennedy was clumsy and, in the view of some observers, insensitive. As the foremost leader in black America's movement toward equality, King possessed the highest profile of any civil rights activist. In the early evening of April 4, during a visit to Memphis, Tennessee, to lend his support for striking sanitation workers, King was felled by an assassin's bullet on the upper balcony of the Lorraine Motel, setting off a series of riots in scores of cities across the country.

This tragedy occurred just days before Major League Baseball was to open its regular season schedule on April 8. President Lyndon Johnson declared Sunday April 7 to be a national day of mourning in honor of King, and baseball's final exhibition games—with the exception of the Indians-Dodgers contest at San Diego—were canceled. Two day games and one night game were slated to start the season: the traditional National League opener in Cincinnati, where the Reds were to host the Cubs; the American League's inaugural in Washington pitting the hometown Senators against the Twins; and the visiting Pirates meeting the Astros in Houston in the evening contest. King's funeral was scheduled for Tuesday morning, April 9, so it was believed that by postponing the trio of openers, baseball would be able to uphold the dignity of King's memory and begin the season with only a minor disruption.

However, on Sunday several teams that were scheduled to begin the season on the day of the funeral announced that they also were postponing their openers. The situation was further complicated when the Pittsburgh Pirates, whose roster was well stocked with black and Latino players, insisted on delaying the first game until Wednesday, April 10, the day after King's funeral. There is no question that those minority players among the Pirates were sensitive to the issue of discrimination, and the staunchest civil rights proponent of that group happened to be the team's brightest star. Roberto Clemente rallied his teammates to embrace what he believed to be the best manner in which to honor King—namely, by not playing on April 9. Clemente promulgated his admiration for King's "ability to give voice to the voiceless," those of any race who were poor or suffered from racial indignities.[46]

There was no small ironic twist to the response of one of baseball's leading franchises. Although the Los Angeles Dodgers had broken the racial barrier twenty-one years earlier with Jackie Robinson's debut during their tenure in Brooklyn, the team did not postpone their final exhibition contest, nor did they propose to move their opener on April 9 to another date. The timing of playing at home on the West Coast meant that the Dodgers' first game could begin after King's funeral, therefore "mourning for him in church [rather than] at the ball field" was a validation of the club's intent to carry on unimpeded.[47] The plan was sanctioned by Dodgers coach Jim Gilliam and outfielder Willie Davis, both of whom were black, as well as owner Walter O'Malley, who did not want to miss out on a large Opening Day crowd passing through the Dodger Stadium turnstiles. However, the visiting team, the Philadelphia Phillies, threatened to forfeit the game rather than violate the sanctity of the day of the funeral, and a settlement was at last brokered by National League president Warren Giles to postpone the contest. Reason finally prevailed across the major leagues with the postponement of all season-opening contests, but the controversies that played out in the press did little to dim the callous image baseball had projected.

In an editorial designed to cast the game in the best light under the circumstances, the *Sporting News* informed its readers that Commissioner William Eckert personally reached out—via telegram—to King's widow to express his condolences, and praised the "yeoman work" he had performed in obtaining "the complete cooperation of major league club owners in honoring Dr. King's memory." No mention was made of O'Malley's initial desire to play on, yet the publication overreached with its fatuous comment that "honoring Dr. King's memory was in keeping with baseball's position as *a pioneer in granting the Negro the opportunities which his skill demanded.*"[48] Apparently the closed-door policy that kept black and Latino players at bay until Jackie Robinson's arrival in 1947 was, in the view of the "Bible of Baseball," only a fiction.

To better commemorate the life of Martin Luther King Jr., Major League Baseball agreed to play an East–West all-star exhibition game with players drawn from current team rosters, but organizing the contest was plagued with difficulty from the start, not least of which was caused by baseball itself. Near the conclusion of the 1968 season, Joseph D. Peters, the sports director for the Southern Christian Leadership Conference, petitioned the commissioner's office for the game to be held toward the end of the 1969 spring training period. Eckert, however, pointed out that all-star games other than the traditional Midsummer Classic were not allowed between spring training and the conclusion of the World Series, and he turned up the rhetoric further when he noted that exhibition games were permitted only during a thirty-day period following the conclusion of the regular season. Rather than demonstrate a spirit of cooperation in honoring King's memory, Eckert was more intent on enforcing baseball's pedantic bylaws.

In early December 1968 Commissioner Eckert and all the club owners approved the hosting of a memorial game scheduled for March 29, 1969. But logistical problems quickly arose due in part to an edict from the baseball commissioner's office that stated, "All arrangements for television and radio coverage, promotion of the event, ticket sales, concessions, etc. is [*sic*] the responsibility of the S.C.L.C." This was in addition to the canvassing that the SCLC had to do to find players willing to participate and then obtaining subsequent approval from each player's club's front office as well as the office of the commissioner.[49] Handicapped by red tape and the bureaucratically infused cooperation of Major League Baseball, Peters at last realized that all the necessary protocols would not be completed in time for a March 1969 game and instead set his sights on March 28, 1970.

Having surmounted the multitude of issues, Peters and his charges successfully staged their production on the rescheduled date, and a galaxy of the major league's best talent gathered at Chavez Ravine, the East squad managed by Joe DiMaggio prevailing over Roy Campanella's West club by a score of 5–1. The game was far from a sellout; nevertheless, 31,694 fans took in the contest, which lasted a crisp two hours and six minutes and featured the likes of future Hall of Famers Tom Seaver, Bob Gibson, Roberto Clemente, Frank Robinson, Lou Brock, Hank Aaron, Ron Santo, Ernie Banks, Johnny Bench, Orlando Cepeda, Al Kaline, and Reggie Jackson. Emmett Ashford, the first black umpire in the majors, had the honor of calling balls and strikes. Despite the ostensible celebrity and goodwill fostered by the game, its lifespan—only one such game was played—was painfully short given the work that went into its planning, although it is better that King's legacy outlasted the staging of a single exhibition baseball game.

—ᴍ—

The shock of the Tet Offensive and the tumult following the murder of Martin Luther King Jr. left the nation reeling, but a further blow was still to come. A late entrant in the presidential campaign of 1968, Senator Robert Kennedy of New York fostered a vision, notably among younger Americans, that a quick conclusion could be brought to hostilities in Vietnam, and a desire to carry on his slain brother's legacy, which had instilled encouragement, especially among the poor and disenfranchised, to break the bonds of poverty and live a better life.

The Kennedy campaign fought hard to make up time against his front-running opponent, Eugene McCarthy, who was victorious in the Oregon primary of May 28. Coming a week later was the most crucial test, the primary in California.

On June 4 Kennedy achieved that short-term goal by out-pointing McCarthy, 46 to 42 percent, prompting a celebratory reception at the Ambassador Hotel in Los Angeles in the wee hours of the next morning. Tragically, as Kennedy exited the hotel's ballroom, he was assassinated by Sirhan Sirhan, thus squelching his vision of a brighter future for the country. For the third time since November 1963, the nation mourned the extinguishing of the life of a leader who inspired better ideals in so many of its citizens. The losses of Martin Luther King Jr. and Robert Kennedy were brutal reminders of how ephemeral life can be, and jointly they "embodied the public protest of their times against a mindless war abroad and racial injustice at home."[50]

Kennedy's body was flown to New York, where it was then taken to St. Patrick's Cathedral in Manhattan for a funeral service on the morning of Saturday, June 8. At the conclusion of the mass, Kennedy was to be borne by rail for the four-hour trip to Washington, DC, where a procession would deliver him to his final resting place at Arlington National Cemetery. However, the journey was complicated by misfortune, including the deaths of two spectators who had come to see the funeral train but were struck and killed by another four-car train heading in the opposite direction, and mechanical problems with the brakes on the car that carried the senator's casket. Because of the delays, the train did not reach Washington until shortly after 9:00 p.m. To honor Kennedy's memory, Sunday, June 9, was declared a national day of mourning by President Johnson.

In the aftermath of the King assassination, baseball's reaction was stilted, to say the least. Working slightly in the national pastime's favor, nonetheless, was the fact that Opening Day schedules are arranged in a staggered pattern, with inaugural games spread out over several days and open dates built into the April calendar to allow for possible inclement weather. The delays in the wake of King's death unquestionably made for a controversial and uneven start to the season, but these proved to be wrinkles that were easily smoothed out of baseball's slate of contests. When Robert Kennedy was slain—at a time when diamonds across the country were at full throttle—the league's response to his passing became emblematic of Commissioner William Eckert's ineptitude. Despite the ally Eckert found when an editorial in the *Sporting News* came to his defense, the lack of a consistent, uniform policy for all teams to follow created a situation whereby the commissioner may have endeavored to set a policy intended to accommodate everyone but that in the end pleased no one.

Contests in New York and Washington set for June 8 were postponed by Eckert's decree because these were the cities in which portions of the Kennedy funeral took place. Figuring that the burial would be complete by late that afternoon, the commissioner further stated that no games were to begin until the completion of the funeral service at Arlington, an ostensibly safe assumption that meant setting back original starting times by only a few hours. But as the holdup in the train's arrival at Washington worsened, several home teams in the Eastern time zone—Baltimore, Boston, Detroit, and Cincinnati—defied Eckert and began well before 9:00 p.m. The Cardinals-Reds game was marred by an imbroglio among members of the home team, who were evenly divided—twelve in favor, twelve against, with one abstention—as to whether they should play the game or force its postponement. Cincinnati player representative Milt Pappas resigned his position in protest of the players' 13–12 vote on the second ballot to carry on with the game. The Cardinals took the field with their regular lineup, but catcher Tim McCarver lamented the inconsistency in implementation of postponements across both leagues, while pitcher Bob Gibson, who was "infuriated" about the death of Kennedy, left no doubt where he stood.[51]

At the Houston Astrodome, the visiting Pirates played the Astros on Saturday, but Houston's Rusty Staub and Bob Aspromonte as well as Pittsburgh's Maury Wills chose to sit out the Sunday game. Astros player representative Dave Giusti revealed that his team's general manager, Spec Richardson, threatened to bring "the strongest economic pressure to bear" on the players who refused to play, and both Staub and Aspromonte forfeited a day's pay for honoring the memory of Kennedy. In San Francisco the visiting Mets, to a man, voted twice not to play on Saturday despite the Giants' efforts to hold the game in order to placate the large crowd expected to turn out for a Bat Day promotion. "We're from New York," said Ed Kranepool, the Mets first baseman who was also the team's player representative. "It's a matter of respect for us not to play."[52]

Kranepool's manager, Gil Hodges, reportedly informed his players of his intention to avoid the ballpark by spending time in a local church, while the team's chairman of the board, M. Donald Grant, firmly stood by his players even at the risk of forfeiting the game and suffering a fine from the league for refusal to play. In the end, all National League clubs played on the national day of mourning, and the circuit's slate featured doubleheaders in Chicago and San Francisco to make up for Saturday postponements.

Back in New York, the Yankees played a twin bill against the Angels, and in the process also took the commissioner's office to task for implying that it was Eckert's decision to call off Saturday's game at Yankee Stadium. The verdict was actually rendered by New York's president, Michael Burke, and the team issued a statement citing American League president Joe Cronin's agreement, as well as that of the visiting Angels, to postpone the Saturday contest. California's player rep Bobby Knoop initially stated his team's desire to forgo the Sunday games but later relented given circumstances of the Yankees' wish to stage their own Bat Day doubleheader, which drew 56,614 fans to the Bronx. For fans who preferred not to attend the twin bill "for personal reasons," the New York front office also offered a ticket exchange for a future 1968 home game.[53]

Excoriated by some sportswriters as "a man asking for chaos" who ended up getting his just desserts, William Eckert failed in coordinating a somber, suitable response to the death of Robert Kennedy. The sports editor of the *Pittsburgh Press* snidely remarked, "Baseball again returned to normalcy—confusion," and Bob August of the *Cleveland Press* chastised baseball for being "thoroughly shabby" at a time that required elegiac comportment. A shred of dignity was salvaged by the late senator's press secretary, Frank Mankiewicz, who wired Aspromonte, Pappas, Staub, and Wills, as well as all Mets players through their manager, Gil Hodges, to acknowledge their show of support in honoring Kennedy's memory by "not putting box-office receipts ahead of national mourning."[54]

In the wake of Kennedy's death, however, much criticism was reserved for the baseball commissioner, who was labeled as "a mere puppet" of the clubs, whose "[m]anagement is money hungry for even thinking of playing on such a day." Through his confused response, Eckert "allowed all 20 clubs to run off in 20 directions," said one fan, while a woman from Maryland lauded the Mets' unanimous decision to not play as exhibiting "more character than all the other teams combined."[55]

Years later, Leonard Koppett of the *New York Times* opined that the furor over the Kennedy tribute had no bearing on Eckert's subsequent dismissal, although he did note that attempts to treat the fallen senator as a head of state— which Kennedy technically was not—did not sit well with some people.[56] But singling out Robert Kennedy for preferential treatment could easily be justified: The legacy of the family name, his past service as the US attorney general and confidant of his slain brother, his strong showing as a prime contender for his party's presidential nomination, and the stance he took against an unpopular war as well as the hope he inspired in so many Americans all burnished Kennedy's credentials. That he had become a martyr evoked an attendant sympathy worthy of the honor many now believed he was due.

Three months after Kennedy was buried, baseball's Executive Council convened. Among the items on its agenda was the group's intent to formulate a protocol for averting the embarrassment recently endured as a result of baseball's response to the deaths of King and Kennedy. In a substantiation of what some fans claimed to be the mercenary attitude of baseball's ownership class, "the Council voted that in the event of death of any national figure, including Presidents of the United States, *games be played as scheduled* and that appropriate tribute be paid at the ball park."[57] This new policy was mildly put to the test in early 1969 upon the death of Dwight Eisenhower. A handful of exhibition games were canceled, and first pitches of other spring training contests were delayed until one hour after the former president's funeral service in Washington, DC, ended on March 31. In the Eisenhower episode, baseball avoided the scorn heaped upon it during the King and Kennedy controversies, but a different kind of tempest raged following the performance of the national anthem as a prelude to one of the World Series games in 1968.

"You Have Created a Commotion"

Prior to Game 4 of the 1968 World Series at Tiger Stadium, a nattily attired Marvin Gaye was accorded the honor of singing the national anthem. Among the vanguard of Motown singers, Gaye was soon to top the popular music charts with his hit song "I Heard It through the Grapevine," and the appearance of a prominent black recording artist in Detroit, a city torn by rioting, made a compelling statement. Gaye performed the anthem in traditional, unembellished fashion, thereby drawing no criticism. But a vastly contrasting version of the same song preceded Game 5, highlighting the wounds that continued to fester in the psyche of an America not recovered from the disconcerting events of recent months.

Ernie Harwell, the announcer for the Detroit Tigers, had asked another pop star, José Feliciano, to present his version of "The Star-Spangled Banner," which the native of Puerto Rico did, accompanied by an acoustic guitar. The blind virtuoso was riding a wave of adoration for his cover recording of "Light My Fire," a 1967 hit song first released by the Doors. However, the tempo of Feliciano's rendition of the anthem was imbued with modest Latino jazz, and to those at the stadium as well as a huge television audience nationwide, the tune was unrecognizable and immediately interpreted as nothing short of profane.

Booing flooded Tiger Stadium, telephone callers registered their complaints with NBC television stations by swamping switchboards, and in some cases grossly offended "soldiers were throwing their shoes at the television." NBC commentator Tony Kubek told the singer, "You have created a commotion," as he broke the news to him regarding the ensuing public outcry. Trying to assuage Feliciano, Kubek told him that he liked the performance and consoled him by saying, "Don't worry kid, you didn't do anything wrong."[58]

Despite the innocence with which Feliciano sang the anthem, a recent pair of anguishing assassinations was fresh in the minds of many Americans, the country was still in the throes of the Vietnam War, and only six weeks before Feliciano appeared at Tiger Stadium, the raucousness and riots that plagued the Democratic National Convention in Chicago had been splashed across the same television screens that now delivered "the [anthem's] first nontraditional version seen by mainstream America."[59] The country simply was not ready to countenance an interpretation of the anthem that failed to conform to the expectations of a divided citizenry.

While one viewer gave grudging admiration to "Jose and the Tiger management for having the guts to let him sing it his way, in his style," more common was the condemnation that labeled the "jazzy, hippy manner" of the performance as "a disgrace to patriotism, to men in service, and to baseball." Admitting that he was "afraid people would misconstrue" his performance, Feliciano quickly paid a price: airplay of his recordings diminished appreciably after his appearance in Detroit, and resentment toward him lingered long after the World Series concluded.[60]

Changes in Attitude

The Cold War had already been at the forefront of current events for some time, but with the introduction of ground troops into Vietnam in March 1965, an undercurrent developed that caused growing numbers of Americans—especially the oldest male Baby Boomers, who had reached an age at which conscription now made them available for military service—to question the war's purpose. In the same way that black Americans continued their difficult fight for equality—with limited success—so too was a nascent activism forming in protest against US intervention in Vietnam. "[I]increasing frustration characterizes the mid-1960s, particularly with the escalation of the war and the failure of public demonstrations to stop it," wrote one historian, noting a corresponding "post-1965 counterculture" trajectory of the Black Power movement.[61]

The voices of antiwar protesters and advocates for racial equality became conflated and served increasingly to undermine a country that the historian

James Patterson had viewed by late 1964 as "a remarkably stable and confident place [in which] to live."[62] The turning away from conservative values, especially by young Americans, fueled a mindset that allowed for questioning authority at all levels—parental, governmental, or cultural—and defiance became a means to an end. Baseball found itself woven into the same contentious strands of a 1960s American fabric that was slowly but surely being ripped apart by the forces of internal pressure, both societal and political.

One of baseball's most visible personifications of the change from a staunchly conservative facade to one that was unmistakably directed at a maturing but still youthful Baby Boomer generation was outfielder Ken Harrelson. When he was traded from Kansas City to the Washington Senators midway through the 1966 season, the twenty-four-year-old Harrelson was frequently at odds with his new manager, Gil Hodges. The skipper's attitude toward Harrelson was reserved because, according to the latter, "[He] just didn't like the way I dressed or wore my hair."[63] Harrelson admitted that the length of his hair served as a distraction from his oversized nose—thus his nickname, "The Hawk"—but when his locks were paired with his wardrobe, which had a style decidedly tilted toward Carnaby Street, Harrelson looked better fitted to be a member of the Beatles' Sgt. Pepper's Lonely Hearts Club Band than a right fielder for a baseball team.

Harrelson's baseball credibility was burnished in 1968 when he was one of the top run producers in the American League, which was no small feat in a season of pitching dominance. Thus Harrelson's superb performance on the diamond earned him a popularity, especially among fans his age, that was among the highest in baseball. Short hair and drab clothing, long a trademark of post–World War II men's fashion, were being pushed aside by a younger generation whose appearances were imbued with freer expression and a concern for impressing themselves rather than catering to the Establishment.

Harrelson was not alone in his tonsorial stand, as evidenced by the minor revolt staged in 1969 by the Oakland Athletics, now led by a former marine who had guided the Baltimore Orioles to the World Series crown three years earlier. When manager Hank Bauer opened Oakland's spring training, he "greet[ed] his charges with a set of dress and behavior codes worthy of a Marine boot camp." Unmoved by Bauer's decrees, several players defiantly "sprout[ed] shaggy weirdness all over the place," and much to the manager's dismay, Oakland owner Charlie Finley approved of the new look, at once undermining Bauer's authority and paving the way for his dismissal six months later after 149 games at the Athletics' helm.[64]

Most iconoclastic among public accounts that provide an unvarnished and unapologetic view into the mind of a ballplayer from that era is Jim Bouton's seminal *Ball Four*, in which he related not only the trials and tribulations of the 1969 expansion Seattle Pilots but also the growing disdain younger ballplayers

Ken Harrelson was not afraid to make a fashion statement at a time when doing so easily rankled those in the baseball establishment. *National Baseball Hall of Fame Library, Coopers-town, NY.*

were exhibiting in fighting the old-fashioned protocols of management, both on the field and in the front office. Players' defiance of authority was not a phenomenon new to the late 1960s, and extracurricular activities such as drinking, womanizing, and carousing had long become rites of passage. But a new edge developed that bolstered a player's confidence in standing up for himself, and the timing coincides with the Major League Baseball Players Association's methodical and continuing advances in gaining rightful benefits for its membership.

Bouton opined that as more senior players retired, those vacancies were being filled by youthful men whose styles were not compatible with short haircuts and staid business attire. The Pilots had a dress code for road trips, which was understandable, but general manager Marvin Milkes was image conscious to the point of trying to persuade players to avoid wearing blue jeans while traveling to and from Sicks' Stadium, their home ballpark. "I don't see how the Seattle Pilots' image is threatened in the time it takes to leave my car and enter the clubhouse," groused outfielder Steve Hovley, who in addition to favoring denim had chosen to avoid seeing a barber for over six months.[65]

By this point in the late 1960s, long hair had been the most overt display of rebellion against authority, having been validated by the wildly popular "mop tops" worn by the Beatles, the first of the 1960s superstar rock 'n' roll groups.

Players with an intellectual bent, such as Bouton and fellow Pilots hurler Mike Marshall, were viewed with suspicion by management, who assumed they were employing their above-average intelligence to thwart deceptive front office chicanery, exercise a freedom they held dear, or perhaps call attention to a situation they believed correctable even at the cost of embarrassment to the front office. This was nothing more than another instance of problematic relations between employer and employee, but the difference with Bouton's revelation was his audacity in bringing such baseball-related issues—unfiltered—into a public forum.

Nor did Bouton limit his narrative to the contemporaneous deeds of the Pilots. The former All-Star pitcher called out some of his former Yankees teammates and managers in an exposé that riled many baseball personnel for having broken the *omertà* of the clubhouse. Drunken escapades, extramarital affairs, and clubhouse pranks were brought to light in *Ball Four*'s narrative, to the delight of many fans who enjoyed a prurient, puerile look at what really took place away from the diamond. In a decade punctuated by a Summer of Love, race riots, and war protests, baseball itself became a target for the antiestablishment crowd in its own ranks. Having been firmly stamped on American culture, the current freedom of expression found favor with those who, like Bouton, dared to embrace it.

Exposure of these once-taboo subjects in the mainstream media was enabled by a group of younger baseball writers nicknamed "the Chipmunks," who "seemed to share a youthful irreverence for the practices of their predecessors" and delighted in covering the game from a vantage point less likely to be taken by the elderly, veteran reporters. Differentiating between this new breed of baseball writers who began coming onto the scene in the late 1950s and the "old timers," George Vecsey of the *New York Times* observed, "We saw the human side of players more than they chose to," and some of the Chipmunks' "stories were more inclined to be found in the clubhouse" than on the playing field.[66] That the editor of Bouton's *Ball Four*, Leonard Shecter, was among this movement in the press was no coincidence.

Taking a candid but more sanguine view from inside the game was Bill Freehan, the All-Star catcher of the Detroit Tigers. Chronicling his team's 1969 season, Freehan wrote an account more suited to family reading, lacking in harsh criticism of teammates and management, and omitting details of salacious behavior and other juvenile antics. In direct, almost cheerful prose, Freehan recounted his "holdout [that] lasted exactly 75 minutes," a brief interlude at the beginning of spring training during which time he quickly came to terms with general manager Jim Campbell on his contract for the year. As the Tigers prepared to defend their World Series title, the mood of the club was diametrically opposed to that of the expansion Pilots. The Tigers were contenders in 1967, fresh off a stunning come-from-behind victory against the Cardinals in the 1968 World Series, and confident they would contend for the pennant of the new American League East division.

Freehan mildly rebuked pitching ace Denny McLain, whom the catcher found to be "a tough guy to understand," and was "disturbed" by the remarks made by new third-base coach Grover Resinger, who expressed concern that the team's pitching staff appeared to be in poor condition because of pitching coach Johnny Sain's lax physical conditioning standards. Projecting the image of a company man, Freehan noted that in addition to his simple negotiations with Campbell, he liked manager Mayo Smith's unobtrusive style of leadership, and, in contrast with Bouton's squabbles with Yankees manager and GM Ralph Houk, Freehan admired Houk and longed for a chance to play for him. And Freehan lauded first-year commissioner Bowie Kuhn, who had secured a new contract in August, for being among those men "who don't beat around the bush" as well as an executive who was up to the task to "protect the future of this game."[67]

Freehan's narrative is colored with optimism as the Tigers gamely—albeit futilely—chase a Baltimore Orioles team that was forming a powerhouse under manager Earl Weaver. Tactful even when disagreement arises and ever-hopeful that Detroit will find a way to catch its chief rival, Freehan furnished a portrait of his team that is Rockwellian and uncontroversial, and it serves as a counterweight to the rollicking, frat house atmosphere of the Seattle Pilots in *Ball Four*.

Tensions between players and managers have long existed, so it comes as no surprise that in 1969 several flare-ups ultimately cost some skippers their jobs. Dick Williams of the Red Sox engaged outfielder Carl Yastrzemski in a tussle because he believed the former Triple Crown winner and reigning AL batting champion was not putting out his best effort, and Minnesota's first-year manager Billy Martin, never one to shy away from any kind of dispute, continued to burnish his pugilistic reputation when he intervened in an argument between hurler Dave Boswell and pitching coach Art Fowler. Boswell was alleged to have skipped out on most of his required outfield running before a game in Detroit, and when the pitcher learned that Fowler had reported the misdemeanor to Martin, Boswell vowed retribution against the coach while drinking in a Motor City bar. Martin, however, happened to be in the same lounge and confronted Boswell, and when the pitcher went after Martin, the streetwise manager decked him in an episode that served as a precursor to other unfortunate incidents in which Martin would be an active participant.

Other notable players—Joe Pepitone of the Yankees and Willie Horton of the Tigers—were fined by their respective teams for unauthorized absences during the same year as the Boswell-Martin imbroglio. By the end of the 1969 baseball season, Williams and Martin, both stern disciplinarians, would lose their jobs in part because they were unable to exercise control over players who, in earlier years, would have been less willing to challenge the power of their superiors.

Having lived through two world wars in addition to the Great Depression, longtime manager Leo Durocher took the reins of the Chicago Cubs in 1966 at sixty years of age. A product of the old school, Durocher served as a Dodgers coach from 1961 to 1964, but he had not piloted a team since 1955, and his return to the managerial ranks was accompanied by no small degree of disillusionment about current young players. The brash Durocher was confounded by the comportment of the "different breed" of players he was now charged with leading, further lamenting, "You can't tell them what to do."[68]

In an era of rising intergenerational tension in America, incidents involving young baseball players and their managers were reflective of a youthful antiauthoritarianism. To be sure, most players did not fight with management, just as most young American men did not burn their draft cards or shirk their military obligations. But the voices of Baby Boomers became emboldened in protesting an increasingly unpopular war and in calling out racial injustice, and they also spilled out into other segments of society, including sports. To the dismay of those of an older generation, open defiance of authority was now in vogue more than ever, be it John Carlos and Tommie Smith with their Black Power salute at the 1968 Summer Olympics, or baseball players demonstrating a willingness to allow themselves freedom of expression.

Drug Use

Defiance of authority and freedom of expression also was manifest in the use of alcohol, drugs, and controlled substances, consumption of which was hardly foreign to society, let alone baseball. "Alcohol and drug use in the national pastime," wrote one scholar, "tells us something about the temptations of American culture," and he further explained that a wide variety of performance-enhancing substances found favor with athletes as far back as the late 1800s.[69] The rush provided by caffeine was especially useful, and beverages laced with it have become permanently ingrained in cultures across the globe. For the most part, alcoholic beverages have the inherent advantage of being both legal to purchase and easily obtainable, and amphetamines have been finding their way into training rooms for decades. Even the psychological boost of a placebo benefited the St. Louis Cardinals in their championship year of 1942, when team members were implored to ingest "pills contain[ing] 'something much more than just vitamins.'"[70]

But the pill of choice appeared to be dextroamphetamine sulfate, a pep pill better known by its common slang term, "greenie." Variations of this drug were used by GIs in World War II, and baseball players who had been exposed to it learned of the pill's ability to keep them "awake for days at a time and still be alert."[71] Returning to the States after the conflict, they imported the pills to their clubhouses and found them a convenient remedy for hangovers or a bad night's sleep.

While Bouton titillated his readers with a humorous tale of a teammate's experience with greenies—an infielder who flew into a rage over being called out on strikes, the tantrum attributed to the pill having taken hold while he was at bat—he also related a more tawdry aspect of this drug. The Seattle Pilots' team policy precluded distribution of greenies, yet their availability in the clubhouse was undeniable because members of the Pilots obtained the pills from friends on other teams, and while Bouton noted the prevalent use of greenies—"A lot of ballplayers couldn't function without them," in his opinion—he sounded an alarm about the "false sense of security" that led some users to believe they were performing better than they actually were. An example of this came on September 7, 1969, when pitcher Don Wilson of the Houston Astros "didn't seem to have a thing" while warming up for his start against the San Francisco Giants, but "after visiting the clubhouse [he] came out throwing BB's."[72] Wilson retired the side in order in the first two innings, allowed two batters to reach base in the third—but no runs—and then came completely unhinged in the fourth inning, yielding a hit, a fly-out, and then four straight walks.

Hank Aaron of the Atlanta Braves tried a greenie in 1968 to try to shake himself from the doldrums of poor hitting, "but when that thing took hold, I thought I was having a heart attack." This was one adverse effect associated with amphetamines, to say nothing of the human body's tendency to build a resistance to them, thus requiring increased usage to reach a higher level of alertness. The stigma of nonconformity also lurked in clubhouses; players who abstained from artificial stimulation could be "ostracized as slackers" for not following the lead of those who were users.[73]

Recreational use of heroin and cocaine vexed celebrities and ordinary citizens far more than baseball players, but this was an era predating by more than fifteen years the notorious cocaine scandal that besmirched the national pastime in 1985. However, marijuana was a less dangerous substance, which may have factored into Joe Pepitone's experimentation with it. The flamboyant Yankee even introduced Mickey Mantle to marijuana, giving the future Hall of Famer a high different from the one to which he had long grown accustomed. Sadly, Mantle had become one of the worst examples of alcohol abuse by the end of his career in 1968, and the condition, attributed to maternal heredity, persisted long after his retirement.

By far, alcoholic beverages have been baseball's constant companion, even during the Prohibition Era, as evidenced in Babe Ruth's prodigious, seemingly unquenchable thirst for them. Whether the purveyor of spirits was a bar, restaurant, nightclub, package store, or speakeasy, liquor's easy accessibility offered the cheapest way to alter the mind, and the varieties in which it was available could satisfy all manner of palates. Socially acceptable and a survivor of the Temperance movement, alcohol remains a virtual staple in American society. The potential to overindulge, however, gives reason for pause, and the travel schedules of baseball teams are filled with much free time away from the ballpark. This "domestic rootlessness" of players can lead them to whiling away the idle hours by drinking or engaging in other unsavory activity.[74]

Trouble can easily find even the most unsuspecting player, a situation that is often compounded by the higher-than-average amount of money well-paid players have at their disposal. For players who found too much refuge in the bottle, rehabilitative help was not as readily available in the late 1960s as it would be a decade later and beyond. The shame associated with addiction and substance abuse has lessened with the recognition that such conditions could be treated successfully, and advancements in science and medicine formed the basis for better dealing with addiction as well as mental illness.

One problem that began to rear its head by the late 1960s was the increasing use of anabolic steroids, a synthetic hormone, taken not as a stimulant but as a means to build muscular body mass and reduce recovery times after injuries. Olympic athletes, especially those participating in weightlifting or track-and-field events such as shot put, found that steroid use enhanced performance. These improvements validated a mindset in which the ends justified the means, and a point was reached where an athlete was virtually obligated to use performance enhancing substances in order to keep pace with his competitors who were steroid users. In the early 1970s, football players in collegiate and professional ranks became evermore influenced by steroids, and they at last spread to baseball, most notably in the late 1990s among a highly visible group of hitters whose stock-in-trade became slugging prodigious numbers of home runs.

The issue is addressed here to emphasize the point that although baseball was only later proven to be susceptible to the influence of steroids, the nature of that influence traces back to the timeframe of this book's focus. One source places the blame for future steroid use in baseball on Commissioner William Eckert, who was cited as having "lost valuable opportunities to be proactive in securing the game's integrity" against the use of steroids, but this argument overreaches in its attempt to censure Eckert.[75]

Indeed, the International Olympic Committee was in the process of formulating a list of banned substances in the wake of the 1964 Summer Games in Tokyo, which in some corners were called the Steroid Olympics because of domination in various weightlifting and weight throwing events by Soviet bloc nations and the United States. A testing program was implemented for the 1968 Olympics in Mexico City, yet the results derived from it were inconclusive because of an inability to "differentiate between ingested or injected testosterone and the testosterone that occurs naturally in the human body."[76] A belief that Eckert—or anyone else in the ranks of baseball management, for that matter—should have been expected to depend upon unreliable data produced by the earliest phase of testing and then apply this policy to baseball is misguided.

Ironically, the same source lauds Eckert's successor, Bowie Kuhn, because the issue of "steroid usage in major league baseball never arose" while he was in office and apparently did not need to be confronted in spite of football's climbing rate of steroid involvement as the 1970s progressed. Later during Kuhn's time in office, he had his own issues of drug and alcohol abuse among players to deal with, but steroids drew no mention in his autobiography. Citing Eckert for failing to institute proactive measures—even though steroids had never been associated with baseball during *his* tenure—while giving Kuhn a pass because the steroid problem did not affect baseball while he was commissioner is simply untenable. There is no record to indicate that Kuhn was sensitive to the steroid issue even though "American sport could now mark its entry into the steroid age: it was 1968."[77]

This final anecdote best captures the devil-may-care mindset characteristic of the era. Tom House, a relief pitcher drafted in 1967 by Atlanta who spent the end of that decade in the minor leagues and whose major-league career was spent during Kuhn's days in office, admitted to using steroids to maintain his physical condition and to keep pace with teammates and opposing players who elected to become users. Fearful of long-term damage as more conclusive evidence became available, House discontinued the practice. Yet in a nod to the free-spirited attitudes of the late 1960s and beyond, he confessed years later that he was a member of "a generation that wasn't afraid to ingest anything."[78]

The Rise of Television

In his sweeping survey of the dynamic decade of the 1950s, the author David Halberstam wrote, "Americans had already begun to adapt their habits to accommodate their favorite [television] programs," and entertainer Milton Berle became TV's first superstar as more television sets found their way into living rooms across the United States and formed another layer of bedrock in American culture and society.[79]

It was only natural that this burgeoning medium would lure sports programming into its realm. Sports teams developed markets in their respective regions in order to secure income generated by their fan base, which was a great advantage of those franchises located in large metropolitan areas such as New York City and Los Angeles. Although the growth of television siphoned some fans away from the stadium gate, and not all market sizes were equal—thus causing an imbalance in income among clubs—the revenue stream created by the sale of broadcast rights served to benefit teams as well as the baseball players' pension fund, thanks to a contract to air a nationwide Game of the Week and major events such as the All-Star Game and World Series.

A key figure who had a major impact on overall sports programming, notably football but less so regarding baseball, was Roone Arledge. When he moved from NBC to ABC in 1960, Arledge commenced to infuse broadcasting with transformative innovations to enhance the experience of viewers by "get[ting] the audience involved emotionally" through the use of microphones to capture the sounds of a game and more cameras that would make viewers feel as if they could look around the stadium and feel more like they were actually at the game.[80] Slow-motion instant replay, introduced by Arledge shortly after his arrival at ABC, has grown into an indispensable part of virtually every sports broadcast, and many of these techniques drew the attention of baseball executives as action on the gridiron—as well as football's increasing popularity—cast an ominous shadow over baseball's once indomitable hold on the American sporting mind.

The bottom line of the balance sheet, however, was what ultimately defined success regardless of the endeavor involved. Legendary football coach Vince Lombardi acknowledged the power of television and the financial benefits it bestowed on sports when he said, "Considering the money involved, [sports teams] do have to put forth some cooperation with television" so that audience size can be maximized to the benefit of the networks, especially for the most important games. Dodgers mogul Walter O'Malley was likewise keenly aware of the hand that was feeding baseball when he stated in 1969, "Without our national Game of the Week program on NBC, many of our teams would be running in the red."[81] Detroit Tigers owner John Fetzer, who made his fortune as a pioneer in radio and television, perhaps best understood the change in relationships between football, a game featuring a lot of continuous action that had greater appeal to a younger male audience, and baseball, which attracted a more cerebral crowd due to its inherently slower pace.

The national pastime had to come to grips with the reality that it no longer held a monopoly over sports fans, Fetzer said, and this sharing of the stage could be traced to the influence of television. But baseball was hardly a helpless victim; money flowing into its coffers by the end of the 1960s was better than ever, with a new three-year contract with NBC delivering $50 million to the big leagues. "Nobody pays that kind of money for a corpse," opined one sportswriter, confirming that baseball, while not as dominant as it once was, would continue to satisfy the fans' appetite for action on the diamond.[82]

Baseball's Centennial Celebration

With the ill-suited William Eckert deposed as commissioner in late 1968, it was fortuitous that his replacement was such an avid, knowledgeable fan. The occasion of Major League Baseball's one hundredth anniversary, which otherwise would have been lost on the bumbling Eckert, was savored immensely by Bowie Kuhn, and also by a man whom Kuhn grew to know well in the ensuing years— President Richard Nixon.

In a generic note to the office of the commissioner—generic in the sense that there was no salutation of "Dear Bowie" or "Dear Commissioner"—dated two weeks after Kuhn's appointment, Nixon reminded the missive's recipient that the honor of throwing out the first ball at the Washington Senators' home opener had usually been reserved for the commander in chief, adding, "I look forward not only to this ceremony but also to attending as many games as possible."[83] The cordial relationship between Nixon and Kuhn flourished in the following months, just in time for one of the highlights of the 1969 season—the All-Star Game, which by fortuitous coincidence would be held in the nation's capital. The showcase contest was scheduled to be played at the former D.C. Stadium, which had been renamed Robert F. Kennedy Memorial Stadium in honor of the fallen senator.

Nixon would indeed fulfill his role as the nation's number-one fan, albeit with an eerie bit of inauspicious foreshadowing when the president dropped the baseball as he was preparing to throw his season-opening pitch prior to the Senators' game against the visiting New York Yankees. The contest, along with two other openers in Cincinnati and Atlanta, marked the beginning of professional baseball's second century, and a commemorative patch adorned the uniforms of all field personnel. Heightening the sense of anticipation for the dawn of baseball's new era, *Sports Illustrated* paid homage to Alexander Cartwright's purported role as baseball's "Johnny Appleseed," then quickly moved to the present day by observing that baseball's previous expansion of 1961 and 1962, which by the end of the decade appeared to be a worthy venture, would seem to bode well for the latest round of new entrants to both the American and National leagues.[84]

Special tribute was paid to the centennial during the All-Star festivities, including the naming of several teams to honor great players from across the national pastime's history. One squad was recognized as "the greatest all-time

Mirroring Bowie Kuhn as an enthusiastic baseball fan, President Richard Nixon tended to Opening Day duties at RFK Stadium. Major figures (in foreground from left) are Washington Senators manager Ted Williams, Kuhn, Nixon, and New York Yankees skipper Ralph Houk. *National Baseball Hall of Fame Library, Cooperstown, NY.*

team" while another saluted "the greatest living players," all of whom, with the exception of Willie Mays, were retired. Fans were presented with the opportunity to vote for the players beginning in the spring of 1969, and the announcement of the winners took place in Washington on the eve of the All-Star Game. In what amounted to a popularity contest, the poll generated a fair amount of controversy when prominent stars such as Mickey Mantle and Hank Aaron failed to pass muster for first honors yet were acknowledged as runners-up for outfield positions. Aaron claimed that Mays was "extremely upset" because he was not named the best of all players still alive, and as for Joe DiMaggio—who did win that distinction—the Yankee Clipper would egomaniacally insist that he always be introduced as "the greatest living ballplayer" at public events, and for many years he continued to harbor a jealousy against Mantle that was "palpable." Real and perceived slights aside, Mays felt comfortable being in company with DiMaggio and among the best of the living players.[85]

At the All-Star break, the *New York Times* informed its readers that an assemblage of "glamorous baseball personalities [and] high-ranking government officials right up to President Nixon, will make the 40th All-Star game a super-social event." A formal dinner the night before the contest drew some of the sport's biggest names, with the exception of Ted Williams. The Senators manager refused to attend rather than break with his tradition of not wearing a necktie, and the afternoon of game day featured a gathering at the East Room of the White House, where guests were personally received by an enthusiastic Nixon. About three hours before the first pitch, guests were treated to a buffet dinner organized by hostess Bess Abell, who indulged them with traditional ballpark fare as well as a buffet of "steamship rounds of beef, . . . clams, oysters, green beans, kidney beans, ice cream cones, old-fashioned cookies, and potato salad." Rather than enjoying the feast in its intended outdoor setting near RFK Stadium, the party had to relocate to a nearby armory because of a downpour that ultimately forced postponement of the game.[86]

Bad weather—and the lingering controversy over Senator Ted Kennedy's involvement in the Chappaquiddick incident, which had occurred just days earlier—notwithstanding, there was a tangible sense of jubilation that underpinned America at this time. Historian Marty Appel placed that spirit in proper context, noting that "everyone was in a great celebratory mood in Washington and across the country" thanks to the recent lunar landing by astronauts Neil Armstrong and Buzz Aldrin, thus making the All-Star Game and its associated agenda more than "a feel-good event."[87]

Improving the State of the Game

With 1968—thankfully—in the past, America was trying to right itself under a new administration in Washington, while in its own parallel sphere, baseball under its new leadership endeavored to rebound from the ennui of the Year of the Pitcher. By midsummer of 1969, *Sports Illustrated* backed its sanguine outlook for the national pastime by pointing out the positive impact of a number of factors that were salvaging baseball from "a sick image" and transforming it into a revitalized sport revitalized with "changes demanded by modern tastes."[88]

The resiliency of the game was manifest in an increase in run production as a result of rules changes assisted further by what the publication claimed to be an enlivened baseball. And in contrast to the singular league pennant races of 1968, the existence of two divisions in each circuit offered the potential for more excitement as teams such as the Mets and Cubs dueled for supremacy in the new National League East, and attendance in Baltimore rose even as the powerful Orioles were running away from their AL East rivals. Several new stadiums were under construction and soon to open, while Commissioner Kuhn—about to be given a new contract since his probationary period was deemed a success—was lauded for recognizing the need to draw younger fans to the game, the better to perpetuate the American tradition of growing to love baseball from an early age. Accessibility to reasonably priced tickets wedded to enhancements such as promotional giveaways were valuable in strengthening the bond between baseball and those supporters who were less likely to be able to afford to attend a pro football game.

To be sure, issues regarding attendance persisted, especially in the American League, where attendance numbers for the White Sox, Angels, Tigers, and Indians fell sharply from their totals of 1968. Problems quickly arose in Seattle over that team's poor stadium and its financial instability, and the Padres stumbled badly in their inaugural season, drawing barely more than a half million fans. But free ticket promotions at Shea Stadium and Candlestick Park contributed to a spirit that breathed fresh life into a game grown stagnant, and the stunning debut of major-league baseball in Canada offered hope of more expansion to markets beyond US borders. Among the clubs in the National League, only Philadelphia and St. Louis showed declines at the gate compared to a year earlier.

To his credit and that of the national pastime, Bowie Kuhn was wise to cultivate positive relationships with powerful public figures, and his cordiality with Richard Nixon was evident as both men began service in their respective offices and warmly exchanged correspondence. The president thanked Kuhn for allowing him the honor of hosting the centennial gala and also for Kuhn's gifts of books, mementos, and a 1969 World Series highlight film. Cheerfully inviting the president to the first American League Championship Series and its NL counterpart as well as the World Series, Kuhn encouraged his attendance by enthusing, "This year your interest in our great game has added very specially to Baseball's lustre [sic]," and expressing appreciation to General Creighton Abrams, his host in Vietnam during the tour of late 1969. Kuhn also stepped beyond traditional political boundaries in September of that year when he sent a gift of several autographed baseballs—"as a manifestation of Baseball's affection and respect for Your Holiness"—to Pope Paul VI.[89]

Indeed, the demons of baseball's poorest-performing commissioner were being exorcised, and all signs pointed to William Eckert's successor being worthy of the praise directed his way. "Bowie Kuhn, the new and progressive commissioner," wrote Arthur Daley in the *New York Times*, "engineered a beautiful promotion that cannot help but reawaken the interest that once made baseball our national pastime."[90] Although Daley was specifically addressing the occasion of the recent All-Star Game, there was no doubt that Kuhn was the right man perfectly situated to shepherd baseball through a crucial time of transition as it began its second century in a new, modern era. Rescued from the approaching peril of moribundity, baseball embarked on a surge in popularity during the decade of the 1970s and beyond.

Zeitgeist, in Conclusion

The years 1968 and 1969 produced seismic events and shifts in America. The abrupt end of the lives of two leaders—one political, the other humanitarian, and both committed to the cause of the nation's citizenry—darkened the shadow already cast over the United States by the war in Vietnam. A shortened war in Southeast Asia would have spared the lives of many soldiers and quelled the protest movement, and while racial harmony has improved since the 1960s, there continues to this day an undercurrent of racism not soon to go away.

That baseball could insulate itself from the milieu of war and racial rifts was unthinkable. Referring to José Feliciano's controversial performance of the national anthem at the 1968 World Series, Tony Kubek opined, "I feel the youth of America has to be served," and while his statement was directed toward the topic of the anthem, a broader meaning can be attached to his comment.[91] Kubek had just turned thirty-three years old two days after the conclusion of the Series, so although he was a member of the demographic whose mere age aroused suspicion in the younger generation—"Don't trust anyone over thirty," or so went the youthful complaint of the day—neither was he too old *not* to have been aware that maturing Baby Boomers were making their voices heard, at times in a most demonstrative way.

By the end of 1969 some of the figures highlighted in this chapter had reached ages that correlate well with Kubek's observation. Dick Allen (twenty-seven), Dave Boswell (twenty-four), Curt Blefary (twenty-six), Roy Gleason (twenty-six), Ken Harrelson (twenty-eight), and Denny McLain (twenty-five) each made an impression on the game of baseball in his own way, whether by display of attitude, an accommodation made for race, or through sacrifice in wartime. Only slightly older, Curt Flood (thirty-one) and Jim Bouton (thirty) also expressed themselves, the former for the cause of labor relations and the latter to unabashedly reveal what most baseball fans did not know about the inner sanctum of the clubhouse. By sacrificing what was left of his career to carry on his fight against "the system," Flood became the highest-profile labor casualty, and his name has been synonymous with the eventual demise of the reserve clause. Bouton performed what could be interpreted as an act of treason by writing *Ball Four*, but the book—which still has not gone out of print more than forty years after its original release—has become an iconic contribution to sports literature.

By the end of the 1960s more was at stake in the world of baseball than the provision of electrical outlets for hair dryers in the clubhouse. Political, cultural, and economic dynamics shaping the United States influenced the national pastime, as did a penchant to question authority overtly and more frequently. Ever evolving, American society and baseball strode into a new decade, a youthful and baseball-savvy commissioner now leading a game better positioned to countenance the challenge posed by its chief rival, professional football.

This was the dawning of baseball's new, modern age.

CHAPTER 8

On the Way Out . . . and Up and Coming

Regardless of the baseball season, the ebb and flow that impact the game are always present, and as time moves forward, it is this never-ending movement that carries away the old faces of the game as it brings fresh characters to the playing field and managerial ranks. By the close of the 1960s an old guard rooted in conservative mores was losing ground to a new generation of players and teams who would carry the national pastime's torch into the 1970s.

The reign of the great New York Yankees teams ended in 1964, but a patchwork of successors to their dynasty had already begun to emerge a year earlier when the Bronx Bombers were swept in the World Series by the Los Angeles Dodgers, who then also captured the 1965 Series crown and the 1966 National League pennant. Trading places with the Dodgers, in a way, were the St. Louis Cardinals, who tried to establish themselves as the successors to the Yankees' throne by taking the 1964 World Series and then ousted the Dodgers in 1967 for their own NL and World Series triumphs before winning another National League pennant in 1968. By the close of the 1960s the Pittsburgh Pirates and Cincinnati Reds, both with a blend of veterans and promising youngsters, were on the brink of creating a regional interdivisional rivalry thanks to the expansion of 1969.

Giving the Yankees direct competition in the American League, the 1965 Minnesota Twins became the first team to oust New York from the top of the AL. Two years later, the Detroit Tigers came painfully close to capturing the pennant and finally achieved that goal the following season, capping it off with a remarkable win over St. Louis in the Fall Classic. The club that became best positioned to stake a claim to dynastic aspirations was the Baltimore Orioles, who swept the Dodgers in the 1966 World Series, but it was not until 1968 that a change in managers facilitated the Orioles' rise to domination that carried into the 1970s. The Twins also contended in 1967 and ruled the new American

League West division in 1969 and 1970, but the burgeoning young talent in the minor-league system of the Athletics—just as the team was shifting from Kansas City to Oakland—would be the catalyst to their three consecutive World Series titles beginning in 1972.

Briefly escaping the grip of mediocrity in 1969 were the Atlanta Braves and the Chicago Cubs, whose won-lost records were nearly identical that year. For the former, it meant a title in the new National League West, but for the latter, the season became one shot through with excruciating disappointment when the team ignominiously collapsed after having spent the first five months of the campaign atop the NL East. Both Atlanta and Chicago proved to be no match for the New York Mets, who cast off the cloak of incompetence and stunned most baseball observers by capturing a World Series title thought to be well beyond their reach.

This chapter will examine the better teams during the time at which the old ten-team American and National leagues transitioned to the revised, ex-panded—and divided—circuits that were central to the new, modern game. During this time, while the struggle for pennants continued, the men who had once been mainstays on the mound or in the field and held sway over the game now were falling to age and injury, thus hastening their exit from the diamond. Some of these players had careers dating back to the early 1950s, and as their shadows lengthened, inevitable segues into retirement ensued. New players filled the voids left by their predecessors, a select few also qualifying for future enshrinement in the Hall of Fame.

The End of the Ten-Team Leagues

The American League contestants vying for the World Series championship in 1968 were no strangers to recent pennant races. Finishing a single game behind the Boston Red Sox in the wild, four-team scramble of September 1967, the Detroit Tigers under manager Mayo Smith hurled and slugged their way to the 1968 AL pennant. Stoked by Denny McLain's thirty-one wins as well as seventeen more by southpaw Mickey Lolich, Detroit's balanced and powerful offensive lineup—which led both major leagues in home runs by a wide margin—included seven players who reached double-digits in homers and one pitcher, Earl Wilson, who belted seven round-trippers. Among the regular-position players, only the .135 batting average of slick-fielding shortstop Ray Oyler seemed to be the weak link on a team that was victorious forty times in contests where it was tied or trailing from the seventh inning on, dramatically winning twenty-eight times in its last at-bat.[1]

Occupying first place for much of the season, Detroit's lead shrank to four games by late August, but the Tigers bolted from the pack by winning all but four of their next twenty-three contests beginning August 28. Detroit's strength was also evident in balloting for the AL Most Valuable Player Award: McLain placed first, catcher Bill Freehan finished second, Willie Horton was fourth, and Dick McAuliffe came in seventh. Smith's bold move of outfielder Mickey Stanley to shortstop in order to get future Hall of Famer Al Kaline in the lineup paid off in the World Series. That year's edition of the Tigers was noteworthy not just for the rallies they staged but also for the camaraderie that they enjoyed as a natural by-product of winning frequently. And no one on the Tigers was more emblematic of those good times than Denny McLain.

At the ripe age of twenty-four, McLain in 1968 became the first pitcher since Dizzy Dean in 1934 to win thirty games in a season, finishing 31–6 and taking MVP and Cy Young Award honors in the American League. An accomplished organist and pilot of his own aircraft, McLain thought nothing of jetting to distant parts of the country on an off day to play a nightclub gig, and he became the unfortunate embodiment of the phrase "live like there's no tomorrow." Fame and the high life came at a cost, and the self-absorbed McLain admitted that during his spectacular run in 1968, "cortisone, xylocaine, Contac, and greenies fueled me."[2] After failing in his first two World Series starts, McLain won Game 6 and watched as Mickey Lolich recorded his third victory of the Series in the finale against the Cardinals.

In 1969 McLain pitched through more pain and followed up with another Cy Young–worthy performance, going 24–9, yet although the Detroit roster remained fairly static from the previous season, the Tigers mustered only ninety wins to finish a distant second to Baltimore. Perennial All-Star catcher Bill Freehan kept a diary of that season and wrote that ultimately the Tigers could blame only themselves for failing to meet the expectations of a defending World Series champion. Freehan confessed that, generally speaking, the players "got away with too much," and a "careless attitude" became noxiously pervasive in all corners of the clubhouse, but singled out for special attention was McLain, who many players felt was allowed to live by a set of rules different from those intended to provide discipline for all members of the team. Al Kaline claimed that McLain's behavior "didn't bother me personally," but he and another veteran, Norm Cash, were urged by many players to ask Mayo Smith to address the issue.[3] Fearing the possibility that McLain would abandon the Tigers if the rules were enforced, the manager let stand the exemption for his ace, and poor team morale continued to fester.

Detroit would segue into the 1970s with the same core of players, with one notable exception. After suspected ties to bookmaking were revealed in a February *Sports Illustrated* cover story, Denny McLain was suspended for the first half of the 1970 season, and he never recovered from the downward spiral into which his career had fallen. While it is doubtful that the Tigers missed McLain's antics and the dissension caused by his insouciant attitude, they did suffer from the lack of a replacement starter who could deliver innings pitched and twenty wins.

In the National League the St. Louis Cardinals reclaimed the glory of their 1964 World Series triumph by outlasting the Boston Red Sox in a thrilling seven-game set in 1967. Enjoying a renaissance following his trade from the Yankees to St. Louis, Roger Maris forced the movement of Mike Shannon from right field to third base, but Maris provided stability to the lineup. However, the Cardinals' acquisition of first baseman Orlando Cepeda from San Francisco was the key transaction that facilitated St. Louis's return to pennant contention. Tim McCarver matured from an overmatched teenager at the beginning of the 1960s to become one of the best catchers in the National League, and the outfield tandem of base-stealer extraordinaire Lou Brock and Curt Flood solidified the top of the batting order. Few weaknesses were evident in the lineup of the team with the highest payroll in baseball.

Cardinals ace hurler Bob Gibson seemed to use his MVP performance in the 1967 Fall Classic as a springboard for his 1968 season, in which he was the apotheosis of what came to be known as the Year of the Pitcher. A consummate professional with a demeanor diametrically opposed to McLain's, Gibson won three games of the 1967 Series while surrendering just fourteen hits and three runs over twenty-seven innings, fanning twenty-six batters in the process.

Not showing any sign of letting up entering the 1968 season, Gibson pitched far better than his early won-lost record indicated. Having but three victories by the end of May due to a lack of run support, Gibson was as close as any pitcher in the twentieth century to being unhittable. Winning fifteen straight decisions from June 2 through August 14, the ace was the undisputed bedrock of the Cardinal rotation and deserving of the Cy Young Award he would capture unanimously. The core of the St. Louis lineup was unchanged from the previous year, and the Cardinals occupied first place in the NL virtually the entire season.

Some cracks soon appeared in the St. Louis armor, however. After gaining a commanding three-games-to-one edge against Detroit in the World Series and holding a 3–2 lead entering the bottom of the seventh inning in Game 5, the Cardinals lost that potentially clinching contest then proceeded to lose the last two games. The finale turned on a costly error in judgment by Flood, the Gold Glove center fielder who misplayed a late-inning line drive by Jim Northrup and permitted the Tigers to break a scoreless tie, giving Mickey Lolich all the runs he would need. Although Flood apologized to Gibson—who was charged with the loss—for the damage he caused, the pitcher later noted that nobody remembers "that Northrup hit the damn ball four hundred feet."[4]

In the wake of the crushing letdown of the World Series loss, the Cardinals embarked on a tour of Japan to play a series of exhibition games, thus making a long season even more fatiguing. Upon the team's return to the United States, contract negotiations between owner Gussie Busch and some players became a source of friction. Cepeda had parlayed his splendid 1967 season into a contract calling for a significant raise from $53,000 to $83,000 in 1968, but when he was vexed by personal distractions and his production fell, the former MVP was shipped to Atlanta for Joe Torre in March of 1969. That same month, Flood sought a salary of $100,000—the elite round figure of the era—but instead settled for $90,000, still a significant increase from the $72,500 he had earned in 1968. However, the acrimony of the bargaining soured Flood to the point that he threatened to quit the game, and Flood's self-inflicted indulgences—"He always seemed to have a vodka martini in his hand and a beautiful woman on his arm," observed his biographer—only hastened his decline.[5] Even after signing his new contract, Flood was the subject of trade rumors as the 1969 season progressed. When the Cardinals did trade him in October, Flood began his trek through the court system in his battle against the reserve clause.

Torre very capably took over first base for St. Louis, and veteran Vada Pinson, acquired from the Reds, filled the gap created by the retirement of Maris, yet Gibson labored through mounting elbow pain to again reach the twenty-victory plateau. The Cardinals played sub-.500 ball through the end of June and never recovered from this poor start, slipping to fourth place in the new National League East division with a record of 87–75. One scribe reported that if the offense had been able to deliver with men in scoring position and less than two out, the Cardinals "could have been contenders all the way."[6] The 1969 season was the first of a lackluster stretch in St. Louis baseball history that extended for more than a decade.

The desultory but quasi-dynastic run of the Cardinals from 1964 to 1968 was built on a foundation of quality pitching enhanced by a core of regulars that was at once youthful and experienced. The departures of Maris, Flood, and Cepeda, along with their playoff-infused acumen, at the end of the 1960s created a breach that was difficult to repair despite the best efforts of manager Red Schoendienst, whose clubs in his later years were competitive but not prime contenders.

The Cardinals and Tigers closed out 1968 as the last pennant winners of the old ten-team leagues, thus ending a golden age of sorts in which the only postseason reward was entry to the World Series. The creation of divisions in 1969 as a result of expansion in both circuits meant potentially twice as many races for first place, and the clubs that took advantage of the revised format earned their rightful places in the game's legacy.

The Pennant Contenders of 1969

Teams vying for first place in their respective divisions generated varying degrees of excitement, and in the maiden voyage of this new configuration, the National League was the clear winner. With the New York Mets and Chicago Cubs dueling in the NL East and nearly every team in the NL West seemingly within hailing distance of first place at one time or another over the course of the campaign, the Senior Circuit captured the attention of many fans as the season hurtled into its post–Labor Day stretch. In the American League, the Baltimore Orioles far outpaced their divisional foes with one of the most powerful rosters assembled in the 1960s—or any decade, for that matter—while the Minnesota Twins fielded a club a bit more pedestrian, finishing with a record that was a full twelve games below the standard set by the Orioles but nonetheless was a very good team fortuitous enough to be in a weak division containing both AL expansion clubs.

Under the guidance of manager Earl Weaver in his first full year at the helm, Baltimore took control of the AL East in mid-April and never looked back, extending its lead at the All-Star break to eleven games and doubling that edge by late September. A quick review of the Orioles' won-lost balance sheet reveals a team with no apparent weaknesses, but in the AL West, Minnesota—also under a rookie manager, Billy Martin—was pursued closely by Oakland throughout

Pugnacious, demanding, but ultimately successful, Baltimore manager Earl Weaver forged the Orioles dynasty that spanned the 1960s and 1970s. *National Baseball Hall of Fame Library, Cooperstown, NY.*

the summer. Charlie Finley's pesky Athletics refused to quit and were just one and one-half games behind in late August, but the Twins asserted themselves by beating Oakland in five of their final six head-to-head contests.

As tentative as Minnesota's grip on their division had been, the Twins proved a worthy opponent in the first American League Championship Series even though they had lost eight of twelve to Baltimore in the regular season. Falling victim to Baltimore in a three-game sweep, Minnesota lost a pair of extra-inning heartbreakers by one run before being trounced in the third game. The confident Orioles were well positioned to take on whatever team emerged as the winner of the National League pennant.

The lack of suspense in the American League division races was offset by a huge amount of drama in the National. In the NL West, only the San Diego Padres were denied a seat at the table of worthy contestants. By early September the five chief competitors were a mere four games apart, and the least of the bunch, the Houston Astros, were the only club to not occupy first place at some point, although they had closed to within two games. Cincinnati, Los Angeles, and San Francisco vied in gamely fashion but ultimately lost out to the Atlanta Braves, who themselves stumbled briefly to fourth place but sprinted to the finish line by taking ten of their final eleven games, leaving the Giants three games behind and the Reds four games out.

But the most prominent baseball story of 1969 was being written in Flushing, New York, where the Mets fascinated the country as they—improbably—shed their reputation as comical losers. Expunging the bugbears of Marv Throneberry and his ilk that gained them a reputation as the Keystone Kops of the diamond, the Mets excelled under the quiet but firm hand of manager Gil Hodges. The only National League team to win one hundred games, New York was merely a .500 club in early June, yet as the summer progressed they tenaciously clung to second place behind the Chicago Cubs. The Mets seemed unable to get closer than four games back, but a crucial showdown in early September against the Cubs swung the pendulum in New York's direction, and they kept rolling while Chicago never recovered and staggered to a disappointing second-place finish.

While Mets' fans were delirious over their team's newfound success, the players remained focused under Hodges's gaze, executing a sweep over Atlanta in the first National League Championship Series. Their ousting of the Braves in three straight games heightened the excitement for their followers, those devoted as well as those recently jumping on the bandwagon. If capturing the NL East was a wonder in itself, and winning the league pennant another marvel, would a third and final miracle—beating the mighty Orioles in the World Series—be conceivable? In the event, the Mets accomplished their version of the 1967 Boston Red Sox "Impossible Dream" by vanquishing Baltimore in five games.

—ᴍ—

The four initial titlists exhibited varied strengths to win their respective divisions, and with the exception of Baltimore, the other three clubs who ultimately surpassed their closest rivals did so by overcoming numerous deficiencies. On balance, the teams with the two best records in both leagues took the pennants of their respective circuits, and the World Series contestants were the only teams to win one hundred games. Upsets were sure to follow, but at least in the first year of the new divisional format, the top clubs advanced as expected.

The best teams of each league took advantage of their assets, so it is appropriate to review what they possessed that made them the class of their circuits.

BALTIMORE ORIOLES

Victorious in 109 games, the Orioles had as complete a team befitting a formidable contender: a potent offense combined with the best pitching staff in baseball to produce the greatest run differential in the American League, all of which was augmented by a stellar defense. Earl Weaver began 1969 with only three months of big-league managerial experience, having replaced Hank Bauer after the All-Star break of the previous season, but he was the right man in the right position to extract what he could from the rich Baltimore lineup.

The Orioles batting order fell eleven runs shy of equaling the Twins' league-leading total of 790, yet balance was evident throughout. Boog Powell led the team with 37 home runs and 121 RBIs, was second in average at .304, and placed second in balloting for the American League MVP; Frank Robinson (.308/32 HRs/100 RBIs) belied his title as the club's elder statesman among position players at the age of thirty-three; center fielder Paul Blair (.285/ 26/76/ 20 stolen bases) was one of the best at his position; Brooks Robinson (.234/23/84) continued to excel at third base; Don Buford (.291/11/64) provided a spark as the leadoff batter, stealing 19 bases and scoring 99 runs; and the catching tandem of Elrod Hendricks and Andy Etchebarren combined for 15 homers and 64 RBIs.

With their gloves, the infield was virtually impregnable as second baseman Dave Johnson, third baseman Brooks Robinson, and shortstop Mark Belanger all received Gold Gloves, and they were joined by Blair in that honor. The primary beneficiary of such a solid defense was a starting rotation featuring a pair of twenty-game winners—Dave McNally and Cy Young co-winner Mike Cuellar—and a young hurler recently recovered from injuries, Jim Palmer, who won sixteen of his twenty decisions. Highlighting the bullpen were three relievers—Dick Hall, Eddie Watt (sixteen saves), and Pete Richert (twelve saves)—who collectively added seventeen wins and whose earned run averages ranged from Watt's 1.65 to Richert's 2.20.

Knowledgeable but demonstrative, Weaver curried no favor with the many umpires he hectored, but the future Hall of Fame manager and player personnel director Harry Dalton were the architects of the Orioles' system that groomed minor leaguers in the early and mid-1960s, and the best of those young players would later join Weaver in Baltimore. He led the Orioles to three straight American League pennants from 1969 to 1971 on the brawn of the lineup he inherited along with a gradual infusion of players he had helped develop in the farm system. Weaver favored veterans who had proven themselves at the major-league level, a philosophy that put newcomers at a disadvantage, and it could be difficult to cultivate a relationship with a man physically undersized yet possessed of a large degree of feistiness. The means of his demands, however, produced competitive teams that were among baseball's best as the 1960s passed into the next decade.

MINNESOTA TWINS

Creating a sporadic dynasty in the fashion of the St. Louis Cardinals—albeit less successful—the Minnesota Twins lost momentum following their pennant-winning season of 1965, and they were thwarted in a quest to hold onto their slim lead on the final weekend of the 1967 campaign, losing twice to the Red Sox. But the new American League West division was weak from the outset, and the Twins found their footing in large part due to a potent offense fronted by slugger Harmon Killebrew, whose 49 home runs and 140 RBIs earned him the 1969 AL MVP honors. His teammates who contributed toward the club's league-leading 790 runs scored included a healthy Tony Oliva (.309/24 HRs/101 RBIs), Rich Reese (.322/16/69), 1967 Rookie of the Year Rod Carew (.332/8/56/19 stolen bases), and César Tovar (.288/11/52/45). On the mound Minnesota relied on three mainstays in the rotation: twenty-game winners Jim Perry (20–6, 2.82 ERA) and Dave Boswell (20–12, 3.23), and Jim Kaat (14–13, 3.49). The key fireman in the bullpen was Ron Perranoski (2.11 ERA), whose thirty-one saves led the majors, but the defense was average at best, even though right fielder Oliva, catcher John Roseboro, and shortstop Leo Cardenas were former Gold Glove winners. Kaat remained a perennial recipient of that award.

Minnesota would finish with a 97–65 record, second-best in the league, thanks to outstanding performances from not only Killebrew but also many of his teammates who drew the notice of MVP voters and ended up bunched between ninth and seventeenth place in the balloting: Perry (9), Carew (10), Cardenas (12), Perranoski (13, tied with McNally of the Orioles), Oliva (15),

Tovar (17). Perry also finished third in voting for the Cy Young Award. But the Twins' path to the AL West title was hardly a foregone conclusion. Chased by a determined band of Oakland Athletics throughout much of the season, Minnesota never gained a comfortable margin over its divisional rival until the month of September. The Twins' dugout was lorded over by its former third-base coach, Billy Martin, who was instrumental to the club's success in its 1965 drive to the AL pennant. Martin proved to be more combustible than his counterpart in Baltimore, and in his first year as a skipper "there were few dull moments," to put it mildly.[7] Never a man to back down from a confrontation, Martin became involved in fisticuffs with one of his starting pitchers, knocking out Boswell during an argument in Detroit. Even the Twins' rise to the top of the division could not save Martin from owner Calvin Griffith's axe when the season ended in the playoff loss to Baltimore, putting the volatile manager on a track toward employment in several other American League cities with similar results—namely, success for his team on the field at the cost of run-ins and unsavory episodes with team personnel and others.

The Twins repeated as AL West champions in 1970—this time under a new manager, Bill Rigney—with a lineup dependent on many of the same faces of the previous year, plus several worthy additions such as Danny Thompson, Brant Alyea, Luis Tiant (who had been acquired from Cleveland), and a future Hall of Fame pitcher, nineteen-year-old Bert Blyleven. But like the St. Louis Cardinals, Minnesota would come to be well-acquainted with mediocrity in the years to come.

ATLANTA BRAVES

Through the late 1950s the Milwaukee Braves had been a strong contender built on run-scoring strength courtesy of a lineup led by power hitters Eddie Mathews and Hank Aaron as well as a pitching staff with stars Lew Burdette and Warren Spahn. By the mid-1960s the Braves had become a middle-of-the-pack team, dating to their most recent years before transferring from Milwaukee to Atlanta following the 1965 season. By 1968 Aaron still dominated the mediocre offense, but beyond the output of the future career home-run champion, only catcher Joe Torre and outfielder Felipe Alou hit with any reliable consistency. The Braves' pitching was similarly less than awe-inspiring, yet Phil Niekro and Pat Jarvis were reliable, and the staff was bolstered by the addition of veteran Milt Pappas.

Entering the new NL West division on the heels of their 81–81 finish in 1968, the Braves were in the process of retooling under general manager Paul Richards, who used trades to import players he believed could return the club to contention. Not all of his moves were well received, as evidenced by Aaron's criticism for Richards's trade of Mathews, but the longtime Braves slugger appreciated the addition of Orlando Cepeda, who was acquired from St. Louis for Torre. "Cepeda was a rah-rah guy who gave [the Braves] that little push we needed," commented Aaron, and Atlanta profited from the lift Cepeda provided on the field and in the clubhouse.[8] For his part, Aaron had been fueled by a rivalry—whether imagined or real—that he felt existed between himself and San Francisco's Willie Mays, and he started to swing more for the fences by 1969 because after reaching three thousand career hits, writer Lee Allen told him he could "create his own niche in baseball history."[9] Aaron had long since discovered that the Braves' new home, Atlanta Stadium, was conducive to pulling the ball for power, and by 1970 he concentrated on home runs rather than simply base hits.

Under manager Lum Harris, Atlanta enjoyed a brief but less significant return to the glory days of their recent past. Cepeda, who batted only .257 but furnished 22 homers and 88 RBIs, was among the catalysts, and after being struck down for the entire 1968 season due to tuberculosis, Rico Carty rebounded—especially in the month of September—and ended the season batting .342 with 16 homers and 58 RBIs, while Aaron (.300/44 HRs/97 RBIs) was true to form. Former Yankee Clete Boyer (.250/14/57) won a Gold Glove while anchoring third base, and in his second full year as second baseman, Felix Millan (.267/6/57) earned All-Star recognition as well as a Gold Glove.

Niekro (23–13, 2.56 ERA) had a superb season and was the only pitcher to prevent the Mets' Tom Seaver from unanimously winning the National League Cy Young Award. Ron Reed won eighteen games against ten losses, and both Pat Jarvis and George Stone logged thirteen wins, although Stone had the better ERA, 3.65 to 4.43. In the bullpen Cecil Upshaw's twenty-seven saves placed him in company with the best in the circuit, and Richards even brought aboard the ancient Hoyt Wilhelm for the season's final three weeks, making the GM look like a genius when the knuckleballer posted two wins and saved four games in just eight appearances. In mid-June Richards exchanged three prospects—including future hitting coach Walt Hriniak—for the Padres' Tony Gonzalez, who contributed with his bat and glove on several key occasions.

Paul Richards's biographer later refuted a contemporaneous charge that the Atlanta roster was not representative of the general manager's strategy in building a team. "Richards's signature was all over the roster," wrote Warren Corbett, noting the Braves' blend of veterans and young talent, to say nothing of the team's emphasis on defense, as Atlanta committed the fewest errors (115) in the National League.[10]

The late-season kick in which the Braves won ten of their final eleven games delivered the NL West title to Atlanta, an accomplishment the Braves proudly made clear in their 1970 media guide when they added a crown to the caricature of their team mascot, Chief Noc-A-Homa. But the Braves' hold on the division was short lived, as the era of the Big Red Machine was very soon to open in Cincinnati.

NEW YORK METS

Baseball's signature moment at the end of the 1960s was undoubtedly the rise of the once woebegone New York Mets to the dizzying heights occupied by a world champion. The plethora of adjectives describing the franchise from its birth in 1962—laughable, bungling, inept, and the like—through the years during which manager Casey Stengel held sway served to romanticize, or even validate, the poor quality of play of Gotham's newest big-league club. Impressive as this turnaround was, however, closer scrutiny reveals it to be slightly less amazing than it seemed because an undercurrent of factors was in motion that fortuitously placed the Mets on their destined course.

Chief among those factors was the young talent arriving at the major-league level within a very short time frame. First baseman Ed Kranepool had been on the roster since he was a teenager in 1962, and he was joined briefly the following year by outfielder Cleon Jones, who was only twenty years old. Former Yankees general manager George Weiss served in that same capacity for the Mets through 1966, and the following year Whitey Herzog came aboard as the director of player development. Herzog's contributions played a crucial role in delivering many future stars to the Mets, but the cavalcade of talent had started in 1965 as a host of players in their very early twenties began making their first appearances in a Mets uniform. Shortstop Bud Harrelson, outfielder Ron Swoboda, reliever Tug McGraw, pitcher Nolan Ryan (1966), catcher Jerry Grote (1966), pitcher and NL Rookie of the Year Tom Seaver (1967), southpaw Jerry Koosman (1967), and pitcher Danny Frisella (1967) began to stake their claim to spots on the Mets roster, although several of them were still shuttling between Shea Stadium and the minor leagues. The Mets in 1967 were still losers of 101 games, but come 1968 a change in managers furnished the second factor that made all the complicated ingredients of a champion begin to coalesce.

Long a favorite of Brooklyn Dodgers fans, former first baseman Gil Hodges returned to New York after serving as manager of the Washington Senators from 1963 to 1967, a tenure in which he demonstrated a knack for gradually improving the fortunes of the team, but this hardly branded him as a miracle worker. Yet Hodges brought with him the salient traits that marked him as the ideal candidate to lead the Mets into the winners' circle. While in the Marine Corps during World War II, he learned the militaristic organizational skills and work ethic that became his guiding doctrine as a baseball manager, and Hodges used a hands-on approach to help his players learn necessary skills or improve talents that were in need of amending. Valuing the depth and flexibility of the twenty-five-man roster, Hodges employed platoons at several positions and took a cue from his own former manager with the Dodgers, Walter Alston, to formulate a lineup based on the strength of the players available.

At the conclusion of Hodges's first year with the Mets, the dividend may not have been obvious in the final standings, with New York mired in ninth place. But only weeks into the 1968 campaign one scribe foretold the signs of hope that were the result of Hodges's command: "[I]t appears that [the Mets] may now be on the verge of abandoning the theater of the absurd and starting to play something that closely resembles big-league baseball," and the collective maturing of Harrelson, Swoboda, Seaver, Koosman, and the others provided the spark to stoke a growing fire.[11] Not alone in his leadership venture, Hodges was accompanied by his pitching coach, Rube Walker, who used a deft hand in cultivating a deep, talented rotation and relief corps. Regardless of the ninth-place finish, the Mets showed an improvement to a franchise-best seventy-three victories, and there was a portent at the Triple-A level of the Mets' system when the fourth-place Jacksonville Mets of the International League surged in improbable fashion during the postseason playoffs and won the IL Governor's Cup, as "catching lightning in a bottle" seemed to breed confidence in some players who carried that winning spirit to Shea Stadium.[12]

With expansion in 1969 splitting each league into two divisions, New York would have to surpass only five rivals to win the NL East, but the Pirates, Cubs, and defending National League champion Cardinals all appeared poised to overmatch the Mets. Yet persistence paid off, and by June 2 the Mets reached the .500 mark at 23–23; the next day they moved into second place, where they remained for over two months. This was unquestionably the best Mets squad in the young history of the team, but their odds of overtaking the division-leading Cubs seemed remote. Chicago's ten-game edge in the standings—to say nothing of their powerful run-producing ability—impressed as insurmountable.

But the pesky Mets countenanced the pressure before them, eschewing lengthy losing streaks yet curiously having great difficulty against their fellow 1962 expansionists, posting a poor 2–10 record versus the Houston Astros. While New York held firm and slowly made inroads against the Cubs, Chicago in turn was staging a revival of the infamous collapse of the 1964 Philadelphia Phillies, and the Cubs' margin over the Mets had dwindled to two and one-half games on September 7. Intent on putting the Mets in their place, Cubs skipper Leo Durocher brusquely "ordered his charges" to "kill them off for good" when the contestants for the NL East title faced off the next day for a critical two-game set at Shea.[13]

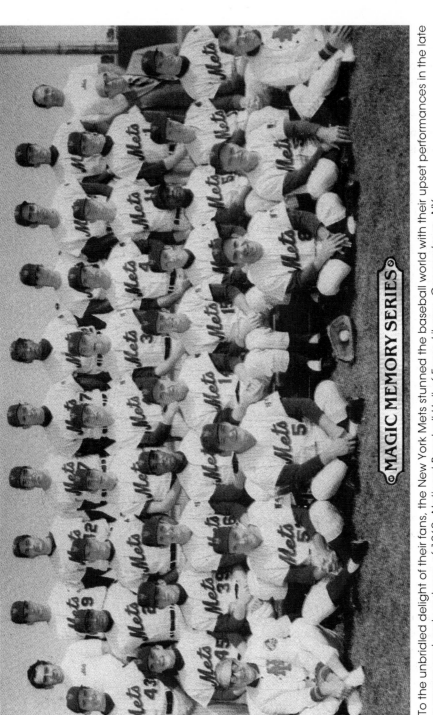

To the unbridled delight of their fans, the New York Mets stunned the baseball world with their upset performances in the late summer and early autumn of 1969. *National Baseball Hall of Fame Library, Cooperstown, NY.*

Momentum clearly favored the Mets, and their sweep of the Cubs extended a winning streak that would grow to ten games by September 13 and put the Cubs in an irreparable tailspin. Durocher clung to his philosophy of old-school tactics, which included having his pitchers intentionally throw at opposing batters, but the Mets were up to the challenge. As the Chicago swoon lingered, "the fingernails of panic begin to dig deep into the back" of the scrappy Cubs manager, but the trend was irreversible and New York forged ahead to clinch the division title on September 24.[14]

Those who believed the Mets to be a one-hit wonder were in for a surprise. After disposing of the Atlanta Braves in the NLCS, New York had one final hill to climb to complete the unlikely journey to lasting fame. In a crisp, two-hour and fourteen-minute game on the afternoon of October 16, the Mets dispatched the Orioles, claiming the World Series crown and touching off a delirious melee at Shea Stadium. Joseph Durso reported in the *New York Times* that seconds after Cleon Jones caught the final out of the contest, "Children, housewives, mature men, all swarmed onto the field where the Mets had marched. They tore up home plate, captured the bases, ripped gaping holes from the turf, set off orange flares and firecrackers, and chalked the wooden outfield walls with signs of success."[15] Donn Clendenon, the subject of the springtime trade imbroglio between Houston and Montreal who landed with the Mets in mid-June, was named the Series MVP, but the winning pitcher of Game 5, Jerry Koosman, could easily have laid claim to the honor with his 2.04 ERA and pair of wins, including the clinching contest. The Mets' domination of the Orioles also was consistent with the pattern of New York–over–Baltimore sporting accomplishments of 1969, beginning with the Jets' upset victory over the heavily favored Colts in Super Bowl III, followed by the Knickerbockers' sweep against the Bullets in the National Basketball Association playoffs. The legacy of the Mets' realization of their own version of "the Impossible Dream" was short lived. Over the next two seasons under Hodges, New York would finish in third place in the National League East, winning eighty-three games each year. As a fresh crop of youngsters was sprouting from Herzog's minor-league system—John Milner, Tim Foli, Mike Jorgensen, Ken Singleton, and future Rookie of the Year pitcher Jon Matlack among them—a second heart attack took the life of the Mets manager on the eve of the 1972 season. Hodges was stoic, calm, and collected under pressure, and although he was outwardly less emotional than several of his contemporaries in the brethren of major-league managers—notably Durocher and especially Weaver—the Mets skipper may have suffered from his reluctance to vent his anger. Hodges's temper could be volcanic, but such outbursts were rare, yet his suppression of emotion may have combined with a relapse of his cigarette habit—which he had given up after his first heart attack in 1968—and the stress of managing to cause the fatal blow that silenced him just two days before his forty-eighth birthday.

A victim of poor health exacerbated by cigarette smoking, manager Gil Hodges kept a smooth but disciplined hand on the Mets' tiller. *National Baseball Hall of Fame Library, Cooperstown, NY.*

But the magic of 1969 lingers and is still a touchstone moment in baseball history. In the summer of that year's NL East race, several New York reporters were asked to offer their opinions—at the behest of a Chicago newspaper—on the team they covered. One snide remark came from a *Newsday* writer who opined, "The Mets have about as much chance of winning the pennant as man has of landing on the moon."[16] As history played out, both events occurred to the delight of millions, and they were emblematic of America's determination and mettle.

CHICAGO CUBS

Juxtaposed against the New York Mets and in the light of what potentially loomed as its own high point in team history, the plight of the Chicago Cubs also warrants special attention for what might have been had they held their course and not fallen victim to the Mets, or, perhaps more accurately, the distressed reactions of manager Leo Durocher as the season wore on.

When Durocher took the Cubs' reins in 1966, he did the seemingly impossible, taking an eighth-place team and sinking it to the cellar of the National League, worse than the expansion Astros and even seven and one-half games behind the ninth-place Mets. Durocher had been away from managing for more than a decade, and the Cubs' young catcher, Randy Hundley, later admitted that the team "had a terrible year trying to learn how Leo wanted us to play the game."[17] But a twenty-eight-game improvement a year later moved Chicago to third place, instilling confidence in the team and enthusiasm among the fans.

In 1968 the Cubs again finished third while winning eighty-four games, three games less than the previous year, but the positive response to two straight seasons over .500—the first such occurrence since 1946—had an enormous impact on the club's morale. The roster was girded by the nucleus of three solid starting pitchers (Ferguson Jenkins, Bill Hands, and Ken Holtzman) along with veteran Phil Regan in the bullpen; Hundley taking charge behind the plate; a solid infield of Ron Santo, Don Kessinger, Glenn Beckert, and Ernie Banks; and Billy Williams patrolling the outfield accompanied by Jim Hickman, who regained his lost power stroke. The prospects on the North Side of Chicago looked bright, and the claque of rabid fans in the cheap seats at Wrigley Field known as the "Bleacher Bums" was as fawning over the hometown team as it was brutal to opposing players.

The 40,796 exuberant partisans on hand for Opening Day at Wrigley set the tone as the Cubs charged from the gate, winning eleven of their first twelve games, the fast start giving credence to Banks's cute prediction that "the Cubs will shine in '69." And shine they did, uninterruptedly so for most of the next five months. "It was great coming to the ballpark all summer," wrote Jenkins in his memoir, adding, "We were a team to be reckoned with." Backup receiver Gene Oliver, a longtime National League veteran, declared his current team to be "the finest piece of baseball machinery I've ever seen."[18] The cogs of that

Never one to back down in any kind of dispute, Leo Durocher of the Chicago Cubs managed the National League East contenders to their most storied pennant run—and subsequent collapse—in the summer of 1969. *National Baseball Hall of Fame Library, Cooperstown, NY.*

machine would, in the final accounting, produce the third-highest offensive run total in the National League, fortified by a quartet of hitters who slugged more than twenty home runs, and a rotation with two twenty-game winners alongside one with seventeen victories.

However, a late August swoon portended trouble, and a five-game winning streak that appeared to halt the skid soon gave way to the coup de grâce in the first half of September during which the Cubs lost eleven of twelve contests, dropping into second place behind the Mets. As the losses mounted and the frequency of Santo's celebratory heel-clicking diminished, Durocher led at least one player to believe that "[he] wanted the regulars to play every inning of every game" rather than giving them a much-needed rest and allowing part-timers to see some action. A heavy reliance on the same starters—Jenkins in particular pitched poorly in September, and Holtzman faltered as the team's slump deepened early that month—who may have benefited from skipping a scheduled start, hindered a turnaround in the Cubs' fortunes, and one of the 1969 Mets who later played for Durocher offered the view that "Leo was the type of manager to cause panic and confusion among his players."[19]

Durocher led the New York Giants in their comeback of 1951 and assumed the role of hunter as his team pursued and overtook the Brooklyn Dodgers, but eighteen years later it was Durocher who was the prey. And it was a twist of scheduling fate that the Cubs faced the Mets when it mattered most at Shea Stadium just as Chicago was unraveling and New York was surging. This juncture of rival teams nearly passing each other in the standings—the Mets actually closed to within a half-game of the Cubs—was an astounding coincidence, later leading Gil Hodges's biographer to speculate that the Mets' skipper—cool under pressure and possessed of a far different tactical mindset when managing his team and an understanding of how to handle personality issues with certain players as well as disputes with umpires—would have successfully guided the Cubs to the NL East pennant had he been *their* manager.[20]

Among the participants in that epic collapse, nonetheless, were five personnel who were later enshrined in Cooperstown—Ernie Banks, Ferguson Jenkins, Ron Santo, Billy Williams, and Leo Durocher—yet the 1969 Cubs remain one of the best teams never to play in the postseason. The miracle belonged to the New York Mets through dint of their effort, while for the Chicago Cubs, "wait 'til next year" continued to be an aphorism for decades to follow.

TEAMS ON THE RISE

The Cubs and the four inaugural division winners were far from competing in a vacuum over the next few seasons, although an argument can be made that in

1969 the Baltimore Orioles were beginning a reign over the AL East that would last for most of the next six years. However, several other teams were approaching turning points as they exited the 1960s ready to stamp their imprint on the game. One of those had a short and low trajectory entering the next decade, but the other two were gifted with a combination of strengths that enabled them to surpass their divisional rivals and remain dominant.

The weakest of this trio was the National League East's Pittsburgh Pirates, second runners-up to the Mets and Cubs in 1969. Entering the 1970s, however, the Bucs handed field leadership to Danny Murtaugh, who managed the club from 1958 to 1964 and led it to victory over the New York Yankees in the 1960 World Series. Murtaugh again worked his skill with veterans Roberto Clemente, Bill Mazeroski, Willie Stargell—all future Hall of Famers—and Matty Alou in tandem with a crop of youngsters who laid a solid foundation for Pittsburgh to win the divisional crown five of the next six years. Manny Sanguillen was shortly to establish himself as one of the best catchers in the NL, Richie Hebner solidified third base for years to come, and outfielder Al Oliver finished second in 1969 Rookie of the Year voting as he secured his place as a consistent hitter. On the mound Steve Blass was the ace of the 1968 Pirates' staff and became the pitching star of the 1971 World Series, while Bob Moose led the NL in winning percentage in 1969. Joining Blass and Moose was Dock Ellis, a spirited right-hander who won nineteen games for the Series champions in 1971.

Another club that matured and became the Pirates' chief rival in the early 1970s was the Cincinnati Reds of the NL West. In 1969 the Reds far outpaced the league, with 798 runs scored and a slugging percentage of .422, tied the Pirates in team batting average at .277, and as a team hit nearly 30 more home runs than their nearest rival. Although a bit weak in the middle of the infield, the other six regular positions were solidly manned by players who at a minimum drove in 82 runs each, with four of them also belting more than 20 homers. The hit parade was fronted by NL batting champion Pete Rose (.338); sluggers Lee May and Tony Perez, with 38 and 37 home runs, respectively; outfielders Bobby Tolan (.305) and Alex Johnson (.315); and Johnny Bench (.293/26 HRs/90 RBIs), the premier catcher in the game in perhaps any era. Tommy Helms, the 1966 winner of the NL Rookie of the Year Award, performed yeomanly at second base but was overshadowed by the rest of the powerful Reds lineup.

Manager Dave Bristol's weak link was the pitching staff, with a collective team ERA that was fourth-worst in the NL, but whose bullpen was led by Wayne Granger's twenty-seven saves. The key to the coming Reds dynasty was neither in Cincinnati nor in the organization's minor-league system, however. Rather, that essential member in 1969 was on the coaching staff of the expansion San Diego Padres, whose third-base coach, Sparky Anderson, had yet to make an appearance in the majors as a manager. Given that chance in 1970, Anderson would commence a stellar career as skipper by immediately guiding the Reds to the NL pennant and by the mid-1970s—thanks to some shrewd player trades—created the juggernaut known as the Big Red Machine. Perez and Anderson joined Bench in the Hall of Fame as Reds from the 1970 squad.

The placement of two expansion teams in the American League's West Division gave that six-team circuit a shallow cast. Such a configuration provided fertile ground for the newly relocated Oakland Athletics to take root in a relatively weak division. Although the Minnesota Twins were the best of the lot, thanks mostly to their offensive punch, the 1969 Athletics were soon to join the ranks of contenders, and, like the Reds in the NL, they would become one of the great teams of the 1970s. Many Athletics had acquired varying degrees of major-league experience dating back to the franchise's waning days in Kansas City, and, built mainly through players selected in the amateur draft created in 1965, Oakland brought together the right pieces at each position and on the pitching staff to furnish balance and depth throughout the lineup.

Owner Charlie Finley's interloping acted as catalyst and irritant, the former in the sense that his baseball and business acumen melded to facilitate his operation of the club, the latter with regard to his irrepressible penchant for interfering with on-field affairs that would have been best left to the manager. Bombast and showmanship aside, Finley's charges included a solid infield with Sal Bando, Bert Campaneris, and Dick Green; two former collegiate stars, Rick Monday and Reggie Jackson, in the outfield; and a starting staff led by Jim "Catfish" Hunter, John "Blue Moon" Odom, and Chuck Dobson, with Rollie Fingers learning the role of bullpen closer. By 1969 several other youngsters made brief appearances with the Athletics, and they too would make significant contributions to the success through the first half of the 1970s, which included three consecutive World Series titles. Vida Blue, Joe Rudi, Gene Tenace, and Dave Duncan would join Hunter, Bando, Jackson, and the others under new manager Dick Williams in 1971 to capture the first of five straight AL West pennants and three World Series titles from 1972 to 1974, although Williams left the team after 1973. Hunter, Fingers, Jackson, and Williams were subsequently elected to Cooperstown.

Managerial Debuts

The ranks of managers evolve just as surely as those of players, although with a season-long ratio of one manager—most of the time—to more than twenty-five players, the turnover rate is lower, but managerial firings and hirings tend to make for bigger headlines when they do occur. Sixteen men opened new careers as big-league skippers in 1968 and 1969, but only three achieved long-term success, while a fourth drew wide attention because of his name recognition.

When Hank Bauer fell out of favor with the Baltimore Orioles front office halfway through the 1968 season, the stage was set to replace him with the man who had been newly appointed as the Orioles' first-base coach that year. Bauer had quickly grown uneasy when Earl Weaver was promoted to his coaching staff by general manager Harry Dalton, a move Bauer viewed as a potential threat to his job security. At the All-Star break, with Baltimore having posted a blasé 43–37 record, Dalton dismissed Bauer and elevated Weaver to the manager's seat. To some players the move confirmed the suspicion that Weaver had been "Dalton's guy" from the moment he arrived in Baltimore and that it was only a matter of time before he assumed Bauer's place.[21] Once given the chance, however, Weaver delivered as Dalton had hoped, and the Orioles finished 48–34 for the remainder of 1968. Building on his success as he moved into his first full season at the Baltimore helm, Weaver adjusted his lineup with spectacular results. Difficult for a youngster to impress, demanding of his players, and caustic with umpires, Weaver left no doubt about who was in charge. But the competitive teams he fielded and the resultant winning record he accumulated distinguished him as one of the great managers through the early 1980s.

John McNamara embarked on his managerial career in 1969 when he replaced Hank Bauer for the Oakland Athletics' final thirteen games. His eventual twenty-year career included a division title with the Cincinnati Reds in 1979 and, most famously, his tenure with the AL champion Boston Red Sox in 1986.

Controversial in his own right, Billy Martin took over the Minnesota Twins in 1969, having served an instrumental role as the team's third-base coach during its drive to the 1965 American League title. Tempestuous and argumentative—and, very unfortunately, also a victim of imbibing too heavily—Martin brought as volatile a spirit to the Twins as Weaver did in Baltimore, but he did so at the cost of rapidly wearing out his welcome. Martin was dismissed after Minnesota was swept in the 1969 ALCS and thereafter stormed through a series of American League managerial jobs, including those with Detroit, Texas, the Yankees—on several occasions—and Oakland.

Lauded as one of the best hitters to ever play the game, Ted Williams retired as a player in 1960 and was content to enjoy promotional work for sporting goods sold at Sears. Yet he valued his privacy and savored the frequent hunting and fishing trips that took him to locales near and far. Turning down several offers to take the reins of even his former employer, the Boston Red Sox, Williams was lured to the Washington Senators after persistent and calculated pursuit by owner Bob Short, who promised a generous compensation package and knighted the Hall of Fame player as "Vice President–Manager."[22]

Named the Senators pilot as spring training commenced in February 1969, Williams arrived at a propitious moment. New rule changes that reshaped the strike zone and lowered the pitching mound augmented the magic Williams seemed to work with the Washington batters, whose team average rose from a torpid .224 in 1968—only the Yankees' .214 was worse in the AL—to .251, tying the Red Sox for third-best in the league. Williams's philosophy held that team chemistry was the simple result of winning, and Senators shortstop Ed Brinkman described his manager as "bubbl[ing] with enthusiasm and it's contagious."[23]

To the delight of Washington baseball observers, the Senators delivered under Williams's tutelage by improving twenty-one games in the win column to third place in the AL East on a record of 86–76, and attendance surged from less than 547,000 in 1968 to more than 918,000. Williams was duly rewarded for the effort by being selected by the Baseball Writers' Association of America as the Manager of the Year, one of the few times the honor was given to a skipper whose team did not finish in first place. Williams's first year as manager was clearly his best, his team's performance deteriorating in each successive season and bottoming out in 1972 at 54–100 with the Texas Rangers.

Coaching Debuts

The years 1968 and 1969 saw the introduction of a number of coaches who went on to lengthy major-league careers serving in that capacity or becoming managers. The former category includes Billy DeMars (Phillies, 1969), Harry Dunlop (Royals, 1969), Johnny Goryl (Twins, 1968, and also briefly as manager in 1980–81), Vern Hoscheit (Orioles, 1968), Elston Howard (Yankees, 1969), future hitting guru Charley Lau (Orioles, 1969), Don Leppert (Pirates, 1968), Lee Stange (Red Sox, 1969), Wayne Terwilliger (Senators, 1969), and Ozzie Virgil (Giants, 1969). Two others are worthy of special mention: Hall of Famer Joe DiMaggio was with the Athletics—at the urging of owner Charlie Finley—beginning in 1968, and the legendary Satchel Paige (Braves, 1968) was signed as a pitching instructor—a sinecure position—so that he would accumulate enough service time to qualify for a major-league pension.

As noted above, Sparky Anderson (Padres, 1969), John McNamara (Athletics, 1968), and Earl Weaver (Orioles, 1968) became coaches prior to their promotions to manager, while George Bamberger (Orioles, 1968), Roy Hartsfield (Dodgers, 1969), and Dick Howser (Yankees, 1969) later advanced to managerial positions, with varying degrees of success.

Fresh Faces on the Field

Stepping back in time a bit further, a host of players made their first appearance in a major-league uniform in 1967 but did not surpass their rookie status until

1968 or 1969. Among those who distinguished themselves were reliever Sparky Lyle (Boston), third baseman Aurelio Rodriguez (California), catcher Ray Fosse (Cleveland), pitcher Pat Dobson (Detroit), outfielder Joe Rudi (Kansas City Athletics), third baseman Graig Nettles (Minnesota), catcher Johnny Bench (Cincinnati), southpaw Jerry Koosman (New York Mets), outfielder Amos Otis (New York Mets), catcher Manny Sanguillen (Pittsburgh), and pitcher Mike Torrez (St. Louis). Two other notables had debuts in 1967 and exceeded the rookie limits that season but then firmly established themselves not long thereafter. Future Cy Young Award winner Mike Marshall (Detroit, 1967) did not play in the majors in 1968 but joined the expansion Seattle Pilots in 1969, while Hall of Fame slugger Reggie Jackson (Kansas City Athletics, 1967) became a fixture in Oakland's lineup in 1968.

Those who opened their lengthy careers in 1968 include outfielders Dusty Baker (Atlanta) and Bobby Bonds (San Francisco); future Hall of Fame manager Bobby Cox (New York Yankees); pitchers Dock Ellis (Pittsburgh) and another future Hall of Famer, Rollie Fingers (Oakland); third baseman Richie Hebner (Pittsburgh); catcher Elrod Hendricks (Baltimore); outfielder Hal McRae (Cincinnati); pitcher Andy Messersmith (California), who would become the focal point of another reserve clause dispute; outfielder Al Oliver (Pittsburgh) and

Soon to stake a claim in Oakland's tenacious lineup, Reggie Jackson went on to become one of his era's top power hitters. *National Baseball Hall of Fame Library, Cooperstown, NY.*

his Pirates teammate shortstop Freddie Patek; and catcher Ted Simmons (St. Louis). After hurling a mere three innings in 1966, Nolan Ryan joined the Mets' starting rotation in 1968 and blazed his path to Cooperstown, while across town 1968 AL Rookie of the Year Stan Bahnsen had a handful of starts in 1966 with the Yankees. Balloting for the 1968 National League rookie award was as tight as could be, with Johnny Bench edging Jerry Koosman, ten and one-half votes to nine and one-half.

Notable players launching careers in 1969 were Ron Blomberg (New York Yankees), who later became the very first designated hitter; pitcher Vida Blue (Oakland); reliever Pedro Borbón (California); outfielder–first baseman Bill Buckner (Los Angeles); catcher Rick Dempsey (Minnesota); third baseman Darrell Evans (Atlanta); future Hall of Fame catcher Carlton Fisk (Boston); outfielder George Foster (San Francisco); All-Star first baseman Steve Garvey (Los Angeles); pitcher Gary Gentry (New York Mets); outfielder César Gerónimo (Houston); southpaw Bill Lee (Boston); catcher Thurman Munson (New York Yankees), who won the 1970 American League Rookie of the Year Award; shortstop Bill Russell (Los Angeles); infielder Ted Sizemore (Los Angeles); and catcher Gene Tenace (Oakland). Kansas City outfielder Lou Piniella won honors as best rookie in the AL—the other only competitor to have a career of substance was Carlos May of the White Sox—and the Dodgers' Sizemore far outdistanced four others, including Pittsburgh's Al Oliver, to capture laurels in the NL.

As Major League Baseball began its second century of play, *Sports Illustrated* mentioned a passel of new third basemen who aspired to be the next Brooks Robinson, provided that "they don't have theirs heads taken off by sizzling line drives between [April] and October."[24] Two of them—Bill Melton of the White Sox and the Pirates' Hebner—had staying power at the hot corner, while a third, Bill Sudakis, served for eight seasons in a utility role for a number of teams. Another pair became star outfielders, Bobby Murcer with the Yankees and Amos Otis, originally with the Mets but who emerged as a catalyst after his trade to the Kansas City Royals. And Coco Laboy of the expansion Expos placed second in NL Rookie of the Year voting but was out of baseball five years later.

The 1969 season was brightened by a comeback by one of the best young sluggers, who had been tragically stopped in his tracks in August 1967. Red Sox outfielder Tony Conigliaro, already a victim of several serious injuries during his short career, suffered a horrific beaning as Boston was fighting its way to the top of the American League that summer. Struck in the left eye by an errant pitch, Conigliaro was sidelined for the entire 1968 season while attempting to regain his full eyesight. A premature comeback that year yielded only frustration for a young player who obviously needed more time to recover, but in 1969 "Tony C.," as he was affectionately known, took remarkable strides toward reclaiming both his sight and old job in right field while, just as importantly, showing little fear when pitches came in high and tight. Hitting the ball again with authority that spring bred confidence in a successful return to Fenway Park, and Conigliaro predicted that he and teammate Ken Harrelson would be "two drunken bums at the end of the year" if they celebrated with champagne each time the returnee hit a home run.[25]

There was much reason for Conigliaro to revel in his reprise—he ended 1969 batting .255 with 20 homers and 82 RBIs in 141 games—but it was a bittersweet experience. During a slump in June, he was hearing boo-birds at Fenway, and he had fallen out of favor with manager Dick Williams, claiming that the Red Sox skipper was "*trying to destroy me.*"[26] Boston dipped to third place in the AL East—no one was capable of catching the Orioles that year—and Williams was fired in late September, yet Conigliaro felt some redemption when he was named the American League Comeback Player of the Year. An even more productive season in 1970 (.266/36 HRs/116 RBIs) ostensibly proclaimed a complete recovery from his ills of the past three years, but a swift decline immediately followed in 1971 and after a three-year absence from the game, Conigliaro failed in a brief final return in 1975.

Ownership Updates

At the highest level of team executive suites, several baseball ownership changes took place. Walter O'Malley, the scourge of Brooklyn who pulled up the Dodgers' stakes and relocated to the West Coast in late 1957, promoted his thirty-year-old son, Peter, to the position of executive vice president. The move, which took place in December 1968, ensured continuity of family control over the storied franchise for decades to come.

That same month in Washington, Bob Short gained full ownership of the Senators. A trucking company and hotel magnate, Short was also a past owner of the Minneapolis Lakers of the National Basketball Association, and his résumé included the role of treasurer of the Democratic National Committee. In Charlie Finley fashion, Short assumed duties as the club's general manager and immediately began courting Ted Williams to be his manager. In addition to audaciously luring Williams out of retirement, Short would demonstrate brashness in late 1970 by trading for controversial pitcher Denny McLain and outfielder Curt Flood; neither player's performance did anything to help Washington. McLain admitted later that Short was "a delightful guy with a dynamic personality," but the owner—with a wandering eye like Finley—had bigger plans for his team and transferred the Senators to Arlington Stadium to become the Texas Rangers in 1972.[27]

On Chicago's South Side, where attendance at White Sox games was flagging in 1968 even though the club had been a pennant contender the previous season, Arthur Allyn had been the face of Sox ownership since his family's holding company assumed control of the franchise from Bill Veeck in 1961. Arthur's brother John had been a silent partner in the team since the acquisition, and in 1969 John took over full ownership from Arthur. When Milwaukee-based interests sought to purchase the Sox and transfer them from Chicago—this coming at the same time that the Seattle Pilots' imbroglio was well underway—the deal collapsed because it was unlikely most American League teams would approve the sale, and with John Allyn now in control of the team there were no guarantees that he would consent to a sale of the White Sox.

The Old Guard

The arrival of new players is always balanced by the departure of those unable to sustain a career in big-league baseball, whether they are overmatched youngsters or old hands who soldiered on for years but have finally lost the battle against time. In 1968 and 1969 a few stalwart veterans exited baseball's biggest stage.

Two Hall of Famers, both members of the 500 Home Run Club, played their final games in 1968. Eddie Mathews, a holdover from the old Boston Braves who followed the team to Milwaukee and on to Atlanta, completed his big-league journey in 1968 with the Detroit Tigers, finishing with 512 career home runs. But the loudest accolades were for Mickey Mantle, a three-time winner of the American League MVP Award and member of sixteen AL All-Star teams. As the switch-hitting author of 536 homers, he ended his career trailing only Babe Ruth, Willie Mays, and Hank Aaron in that category. On June 8, 1969, when his number 7 was retired by the Yankees, the roar of the crowd lasted for nine minutes when Mantle was introduced to more than sixty thousand admirers at Yankee Stadium. The man in full—including the tales of Mantle's carousing—would be revealed later, but on the day of his tribute he was humble in acknowledging the honor paid to him by echoing the sentiments that Lou Gehrig had expressed three decades earlier. If the "Iron Horse" considered himself "the luckiest man on the face of the earth" despite knowing that he was dying, Mantle too conveyed how fortunate he himself had been when he told the gathering, "Now I think I know how Lou Gehrig felt."[28] Mantle would be elected to the Hall of Fame in 1974, his first year of eligibility.

The other half of the Yankees' "M & M" tandem through their glory years of the 1960s also retired at the close of the 1968 campaign. Just thirty-four years old, outfielder Roger Maris spent his final two seasons with the St. Louis Cardinals following his trade from the Bronx. Maris felt lucky as well, but his reasoning was far different from that of Gehrig or Mantle. During his chase of Babe Ruth's single-season home run record in 1961, Maris was hounded by the media and vilified by those who believed the standard set by the Babe was sacrosanct. Having accomplished the feat of surpassing Ruth—and winning American League MVP honors for a second straight year—Maris was a victim of his own success and never came close to repeating his run production of that illustrious season. Broken in spirit and suffering from injuries, Maris was exiled in 1967 to St. Louis, which valued his professionalism and the contributions he made to the Cardinals in the pennant-winning seasons of 1967 and 1968. At his celebratory day before the Cardinals' final home game, Maris modestly told the crowd of more than twenty-three thousand, "I want to thank all the fans *for accepting me the way they did.*"[29] Only with the passage of time would Maris's bitterness lessen as many fans came to better appreciate his astounding home run feat and understand the personal ordeal he endured in 1961 and thereafter.

One last Yankee from New York's great dynasty who was a past AL MVP, Elston Howard, ended his career with the Boston Red Sox in 1968. A stalwart among catchers who won a pair of Gold Gloves, Howard was the first African American to appear in pinstripes, and the BoSox acquired the nine-time All-Star to help them in their drive to the pennant in 1967.

The 1968 season was the curtain call for another renowned American League slugger, Rocky Colavito. Totaling 374 homers over a fourteen-year career, the outfielder spent the majority of his time with the Cleveland Indians and Detroit Tigers, topping the thirty-home-run mark seven times. He had several short stints with the Kansas City Athletics, White Sox, Los Angeles Dodgers, and Yankees, even using his powerful arm in an emergency relief appearance for New York only weeks before playing in his final game.

The following year would mark the final games for other memorable players. Among the last of the active fabled Boys of Summer, Johnny Podres spent most of his time in the rotation of the Brooklyn and Los Angeles Dodgers, and he excelled in six World Series games, winning four of five decisions and posting a 2.11 ERA. With Detroit in 1966 and 1967, Podres was away from the majors in 1968 but then joined the expansion San Diego Padres for the first half of the 1969 campaign.

Podres's teammate, Don Drysdale, became the last Brooklynite to play in the majors. Burdened by shoulder problems, Drysdale quit in early August 1969, but by then he had already left his mark on the game. Intimidating at six-foot-five and unapologetic about moving batters away from the plate, Drysdale teamed with the great Sandy Koufax to give the Dodgers' rotation baseball's preeminent righty-lefty combination. Drysdale went on to hurl fifty-eight consecutive scoreless innings in 1968 and was inducted into the Baseball Hall of Fame in 1984.

Five-time All-Star Bill White, a smooth-fielding first baseman with St. Louis for most of his major-league career, played his final three seasons with the Phillies and retired after the 1969 season. With broadcasting experience dating back to his days with the Cardinals, White joined the New York Yankees network from 1971 to 1988 and then replaced A. Bartlett Giamatti as president of National League in 1989.

Cardinal third baseman Ken Boyer captured honors as the 1964 NL MVP in leading St. Louis to its World Series title, and, like White, was a Gold Glove winner and All-Star multiple times. Ken closed out his career in 1969 with the Dodgers after compiling a .287 lifetime average with 282 home runs and 1,141 RBIs, totals that were far ahead of his brother Clete (.242/162 HRs/654 RBIs with the Athletics, Yankees, and Braves).

Roy Face, the mainstay of the Pittsburgh Pirate bullpen in the early 1960s, pitched his final games in 1969 while wearing the uniform of the expansion Montreal Expos. The diminutive right-hander led the National League in saves three times and posted a remarkable 18–1 record in 1959.

Another long-ball threat of the early 1960s was Leon Wagner, who averaged twenty-nine homers a year from 1961 to 1966 while playing for the expansion Los Angeles Angels and the Cleveland Indians. Wagner's output declined significantly thereafter, and he played his final games in 1969 with the San Francisco Giants, his original team.

CHAPTER 9

The Year of the Pitcher, and Changes to the Rules

As major-league teams prepared for the 1968 season, the status quo held forth with regard to the primary rules governing the game, although another attempt at thwarting use of the spitball would be made. In addition, one minor bureaucratic adjustment would now be in effect: Previously, clubs were allowed to carry three players above the regular twenty-five-man limit for the opening month of the campaign, but beginning in 1968, rosters would be capped at twenty-five beginning on Opening Day. Concerning overall regulation of the game as played on the diamond, however, the relative lack of change remained a testimony to baseball's tradition and stability.

Yet hiding just below the surface of baseball's landscape was empirical data, which, when scrutinized, showed a steady year-by-year decline in American League batting averages and earned run averages since the AL's initial round of expansion in 1961. In the National League, those same averages, rather than showing a straight-line downward trend, wavered along a more desultory path following the addition of the Mets and the Colt .45s in 1962.

Not a cause of immediate alarm—perhaps because the vacillating figures in the NL may have masked the overall descent of those averages in the major leagues—a slow but progressive rise in pitching dominance could be traced to an alteration of the strike zone originally proposed in 1961 and implemented in 1963, which redefined it as extending from "[the] top of the armpit to the bottom of the knee," a subtle yet discernible change from the 1949 definition that had set the parameters "between the batter's arm-pits and the top of his knees."[1] The baseball commissioner at the time of the revision, Ford Frick, grew concerned about the spike in runs scored in the expanded American League, where the 1960 average of 677 runs per club leapt to 734 in the year in which the Los Angeles Angels and the new Washington Senators joined the circuit. In the National League in 1962, runs scored per team experienced a more modest increase over pre-expansion clubs, from 700 to 728, and even though the AL average in 1962 dropped to 718, Frick was convinced that such totals spelled doom for the future of quality pitching.

Frick's belief was myopic, but rashly intent on nipping this perceived problem in the bud, he successfully lobbied the Rules Committee to assist pitchers by enlarging the strike zone. The results may have been more to the commissioner's liking in the American League than in the National, but by the end of the 1967 season there was no doubt that both leagues were in the throes of an offensive swoon. The falloff of offensive output and corresponding drop in earned run averages are shown in table 9.1 for the NL, and table 9.2 for the AL, with a more pronounced downturn evident in the latter.

At the conclusion of 1967 the league batting average of .249 in the Senior Circuit equaled the second lowest such figure since expansion, while the league ERA of 3.38 was only marginally above the ERA in 1963, the first year using the revised strike zone. In the Junior Circuit the .236 league batting average continued on a straight downward line and was twenty points lower than the first year of expansion, while the league ERA of 3.23 was nearly a full run less than it had been in 1961 (4.02).

"The ultimate ridiculousness," according to writer Leonard Koppett, "was made vivid by the 1966, 1967, and 1968 All-Star Games," in which a total of seven runs were scored. But this observation augmented Koppett's own earlier analysis citing a range of factors that collectively had a negative impact on batters. Broadly stating "improved pitching"—meaning the onset of relief specialists, more knowledgeable pitch selection, and a wider selection of pitches to

Table 9.1.   National League Data, Season by Season

Year	Number of Teams	League Batting Average	Total Hits–Hits Per Team	Total Runs–Runs Per Team	League ERA
1961	8	.262	11,029–1,379	5,600–700	4.03
1962	10	.261	14,453–1,445	7,278–728	3.94
1963	10	.245	13,434–1,343	6,181–618	3.29
1964	10	.254	14,032–1,403	6,517–652	3.54
1965	10	.249	13,794–1,379	6,558–656	3.54
1966	10	.256	14,202–1,420	6,624–662	3.61
1967	10	.249	13,698–1,370	6,218–622	3.38
1968	**10**	**.243**	**13,351–1,335**	**5,577–558**	**2.99**
1969	12	.250	16,461–1,372	7,890–658	3.59
1970	12	.258	17,151–1,429	8,771–731	4.05
1971	12	.252	16,590–1,383	7,601–633	3.47
1972	12	.248	15,683–1,307	7,265–605	3.45

Source: *The ESPN Baseball Encyclopedia* (New York: Sterling, 2007), 76–98.

Table 9.2.   American League Data, Season by Season

Year	Number of Teams	League Batting Average	Total Hits–Hits Per Team	Total Runs–Runs Per Team	League ERA
1960	8	.255	10,689–1,336	5,414–677	3.87
1961	10	.256	14,037–1,404	7,342–734	4.02
1962	10	.255	14,068–1,407	7,183–718	3.97
1963	10	.247	13,609–1,361	6,599–660	3.63
1964	10	.247	13,637–1,364	6,607–661	3.63
1965	10	.242	13,158–1,316	6,388–639	3.46
1966	10	.240	13,005–1,301	6,276–628	3.44
1967	10	.236	12,766–1,277	5,992–599	3.23
1968	**10**	**.230**	**12,359–1,236**	**5,532–553**	**2.98**
1969	12	.246	16,120–1,343	7,960–663	3.62
1970	12	.250	16,404–1,367	8,109–676	3.71
1971	12	.247	15,957–1,330	7,472–623	3.46
1972	12	.239	14,751–1,229	6,441–537	3.06

Source: *The ESPN Baseball Encyclopedia* (New York: Sterling, 2007), 77–101.

choose from, including the slider—that worked to the hitters' detriment, Koppett also postulated that fatigue from long-distance travel, the increased number of night games, newer stadiums that replaced older—and smaller—ballparks, and an emphasis on defense were the among the answers to his rhetorical question: "Whatever became of the .300 hitter?"[2]

The nadir was about to be reached in both the NL and AL, a point at which sea changes would be instituted to offset the effects of what occurred in the "Year of the Pitcher."

Reaching Rock-Bottom in 1968

As spring training was underway in early 1968 at least one general manager and one scout were aware of the recent offensive struggles. Executive Paul Richards of Atlanta proposed moving the pitching mound back several feet in order to increase the distance to home plate, but Frank Lane, scouting at the time for the Orioles, suggested a less radical amendment. "By reducing the incline of the mound just five inches . . . the hitter would be able to better follow the ball," reasoned Lane.[3]

With the mound at its present fifteen-inch height and no authorized rule changes on the horizon, several teams were getting a foretaste of what was to follow beyond Opening Day. The Mets scored two runs or fewer in ten of their first fifteen exhibition contests, and their crosstown rivals, the Yankees, failed to produce a run for more than twenty-three straight innings midway through their Grapefruit League schedule. Once the regular season commenced, and as if to validate the coming drought of runs across all of baseball, the visiting Mets and Astros locked up in a scoreless duel for an agonizing twenty-three innings on April 15 before the six-hour affair mercifully ended when Houston plated the only run of the contest on a bases-loaded error committed by New York's shortstop, Al Weis, in the bottom of the twenty-fourth frame.

The paucity of runs in the Astrodome was a prelude to what followed for the rest of the season. On May 9, Jim "Catfish" Hunter of the Oakland Athletics threw the first perfect game in the American League in forty-six years by blanking the Minnesota Twins, 4–0, which some may view as an anomalous, one-game feat. However, over the course of the season, a trio of pitchers accumulated streaks of more than forty consecutive scoreless innings. Cleveland's Luis Tiant (forty-two innings), Bob Gibson of St. Louis (forty-eight), and the Dodgers' Don Drysdale (a record fifty-eight) were unrelenting in their ability to keep the opposition off the scoreboard over the long haul, with Gibson ending 1968 as the National League winner of both the Cy Young and Most Valuable Player awards for his 1.12 ERA, the lowest in the live-ball era. Another singular achievement was Denny McLain's total of thirty-one victories, the first thirty-plus season since 1934, which earned him dual Cy Young and MVP awards in the AL.

Setting a new record in 1968 for consecutive scoreless innings pitched, the intimidating Don Drysdale was humbly forced into retirement by injury the following year. *National Baseball Hall of Fame Library, Cooperstown, NY.*

As the 1968 campaign played out during America's turbulent summer, "batting anemia which suddenly ranks as baseball's big headache" was thought by Detroit manager Mayo Smith to be a short-term problem that would be cured when "the hitters eventually catch up with the pitchers." With the season barely two months old, columnist Rex Lardner complained that "the pitchers are ruining the game," citing as evidence a comparison of the first forty-five games played in 1968 versus the same period of the prior season and finding that the "National League's collective batting average was down by eight points, the American League's by 12."[4] With tongue in cheek but nonetheless intending to emphasize the dystopia into which baseball was heading, Lardner's essay included a fictitious account of a game that featured but one base hit as the contest's only offensive production. As if to make Lardner a prophet, the Chicago Cubs during one stretch in mid-June went forty-eight innings without scoring a run and suffered three 1–0 losses in the process, and on August 26, a record-tying seven shutouts were thrown in the majors.

Lardner's mockery aside, the alarmists were being proven correct on actual playing fields, and as the decline in hitting continued, the *Sporting News* revealed that fans, especially those in the National League where Gibson and Drysdale were wreaking havoc, appeared to be voting with their feet. Although overall attendance in American League stadiums was nearly identical to that in the first half of 1967, NL parks experienced a drop of 10 percent. The 1968 All-Star Game played in Houston's Astrodome reflected the utter domination of pitching—even though Gibson did not appear in the contest—as both squads produced a total of just eight hits in the National League's 1–0 victory.

Nor was hitting becoming the only scarce commodity. For all the publicity the frontline pitchers were garnering in the media, a larger number of lesser-known hurlers were "savor[ing] success for a short time and then silently fad[ing] into the obscurity of El Paso or Waterbury." In some respects this was hardly a new phenomenon—flash-in-the-pan performers are omnipresent in every sport—but what raised concern in the era of increasingly superior pitching was the headlong rush made by many teams to capitalize on the trend toward dominant pitching at the expense of the health of youthful, newly signed pitchers who were now subjected to "intolerable pressures" to quickly reach the major-league level.[5] Those pressures were exacerbated by a lack of competent coaching in the minor leagues as well as deficient—or nonexistent—medical care to tend to young pitchers' ailments. The struggle to reach the big-league stage, fraught with peril to begin with, was even more treacherous when the risk of permanent health problems was taken into account.

At a gathering of baseball's Executive Council in early September 1968, major-league club owners and even commissioner William Eckert took note of

A superb athlete, Bob Gibson of the Cardinals enjoyed one of the most dominant seasons of any pitcher, ever. In 1968 he posted a 1.12 ERA over the course of three-hundred-plus innings. *National Baseball Hall of Fame Library, Cooperstown, NY.*

the disturbing plunge in batting. The issue of "the imbalance between current pitching and hitting" had been forwarded by Eckert to the Rules Committee and the teams' general managers for their consideration as to how to address the problem.[6] Walter O'Malley of the Dodgers blamed some of the newer, more spacious ballparks for robbing hitters of home runs that cleared the fences of older stadiums, and although he may have been correct to a limited degree, reviving baseball's offense required more attention than recalibrating the distances of outfield walls from home plate.

Mere days after the Executive Council meeting, Detroit's Denny McLain benefited from a late Tiger rally to register his thirtieth win of the season, becoming the first pitcher since Dizzy Dean in 1934 to reach that plateau. Praised by umpire Bill Kinnamon for "[throwing] more different pitches for strikes than anybody I ever saw," McLain was unquestionably due the accolades he received, but heading into the same mid-September weekend on which he reached the coveted milestone, lists of the AL and NL averages showed that a quintet of National Leaguers—Pete Rose (.342), Matty Alou (.330), Alex Johnson (.320), Felipe Alou (.312), and Tito Francona (.305)—

were the only hitters in all of Major League Baseball above the .300 mark as the season wound down.[7] Rose retained his lead and won the NL batting crown despite slipping to .336, but Boston's Carl Yastrzemski (.3006) barely climbed over .300 as the lone AL hitter to do so. Meanwhile, seven pitchers posted earned run averages of less than 2.00, with the Cardinals' Bob Gibson's 1.12 the best in the majors.

In the final accounting for baseball's top awards, McLain in the American League and Gibson in the National League took home their circuit's Most Valuable Player Award and, unanimously for both, the Cy Young Award. Gibson edged Rose for MVP laurels, but McLain swept all twenty first-place ballots for the AL honor to outpace his batterymate, Bill Freehan. While Gibson proudly noted that his greatest feat in the "Year of the Pitcher" was throwing twenty-eight complete games in thirty-four starts, McLain, who also was tabbed the *Sporting News* "Man of the Year," was more absorbed with his concert appearances and intended to cash in on his rising stock value by demanding a $100,000 salary for 1969, finally settling for around $60,000. And as Gibson continued his stoic, workmanlike approach to his pitching assignments and won at least sixteen games in each of the next four seasons to build up his Hall of Fame credentials, McLain had but one more good year remaining in his ailing right arm, thereafter tumbling into a multitude of troubles inside and outside of baseball.

Denny McLain, the last of baseball's thirty-game winners. *National Baseball Hall of Fame Library, Cooperstown, NY.*

—ɯ—

The upper hand of pitching that had turned offense back to that of the dead-ball era needed to be reined in. The toll on composite 1968 major-league averages gave the season a curious resemblance to 1908.[8] Of all games played in 1968, 340 of them—or 21 percent of the total—were shutouts, the highest percentage in sixty years, and 82 of those contests were by scores of 1–0. The combined average runs per game for both teams was 6.84, also the lowest in sixty years, and the composite major-league batting average of .236 was also the worst since 1908. Home runs per game were only 1.23, an average that was marginally above the 0.98 of 1946, when many major leaguers were adjusting to their return from military service. If Ford Frick's intention was to take the sting out of hitting and run production, the fruits of his effort via the 1963 rule change he instigated were by now abundantly clear.

Fears of dilution of major-league pitching resulting from the expansion of 1961 and 1962 were also proved to be unfounded. In fact the aggregate major-league batting average was incredibly consistent from 1955 through 1962: A .258 average was logged each year, with the minor exception of 1959 and 1960, when the averages were .257 and .255, respectively. Bemoaning "the present hitting famine that has persisted since 1963," the *Sporting News* urged adjusting the strike zone to its boundaries prior to Frick's 1963 edict, and the publication further recommended a reduction in the height of the pitcher's mound, although it neglected to specify the number of inches.[9]

The offensive drought brought attention to an unsettling trend that was clearly more than a one- or two-season aberration. In their study of all aspects of pitching, Bill James and Rob Neyer blamed batting woes on the rise in popularity at this time of a variation on the fastball as yet another weapon that pitchers had at their disposal. Citing two-seam and four-seam fastballs—which sink and rise—that had been used earlier with little distinction until Curt Simmons of the Philadelphia Phillies employed them beginning around 1950, James and Neyer observed, "[T]here is little evidence of other pitchers throwing the two fastballs until the mid-1960s, when the practice suddenly exploded." Using both types of fastballs for profit, the authors noted, were a group of pitchers who began their service in the major leagues at that time, notably future Cooperstown inductees Steve Carlton, Fergie Jenkins, Jim Palmer, Tom Seaver, and Don Sutton. The forkball, later to be recast as the split-finger fastball, lost its appeal—"by the late 1960s, virtually the only people left who threw [it] were old guys like Elroy Face and Diego Segui," according to James and Neyer—but the slider, once viewed as an effeminate pitch by hardliners such as Sal Maglie, was growing in popularity at this time. When coupled with the nascent but increasing emphasis on specialized relief pitching—by 1970, complete games would be outnumbered by saves for the first time in the major leagues—the currency of the sinking fastball, or sinker, and the slider spelled more trouble for batters.[10]

As the pendulum of advantage swung to the side of pitching, Leonard Koppett promoted his argument, made shortly after the conclusion of the 1968 World Series, that the main culprit was the strike zone change of 1963. "Some specific steps to restore balance—to bring back the nine-runs-a-game average that was normal until 1963—must be taken," he wrote. "The strike zone is a good place to begin."[11]

Proactively addressing baseball's offensive woes, Walter O'Malley announced a month after the World Series that his Los Angeles Dodgers were going to move home plate at Dodger Stadium ten feet closer to the outfield fences in the hope of stimulating the Dodger bats. The White Sox, Braves, Athletics, Phillies, and expansion Kansas City Royals followed suit by altering outfield distances in their respective ballparks for 1969, with the ChiSox changing the power alleys by a modest five feet but encouraging dead-pull hitters by moving the left- and right-field corners in by seventeen feet. Enlivening the baseball itself, a plea made by the Orioles' Frank Robinson, would assuredly help hitters rebound from the precipitous drop in home run production throughout the game. So anemic had the long ball become that total home run output was down by more than one thousand since 1962. In 1968 half of the major-league teams hit fewer than one hundred homers, adding fuel to the argument that the national pastime had become a bore.

The Battle against the Spitball

As much a part of the game as bats, balls, and bases, cheating has been a bugbear of the national pastime since its inception, as players have used various means to gain an edge over their opponents. For some pitchers, the employment of a scuffed baseball or a ball to which a foreign substance has been applied became a stock-in-trade, and to this day pitchers are still being caught loading up the ball. Although the spitball was banned in 1920, its prohibition suffered from lax enforcement.

In 1967 baseball attempted to crack down severely on violators by mandating umpires to eject pitchers who ignored the warning not to touch their mouth or lips while on the mound or within the eighteen-foot pitching circle. The major thrust of the rule update was to rid the game of foreign substances and speed up playing time of contests that dragged on because of running disputes instigated by batters asking for umpires to check the ball before the pitcher delivered it. Although such psychological warfare is inherent in the matchup between pitcher and batter, the pace of the game suffered.

The Playing Rules Committee in 1968 lessened the penalty to simply forcing the umpire to call an automatic ball or a balk, unless the batter reached first base and any other runners on base safely advanced one base on the illegal pitch. Also codified was the outlawing of a pitcher spitting on either of his hands or his glove. Regardless of any legislation or subsequent amendments, at least one hardline manager believed the specific rules would all be in vain. "You're not going to stop pitchers from throwing the spitball, no matter what you do," argued Cub manager Leo Durocher.[12]

One pitcher reputed to make good use of the spitball was Don Drysdale of the Los Angeles Dodgers, as if his six-foot-five physique and tendency to throw at batters were not intimidating enough. A teammate of Drysdale and fellow Dodger Bill Singer—another pitcher known for loading up the ball—was Phil Regan, who became the center of controversy in the summer of 1968 when he was cited by home-plate umpire Chris Pelekoudas for throwing spitters three times in an August 18 contest. The umpire claimed further that Regan's cap contained Vaseline, but Pelekoudas did not receive the backing of National League president Warren Giles, who exonerated Regan after interviewing him. Pelekoudas complained that although umpires had been instructed to enforce the rules, league officials were reluctant to support them when disputes arose, and the umpire said he would no longer perform a physical search for foreign substances.

One future Hall of Fame pitcher who would reap his own share of notoriety was at this time in the employ of the San Francisco Giants. Established as a member of the Giants' starting rotation by the end of the 1960s, Gaylord Perry galvanized his reputation for using the spitter especially in the following decade by frustrating batters—and umpires—with the antics and gestures he performed on the mound, always planting the seed of doubt as to whether he was actually picking up a hidden substance from his head, cap, or uniform, or simply trying to psych out the batter.

The futility of nabbing pitchers thought to be doctoring the ball endures, and just as Prohibition was ineffective in stemming the consumption of alcoholic beverages, so too the ban on the spitball "merely makes lawbreakers of otherwise law-abiding folks and hypocrites of the rest."[13] Some pitchers operating outside the bounds of fairness are caught on occasion. However, other rule changes of 1969 were intended to help batters, and one of these amendments literally leveled the pitching mound, if not the playing field.

Redefining the Strike Zone (Again) and Lowering the Mound

When a call to action was finally sounded to pull baseball out of its batting slump, the game's executives undertook a two-pronged effort to be made effective in 1969. The first of these endeavors shortened the top of the strike zone from the batter's shoulders to the armpits, with the lower boundary raised to the top of the batter's knees. This reduction of the strike zone meant batters could be more selective at the plate rather than having to swing at offerings less to their liking. Bob Gibson, completely overwhelming throughout 1968, would be very critical of the new strike zone because, in his opinion, "suddenly there was no such thing as a high strike."[14] Pitchers accustomed to getting calls in the upper and lower stretches of the strike zone were now to be disappointed with the revision.

The second measure served to lower the pitching mound from its height of fifteen inches, a standard in place since the early 1900s, to ten inches. Because even this regulation was loosely policed, some teams tailored the height of the mound in their home ballpark to the benefit of their pitching staff, such as the Phillies' use of a short mound that benefited their ace, Jim Bunning, who used more of a sidearm delivery. The change to the ten-inch mound meant that umpires would have to be more vigilant to ensure its correct height.

This five-inch reduction meant that as a pitcher delivered the ball, his front foot would touch the slope of the mound sooner than he was accustomed to, and this change required a period of adjustment. Jim Palmer of the Orioles and Houston's Denny Lemaster were two pitchers who were challenged in adapting to the new mound, with Palmer further noting the difficulty in making corrections because of his extreme overhand motion. "The lowered mound flattened out wicked curveballs and sliders and took the hop off all but the elite of fastballs," observed historian John Thorn, and Dan Osinski of the White Sox, referring to Chicago's staff of low-ball hurlers, felt that sinkerball pitchers would "find the lower pitching plane to their advantage." For Gibson's part, he believed that the mound change affected him minimally because he did not depend on an overhand curveball with its attendant drop as it approached the plate, but other hurlers, like his teammate, Nelson Briles, were challenged to embrace the new mound. San Francisco ace Juan Marichal "struggled to keep his pitches down" and injured a rib cage muscle in his seventh start of the 1969 season. Marichal had to make an accommodation in his trademark high leg kick because of the lowered mound. Longtime AL hurler Camilo Pascual conceded that he was "having trouble forcing [his] arm and body down onto the ball," which prompted him to consider "go[ing] with the side-arm fastball more than in the past."[15]

Other far-flung suggestions for improving the languishing offenses that were not implemented include Atlanta general manager Paul Richards's proposal to move the pitching rubber two to five feet further away from home plate, and another, courtesy of an engineer at the University of Illinois, theorized that widening the angle of the playing field at home plate from 90 degrees to 96 degrees, "would increase the probable hitting area [i.e., fair territory] by 7%."[16]

Whether the rule changes would help or hinder batters remained to be seen as the 1969 season opened. Major League Baseball took a step toward improving the performance of umpiring that year when both the American and National leagues supported the establishment of their own umpiring school. Bill Kinnamon, an AL ump who was no longer able to serve due to arthritic hip problems, was charged with creating instructional sessions for the new academy. Central to those lessons was Kinnamon's tenet that the duties of the home plate umpire—the most important on the field—should be carried out as efficiently as possible, and the modified strike zone of 1969 certainly became a factor. "We pioneered in using a pitching machine for plate instruction," he later explained, emphasizing further that although the strike zone was taught as defined in the rule book, he "squeezed the strike zone" as he worked his way from lower to upper minor leagues—in other words, as the overall quality of play improved at different levels.[17]

Years later, future Hall of Fame umpire Doug Harvey wrote that he did not want to "cheat in any direction" in order to favor the pitcher, so as to better his own chance of obtaining an umpiring job in the majors. Yet after 1969 "the strike zone progressively shrunk in practice, [and] strikes above the waist were seldom called" in subsequent years as batters adjusted and home run production rose. But another noticeable difference quickly became evident when some players discovered that the baseballs themselves "feel much, much harder" than they did in the "Year of the Pitcher."[18] Taken collectively, the agents of change delivered the prescription that baseball sought to end its hitting slump.

1969—The Year of the Big Bang

The lowering of the pitching mound, in the physical sense, was in stark contrast to the heightened expectation of the opening of a fresh and very different baseball season. Expansion teams, divisional formats, rules changes, and a celebration of baseball's centennial were all to be presided over by a new commissioner, and the sweeping reform in so many aspects of the national pastime impressed as nothing short of revolutionary. When "Play ball!" was shouted in the dozen Opening Day venues that inaugurated the 1969 campaign, more than 401,000 fans clicked the turnstiles, surpassing by 64,700 admissions the old record set in 1960.

After roughly one month of play, the early evidence indicated that the rules changes, alterations to the outfield distance at several stadiums, and a livelier baseball had pitchers back on their heels. A host of batsmen who struggled through 1968 were raising their averages with ostensible impunity, and formerly punchless teams like the White Sox and Dodgers were flexing their muscles to the delight of everyone except the pitchers against whom all the changes were initiated. One pitcher, Ray Sadecki of the Giants, made a sobering observation that once the tally of improved offense was taken at season's end and position players began to ask for huge raises based on vastly improved performance, "Then the owners will be sorry they lowered the mound, shortened the fences, and narrowed the strike zone."[19]

The season continued to unfold as hoped, and baseball's report card at the midway point of the campaign showed excellent marks. On average, scoring in the American League was up by almost 1.5 runs per game over 1968, and in the National League the run increase was 1.7 per game. Strikeouts per game were down marginally in the AL—and actually up in the NL—but this may be attributed to batters taking the opportunity to swing for shorter fences and take advantage of the more animated baseball.

At the end of the 1969 season baseball breathed a tentative sigh after the maiden voyage of the modern divisional era. Run production per game—at 8.16—was at its best level since 1962, although this average was still short of runs per game compared to each year of the 1950s. Composite batting averages for both leagues rose from 1968's .237 to .248, and home runs per team increased from an average of 100 in 1968 to 130.[20] Bearing the brunt of the revived batting were the pitchers, whose ERAs rose from 2.98 in the AL and 2.99 in the NL to 3.62 and 3.59, respectively. The run-scoring improvement was welcome, but it remained to be seen if the trend would continue. And in 1970 the upswing gained momentum when batting averages rose four more points to .250 in the AL and eight more to .258 in the NL. A nominal increase in ERA occurred in the AL, to 3.71, but in the NL it spiked to 4.05, nearly half a run higher. The gamble taken in shrinking the strike zone and lowering the pitching mound appeared to invigorate hitting as had been hoped.

Shortly after the Mets' stunning World Series triumph, commissioner Bowie Kuhn was presented with a study that compared offensive performance in the first half of the 1969 season versus the second half. The analysis was undertaken by Kuhn's assistant, Cal Gauss, to determine whether hitting and runs had increased from Opening Day in 1969 until mid-July because of the effects of expansion and the strike zone/pitching mound changes, and whether pitching caught up with hitting in the second half of the season to cause a decrease in offensive output. The research provided a corroboration of sorts to a *Sports Illustrated* article as well as a rebuttal to another story in that same publication. The first one, from May 12, titled "Here Come the Hitters—Maybe," sounded a cautionary note implying that once the pitchers adjusted to the rules revisions and made up for time lost when spring camps opened late because of the labor dispute, they would regain an edge over the batters. By midsummer, the edition of August 4 trumpeted: "Baseball Booms Again," a sanguine feature that praised, among other things, the inflated major-league home run output.[21]

Gauss found that the thrill of the long ball was ultimately a red herring that veiled the actual slippage in offensive output in the second half of 1969 across the combined leagues' batting average (from .249 to .247), hits per game (from 16.8 to 16.7), runs per game (from 8.32 to 7.97), and home runs per game (from 1.63 to 1.58). There had been an initial boom, but the question of its staying power was causing concern.

"There can be little question that the offensive-defensive balance reverted back to the latter in the second half of the 1969 season," Gauss informed Kuhn, prompting the commissioner to brainstorm ways of heading off another swoon like the one experienced after the 1963 strike zone change.[22] Kuhn acknowledged use of a pinch hitter in place of the pitcher among the possibilities suitable to averting another offensive stall.

Kuhn's chief assistant, Joseph Reichler, also expressed reservations about the supposedly improved hitting production in 1969 because it came on the heels of a season so dominated by pitching. Reichler pointed out to the commissioner that batting and run totals "are nowhere near the levels that were normal from 1921 to 1963, except for the years 1942–46 when we had war-time baseball."[23]

Even before the first pitch was thrown in 1969, movement was afoot to allow pitchers their rightful place on the mound but prevent them from stepping to the plate. Relatively few hurlers were able to avoid embarrassing themselves with a bat in their hands, and most pitchers were fated to bat .200 or worse. Corrective measures had to be taken before baseball fell out of favor with fans who expected more hitting and scoring to retain their interest.

"We Must Supply More Action"

Bob Gibson, a superb athlete whose best years included batting averages of .303 (1970), .263 (1962), .246 (1969) and .240 (1965), and Earl Wilson, who belted thirty-five home runs in 740 at-bats over the course of his major-league career, were two pitchers who proved they could be forces at the plate. Twice in his career Don Drysdale launched seven homers in a season, including the 1965 campaign when he accounted for almost 10 percent of the Dodgers' paltry team total of seventy-eight home runs. But such exceptions could not redeem the failures of the overwhelming majority of pitchers who were simply lost at the plate.

By 1969 the commissioner's office had solid evidence that pitchers literally could not hit their weight in the two years prior to the divisional split in each league. Juxtaposed against this unfortunate data was a shorter series of figures indicating that pinch hitters could hit roughly seventy points higher than ordinary, woebegone pitchers (see table 9.3).

Table 9.3.   Batting Averages of Pitchers versus Pinch Hitters

	1967 AL	1967 NL	1968 AL	1968 NL
Pitchers	.139	.137	.131	.134
Pinch Hitters	.209	.200	.218	.202

Source: Papers of Bowie Kuhn, National Baseball Hall of Fame.

A memorandum to Bowie Kuhn summarized the milieu of the era and baseball's predicament:

> We are in the midst of an age of jet propulsion, supersonic speed, violent uprising and youth rebellion. As you know, football and basketball and hockey are sports more geared to this type of instant and violent action. I believe it's not enough to simply say that our game is one of finesse, drama and suspense, aimed more to entertain the fans. We must supply more action because the public demands it. What is the best inducer of action? Bat and ball contact. When a batter hits a ball, it causes action in base running and fielding. There is little action when the pitcher monotonously keeps striking out the batter [opposing pitcher at bat]. Few pitchers capture the imagination of the public. Hitters do.[24]

The idea of a pinch hitter coming to the plate each time the pitcher was scheduled to bat drew closer attention near the end of the 1960s. The role of the pinch hitter was deemed important enough that the White Sox were preparing rookie Gail Hopkins in 1968 to serve as a pinch-hit specialist in the way that Jerry Lynch (.264 lifetime) and Smoky Burgess (.285 lifetime) had performed for many years. In his early duties coming off the bench Hopkins was 3-for-10 as a pinch hitter and impressed Sox manager Eddie Stanky to the extent that he was willing to hold a roster spot for the youngster who would rarely appear as a defensive player.

Advocating for a permanent pinch hitter was former Dodger slugger Duke Snider, who, while scouting for the San Diego Padres, reported that he saw several players who hit well but were not able to play full-time in the field. "The day of the substitute pinch-hitter is coming," he predicted, adding that permanent pinch hitters would add a specialist-related dimension to baseball and lengthen the careers of players like Mickey Mantle who were still capable of batting but were hard-pressed due to age or injury to play adequately on defense.[25]

Purists like American League president Joe Cronin, however, bristled at the notion of adding a tenth man to the lineup, believing it would "take something away from the traditional grand strategy of the game," in large part because the "battle of wits between managers, which I'm sure the spectators enjoy, would be virtually eliminated." Cronin, who was sixty-two years old when he made this statement, was content to let baseball plod along with the status quo, but the energetic commissioner—Kuhn was twenty years Cronin's junior—felt that adding a designated hitter (DH) would prove to fans that "we were finally awake." Variations of the DH were being used in five minor leagues by 1969, according to Kuhn, and the current head of the new expansion Seattle Pilots, Dewey Soriano, had been president of the Pacific Coast League in 1961 when that circuit adopted the DH as a "radical change" in order "to make the game more entertaining."[26]

When the 1969 spring training exhibition season opened, approval had been given for all teams to use the DH, but—perhaps not surprisingly—there were differences between rules to be used by American League teams and those in the National League. Inconsistencies in the number of pinch hitters and pinch runners, as well as the number of times they could appear in a game, led to much frustration and confusion. White Sox manager Al Lopez complained that the introduction of a tenth man was going to cause problems because the revised strike zone and lowered pitching mound were already major changes to which players needed to become acclimated. Lopez was willing to employ the DH "most of the time" in the exhibition games, but he also had a duty to ensure that his regular pitchers spent time at bat so that they would be ready—relatively speaking—when the regular season began rather than devote too much effort to an experiment. Lopez's crosstown counterpart, Leo Durocher of the Cubs, at first was open-minded about the trials, saying, "I'm all for progress, and if some of the people seem to think this is a step forward, then I see no harm in giving it a try." But in an exhibition game against California when a National League umpire erroneously allowed the Angels an illegal substitution but denied the Cubs a similar move, Durocher was livid. "These rules are going in my wastebasket," fumed Durocher, who vowed to abandon further trials of baseball's latest experiment as several other NL managers pledged to follow suit.[27]

Most managers were cool to the whole concept because they believed it compromised game strategy that they had learned and used their entire career, and one columnist opined that the performance of the pinch hitters, which was hardly awe-inspiring, might be attributed to a psychological barrier that made it "hard to get into the game" for players also accustomed to being in the field on defense. As the spring-training schedule ran its course, data were being compiled to determine how effective the pinch hitters were in virtual comparison with pitchers assumed to be their typical poorly hitting selves had they batted under regular conditions. After roughly half of the exhibition games had been played using the DH, Joseph Reichler of the commissioner's office estimated that projected out to a full season, the pinch hitter would produce a tepid .219 batting average, 13 home runs, and 68 RBIs, "not too good," he confessed, but immediately qualified this assessment by stating, "but not too bad considering a number of the designated pinch hitters were youngsters who probably will be back in the minor leagues this season."[28]

When the final figures were gathered across the seventy-three games in which the DH was used, the batting average of .219 (109 hits in 497 at-bats) was complemented by seventeen doubles, four triples, ten home runs, and sixty-one RBIs, very close to Reichler's projection.[29] Five NL teams opted out completely from the experiment, but of the other seven clubs, three showed excellent DH averages, with the new Montreal Expos leading the pack at .353 (12-for-34), followed by the Dodgers (.308 on 4-for-14) and San Diego (.304 on 7-for-23). In the AL the Angels (.382 on 15-for-39) and Orioles (.344 on 11-for-32) showed the most clout, but half the league posted numbers that mirrored any run-of-the-mill pitcher with a bat in this hands.

Yet the trial was hardly a total failure. Some players who served as the designated hitter that spring would also appear in that role years later when the DH was officially instituted in 1973. Hank Aaron, Harmon Killebrew, Rod Carew, Don Baylor, and Frank Howard would be called to duty just as they had been in March 1969. More evidence of the success of the DH, albeit in the minor leagues, was found in the International League, where use of the designated hitter in 1969 not only spared poor-hitting pitchers from embarrassing trips to the plate but sent to bat in their place DHs who were likely to bat around .270. "The figures show that not only is the hitting improved, but the pitchers last through more complete games and the fans get more action," reported *Sports Illustrated* in early August, and a further bonus was realized because "the use of Designated Hitters has cut as much as 10 minutes off the average times of games." All told, eighty-nine pitchers in the International League took the mound yet never stepped to the plate.[30]

Sportswriters were hardly the only people taking notice of the offensive boost inherent in the DH. Oakland Athletics owner Charlie Finley, never one to pass up the chance to enliven the game in whatever form such an endeavor would take, sent his New York Yankees counterpart, Michael Burke, a newspaper article in which columnist David Condon of the *Chicago Tribune* cited his willingness to ignore the "howls from traditionalists" who preferred a perpetuation of the current condition of pitchers pretending to be hitters and instead cast his lot with those in favor of a designated hitter.[31]

"Baseball is dying on the vine—only because we owners do not realize what the fans enjoy," Finley vented to Burke. "Baseball fans want ACTION and plenty of it. Other sports realize what their fans want and have taken action to provide it. We in baseball don't seem to give a damn." Burke, in his reply to Finley, decried the negativity expressed over the DH issue by many attendees of a recent meeting of general managers, especially in light of the .321 batting average of the DH at the Yankees' Triple-A farm team in Syracuse. "I personally believe we should make every effort to have the [DH] rule adopted by the Major Leagues for the 1970 season," implored Burke.[32]

Regardless of the urgings of proponents like Finley and Burke, Major League Baseball would not employ the DH until 1973, and then only in the American League. The delay in its adoption meant that pitcher Dean Chance of the Cleveland Indians, whose legendary ineptness at bat should have single-handedly swayed the hidebound attitudes of many baseball executives, was given the opportunity to redeem himself and his pathetic .042 batting average of 1969 when he was with the Minnesota Twins. The next season Chance batted .071, his best showing in five years, yet he provided still more fodder for the AL, at least, to consider heeding the call of Finley and Burke.

Other Rules Issues

The modern evolution of the relief pitcher rescued some hurlers from the obscurity of the bullpen and put them in the role of today's indispensable closer. As the value of a pitcher who was capable of shutting down opponents' bats at the end of a game came to be increasingly clear, especially in the post–World War II era, the save was devised to acknowledge the deeds of a reliever who maintained his team's margin of victory.

Kept on an unofficial basis by the *Sporting News* beginning in 1960 thanks to the efforts of baseball writer Jerome Holtzman, saves received their rightful place among baseball statistics when the Scoring Rules Committee in December 1968 sanctioned his definition of a save as being awarded to a pitcher who "holds the lead for the remainder of the game, provided he is not credited with the victory." The value of the save became adulterated when some relievers were given credit for closing out a game in which their team had a commanding lead, so the criteria for awarding a save were eventually refined to include size of the lead inherited by the reliever as well as the number of innings he pitched. Nonetheless, the save became a barometer for gauging the value of relief pitchers and provided them with a statistic "to argue their worth at contract time."[33]

Another change in earned-run scoring adopted at this time was intended to penalize ineffective pitchers coming out of the bullpen. Relievers would now be held responsible for the runs they personally surrendered regardless of how those runs were charged to the ERA of the team. As the Minnesota Twins' 1969 media guide tried to explain,

> This new rule puts a new light on those occasions when a relief pitcher enters a game with two out and after an error or two. Under the old scoring rule, the reliefer [*sic*] could not be charged with an

earned-run under those circumstances no matter how many runs he subsequently gave up that inning. Now, runs scored by batters who reach base off the reliefer [*sic*] will be charged as earned on that pitcher's record.[34]

These scenarios could create slight differences between the aggregate team ERA and those of some individual pitchers, but the rule change would remove the unfairness that previously existed when a reliever had a bad outing and walked away from it with little or no impact to his earned-run average.

In addition to the save and ERA amendments, other scoring regulations were put into effect in 1969. As a follow-up to the 1967 ruling on batting average and slugging average, which mandated 3.1 plate appearances for all contests on the schedule, Major League Baseball adopted qualifications for leaders in several categories that previously had no fixed standard. Relievers now needed eight victories to be placed among leaders in winning percentage, and they had to pitch at least fifty-four innings—or one-third of an inning over the course of a 162-game season—in order to qualify for the best ERA. Also, pinch hitters would need to total at least thirty at-bats to be eligible for the best batting average among pinch hitters.[35]

Enforcement of the rule whereby pitchers were supposed to deliver the ball to the plate within twenty seconds when no runners were on base was also impressed upon umpires for the 1969 season. Encouraging them to use stopwatches if necessary to enforce Rule 8.04, which penalized the pitcher with a called ball but was long ignored by most arbiters, American League president Joe Cronin suggested having the second-base or third-base umpire assigned the duty of tracking the elapsed time, and the White Sox installed a "Pitchometer" on their scoreboard at Comiskey Park to assist in that endeavor.[36] The policing of the twenty-second rule was intended to speed up the game, especially when slow-working pitchers like Sonny Siebert, Gaylord Perry, and Claude Osteen were on the mound. However, little evidence exists as to the overall effectiveness of the timers across the breadth of major-league games.

To head off further controversies involving a traded player who then refused to report to his new team—as in the cases of Donn Clendenon and Ken Harrelson in 1969—major-league general managers after that year's World Series invoked caveat emptor in all future transactions. "Once made, a deal would be a deal," summarized the *Sporting News*, adding "the burden would be on [the player's] new club to persuade him to return" should he elect to hold out for any reason.[37]

One final rule was instituted to the dismay of the players' association that was directly related to an injury suffered by the American League's 1967 Cy Young Award winner, Jim Lonborg of the Boston Red Sox. Lonborg's exploits that season enabled the Red Sox to win the AL pennant and nearly capture the

World Series. Two months after the Series, he signed his contract for 1968—at a hefty raise from $20,000 to $50,000—and went on a ski vacation in December.[38] While on the slopes, Lonborg tore two ligaments in his left knee, underwent surgery to repair the damage, and was unable to pitch for nearly two months. During his recuperation, he nevertheless collected all that was due him under his new contract, which contained no stipulations that prohibited him from partaking in skiing.

As a future safeguard against having to pay a player who was hurt while engaging in what could be deemed risky activity, team owners devised a new "temporary inactive list" after the 1968 season to which a player would be assigned if he was "unable to render service during the championship season due to a bona-fide illness or injury not related to baseball."[39] The injured player would be deprived of his salary until he was reinstated from the new inactive list.

The issues confronting baseball after 1968 were serious enough to prompt its awakening to the realities of the times. Although expansion for 1969 was already in progress, baseball acted properly by taking extra steps to address the steep offensive decline and prevent the game from losing more fan appeal to professional football. The confluence of expansion and revision of rules in 1969, neither of which were initiated by Bowie Kuhn but nevertheless were matters inherited by him, presented the new commissioner with the perfect opportunity to guide baseball out of the wilderness.

The sclerosis of a national pastime burdened with a style of play better suited to the dead-ball era was destined to be an unfavorable match against the continuing dynamism of professional football, and history has proven that baseball's course correction at the end of the 1960s prepared it to move forward in the succeeding decades.

Just as the "Year of the Pitcher" was beginning, columnist Joe King wrote, "The great strength of baseball is its stability," and indeed the bedrock of that constancy was the foundation upon which the popularity of the game was built, enabling baseball's legacy to be passed from one generation to the next.[40] There is much truth to King's statement even today, but in his defense of his comment—in which he said, "A man can take his grandson to the game and explain the action the way he recalled it from bygone times"—a flaw was revealed. Those olden days in which baseball took root carried into the 1960s the faces of men who related better to yesteryear. The grandfather was likely recalling Connie Mack, Branch Rickey, Casey Stengel, and other luminaries of the game dating to the 1930s. But as the 1970s approached, those men were making way for a new breed of players who were more defiant and hardened by the social and cultural milieu of the modern era.

The transformation of baseball's image included plans to update the venues in which the major-league game was played. The quaint ballparks that hosted contests for the vast majority of the twentieth century were becoming fodder for the wrecking ball, and in their places were constructed stadiums that became showpieces of the age of concrete and plastic.

CHAPTER 10

From Ballparks to Stadiums

Entering the 1969 season Major League Baseball had the potential to surpass its record for total single-season attendance of just over 25.1 million established in 1966. And with four new teams set to take the field, baseball had already drawn more fans from 1961 to 1968 than in any previous decade going back to 1901.[1] That baseball could draw a total of 200 million fans from 1961 to 1970 testified to its resilience in the face of recent and heated competition from professional football.

To better accommodate the increasing numbers of spectators and provide them with a more comfortable experience at the ballpark, baseball abandoned many of its old venues and sought homes in new, modern facilities. It is important to note that the term *modern* is used relative to the time during the 1950s and 1960s when the movement of franchises and the initial rounds of expansion were occurring.

Thus, the Brooklyn Dodgers—late of Ebbets Field, which was built in 1913, and relocated in 1958 to the Los Angeles Coliseum, built in 1923 but now reconfigured for baseball—finally moved into newly completed Dodger Stadium in 1962, which was a marvel in its day. Although some resentment over the Dodgers' relocation still smolders among steadfast Brooklyn loyalists, the transformation from Flatbush to Chavez Ravine was remarkable.

Credit is due the Dodgers' western partner, the San Francisco Giants, for having inaugurated an era in new stadium occupancy in the early 1960s. Fleeing the Polo Grounds for temporary residence in Seals Stadium, the club moved to its permanent home in April 1960 at redoubtable Candlestick Park, where the chill, wind, and fog turned playing baseball into a meteorological challenge. The contours of Candlestick were not identical to a classic ballpark like Dodger Stadium, but it served as a single-purpose stadium for more than a decade before the NFL's 49ers became co-tenants in 1971.

Stadiums had long been used for both football and baseball, but Washington's D.C. Stadium, built in 1961 and renamed Robert F. Kennedy Memorial Stadium in 1969, took on a new dimension of architectural form. Whereas Cleveland's Municipal Stadium, Yankee Stadium, Wrigley Field, and other venues that hosted the two major sports were open-ended, RFK Stadium, home of the NFL's Redskins and the AL expansion Washington Senators, was fully enclosed. But in the opinion of one critic, the stadium's "ugly modern lines seemed designed by Stalin."[2] Utilitarian sterility served a purpose for some buildings, but when applied to an outdoor sports arena, the intimacy long associated with baseball's old ballparks and the closeness fans felt to the game they were attending began to erode. The communion previously enjoyed was now being subordinated to the economy of larger—and less personable—venues with cheaper maintenance costs inherent in municipally financed multipurpose stadiums.

As the 1960s progressed and taxpayer-funded stadiums began to replace antiquated ballparks, some "cities decided to locate their new facilities in the suburbs along major freeways to accommodate affluent suburbanites."[3] Such strategies catered to the growing dependence of Americans on the automobile and enabled sports teams to flee urban areas falling into blight or otherwise suffering from the ills of social decay. When teams were created through expansion and others relocated—either to different cities or within their metropolitan region—new stadiums became a necessity. The Dodgers used the ill-suited Coliseum until Dodger Stadium could be built north of Los Angeles's downtown area, and the New York Mets bided their time in the aged Polo Grounds waiting for Robert Moses's showpiece, Shea Stadium, to be ready in conjunction with the 1964–1965 New York World's Fair.

Following in 1965 were Atlanta Stadium, envisaged as early as 1962 to serve as an enticement to lure a major-league team to Atlanta—which it eventually did, in the form of the Milwaukee Braves—as well as the Houston Astrodome, dubbed the "Eighth Wonder of the World" as baseball's first indoor stadium, which soon required a replacement for the natural grass field incapable of growing in such an environment.

The following year, three new stadiums joined the ranks, with only two of them having immediate baseball tenants. In St. Louis, Busch Memorial Stadium displaced the third edition of the site known as Sportsman's Park, and the new stadium was ablaze with the modernity manifest in its usage of "enough electricity with its 35,000 lights to illuminate 450 homes." The early games at spacious Busch drew the notice of the *Sporting News*, headquartered not far from the stadium, which commented in an editorial that although home run production was lacking, "instead, we've seen the three-base hit revived as an effective and exciting weapon."[4] In Southern California the Dodgers became sole tenants at Chavez Ravine when the Angels moved to their new stadium in Anaheim, just minutes from Disneyland. Renamed the California Angels, the team relocated to an agrarian site where oranges, alfalfa, eucalyptus, and corn had once grown, and the facility soon acquired the nickname "the Big A" in tribute to a gigantic twenty-three-story-high scoreboard shaped like an uppercase letter *A* and adorned with an illuminated halo. Farther north across San Francisco Bay, construction of the Oakland–Alameda County Coliseum was well underway in 1965 and was already in Charlie Finley's sights as a potential new home for his Kansas City Athletics. Completed in 1966 as the new home of the American Football League's Raiders but lacking a baseball team, the Coliseum would add the Athletics as a tenant beginning in 1968.

Another West Coast venue temporarily without a big-league team was San Diego Stadium, which was completed in 1967 and would be the home of the National League's Padres beginning in 1969. And when the city of Montreal was awarded the NL's second expansion club, Jarry Park was hastily converted from a public park, equipped with accommodations for various athletic activities, to a stadium intended to be in service for only one season. Slapdash in design since its lifespan as host for major-league baseball was assumed to be short-term, Jarry Park's "closeness of the seats to the field provided an intimacy to the game which may not have materialized in a larger stadium."[5]

When the 1969 baseball season opened, the National League was better poised to accommodate fans because eight of its twelve stadiums were less than a decade old. By contrast, only three of the dozen ballparks in the American League could make the same claim, although Metropolitan Stadium in Minnesota was modernized somewhat when the Senators became the Twins in 1961, and in Baltimore a second tier was added to Memorial Stadium in 1954 when the St. Louis Browns relocated to become the present-day Orioles. All other ballparks, however, soldiered on with varying degrees of old-world charm or bleakness, depending on one's point of view.

In Chicago, a city trying to settle down following the riotous Democratic National Convention in the summer of 1968, White Sox president Arthur Allyn tried to quell rumors that his team would move to Milwaukee by proposing the Sox play eleven games annually over the next few seasons at Milwaukee County Stadium and scheduling these contests far enough in advance to convince many fans that no permanent move was afoot. Allyn intended to keep the White Sox in Chicago in order to play at a proposed $46 million sports complex that was to be built on a fifty-three-acre site over the Dearborn Street railroad station. This grand plan did not materialize, but in 1969 the home of the Sox received a makeover of sorts to improve the lighting in the vicinity of the stadium. The new team motto, "White Sox Park is the Light, Bright and Right One," was intended to promote a safer image to those fans who were reluctant to venture to a night game on Chicago's South Side.[6]

Still in use today, Fenway Park in Boston and Wrigley Field on the North Side of Chicago have not only cheated time and the wrecking ball but have become enduring landmarks that continue to serve as they have for more than a century. But several other stadiums of advanced age still in use during baseball's 1969 centennial were destined not to be as fortunate as Fenway and Wrigley.

Newer Stadiums through the Mid-1960s

As construction took place throughout the 1960s, the design of the new ballparks in some instances catered only to baseball tenants, such as those in Los Angeles and Anaheim, which had the footprint of a classic facility like the original Yankee Stadium. In these configurations, the main grandstand extended from the left-field foul pole toward home plate along a relatively straight line, with this symmetry mirrored along the right-field side, and the upper decks were similarly contoured.

The first of the round—or mostly round—multipurpose stadiums was D.C. Stadium, which had been under construction at the time of the original Senators' move to Minneapolis after the 1960 season. Nearly circular in its footprint and fully enclosed by stands that surrounded the field, the stadium also inaugurated the use of a mechanism to reposition the grandstand section on the third-base side to change the playing area from a baseball field configuration to one for football. Although some older stadiums—Municipal Stadium in Cleveland, Chicago's Wrigley Field and Comiskey Park, as well as the Polo Grounds and Yankee Stadium, both in New York—hosted the two major sports, there was no technology available when they were built to support movable sections. For better or worse, D.C. Stadium became, at a cost of $24 million, the de facto template for future multipurpose facilities.

In the early part of the decade, as plans were being formulated for New York City to host the World's Fair in 1964 and 1965, a key portion of the fair's agenda included the construction of a stadium as a new home for the Mets. The mastermind behind the effort was Robert Moses, who for decades autocratically shaped nearly every major civil engineering project in the greater metropolitan area. Moses's ego demanded the creation of spectacular public works, and the iron hand he employed to bring them to fruition was legendary. He envisioned Flushing Meadows, the site east of Manhattan where the fair would be built, to serve as a new Robert Moses Park once the fair had run its course.

Besides the exhibition halls and pavilions scheduled to be built for the fair, a new sports stadium costing more than $28 million also was slated for construction, and this facility would be, in the words of Moses's biographer Robert Caro, "consciously shaped to resemble Rome's Colosseum" and thus imbued—at least in Moses's mind—with the same significance and immortality as its ancient counterpart. It was no coincidence that as contingents of World's Fair executives visited many foreign countries to encourage those nations to participate in the fair, Moses ensured that he was booked to travel to Italy, specifically Rome, where the 1960 Summer Olympic Games were to be played beginning in late August. His goal was to "pick up ideas on events, exhibits, etc.," but he also asked William Shea, the man primarily responsible for returning National League baseball to New York following the flight of the Dodgers and Giants in 1957, "Don't you think you ought to go [to Rome] in connection with the uses, etc., of the new Stadium?"[7]

It was soon suggested that a running track be incorporated into the stadium's layout, with the notion that the stadium "could be used for Olympic trials in 1964 and for the games in 1968 if New York is the host City." However, the track proposal was quickly abandoned when Branch Rickey, who was consulted on the stadium, voiced his disapproval, as did Stuart Constable, Moses's Park Department executive officer. "[N]o major league team would lease [the stadium] from us with a cinder track in it," warned Constable, who further noted, "Track and baseball don't fit on the same field as track and football do." Even as the stadium was in the design phase, Shea made known his opinion that accommodation for a roof was central to its construction, but Moses demurred. Citing the similarly planned roof for a proposed new facility in Pittsburgh, Moses feared that the addition of "all sorts of movable schemes, plastic bubbles, thin concrete, etc." would push construction "to the absolute limit if you build the Stadium strong enough to hold a roof later on if it proves desirable."[8] Moses also revealed his practical side by further observing that the roof would provide a safeguard only against rain, since the stadium was not intended to be heated or cooled and events were not to be scheduled during the winter months.

The circularity of the Colosseum was incorporated in the design of Shea Stadium by the architectural firm of Praeger-Kavanaugh-Waterbury for a very practical purpose. In order to allow the playing field to be transformed from baseball mode to football, the field-level stands containing more than ten thousand seats were installed on a pair of independent sections mounted on a track system that rotated using electric motors, the third-base section moving clockwise toward the outfield while that on the first-base side shifted counterclockwise. Although D.C. Stadium in Washington had one movable section, Shea Stadium was the first to use two, and this dual rotation scheme was employed with other facilities soon to be constructed. Because the area beyond the outfield fence was open, the stadium could be expanded by twenty-five thousand seats "without disturbance to the initial construction," and in 1964 the New York City Department of Parks noted further that "provision has been made in the design of the stadium for future installation of an all-weather retractor cover." A proposal to privately fund the building of the additional grandstand as well as creation of a covering of "giant louvers which can be opened for fair weather and summertime events and closed tight for comfort and protection from the elements" was advanced by the sports commissioner of New York, but this plan never materialized.[9]

Round in shape but constructed with no movable stands, Atlanta Stadium opened in 1965 but did not have a major-league tenant because of the legal wrangling that prevented the Milwaukee Braves from transferring to a new southern home. Instead the International League's Atlanta Crackers used it for one season before the Braves officially moved in for the 1966 season. Atlanta Stadium was conceived by mayoral candidate Ivan Allen during his successful 1961 campaign and was built only on hopeful speculation of attracting a major sports franchise to the Deep South. Allen was credited with creating "the magnet that drew Atlanta into the big leagues," and the stadium also became home to the expansion Falcons of the NFL in 1966.[10] Atlanta Stadium's field served as a template of sorts for a companion stadium on the West Coast, its football gridiron laid out in the direction from third base to first base rather than from home plate out into centerfield.

With the Crackers soon to take the field at their new home in the spring of 1965, the realm of modernity was bestowed with a new showpiece in Houston, Texas, where the "Eighth Wonder of the World" was opened. Also drawing inspiration from the Colosseum in Rome, Judge Roy Hofheinz envisioned "a round facility with a cover" that would differ in layout compared to "most of the stadiums in the United States [that] had been built to conform to the shape of the playing fields." Lauded as "a structure 710 feet in diameter which may very well make obsolete all other stadiums in the world," the Astrodome was replete with amenities found nowhere else: a gigantic scoreboard, oversized dugouts, a press area to comfortably accommodate 276 members of the media, luxury boxes for wealthy patrons, dining selections offering more than traditional ballpark fare, and—not least, to the benefit of players and fans alike—an air-conditioned environment to provide relief from the sweltering Texas heat and humidity.[11]

On February 8, 1965, the Astros participated in a late afternoon workout at the new facility, a total of three million watts of lighting power illuminating the playing field and evoking favorable reactions from players who found the visibility of batted balls "much easier to follow" than in traditional outdoor stadiums. For the time being, it appeared that while adjustments would need to be made in order to get acclimated to the Astrodome, the success of indoor baseball was in the offing, and the "mild concern express[ed] over the problem fielders *might* have in a day game," while not entirely dismissed, was duly noted as another difficulty to "be solved as skillfully as those which preceded it."[12]

The Astrodome was a huge success when it opened on April 9 for an exhibition game featuring the Astros and the visiting New York Yankees. Throughout the season, fans sat in air-conditioned comfort and were treated to displays on the gigantic scoreboard featuring cartoons of pistol-packing cowboys, cattle, and rockets, as well as animated fireworks. At least one observer, however, was not impressed by the garish amusements. Roger Angell of the *New Yorker* felt that the attention of the fans was being appropriated by "'distractions' as exemplified by the scoreboard's antics," and, critical of those charged with running the Astrodome, the writer feared that baseball at that venue would devolve into "mere entertainment and thus guarantee its descent to the status of a boring and stylized curiosity."[13]

Not foreseen in the grand vision of the Astrodome's designer or that of team owner Hofheinz was the stadium's inability to accommodate one of its most important logistical assets. The stadium roof of nearly forty-eight hundred skylights made of Lucite was supposed to allow the three-plus acres of special Bermuda grass below—chosen for its indoor growth traits—to continue growing after being transplanted from a farm in Wharton, Texas. But when the sun was out during afternoon games, the glare from the panels made conditions nearly impossible for players to follow the flight of the ball, and even Houston GM Paul Richards feared that contests would resemble a "Keystone Comedy" unless a remedy was implemented.[14] The immediate solution called for painting two of the dome's eight overhead sections, but the unintended consequence of this remedy deprived the grass of its natural sustainability: sunlight. To address the issue of dying grass, a new experimental surface first used in 1964 was given a trial at the professional level.

Entering the Age of Plastics and Electronics

The crisis developing under the roof of the Astrodome during 1965 called for prompt action, and a solution was closer at hand than some people may have thought. Created in 1962 by a subsidiary of Monsanto Company known as the Chemstrand Corporation, a synthetic turf dubbed "Chemgrass" was first placed on the floor of the field house at Moses Brown School in Providence, Rhode Island, in June 1964. Chemstrand tested variations of the carpet to determine "foot traction and cushioning, weather drainage, flammability, and wear resistance."[15] Developed with the intention of providing a more useful surface for school sports in urban settings, an updated version of the product was formulated and later issued United States patent #3332828. When the Astros opened their 1966 season in Houston, the Astrodome was the first major sporting venue to use the artificial turf—rebranded as AstroTurf—thus ushering in a new era in which baseball abandoned real grass for a substitute that held many advantages over a natural surface.

In 1969 the head groundskeeper at White Sox Park, Gene Bossard, was very enthusiastic about his stadium's new artificial surface—on the infield only—because its durability eliminated the monthly chore of resodding heavily used portions of the infield near home plate, the coaching boxes, and the fungo circles. Although Bossard overreached with his prediction that AstroTurf would become a standard feature in all stadiums, he embraced the ease of upkeep inherent with the carpet. "[A]s far as maintenance is concerned, there's no comparison between natural and synthetic grass. With a special power-driven vacuum cleaner, it takes me only forty-five minutes to do," he said, adding that an occasional washing of the carpet with a hose kept its appearance fresh. At the time of Bossard's testimony, two dozen professional, college, and municipal stadiums were using AstroTurf or had committed to installing it, with the mayor of Cincinnati announcing his city's decision to employ the turf at its new facility. Running counter to Bossard's belief in ease of maintenance, however, was the unfortunate fact that tobacco juice stains were a chore to clean from the turf, leading Pittsburgh manager Danny Murtaugh to wonder if he should "switch to bubble gum or attach a spittoon to my belt."[16]

Monsanto boasted about the rapid conversion time from a stadium's baseball configuration to one for football—"Two sports, one field. The answer: AstroTurf and eight hours," chirped the company's advertisement in *Sports Illustrated*—with Busch Memorial Stadium in St. Louis serving as the new example of technical efficiency.[17] Baseball players were further assured of truer bounces on the turf compared to the hazards of divots or other flaws inherent with natural grass and dirt surfaces, although those in the outfield had to exercise caution that high bounding balls did not bounce over their heads.

What Monsanto neglected to mention were the brutal working conditions to which players and umpires were exposed during games—especially those in the daytime—in the peak summer months. Although contests in the Astrodome were protected from extreme heat, veteran umpire Ed Sudol noted in games played outdoors on such surfaces in July and August, the field temperature was often more than 20 degrees hotter than the air temperature, which could already be stifling in the high 90s. Players could at least get a temporary respite by repairing to their dugout in their half of an inning, but there was no such opportunity for the men calling the game.

Sudol also pointed out the one hazard no one could avoid regardless of the weather: "The artificial turf is murder on your legs and feet. It's like standing on concrete." Indeed, that was basically what those in the field *were* standing on. At Cincinnati's Riverfront Stadium, a substratum of seven inches of crushed rock was overlaid with five inches of asphalt, which was then topped by three-quarter-inch padding. Finally, fourteen-hundred-pound spools of carpet fifteen by two hundred feet were rolled out over the pavement to create the completed field.[18]

The evolution of plastics moved apace. Roof panels, playing surfaces, and grandstand seats—all developed from one type of manmade substance or another—became integral to stadium construction as the 1960s progressed. The American Seating Company of Grand Rapids, Michigan, had captured most of the market for providing seats to big-league stadiums, and its products were "subjected . . . to a series of grueling tests" to ensure both quality and durability, including "an ultraviolet aging test" for exposure to sunlight and "a salt spray bath [to test] the rust-resisting qualities of the paint finish."[19] Seats made from wooden slats and natural grass playing fields were now being slowly but surely supplanted by more durable and economically feasible materials.

But as efficiency of multisport facility construction, operation, and maintenance gained increasing ground, the ambience of the traditional ballparks and the traits that gave them their defining character were lost. A rounded yet slightly rectangular stadium footprint, also known as an octorad, for all intents and purposes demanded the use of symmetric outfield walls, leading National League infielder Richie Hebner to observe, "I stand at the plate in [Veterans

Veterans Stadium in Philadelphia, which did not look substantially different from its earlier-built rivals in Cincinnati and Pittsburgh. *National Baseball Hall of Fame Library, Cooperstown, NY.*

Stadium] in Philadelphia, and I don't honestly know whether I'm in Pittsburgh, Cincinnati, St. Louis, or Philly. They all look alike."[20] The advantages gained via new construction—broad concourses, more restroom facilities, and an airiness not found in the cramped quarters of old parks—were offset by a synthetic homogeneity that spread from city to city as new stadiums came into existence.

Modern entertainment in the form of elaborate scoreboards and music produced with the aid of new electronics also made an appearance as the 1960s drew to a close. Cartoons displayed on new scoreboards added a creative dimension to key moments during a game, whether to encourage the crowd to exhort the home team with a boisterous "*Charge!!!*" or to celebrate a big base hit. Even in an age before large television screens and video systems arrived in stadiums, fans could be presented with more information—such as player statistics or messages—than was possible on old, manually operated scoreboards.

By the middle part of the twentieth century, organ music was in the midst of a migration from church settings to other public and commercial venues. Technological advances led to the development of electric organs that gained in popularity, and, as one scholar noted, when coupled with improvements in loudspeaker systems, the country soon became "an increasingly electrically mediated society" whose experience at a ballgame could be musically enhanced.[21] Organists such as Gladys Goodding, John Kiley, and Jane Jarvis, who plied their trade with various major-league teams in the 1950s, served as inspirations for a new group of keyboardists whose ranks by 1970 included a young Nancy Faust of the Chicago White Sox, who later gained much favor with the home crowd for her rendition of the 1969 hit song "Na Na Hey Hey Kiss Him Goodbye."

The use of songs was no longer limited to the simple provision of musical diversion, as was Kiley's approach, and for some organists music became the soundtrack to the pulse of a baseball game. Faust thus deemed it necessary to peruse the sports pages in order to create "a repertoire that includes a song for every baseball situation and a musical salute to every [American League] player."[22]

As the decade of the 1960s progressed, it bore the stamp of plastics and electronics, which found their way into all manner of American society, so it is not surprising that they would be incorporated into the new stadiums then being constructed. Yet also of prime concern was the location of the building sites of those facilities, which was as important as the ability of the stadiums to accommodate multiple sports. Several multipurpose stadiums were built with the intention of enhancing a broader plan of urban redevelopment, as was the case with a trio of stadiums under construction at the close of the 1960s. These also were the latest in a series of what were derisively called "cookie cutters," a label that emphasized the lack of originality in their design, and the architectural adage of "form follows function" was never more true than in Cincinnati, Pittsburgh, and Philadelphia.

A Path to Redevelopment

In 1966 the introduction of Busch Memorial Stadium in St. Louis served as a template soon to be copied by the next three National League cities in line to replace their aging ballparks. On the banks of the Mississippi River was the new home of the Cardinals, which was built under the auspices of the Civic Center Redevelopment Corporation of St. Louis at a cost of $27 million. The corporate entity was established in 1959 aiming not only to build a new stadium but also to redevelop the city's former warehouse district. From start to finish this process took more than a decade to complete, with the most prominent structure being Eero Saarinen's landmark Gateway Arch, which opened in 1963.

The multipurpose design of the stadium was deemed as crucial in preventing a possible move of the NFL Cardinals, who had been wooed by the city of Atlanta to play in its new stadium. From a financial perspective Busch Memorial Stadium in itself was not anticipated to be a profitable entity. Rather, as O. O. McCracken, the head of the redevelopment group, stated, the overall project was "considered a civic investment," and the stadium was being relied upon to provide a "rippling effect" that in turn would draw other commercial interests to the area.[23]

Such rippling was important to the stadium itself, whose football and base-ball tenants were incapable of generating a revenue stream sufficient to keep the whole enterprise viable. Other construction projects, events such as concerts hosted at the stadium, and real estate holdings of the redevelopment corporation were necessary to keep money flowing into its coffers. The status of the NFL Cardinals changed over time, but in the early years following Busch Memorial Stadium's debut the redevelopment corporation was "solidly in the black."[24] The experiences of several cities in forging new sporting venues were replete with their own travails on the path to redevelopment.

Building Anew in Cincinnati, Pittsburgh, and Philadelphia

Between the fall of 1967 and the spring of 1968, three groundbreakings ushered in the latest wave of stadium construction. The earliest of these took place in Philadelphia on October 2, yet this head start failed to ensure a timely grand opening for that city's new sports venue. Better luck was experienced by the Queen City of Cincinnati, which began its project on February 1 when a host of civic leaders joined Reds president Francis Dale and legendary football coach Paul Brown to set off a ceremonial explosion marking the commencement of the project. And on April 24, Pittsburgh baseball mogul John Galbreath and his gridiron counterpart, Art Rooney of the Steelers, launched the initial building phase of a stadium slated to replace the one built in 1909 by the Bucs' owner, future Hall of Famer Barney Dreyfuss.

—⁓—

The construction endeavor in Cincinnati followed a route that took years to navigate. A twenty-year master plan of development for the city was drawn up in 1948, with a new stadium in the riverfront area incorporated into its agenda. But with other civic initiatives taking priority, less attention was devoted to a replacement for aging Crosley Field. After the Dodgers vacated Brooklyn and the Giants likewise moved from New York in 1957, genuine fears arose that the Reds might be wooed east as a replacement franchise. The situation was defused temporarily when parking problems near Crosley Field were addressed, and the Reds agreed to remain in Cincinnati for five more years while new stadium plans could be explored.

By 1965 new Reds owner William O. DeWitt renewed a commitment to keep the team in place for an additional six years, and at last a committee was formed at the end of that year to formally begin a bona fide effort to construct a new stadium. Adding much weight to the venture was the governor of Ohio, James A. Rhodes, a sports enthusiast gifted with "unbelievable energy and his genius as a salesman" who was no stranger to the crucial negotiations and maneuvering necessary to bring about intended results. Selection of the intended site along the Ohio River was met with trepidation by those, including the Reds' ownership, who feared that flooding would have disastrous consequences. But despite its relatively small acreage compared to other potential locations under consideration, the biggest advantage to the riverfront area was its proximity to the downtown area. A stadium here "would pump adrenalin into the life blood of the city," and financial aid from the federal government was already in hand to assist in clearing the area for construction.[25]

In the spring of 1966 two architectural firms from Atlanta, who had created that city's new stadium, were chosen for the riverfront project, but a standoff developed between Cincinnati officials and the American Football League. The city was reluctant to build a stadium unless assurance was given that a new football franchise would be awarded—this turned out to be the expansion Bengals—while the AFL was hesitant to grant a franchise to Cincinnati until guarantees could be provided that the new team would have a new home field. When *Cincinnati Enquirer* publisher Francis Dale purchased the team from De-Witt in late 1966, he financially supplemented the design phase and consented to a forty-year lease that assured the Reds would stay in Cincinnati. Governor Rhodes "'cracked heads' in political circles in Cincinnati to get city-county cohesion in financing the new riverfront stadium."[26]

Nearly a year from the date of the groundbreaking, the Reds' board of directors authorized team president Dale to petition the mayor of Cincinnati to seek the inclusion of artificial turf rather than a natural surface for the stadium. AstroTurf was ultimately selected by the Reds and the stadium's other primary tenant, the pro football Bengals, but there was a twist to the manner in which the turf was to be employed. At the major-league general managers meeting in December 1969, the Reds received approval for a one-year trial "to cover its entire field—including what normally would be the 'dirt' infield—with artificial turf" as long as "the portion of the field usually skinned would be painted, colored or stained to give the appearance of a 'dirt' infield." A proposal to "spread 'granules'" near the bases to facilitate sliding for base runners ultimately transformed into the creation of dirt sliding pits installed at the three bases, with dirt also used for the pitcher's circle and the greater area around home plate.[27] Just as the GMs were sanctioning the full-field turf for a trial now amended to five years, other major-league executives selected Cincinnati to host the upcoming 1970 All-Star Game. But ongoing construction was not keeping a pace that would allow the stadium to open in time for the Midsummer Classic, and there was a genuine fear that Cincinnati would have to forfeit its hosting opportunity.

Understandably concerned that chaos would arise as the date of the game drew closer and the stadium had no clear completion date, commissioner Bowie Kuhn established a deadline of May 30 for a decision to proceed with playing in Cincinnati or move the game to the alternate city of Atlanta, with its five-year-old stadium. Despite a strike on June 1 by several labor unions working at the site in Cincinnati, the laborers agreed to remain on the job, and the two-to-three-week task of turf installation continued. Enough confidence was gained in construction progress that the Reds committed to move out of Crosley Field, where the final game was played on the evening of June 24. After the last out was recorded, the crowd sang an emotional "Auld Lang Syne," and home plate was dug up to be whisked by helicopter to its new location at the now officially named Riverfront Stadium.

Although Riverfront was not fully completed and its grand opening created huge traffic snarls, the stadium's maiden voyage was a success for the hometown team, which defeated the Astros on July 5. The new stadium was equipped with a seventy-five-ton scoreboard comprising more than 350 miles of wiring and more than thirty-one thousand lamps that flashed messages and cartoons, while twenty-five men's rooms and a like number of ladies' rooms provided for sanitation needs. Nearly three dozen concession stands catered to the hungry, and flooding concerns were addressed by the installation of a "flood wall [that] completely circles the outer perimeter of the stadium" along with "sub-surface pumps within the confines of the flood wall [to] ensure protection of the playing field." The barrier was designed and constructed to restrict potential flooding from the Ohio River of up to seventy-eight feet, keeping the field and five club-houses safe while confining waters to the underground parking area. Capacious locker room facilities and a pair of "theater-type meeting rooms complete with projector rooms" added to the state-of-the-art amenities.[28] Four elevators and sixteen escalators were available to convey people to and from various levels of the facility, and the playing field was awash in light from nearly seventeen-hundred 1,000-watt Metalarc lamps manufactured by Sylvania Electric Products, the better to illuminate the field for the benefit of broadcasts via color television.

However, little time passed before for the first complaints about the playing surface were registered. The bugbear of high temperatures and the discomfort caused underfoot became occupational hazards as the outdoor turf genie, already let out of its bottle on the fields at White Sox Park and Busch Memorial Stadium, took ever firmer hold. To good effect, AstroTurf would migrate to San Francisco, thereby eliminating the bothersome issue of dust storms that plagued windswept Candlestick Park.

—–∿∿––

Several hundred miles farther up the Ohio River, at the confluence of the Allegheny and Monongahela Rivers in Pittsburgh, plans for the replacement of aged Forbes Field and Pitt Stadium began in April 1968 when base bids of $26 million were obtained by the Pittsburgh Stadium Authority. In the 1950s a multipurpose stadium was intended to be constructed over the Monongahela to take advantage of the view of the Pittsburgh skyline, but those ambitious plans, which included hotels and an adjoining marina, were scrapped due to the cost of such a project. Revisions to the design and placement of the stadium were formulated in 1958 that would have situated the new facility in an inconvenient location, at a place occupied by Exposition Park, the Pirates' former home at the turn of the century. Debate over ease of fans' access to the area known as Northside and other bureaucratic delays stalled the project for years, and it was not until 1968 that construction began in earnest, with the new stadium finally opening on July 16, 1970.

Three Rivers Stadium was surfaced with Tartan Turf, a counterpart to AstroTurf manufactured by the 3M Company that was capable of "surviv[ing] six years of horses' pounding hoofs at race tracks without appreciable wear" and was developed so that baseball and football players could continue to use their accustomed spiked shoes rather than special cleats. The playing surface included the traditional dirt infield rather than a completely carpeted field, and a vacuum cleaner could be employed to transfer water from the soaked field to the warning track, where a drainage system removed it from the stadium. Fans able to partake of the exclusive seats in the Allegheny Club were protected by "1/2-inch-thick laminated Herculite safety glass . . . that stands up to baseballs fired out of a cannon" and was developed, not surprisingly, by Pittsburgh Plate Glass. Although the original marina plans failed to materialize, an executive with the Three Rivers Management Corporation noted, "Generous boat docking facilities will be provided for private boats as well as public excursions and taxi boat service to and from the Stadium events."[29]

A partner of the firm responsible for the stadium's design, Deeter Ritchey Sippel, claimed that the architects "did extensive research on what makes a really good stadium. We traveled with baseball and football teams, talked to the players and asked them what they liked or disliked about the stadiums they played in."[30] For better or worse, the resulting facility was contemporaneous modernity in design and construction, and the Pirates, in keeping with the growing omnipresence of synthetics, shed their old tank-top uniforms in favor of new polyester togs when they played the opening game at Three Rivers in July 1970.

Gone also were the quirky dimensions of Forbes Field, with its discrepant foul lines—365 feet to left, only 300 to right—cavernous 457-foot distance to center, and variable-height outfield wall measuring twelve feet from the left-field corner to the gap in right-center and ten feet high behind most of right field, with the section in the right-field corner protected by a screen nearly twenty-eight feet in height. Three Rivers Stadium now featured a homogenous dimension of 340 feet down both lines and 410 feet to straightaway center.

At the eastern end of Pennsylvania, a series of difficulties delayed the construction of a replacement for Connie Mack Stadium—known as Shibe Park until 1953—in Philadelphia. An opulent showcase at the time of its opening in 1909, the stadium in the city's north end was an attraction for the neighborhood's largely white yet ethnically diverse population. As the area in succeeding decades grew less desirable and the thrill of the 1950 Whiz Kids wore off, the Phillies were reluctant to provide upkeep for a ballpark increasingly plagued with the odious "smell of mustard, urine, stale beer, and cigar smoke," which did little to encourage fans to venture to Connie Mack to watch a baseball team that finished in the National League basement each year from 1958 to 1961.[31]

In the early part of the 1960s, much discussion among city planners led to a handful of potential sites for a new stadium. But a major factor complicating the situation concerned the assumed co-tenancy of a new stadium by the Phillies and the NFL Eagles. The baseball team was in need of an updated venue, but the football club was content to remain at Franklin Field, located on the grounds of the University of Pennsylvania, where the Eagles had moved after abandoning Connie Mack in 1958. A proposal to construct a new stadium in 1962 failed when a referendum on the ballot was defeated by heavy opposition in the affected neighborhood in the southernmost area of Philadelphia.

In late 1964 a loan in the amount of $25 million was secured, but when the architect's initial stadium design was deemed by the Phillies as "completely unsuitable for baseball," the plan was scrapped and resulted in a delay for redesigning.[32] Controversy also erupted over Phillies owner Bob Carpenter's proposal to build the stadium in Cherry Hill, New Jersey, but the site ultimately selected was at the lower end of Broad Street—but not as far south as originally proposed—and put the stadium in a sporting row of sorts, with the soon-to-open Spectrum for basketball and hockey immediately to the south, and JFK Stadium just below the Spectrum.

After the Eagles were finally convinced to join the venture as co-tenants, fresh controversy ensued over the design of the new stadium. When renderings for the multipurpose facility were made public at a special event hosted by Philadelphia mayor James Tate, both the Eagles and Phillies were repulsed by the configuration. When an acceptable revision was drawn up suitable for baseball and football, the new design came with a 50 percent increase over the original cost and had to be put before a public vote. Soil testing at the building site revealed it to be a former landfill, and "[by] September 1966, the city had already spent nearly $5 million without one shovel having been stuck in the ground."[33] In mid-May of 1967 and by a margin of fewer than five thousand votes, Philadelphia citizens sanctioned additional funding of $13 million to allow construction to move forward at last.

As frugality became an increasing concern in the minds of civic leaders, "the architects were instructed to cut the frills" in order to lower the cost to $37 million, just below the total of the initial price plus the supplement just approved by the Philadelphia electorate.[34] Another year was expected to pass before bids would be sent for the project, but hopes prevailed for a groundbreaking ceremony in the autumn of 1968, with the new stadium to open in the spring of 1970.

Good intentions notwithstanding, the construction process suffered from delays that drove the timeline for completion into 1971 and forced the opening of the stadium into the spring of that year. Controversy even erupted over the name of the new stadium, but Veterans Stadium ultimately prevailed by an 11–5 vote of the city council.

Enduring what one historian described as "the usual ills to which a public project in Philadelphia is subject," work at the site was not only plagued by typical cost overruns—leading to a final price of $52 million for the stadium—but corruption also played an unwanted role when "a grand jury investigation resulted in the indictment of the stadium manager and more than a half-dozen others involved in the stadium's construction."[35] Venality, labor disputes, theft of building material and tools, and inclement weather that temporarily created a ten-foot-deep pond on the building site all conspired to prevent the stadium's timely completion. The surfeit of problems forced the Phillies to confront the reality that they would play their 1970 home games at Connie Mack Stadium before at last moving to their new home.

When Veterans Stadium did open in 1971, it was not an exact copy of its brethren in Cincinnati or Pittsburgh, but it did bear a strong resemblance. Corporate patrons were invited to spend up to $15,800 per season for special "Super Boxes," each lavishly furnished with a bar, refrigerator, color television, sofa, tables and chairs, and seating for up to thirty people for luxurious viewing of the playing field. White-miniskirt-clad usherettes called Fillies would show attendees to their seats, and a private restaurant club featuring a two-hundred-foot-long bar was added to the right-field area. Players had use of four clubhouses, two handball courts, and a sauna, splendor that was undreamed of at Connie Mack Stadium. To complete the makeover, the Phillies announced a sartorial update to their uniforms that were to be adorned with an updated logo: "[T]he new symbol is a 'P' that grows out of the red stitches of a baseball and swirls into the letter with the ball in the middle."[36]

Famed architect Hugh Stubbins Jr. was a consulting designer for the stadium, but his reputation for delivering structures with noteworthy characteristics—such as Manhattan's Citicorp Center and the Ronald Reagan Library—was diminished when his firm gifted the American sporting scene with yet another stadium that was vapid to the eye. Relatively round in shape and replete with concrete, plastic seats, and AstroTurf, Veterans Stadium followed what was by now formulaic construction in the athletic outdoor arena of the era.

Seeking Synergy of Stadiums and Local Commerce

The above sketches of the newer baseball facilities in use or under construction at the end of the 1960s are presented to give context to the evolution of those physical plants from what may be quaintly referred to as "old ballparks" to the "stadiums," the latter term perhaps lending a connotation of a greater sense of industry or efficiency to the project. In several instances, a new stadium was part and parcel of a broader civic goal—namely, the revitalization of a specific area that would benefit from its construction.

The tenancy of a professional football team in such places was obviously important, but football games would draw large crowds on perhaps only a dozen or fewer occasions each year. On the other hand, baseball teams, with their home schedules of around eighty games per season, were in a position to add significantly to the economic impact on local businesses, especially those in the area surrounding the stadium that catered to fans attending games or other events being held. The operative phrase describing the locale of interest is central business district (CBD).[37]

In the case of the Astrodome, its location five miles from Houston's CBD was a disadvantage, but the stadium site was just two miles beyond Rice University and the Texas Medical Center, all of which were along the South Main Street corridor, which at the time was being developed in support of the school and medical facility. When the Astrodome first opened in 1965, the spectacle of its newness ensured that the novelty would not quickly wear off, and the baseball team drew a robust 2.3 million fans. Yet as the thrill inevitably diminished and attendance fell to under 1.6 million in 1969, the total of those drawn to the Astrodome for all events—rodeos, bullfights, football games, circuses, guided tours, and the like—remained relatively consistent at about 3.6 million people.

But the Astrodome's immediate vicinity remained static for a number of years because the stadium became a destination in and of itself rather than a catalyst to spur further development. "Early efforts at hotel development suffered from a lack of steady support until completion of the Astro World [in June 1968] and the Astro Hall [in late 1973] provided a more even flow of support during the entire year," noted one economic survey.[38] With the Astrodome at such a remove from the CBD, incentives to construct other commercial properties were few.

In St. Louis the circumstances were vastly different because of the location of the new Busch Memorial Stadium. Built in 1966 just to the south of the downtown area, the stadium site was targeted by the Civic Center Redevelopment Corporation "to facilitate the redevelopment of a deteriorated area," and, as noted above, parking to accommodate automobiles, hotel construction, as well as the opening of the Gateway Arch and its associated park proved to be an overall success. But the projects in Cincinnati and Pittsburgh had their own obstacles to overcome on the way to entering the modern era of stadiums.

Riverfront Stadium in the Queen City looked very much like its companion upstream in Pittsburgh and may have been the epitome of stadium design catering to the automobile. Built just to the south of an interstate highway, the facility was situated "directly in the middle of the world's largest three-story parking garage," and although Cincinnati was among baseball's smaller markets, the Reds' fan base extended to eastern Indiana, northern Kentucky, and even into West Virginia.[39] The opening of the stadium in 1970 was most propitious in that it coincided with the arrival of Sparky Anderson as the Reds manager and the coalescing of a lineup that featured a number of future Hall of Fame players whose deeds prompted fans to flock to Riverfront to see the team win several championships in the first part of the decade.

Despite Riverfront Stadium's cost and the fact that, like Busch Memorial Stadium, the facility had an operating deficit, its overall impact on the community grew into a success, albeit at a slow pace. The transmogrification of "a deteriorating industrial slum along the Ohio River" into a section of Cincinnati featuring a new stadium made it "aesthetically pleasing and . . . recognized as being important to the economic vitality of the Cincinnati CBD."[40] As the 1970s progressed a new indoor arena for basketball, hockey, rodeos, and concerts was built, and plans for high-rise residential buildings and offices were in the development stage.

The distinct advantage for business interests in Cincinnati—and in St. Louis, for that matter—was the placement of the new stadium in close proximity to an area that could benefit greatly from its construction. The appeal of Riverfront was enhanced by the addition of connecting pedestrian walkways that linked the stadium to the city's business district just blocks to the north beyond the highway, creating a synergy that aided both local businesses and a new stadium that served as an emblematic centerpiece for the repurposing of a small portion of the Rust Belt.

To the east, Three Rivers Stadium and the city of Pittsburgh did not derive the same mutually beneficial result. Upon the completion of the facility, the new, modern home for the Pirates and NFL Steelers proved a huge improvement over their past respective playing sites, and, as was the case in Cincinnati, the stadium reclaimed a commercial wasteland. But its location was not connected to the CBD of Pittsburgh's "Golden Triangle," which was on the other side of the Allegheny River, and the new stadium was also at a remove from the Pirates' former ballpark, Forbes Field near the University of Pittsburgh.

Like the Astrodome, Three Rivers Stadium was a destination, and its separation by a waterway from the CBD hampered accessibility to local businesses. The spin-off development of new commercial entities in the stadium's immediate vicinity failed to take root even years after the opening of the stadium, the few tangible advantages of the project being the reclamation of industrial land formerly saddled with "blighted buildings which inhibit new construction" and the creation of "new vistas" of the main part of the city that the stadium was supposed to benefit.[41] Credit was given nonetheless to Three Rivers Stadium for its catalytic results by improving the drawing power of the Pirates—who at this time also began enjoying some of the best years in their franchise's history—and complementing the various commercial enterprises associated with the entertainment industry.

Located on the south side of Philadelphia, Veterans Stadium was at a distance from any business district to which it would offer any residual benefit, and a special mass transit line had to be built to facilitate the public's access to the venue. The price of the new line was "wrapped in the same $162 million loan authorized on the 1964 ballot" for civic initiatives that also included the building of the stadium, and creative bookkeeping and loan refinancing in subsequent years obscured the true cost of such ancillary projects to the city.[42] Indeed, by the time the stadium was demolished in early 2004 after a meager thirty-two-year existence, the fact that bond debt obligations outlasted the life of the facility rankled some officials at the Philadelphia city treasury.

Much controversy has accompanied the justification for the construction of new stadiums. These facilities were promoted as likely boons for local economies in order to fortify the case for their construction and validate the private funds and public money spent on them. But by the 1980s—when several years had passed since the opening of the newer stadiums to allow time for rational observation—some economic surveys began to indicate a different reality. Closer scrutiny of the aftereffects of construction revealed only "[redistribution of] pre-existing local leisure spending" rather than creation of new revenue streams, and "[m]ost significantly, there is no evidence whatsoever that new stadium construction necessarily generates significant ancillary development." Bolstered by an assumption that newer would always be better and funded in part by governments—state and especially local—eager to improve a city's image, the lure of the new seemed irresistible. Future construction endeavors beyond the concrete-and-plastic stadiums of the 1960s and 1970s would need to strike a balance in which "a channeling of fans through carefully planned commercial corridors could help maximize secondary economic activity" while also catering to the aesthetics that made older, traditional ballparks attractive through their intimacy.[43]

The Segue from Ballpark to Stadium

As the old ballparks built in the first half of the 1900s faded away and the new "cookie cutters" assumed their place, modernity cast a shadow over the nostalgic. Conflicted about the stadium upgrades, Hank Aaron wrote, "The old parks had dirty, smelly clubhouses, and the players were generally glad to get into new, spacious clean ones," but he believed that the comfort of comparative luxury unfortunately created a distance among teammates who "weren't quite as close anymore [as they] became a little more pampered and a little more selfish."[44]

Newer methods of construction technology allowed for the removal of structural beams that previously obstructed the view for those unfortunate fans sitting behind them, demonstrating one benefit of the new, round stadiums of the 1960s. Although all seats now had clear sightlines, this came at the cost of increased distance from game action on the field. Janet Marie Smith, the noted designer who in the early 1990s led the movement away from plastic stadiums in favor of what are termed retro ballparks, observed that although the multipurpose stadiums may have been emblematic of "America's trend toward modernism," these types of facilities failed both baseball and football; thus, in the end, "multipurpose meant multipurposeless."[45]

Thanks to other governmental subsidies by the end of the twentieth century—and beyond—the multipurpose stadiums of the expansion era were demolished as the next series of ballparks reclaimed the space of their cookie-cutter predecessors, showing that baseball was capable of reinventing itself in order to cure the ills of a previous wave of modernity. Beginning in the 1960s and early 1970s, a decades-long transition from older ballparks to impersonal stadiums—and, in some cases, to retro ballparks—coursed through many major-league cities. What had been new was now old, and what had been thought to be passé slowly made a comeback to the delight of new generations of fans.

CHAPTER 11

Does IT Matter?

THE RISE OF THE INFORMATION AGE

In the aftermath of World War II, an emerging series of "ages" began to make their enduring marks on the Western world. The nuclear age, the jet age, the space age, the plastic age, and the computer age were born out of technological innovations of the era as the products of those respective ages and their applications in both military and civilian life increased and grew in sophistication. Such endeavors became further entrenched as the 1950s progressed to satisfy the demands of a new American consumer-based economy. The historian James T. Patterson wrote of the "grand expectations" held by many Americans at the conclusion of the war that would contribute to a feeling that "the future promised a great deal more than the past."[1]

Running concurrently in many cases, these ages fueled the burgeoning period of modernity that advanced into the 1960s and beyond. Baseball was not left by the wayside as it, too, became an active participant in the jet age that facilitated long-distance travel and the age of plastics that contributed to its new stadiums. As electronic data processing expanded from its nascent military beginnings and took root in American business and industry, it was only natural that this technology would eventually find its way into the realm of sports.

Several aspects of computer technology would come to enhance our knowledge of the game of baseball, force a revision as to how the national pastime's traditional statistics were viewed, and create ways to present the game in a more fan-friendly manner. Conspiring with the latest trends in aircraft and the newest building materials, the computer abetted the advancement of baseball in previously unimaginable ways. As the reach of electronic data processing extended deeper into a growing number of facets of American business and society, baseball would also come under its influence in matters of record keeping, statistical analysis, scouting, marketing, and other ways in which the game's appeal to fans was broadened.

"Electronic Brain"

Primitive by twenty-first-century standards but state-of-the-art in their heyday, computers produced by Burroughs, RCA, Sperry, IBM, and other manufacturers embarked on the journey toward a new technological frontier. The earliest use of the machine for a baseball application, not surprisingly, was initiated by Branch Rickey in early 1955. Late of the Brooklyn Dodgers and now working in what would be his final season as the general manager of the Pittsburgh Pirates, Rickey devised a complicated formula to determine a ranking of National League players based on a number of factors.

In an early attempt to look beyond batting average as the sole means of rating a player's offensive value, Rickey presaged the era of sabermetrics by using "on-base percentage, isolated power, and clutch hitting" as the ingredients in a recipe that was used as input to an "electric brain," which in reality was a "$25,000 high-speed computer acquired by a Pittsburgh industrial firm."[2] In total, the formula relied on thirty different statistics, and although this computer took five days to produce output for all NL players and teams, this method was still found to be preferable to the manual processing that left one of Rickey's analytical assistants at wit's end when he attempted the same computation on his own. The machine determined that the performance of some players and several teams matched the expectations found in traditional statistics, but it also revealed that the batting average of a player such as Don Mueller of the New York Giants, whose .342 placed second among NL hitters in 1954, translated into a far lower ranking—twenty-sixth—when combined with Rickey's other criteria.

A year after Rickey's advanced statistical endeavor, the prognostication capabilities of the computer were put to the test. The *Sporting News* announced that an "electronic brain" called Datatron, which had correctly forecast the winner of four college football bowl games a few months earlier, predicted that the Brooklyn Dodgers and Detroit Tigers would claim the pennants of their respective leagues.[3] This gave the computer a .500 average when the dominant Yankees, picked to place third by the machine, again outpaced their AL rivals. And one fan who was outraged by the baseball writers' failure to choose Boston's Ted Williams as the American League Most Valuable Player in 1957 strongly suggested that the voting should be left to a computer, whose internal workings were presumed to be without bias.

In the summer of 1956 a Reeves analog computer that had been employed by the US Navy to determine trajectories of guided missiles was trusted with the task of determining the distance traveled by one of slugger Mickey Mantle's prodigious home runs at Yankee Stadium. Had the ball not struck the upper facade in right field it would have left the ballpark, yet the computer found that the blast, while still impressive, likely would have traveled about 482 feet to its calculated landing spot. The following year, some US Army officers employed an RCA machine to track 1957 American and National League batting averages when it was not being used for ordnance purposes.

There was discernable reluctance to embrace prognostication via computer, some of this expressed in satirical fashion. To find who the World Series contestants would be in 1959, one scribe wrote, "You oil up the Univac, and throw in the official averages for 1958 and two fifths of bourbon." When sports columnist Joe King was dispatched later that summer to see how a Univac system was being used to create the National League's schedule for the following season, he came away with little understanding of how this would be accomplished, but King was delighted to report on some of the specifications of the hardware. The less tongue-in-cheek writers informed readers that the computer occupied floor space measuring around nine feet by twelve, was able to store 24,000 characters of data, and had an execution rate of 800 instructions per minute.[4]

Also taken seriously was an attempt to predict Stan Musial's batting average for the 1961 season. The forty-year-old star was forecast to hit .303 by an IBM 7090 computer belonging to McDonnell Aircraft—Musial was on hand to set the machine in motion—but he came up short of expectations, his actual .288 falling shy of the prediction. And a company known as Statistical Tabulating Corporation lost out in its bid to predict the outcome of that year's home run derby between Mantle and his Yankees teammate Roger Maris. On twenty occasions the computer failed to come up with the correct totals for each player when the 154th game of the season had been reached, keeping in mind Ford Frick's edict about breaking Babe Ruth's record within the time frame of the pre-expansion schedule. But the computer did come very close in one respect: It predicted that Maris would hit sixty-one homers over the course of 161 games.

Some later forecasts of pennant races yielded mixed results as well. Programmers at Philadelphia's Franklin Institute may have been tainted by that city's lingering ill memory of the Phillies' 1964 collapse. In mid-September 1965 the institute's computer listed the Minnesota Twins—in first place by nine games with sixteen left in the season—as having an incredulous 10,000-to-1 chance of capturing the American League pennant, but it more realistically had the San Francisco Giants—ahead by two and one-half games with eighteen to go—at 4 to 1 to win the National League race. In the event, the Twins easily outdistanced their AL rivals while the Giants swooned and lost seven of their last twelve games to place second behind the Los Angeles Dodgers. And the seemingly impossible was nearly achieved in 1967: Honeywell Systems calculated odds of a four-way tie in the American League to be more than 30 million to 1, but those teams— the Red Sox, Twins, Tigers, and White Sox—came close to overcoming those staggering odds.

An IBM Model 7090 computer, circa 1965. *Courtesy of the Library of Congress, HAER AK-30-A-98.*

One operations researcher at the Massachusetts Institute of Technology, whose analysis of baseball data irked some traditionalists, used an IBM 7040 computer to discover that "if you want to win games you neither steal nor sacrifice, but belt the ball for hits—and more runs," a game philosophy that predated Earl Weaver's arrival in Baltimore by a decade.[5] The human element and the judgments rendered by those on the field and in the dugout, argued the purists, were still held to trump anything that could be produced by a computer.

But the Pandora's box of the computer age had been opened, for better or worse. By the beginning of the 1960s an IBM Ramac computer had a storage capacity of 20 million characters and was the first to use magnetic disk storage. This type of machine was used to answer questions posed to it by a panel of baseball writers, the queries intended to test the computer's strategic acumen. In one situation the Ramac picked a pinch hitter who was most likely to succeed among the three choices available in a particular game situation, and in another it selected a starting pitcher based on a series of variables pertinent to the site of the game and the opponent. By the middle of that decade, Paul Richards, recently fired as general manager of the Houston Astros, decried the growing influence of the computer over baseball. Without saying specifically who was "trying to peddle systems that will make a player hit .400," Richards feared that if "everybody hit .400" the game would surely be in a sorry state.[6]

To add a bit of fuel to Richards's argument, the *Sporting News* lamented the poor quality of the daily box scores being printed in many newspapers across the country. "The computer age was supposed to open new vistas of information," carped the weekly publication in the spring of 1967, but instead it felt that, in some instances, less data was being disseminated due to the overzealous abbreviation of players' names shown in "the computerized version of box scores."[7] This practice led to a bewildering array of letters that left many readers wondering who really played in the game.

Box score illegibility aside, some tangible benefits were being derived from computers, the use of which was at this time beginning to percolate down to the minor-league level. The Erie club in the New York–Penn League announced that medical information obtained for each player would be used as input to generate a customized conditioning regimen as a means of preventing future injuries.

In the midst of this technological milieu, the introduction of the IBM System/360 in 1965 ushered in a new era of the mainframe computer that was capable of handling a range of business and scientific applications. IBM became adept at marketing its wares to customers based on their current needs while also assuring their client base that upward compatibility to bigger systems was viable to meet the demands of future business.

The smallest System/360 model delivered in June 1965 had a maximum memory of just 64 kilobytes, but by the end of the decade that capacity in some units had grown to 4,096.[8] Execution rate increased from 34,500 instructions per second on the slower models announced in 1964 to more than 16 million three years later. As the computer gained a stronger foothold in business, the attendant need for personnel to write instructions for it prompted a swelling demand for programmers, and even the *Sporting News* ran advertisements for correspondence courses. Offering the lure of "big earnings in the world's newest, most exciting profession," extension divisions of some colleges and universities specifically promoted the System/360 as the computer of choice for their programming training curriculum.[9]

The advances in computing power and storage volume grew at exponential rates and reflected a burgeoning industry rising higher on the American scene. Supporting hardware in the form of magnetic tape drives, keypunch machines, card sorters, and impact printers was very much in use and would remain so through at least the 1970s. So much paper was being generated by printers—and, in turn, taking up so much physical space, especially in the office environment—that microfilming began to come into vogue by 1967, even though its origins dated to nearly a century earlier. Some of this media became unwitting confetti in the wake of the New York Mets' resounding World Series title in 1969 when "many businessmen awoke to a horrible hangover brought on by the fact that enthusiastic employees had tossed valuable computer tape and punched cards out office windows" during the Mets' celebratory ticker tape parade.[10]

These perils notwithstanding, all this technology was not lost on other sports, and as the 1960s progressed computers analyzed golf swings and helped horse-racing aficionados pick winners. But machines were capable of storing and processing large amounts of data, and it was in this milieu that enterprises such as the Elias and Howe baseball bureaus, both of which held positions as official statisticians for Major League Baseball, joined the age of the computer.

Prominent Statisticians in the Early Years

Baseball and statistics have had a close relationship going back to the mid-1800s, although the earliest data can be thought of as quotidian. The nascent box scores of Henry Chadwick would evolve in the coming decades to take the form we know well today, but Chadwick's fixation with data contributed to what historian Harold Seymour called "a new arithmetic" that gripped the still-developing United States.[11] Chadwick created "a staggering statistical portrait" of the 1869–70 Cincinnati Red Stockings ranging "from the routine (runs and total innings played) to the hopelessly esoteric (Times Forced Out on the Bases,

. . .)," this mélange of numbers joining those produced at the time by Albert Spalding, Irwin Beadle, and Albert Reach in a competition for the best statistical compilations.

Near the close of the nineteenth century, Ernie Lanigan began to cut his teeth with the *Sporting News*, a publication founded by his uncles, Albert and Charles Spink, and he became a staunch proponent of a statistic that fell in and out of favor—the run batted in. Meanwhile, John Heydler, the secretary of the National League, also immersed himself in the circuit's statistics, with particular attention to those related to pitching. In the early 1900s F. C. Lane took charge of *Baseball* magazine and revealed his passion for statistics that presaged sabermetrics for the nonstandard manner in which he viewed the values of batting and fielding averages.

In 1914 a stickler for statistics came on the scene trying to peddle his personally compiled data to news agencies in New York. Al Elias, a native of South Carolina, joined forces with his brother Walter to generate figures that were as exacting as possible—"There are only two kinds of statistics: [a]ccurate and worthless," was Al's mantra—and they achieved a breakthrough by providing the daily leaders of numerous major offensive and pitching categories to several metropolitan newspapers.[12] Founding the Elias Baseball Bureau in 1916 and setting up shop in the heart of Manhattan by 1918, the Eliases were retained by the National League to be that circuit's official record keeper. A few years prior, Irwin Howe had begun his tenure in that same capacity for the American League and later also for the Negro Leagues and several minor leagues. The Elias and Howe bureaus carried on for decades providing statistics for various news services and publications such as the Associated Press and the *Sporting News*.

About the time that the Eliases' business was growing by leaps and bounds, another Figure Filbert was born in Brooklyn who would join them in 1943 after his graduation from St. John's University. Seymour Siwoff was hired to handle minor-league data and other lesser chores, then served in World War II, not returning to the Elias agency until 1948. By this time Al Elias had passed away and the business was on poor financial footing, but Siwoff took the reins in 1952 and held firm, "pick[ing] up the pieces, reorganizing the bureau but keeping the Elias name."[13] Doing that name proud in the ensuing decades, Siwoff expanded his services by publishing an annual *Elias Baseball Analyst* from 1985 to 1993.

Plying his trade in a different country but soon to place his own stamp on baseball was Allan Roth, a native of Montreal, Quebec, who as a teenager put his love of numbers to good use by creating statistics for International League teams, including the Montreal Royals, the top Brooklyn Dodgers affiliate at the time. In late 1940 the twenty-three-year-old Roth approached Dodgers president Larry MacPhail about the possibility of joining the team as its statistician, but the "Roaring Redhead" declined to hire him. After finding favor as a statistician for the National Hockey League the following year and serving briefly in the Royal Canadian Army during World War II, Roth continued his data compilation for the Montreal Canadiens, "but he kept his focus on the Dodgers because he considered Branch Rickey, MacPhail's successor as Dodger president, the most innovative man in sports." When Roth impressed Rickey by proposing to assemble an array of intricate statistics "that would reveal tendencies which the front office and the manager *could use to win ballgames*," the mathematician garnered the attention of the Mahatma, who convinced Dodgers ownership to offer Roth a job.[14]

Roth embarked on a career beginning in 1947 that spanned eighteen years with the Dodgers, adding his newly developed spray charts to his repertoire of information. By 1954 he was furnishing data to those broadcasting Dodgers games, including the inimitable Vin Scully. Roth's position as team statistician was unique, and he was credited with deriving the famous Rickey equation mentioned above. When the Dodgers moved west, his duties expanded to include player consultations in spring training to advise them what areas of their game needed improvement. But when Roth was dismissed by the Dodgers near the close of the 1964 season over a reputed interracial extramarital relationship, he was taken on by NBC to work as the statistician for the Game of the Week broadcast, a position that thrust him onto the national stage as the integral accompanist for announcers Curt Gowdy and Tony Kubek.

Through his perception, innovations, and the notoriety he received for his on-air work from 1966 well into the 1980s, Roth was sanctioned by no less a figure than Bill James as the man who could be given credit for "[taking] statisticians into a brave new world."[15] That frontier included new ways of looking at old data, mountains of it that seemed to grow exponentially as the age of the computer moved forward.

Metrics for the Cubs

As noted above, many years ago there were baseball men who sought to look beyond the typical batting average and probe deeper into the numbers to find a truer indicator of a batter's value. Leonard Koppett astutely observed, "The first thing to remember is that statistics merely count what has already happened; they say nothing about why," but as computers allowed growing amounts of data to be analyzed, "why" would slowly become less of a mystery.[16] The bromide "figures don't lie, but liars can figure" held as much truth in baseball as in virtually any other application, especially when players tried to plead their case during contract negotiations. For example, a high number of runs batted in could be viewed in a positive light—any amount greater than ninety can be seen as indicative of a good season's production—yet an examination of *when* those RBIs were registered may reveal that a significant number of them came in lopsided games, indicating the runs were driven in during less pressure-filled opportunities and therefore casting such production with a skeptical glow.

Owner Philip Wrigley hired several statisticians in the late 1930s who were charged with analyzing game data through what was called the Chicago Cubs Experimental Laboratories, a spinoff of the Athletic Research Laboratory at the University of Illinois. In his study of the Cubs' analytical endeavor in the succeeding decades, Alan Kornspan noted that Wrigley's primary focus—besides behavioral and psychological aspects to player traits—was to collect data "for player-evaluation purposes and also for determining the best methods to help players improve their baseball performance."[17]

Analysis done by a small group of Wrigley's data specialists beginning in 1938 then delineated how batters fared against each pitcher they faced, and by the 1940s, Wrigley determined that this information should be given to the team manager to assist him in making decisions in the course of a game. This methodology drew the attention of Cubs skipper Jimmie Wilson, who sought data to inform his judgment on whether to leave a pitcher in the game or place a call to the bullpen.

Other teams embraced the advanced data analytics, many of the original sixteen major-league teams doing so by the late 1950s. In 1961 Wrigley announced that his club would be using an IBM computer to assist in processing the data in a more timely fashion. Earlier collections of numbers were so cumbersome that a full review could be done only at the conclusion of the season, but electronic machines could generate information on a weekly basis that could be used during the season and thus have a more immediate impact. Analyst Ed Whitlow charted pitches for the Cubs in 1963 and fed a multitude of other data into the team's computer in order to create output helpful to the manager in preparing for upcoming games. As the mid-1960s approached, Cubs general manager John Holland was arming himself with computerized statistics to figure out how players performed—in the negative sense—so he would have points to make in keeping salaries low during contract negotiations. And a closer look into the typical 1965 American League batting average was performed the following year in an effort to find the best clutch hitters in that circuit.

The Search for Clutch

Venturing to General Electric headquarters in Phoenix, Arizona, in the spring of 1966, sportswriter Bob Sudyk reported that a GE-235 computer was programmed to generate a list of AL batters and their averages based on a series of pressure-related criteria, the input derived from the actual performance of players in those situations during the 1965 season. The theory was to prove—or disprove—a correlation between a player's batting average over the full season and his average in specific game situations. The six scenarios ranged from low pressure—coming to bat in the first inning with the player's team already ahead—to very high pressure, where the score was tied in the ninth inning or the player's team trailed by a run. Sudyk gave a nod to the previous work done by the Cubs, but he noted that the effort by GE was the first to examine data across an entire league.

With the data "gulped down" by the computer and results "burped out" quite likely on green-stripe paper, Harmon Killebrew of the Twins was tabbed by "computermen in their antiseptic white coats" as the best at displaying more or less "a steady upward curve of their batting averages as the percentage of pressure rose."[18] (See table 11.1.)

Killebrew hit only .269 for the season, but he batted .304 at the 50 percent mark, .275 at 75 percent, .421 at 100 percent, and a resounding .886 at 120 percent. A banged-up Mickey Mantle also did well in the clutch, his .292/75%, .357/100%, and .333/120% all outpacing his modest batting average of .255. But several star-quality hitters came up short with the pressure on, including Tony Oliva (.321 average but .288/100% and .190/120%) and Brooks Robinson (.297 average yet only .259/100% and .224/120%). Thankfully for those susceptible to the ill effects of tension, the figures were published only as the 1966 season was about to begin, meaning the players were not subjected to negative publicity as they were haggling over their contracts for the upcoming campaign.

Table 11.1. Pressure Situation Criteria for GE-235 Computer Program

Pressure	Inning	Score	Outs	Men On
5%	1st	+2	0	None
5%	9th	+4	0	None
25%	9th	+2	1	First
25%	9th	–6	2	First, second
50%	9th	+1	0	Third
50%	9th	-4	1	Third
75%	9th	+1	1	Second, third
75%	9th	–2	0	First
100%	9th	Tied	0	Third
100%	9th	–2	1	Third
120%	9th	Tied	1	Second, third
120%	9th	–1	0	First, third

Source: Sporting News, April 16, 1966, 13.

The New Math

Speaking of Earnshaw Cook, the *Sporting News* editorialized in 1966 that the author of *Percentage Baseball* had presented "math [that] goes over our head." Indeed, when even the casual fan takes a cursory look at portions of Cook's text, it becomes clear that the reader needs to be at an advanced level of mathematical skill. Cook conceded that "the computer cannot *think*; it can only do exactly as it is instructed to do within the knowledge and wisdom of the fallible creatures who operate it."[19]

Cook admitted that his approach was not for the faint of heart, but he made several observations that cut against the traditional execution of baseball strategy. Among them were use of relief pitchers for the first two innings and again for the last two frames while employing a starter for the middle five frames, elimination of platooning in favor of "the eight most valuable non-pitchers"—and arranging the batting order in accordance with their ability—and limiting bunting only to poor-hitting pitchers. The radical ideas promulgated by Cook were directed toward managers who lacked a competitive team: "What do you have to lose by trying a new approach?" he argued.[20]

Around the time Cook was engaged with his data and formulas, an associate of Rutgers University devised a "utility average," which was "defined as how the player contributes to his team's probability of scoring a run."[21] Although the details of the formula were not revealed, the data that was tabulated by a General Electric computer included traditional figures such as at-bats, hits, extra base hits, walks, and stolen bases. For the 1968 National League season, the best performers according to their utility average were Willie McCovey (.314), Hank Aaron (.307), and Dick Allen (.303).

Another breakthrough was achieved by a pair of siblings, Eldon and Harlan Mills, who were soon to answer the plea from a fan in New York who asked, "Where do we find the critical hits that tie and win ball games? Where is the information on spectacular fielding plays that often turn a pitcher from a quivering mass of ineffectiveness to a resurgence of power and confidence? Which r.b.i.'s are meaningless and which turn the tide, winning ball games and pennants?" Eminently qualified—Eldon Mills was a retired air force lieutenant colonel who headed up the automation of that military branch's personnel operations, and his brother Harlan was a mathematics consultant to computer giant IBM—they were cited by statistics expert Pete Palmer for creating a prototype to "calculat[e] win probability as a function of inning, score, and base-out situation and then measure the change for each at-bat during the 1969 season for every batter and pitcher."[22]

With the Elias Sports Bureau in charge of the Mills's data, they devised their methodology based on what they called win points and loss points, the former based on a player's positive contributions to the team and the latter awarded when he did not come through. "What we are really keeping track of is a player's clutch ability," they stated, and the Mills brothers had to account for all player performances on a play-by-play basis in order to compile this new statistic they called player win average (PWA).[23]

The tremendous task in front of them was to determine *what* a player did in a game—a factor consisting of twenty variables such as a hit, walk, stolen base, and so on—and couple those deeds with *when* they occurred, which they found to be almost eight thousand possible instances.[24] Their data was placed on punch cards, which were in turn fed into a computer programmed to analyze it based on an actuarial analogy.

Of most relevance at the time of their foray into player win averages, the Mills brothers used the 1969 New York Mets as an example. Their investigation revealed that the typical focus on high batting average as the standard measurement worked in some cases, such as Cleon Jones and his .340 average, as well as Art Shamsky (.300) and Tommie Agee (.271). Traditionalists could look at Ron Swoboda's .235 in a less favorable light. The player win averages of Jones (.567), Shamsky (.582), and Agee (.548) were well above average, but when Swoboda's PWA was discovered to be .571, almost on a par with his high-ranking teammates, it showed that he was still very valuable to the Mets despite his mediocre batting average.

"Keep in mind that Player Win Averages measure only one thing," the brothers implored—namely, "how much a player helps his team win games." When their PWA results of the 1969 season are placed in context with the players recognized in voting for the Most Valuable Player and Cy Young awards, there are some interesting differences.[25]

In the National League Willie McCovey of the Giants led with a .677 PWA and edged the Mets' Tom Seaver for MVP, while Cy Young winner Seaver's .609 PWA was second among NL starters to Houston's Larry Dierker (.612), who received not a single Cy Young vote. In the American League the Twins' Harmon Killebrew easily outpaced his rivals for the MVP but his .608 PWA was actually fourth among everyday players. Mike Epstein of the Senators was the best with .641, yet he drew only four MVP points. For the AL Cy Young Award, co-winner Denny McLain of Detroit tied Baltimore's Jim Palmer for the best among starters at .585, yet co-winner Mike Cuellar of the Orioles (.569) fared no better than sixth-best for PWA.

As spring training camps were about to open in 1970, Eldon and Harlan Mills brought their findings to market in the form of a book introducing "[t]he first significant new baseball statistic in 50 years," one using a "computer-age approach" that was "sure to generate discussion and controversy in the season to come." Many years later, baseball historian John Thorn stated, "Good hitters are good hitters and weak hitters are weak hitters regardless of the game situation," but he also gave a firm nod to colleague Dick Cramer, who in 1977 pondered the primary trait of a clutch hitter: "Was he really a batter who didn't fold under pressure—or was he a lazy batter who bothered to try his hardest only when the game was on the line?"[26]

    Clutch—elusive and esoteric in nature—may be hard to define, but we know it when we see it.

Settling Arguments

Perhaps no sport has been as steeped in trivia as much as our national pastime, and since baseball's formation in the 1800s, countless disputes have arisen over the gamesmanship one fan can pull off by outsmarting another regarding knowledge of the game. Who led a particular league in home runs for a certain season? What pitcher had the most victories—or losses—for his team? Who managed a club in its most miserable years? These samples only scratch the surface of an endless stream of possible questions. The answers could be found in one of the many volumes published, such as the Reach and Spalding guides dating to the late 1800s.

    Other important books, including *The Sporting News Official Baseball Guide* and its companion *Register*, later became staples that chronicled baseball on an annual basis. By 1922 a former *Sporting News* writer and baseball editor named Ernest J. Lanigan produced—under the aegis of the *Baseball* magazine—an interesting compendium titled *Baseball Cyclopedia*, which contained a synopsis of the early development of the game, a summary of baseball history among cities in the highest-ranking leagues, a recap of batting and pitching leaders, all-time record holders, and other sections related to leagues, teams, and players. Dating to the mid-1920s, *The Pocket Cyclopedia of Major League Baseball* was a publication of the Elias Baseball Bureau, and in the mid-1940s a chance encounter between a baseball hobbyist, S. C. Thompson, and a sports reporter for the *New York Daily News*, Hy Turkin, led the pair to join forces and create *The Official Encyclopedia of Baseball* in 1951. Designated as a Jubilee Edition to commemorate multiple significant anniversaries in baseball history, such as the seventy-fifth anniversary of the National League and the fiftieth anniversary of the American League, the volume was intended to be published as "the complete record of just about every player in the majors since the first year of pro ball, 1871."[27] The finished product of their massive undertaking included a 375-page register of players and managers; histories of the major and minor leagues, plus a look at college, semipro, and Negro League baseball; a review of baseball's administrative apparatus; summaries of each team and diagrams of their respective ballparks; rules of the game and a guide for keeping score; synopses and line scores for all World Series played; a list of record-setting performances and the best-known players, including Hall of Fame members; a register of umpires; playing tips for each position according to some of the best major-league players; a section on baseball songs and poetry; a bibliography of the game's books, periodicals, and other publications; and features that dealt with ballpark minutiae, such as the background of concessionaire Harry M. Stevens.

The layout of the player entries was simplistic and remained that way in subsequent editions, which were enhanced with career totals and batting/throwing information (see table 11.2).

The Jubilee Edition was a first of its kind, noteworthy for its inclusion of so much data and information but also for its broad range of topics, covering nearly every imaginable area of the game of baseball.

If the 620-page Turkin-Thompson opus set a standard for other future encyclopedias, the challenge was duly met by another reference book endorsed by commissioner Ford Frick and edited by Joe Reichler, the *Ronald Encyclopedia of Baseball.* Expansive in its own way, this volume presented standard fare in addition to esoterica, including a chapter highlighting "Spectacular Achievements"

Table 11.2. Sample of Player Data for an Outfielder and a Pitcher, Turkin and Thompson *Encyclopedia*

Yr	Cl	Lea	Pos	G	Rec
ABERSON, CLIFFORD ALEXANDER					
b. Aug. 28, 1921 Chicago, Ill.					
1947	Chi	N	O	47	.279
1948	Chi	N	O	12	.188
1949	Chi	N	O	4	.000
		BRTR		63	.251
ACOSTA, JOSE					
b. Mar. 4, 1894 Havana, Cuba					
1920	Was	A	P	17	5–4
1921	Was	A	P	33	5–4
1922	Chi	A	P	5	0–2
		BBTR		55	10–10

Key: Yr = Year; Cl = Club; Lea = League (A = American, N = National); Pos = Position (O = Outfielder, P = Pitcher); G = Games; Rec = Record (batting average or won-lost record); BB = Batted Both; BR = Batted Right; TR = Threw Right

Source: The Official Encyclopedia of Baseball, Jubilee ed. (New York: Barnes, 1951), 68, 69.

such as the new home run record set by Roger Maris, and complete—or as complete as possible—registers of all players and pitchers, the formats of which were similar to those found in Turkin-Thompson but included shutouts for pitchers as well as home runs and RBIs for batters. In late 1968 the fourth revised edition cost $9.75, and its publisher, A. S. Barnes and Company, also offered a book of World Series records for $5.95.[28]

As the 1960s progressed, revisions of the Turkin-Thompson works were published, and in the early part of the ensuing decade, Seymour Siwoff released "the most accurate baseball record book ever published," listing lifetime, yearly, game, and inning standards for regular-season, league championship series, World Series, and All-Star games.[29] But with advances in information technology growing ever more prevalent, a massive, newly created tome that was typeset by computer—the first to be done so for commercial purposes—came into the sports publication market in the summer of 1969. Fans, librarians, and bookstore clerks may have been challenged to wrestle with its six-and-one-half-pound weight, yet the simple title, *The Baseball Encyclopedia*, belied the contents of the more than twenty-three hundred pages contained therein.

"Big Mac"

The alphabet soup of modern acronyms, especially in what back in the 1960s was referred to as EDP—electronic data processing—included not only the most renowned trio of letters (IBM) but those of another company specializing in computer systems software. Information Concepts Incorporated (ICI) in 1965 had hired the chief statistician at the Lou Harris polling enterprise to put its computing capacity to work in fresh ways. David Neft foresaw a new baseball encyclopedia, created with the assistance of a computer and replete with as much statistical data available for every player dating back to the previous century.

A graduate of Columbia University with a degree in statistics, Neft sought to develop a book that contained more than just the primordial data of games played in a season plus corresponding batting averages and won-lost records that were the stock issue of Turkin-Thompson and *Ronald*. The daunting project was extremely ambitious, and although Neft's proposal gained favor with ICI, more personnel had to be enlisted to be sure the accuracy of the information on each page was at the highest level possible. Neft drew the assignment as the project leader, and he created a staff that included four research positions charged with scouring libraries around the country to find old newspapers containing records of players from yesteryear. The necessity of "completely rebuild[ing] the game's statistical history, brick by painstaking brick" became the overarching goal.[30]

Besides scaling this difficult precipice of data gathering, Neft also had to get a publisher on board to print the finished product, which would be a tough sell to any printing house. In 1967 Neft pitched the idea to the Macmillan Publishing Company, whose executive editor, Robert Markel, was a baseball enthusiast. While it was easy to convince Markel of the project's merit, the publisher's president, Jeremiah Kaplan, blanched at the likely price tag of twenty-five dollars per copy, which he thought would put the book beyond the reach of most fans in an era when hardcover editions of bestsellers were about one-third what the encyclopedia would cost.

Yet Markel was successful in pleading his case, and, now moving forward with greater resolution, more than a dozen researchers were added to the mission. Crucial for the assistance they also contributed were the historian at the Baseball Hall of Fame, Lee Allen, whose own collection of personal data became the framework for each of the encyclopedia's player entries; John Tattersall, owner of a trove of pre-1900 information and author of a home run log; Jordan Deutsch, one of the first researchers originally hired by Neft; and Neil Armann, a former Peace Corps worker who made up for his dearth of baseball knowledge by demonstrating an expertise in his newfound skill of computer programming with a language known as COBOL (common business-oriented language). An IBM System/360 provided the power for executing Armann's programs.

Working collaboratively to fuse together biographical information with accurate statistics, some of which had to be created from scratch using old newspaper game accounts, Neft's charges labored occasionally in uncharted territory. A newly minted system of checks and balances was devised to reconcile individual player figures with the totals for their teams, and not surprisingly, a vast number of errors and inconsistencies emerged in the course of assembling so much information. "The group had to balance correctness against the impression of monkeying willy-nilly with baseball's hallowed statistics," observed Alan Schwarz in his examination of the encyclopedia's formation.[31] Among these was a potential change that would have increased Babe Ruth's time-honored record of lifetime home runs to 715, but it was ultimately determined that a homer Ruth hit in 1918 was properly scored as a triple under rules in force at the time.

Indeed, the mere task of backfilling missing data from the earliest decades of baseball, a mission made more difficult by the necessity of combing out errors and inconsistencies, was by necessity Herculean. The period prior to 1920 was described as "a time that was somewhat chaotic in baseball for record-keeping procedures," and bringing old data into alignment with a fuller set of new information was often an ordeal. The research staff also confessed that deriving accurate won-lost records for managers proved to be most formidable because individual marks had to be found for each man in charge. "A manager in early baseball was often designated as a field captain, not a manager, as he would be known today," the first edition of MacMillan's *The Baseball Encyclopedia* explained.[32]

While the inaugural issue was hardly 100 percent accurate, it nonetheless firmly placed a stake in the ground of modern statistics. "In March of 1969 the work on this volume came to an end," wrote the editors, and anyone reading the four-page preface may have detected a palpable sigh of relief from the staff who had toiled for years to bring the project to a conclusion. As cruel fate would have it, Lee Allen, whose biographical information was crucial to the book's formation, passed away three months before the encyclopedia was released for sale to the public.

The contents of the first edition were remarkable for their inclusiveness and quantity. Separate sections gave a history of the game's evolution; pitching, batting, and fielding leaders for individuals and teams, both single-season and lifetime; year-by-year, team-by-team rosters that included statistics for each player and pitcher; registers of National Association players, all major-league players, pitchers, and managers; summaries of all World Series and All-Star games; appendices listing verdicts of the Records Committee and how they were incorporated into the book; major updates to scoring and playing rules; and notes on source material. Three full pages of thanks and acknowledgments were printed in the beginning as a tribute to the wide-ranging assistance rendered during the course of the project. Recognition of individual contributors was complemented with kudos to many libraries, historical societies, and other institutions across the country that furnished information or otherwise facilitated the encyclopedia's production.

Once a fan dared to venture between the covers of the overweight opus, an unending bounty was there to provide ostensibly endless exploration. The player register displayed seventeen different categories, while the corresponding section for pitchers held nineteen. Nearly three-quarters of the encyclopedia's more than twenty-three hundred pages contained the records of individual players, from the famous to the obscure and long-forgotten, if they were ever known at all. Some of those truly unknown participants, or "phantom players," as they were termed, were deleted from the official record after sufficient investigation proved that the name appearing in an old box score may have been the result of a problem with transmission—by telegraph—of a game account or some other typographical error.[33] While the number of such players was very few, the issue, which was addressed in an earlier version of the *Ronald* encyclopedia, drew further scrutiny in the latest attempt for perfect accuracy.

The introduction of *The Baseball Encyclopedia* at a press conference at Mamma Leone's Restaurant in Manhattan on August 28, 1969—just over five weeks after the first men walked on the moon—could be seen by sports enthusiasts as no less important an end product thanks to the use of modern technology.

Neil Armann's programming allowed for cross-referential verification of various categories of data, yet the fact that so vast an amount of information could be reined in with a computer system and brought to heel in printed form was a true marvel. No accounting could possibly total up how many man-hours would have been required to generate the tome that project director David Neft said "took seven hours to print . . . but a year and a half to tell the computer what to do."[34]

While *Sports Illustrated* found fault with *The Baseball Encyclopedia*, pointing out the umbrage some purists took at the alterations of select statistics, the weekly also praised the book for "its magnificent detail" that made it "so engrossing." Yet the verdict on the book would rest with the sporting and book-buying public, and the reception received by *The Baseball Encyclopedia* was overwhelming, not just on the part of the critics but also by those willing to shell out $25 for a copy. Readers of the June 28 issue of the *Sporting News* were enticed with a prerelease offer of the encyclopedia and a copy of Lawrence S. Ritter's *The Glory of Their Times* for $19.95. The ad appeared to underestimate the number of facts contained in the encyclopedia—1.3 million—given its size, but the claim of $1.5 million in production costs and three and one-half years of research was certainly believable. "[B]ig for a book, small for an amusement park," was the quip offered by one reviewer, who with each turn of the page seemed to be "sent . . . off on another tangent" in search of an answer to whatever baseball question happened to come to mind.[35]

The return for Macmillan was impressive as more than one hundred thousand copies were sold, and even as large and heavy as the encyclopedia was, it became a fixture on the shelves of many serious baseball fans. Among the recipients was President Richard Nixon, who was gifted with a pair of copies courtesy of Bowie Kuhn and informed the commissioner through his secretary, Rose Mary Woods, that he was intending to share one of them with his son-in-law, David Eisenhower. Whether *The Baseball Encyclopedia* gained more importance by being an authority in settling disputes over baseball trivia or simply by providing access to seemingly every statistic known to fans matters little. Its publication was a sea change in the world of baseball, and, as author Alan Schwarz correctly observed, "The book began a new era of fanaticism for baseball statistics."[36]

Not only did *The Baseball Encyclopedia* spur interest in statistics and their modernistic offspring, but it also kindled a greater general appreciation for the game's history. Riding the momentum of the recent, dramatic World Series upset, Macmillan released in early 1970 a book authored by Leonard Koppett, *The New York Mets: The Whole Story*, which featured one hundred thousand statistics worth of data—"all of it computer-authenticated"—for a team only eight years old, plus a narrative telling the "complete history of the Mets. . . . This one could come only from the publishers of *The Baseball Encyclopedia.*"[37] With the availability of smaller, less expensive derivatives that were still packed with information, fans could delve deeper into their favorite team—at about ten dollars a copy—without having to purchase the oversized and pricey encyclopedia.

Macmillan's triumph did not completely leave its competitors in the dust, however. The Turkin-Thompson encyclopedia carried on in its comparatively limited format throughout the 1970s, but Macmillan had clearly created a new standard. Their encyclopedia would be updated every three years, adding data for the most recently completed seasons as well as continuing to ferret out pesky mistakes and inaccuracies. But perhaps the most enduring legacy of the Macmillan effort came not in the form of another book but in the creation of an organization that brought together some of the most devoted baseball minds.

Two years after the release of *The Baseball Encyclopedia*, a gathering took place in Cooperstown, New York, and the attendees formed the core of what became the Society for American Baseball Research, whose work in the fields of statistical and historical research over more than four decades has created a vast corpus of scholarship on the national pastime. "Once the [encyclopedia] was in place, a new world opened," wrote law professor Robert C. Berring, who, like Schwarz, recognized the connection between Macmillan's product and a surge of newfound interest in baseball that set both casual fans as well as serious students of the game on a path to more passionate exploration.[38]

Scouting

The "electronic brain" mentioned earlier was used to predict certain player performances and outcomes of pennant races. A natural extension of this sort of forecasting was an application for scouting purposes. But even though the computer age was swinging into high gear by the end of the 1960s, some people, like Orioles manager Earl Weaver, clung to a more old-fashioned means of data collection so they had a bank of information at their disposal when needed. A vast parcel of index cards served as the file from which Weaver could extract "four or five things that give you an idea of a player's strengths, weaknesses, and tendencies." For pitchers or players Weaver's team had not faced, the manager sought an appraisal from Baltimore scout Jim Russo so that he could "get an index card on the guy as soon as possible."[39] Weaver, in essence, was manually mimicking the system used by the Cubs' Ed Whitlow, only tailoring the application to his personal non-computer usage. Relief pitcher Bob Locker maintained his own personal records so that he did not have to rely on potentially faulty recall in preparing for opposing batters he might face.

In the wake of the conclusion of the 1968 regular season, personnel in Seattle and Kansas City were making ready for the American League expansion draft of major-league players. At the Sheraton Hotel in Boston, where the draft was to be held, "an inconspicuous-looking van containing a desk-sized computer system . . . will provide the interested parties inside with a wealth of instant information on the progress of the draft."[40] The service came courtesy of IBM, whose sports data division also furnished efficient information capabilities for professional golfing events. Several key components were to be tracked during the draft, including the players formerly available but then reclassified as protected after that team lost a player, as well as the names of players by position still available for selecting. A pair of monitors were placed in the hotel, one containing information for the expansion team personnel and another for the benefit of the other clubs. Although Seattle and Kansas City still had to rely on their own scouting reports to determine specifically whom to select, the assistance furnished to all parties on draft day was quite helpful: The AL's computer-assisted draft was four hours faster than the one held for the National League.

One notable skeptic needed convincing as to the worthiness of some applications of the latest technology. In a postdraft editorial, the *Sporting News* acknowledged the efforts of the Houston Astros to cast their lot with punch-card data for scouting purposes, but the publication also derided the poor accuracy rate—41.2 percent correct—of Penn State's IBM computer in foretelling home run output for the campaign that had just ended. "The formula resulted in some rather absurd predictions," said the opinion piece, which also cited Penn State's own concession about the foibles of the machine: "Unfortunately for the computer, talent cannot be measured in any meaningful or quantitative way that would enable a computer to include it in a mathematical formula."[41]

Taking fuller measure of the technology was Baltimore second baseman Dave Johnson, who, in the process of studying for a degree in mathematics, tried his hand with the computer at his offseason employer, the Institute of Computer Management. Coming off the year of his first All-Star Game selection but still seeking ways to help his team improve, Johnson looked to the computer to process "percentages" of a number of factors to determine an optimal batting order.[42]

One year after the expansion draft, World Series hero Jerry Koosman was on hand at a sports forum in New York to promote "the use of the computer in baseball as a scouting tool and a gleaner of talent."[43] The event was also highlighted by a film that extolled the computer's virtues in assisting the scouting endeavors related to football players, and the new technology was embraced by the National Basketball Association's Philadelphia 76ers, who were employing computer assistance to sift through the many players available for the next NBA draft.

Pitcher Jack DiLauro, Koosman's teammate on the Mets, was scouted after the 1969 campaign by the Houston Astros, who were looking for a left-handed reliever in the upcoming Rule 5 draft. "Personnel director Tal Smith fed the data processing machine the scouting reports on some 300 lefthanded pitchers available in the draft," and Houston had previously used computers to evaluate trade prospects from other teams.[44] In DiLauro's case, his rating paid off when the Astros chose him for the $25,000 draft price and he became one of the best relievers in the National League in 1970, especially from late April until early July when he yielded no earned runs.

The pitfalls of any computer, regardless of its application, often point to the adage of "garbage in, garbage out," and no machine can predict the outcomes of personality clashes that can short-circuit a career, which was what happened to DiLauro when a dispute with Astros management made him persona non grata in Houston and to all intents and purposes ended his days as a major leaguer.

Scheduling

Unlike the various attempts at foretelling player performance or pennant winners—the results of which could be inconsistent, to say the least—another facet of baseball that had a completely predictable outcome was the scheduling of regular-season games in each major league. Until 1960 every team played 22 games against each of its intraleague rivals, for a total of 154 contests, and upon expansion in 1961 and 1962 the formula was altered to 18 matches per rival, for a total of 162 games. The American League pennant frenzy of 1964 drew notice as well as a bit of criticism because the top contenders in September—the White Sox, Yankees, and Orioles—would not face each other head-to-head as the season wound down. The blame was placed by the league office on the "sectional" way in which the schedule was initially drawn up.

AL administrative assistant Bill Cutler said that parsing the calendar into three roughly equivalent timeframes of eight weeks apiece allowed for balancing the slate so that every club played all other teams home-and-home in each of the trio of sections. The first part ran from Opening Day until June 7, the second from June 8 to August 5, and the last from August 6 until the end of the season. "Now it so happened that this year when the schedule reached the last third on August 5, the contenders [had] played each other early in this segment," Cutler explained. Cutler's boss, AL president Joe Cronin, defended the manner in which the slate was created and had no envy for the task with which Cutler and his National League counterpart, Fred Fleig, were charged. When Cutler and Fleig sought help from IBM's Boston office, disappointment followed—"They were sorry, but they couldn't handle it," was the reply—and a further entreaty to United Airlines, which dealt with travel arrangements for many teams, only led to more frustration as the carrier "threw up their hands" saying "there was no mathematical answer" to the conundrum."[45] Not only could logical travel routes be problematic, but accommodating the special requests of teams played further hob with the schedule makers. For example, the Baltimore Orioles wanted to avoid poor attendance during the mid-May weekend when the Preakness, the second leg of horse racing's Triple Crown, was being run at nearby Pimlico. In addition, the three cities that hosted two teams each—New York, Chicago, and Los Angeles—preferred to avoid conflicts by not playing at home on the same dates.

Little improvement was evident as 1965 came to a close. Fleig stated that besides IBM and United being enlisted, "firms of specialists [tried] to arrange a schedule on their computers, and all attempts have either been abandoned or have proved unsatisfactory." To solve its own scheduling problems, the National Football League, now increased in size to sixteen teams for the 1967 season with the addition of the New Orleans Saints, also decided to forgo use of a computer in favor of an oversized checkerboard on which "coat tags are labeled with team names and [hung] up on nails."[46] NFL commissioner Pete Rozelle had sought computer assistance but decided that the manual alternative was preferable.

Baseball, however, demanded more attention to detail because of the far greater number of games to be played. By early 1969 the persistent Fleig announced that both human and artificial intelligence at Harvard University had been brought on board to solve the problem. Two professors and a graduate student who was working directly with the American League office to devise a computer-generated schedule finally succeeded—to a degree—later that year, although manual intervention was required to complete the mission. Among the pet peeves that were given at least some attention were allowing for more sensible travel across time zones as well as scheduling daytime "getaway" games during the week so that teams could reach their next destination with less of a fatigue factor.

Fred Fleig again partnered with William Cain, the former Harvard graduate student who had now become a Georgia State University professor, to create the 1970 schedule. The expedient processing capabilities of the computer drastically reduced the time needed to resolve discrepancies that would otherwise have consumed an untold number of hours for humans to conquer. This latest schedule was estimated to have pared about seven thousand miles of travel from the previous year's National League slate alone, and although cross-checking against the American League schedule remained a chore, the experience gained from increasing reliance on computers would help tame the "gigantic jigsaw puzzle" that by its very nature was the schedule of Major League Baseball.[47]

Marketing Aspects

Once all those games were set on the calendar, the business of filling seats through ticket sales and generating interest in a team through an effective marketing strategy played a crucial role in helping the clubs' revenue streams, and taking advantage of television broadcasting would become increasingly valuable as the 1960s progressed. Information technology began playing a role in these pursuits as well.

Computer-related offerings made conspicuous appearances in the *Sporting News*, whose advertisements from several enterprises catered to the male fan. One ad sponsored by the Fort Lauderdale Technical College told of programming correspondence courses to train users on the IBM 360 mainframe, while a more seductive notice for a matchmaking service tempted lonely men with the picture of a dark-haired siren shown with a tagline of "She Wants to Meet YOU Now!"—a rendezvous to be arranged "thanks to the electronic memory computer."[48]

The use of high tech to lure baseball fans to watch the game from the comfort of home began in the early part of the decade. TelePrompTer, a closed-circuit television company, employed a "new gimmick box tied to an automatic computer," and viewers in New York would push buttons on the TelePrompTer console to select a pay-per-view broadcast such as a sporting event. The signal relayed to the transmission company would not only cue the signal to the viewer's home television but also feed information into a "mechanical brain" that would generate a billing statement.[49] Such a scheme was believed to be an improvement over coin-operated implements in vogue at the time.

Watching such a system with keen interest—both literally and figuratively—were the Los Angeles Dodgers, who premiered their version of pay-per-view in the summer of 1964, two years after the New York trial. Enlisting the services of Subscription TeleVision, Inc. (STV), the Dodgers sent their July 17 contest against the Cubs to cable subscribers who paid a $5 installation fee and $1.50 for the game, one of three offerings on different channels on the STV system, "with an electronic computer figuring each subscriber's tab by the month." A resourceful Little League team in the Los Angeles area found STV to be an attractive alternative to a Saturday afternoon movie. "They watched [a Dodgers game] in a private home, chipping in ten cents apiece," and some commercial outlets such as bars and restaurants were expected to subscribe—at $18 per view—as a drawing card for their businesses.[50] Although baseball cablecasts would cut into attendance at the ballpark, the revenue generated from viewers' fees would offset some of those losses.

As more major-league cities were wired for cable television, the computer was being used by at least one team to sift through fans' questionnaires to determine expenditures by those actually coming to the ballpark. With the novelty of the Astrodome at a high level after its 1965 debut, attendees of events there were calculated to spend about $40 per visit, with "the average out-of-town fan see[ing] five baseball games a year in the Dome, which represents a large increase from the days when the Houston Colts [*sic*] played outdoors at Colt Stadium."[51] Not only were tickets purchased by fans, but parking and concessions also factored into their outlay of cash.

And this on-site expenditure could only take place when the turnstiles clicked, so as cablecasts—with built-in electronic customer billing—competed for the fans' dollars, the computer was used to make ticket purchases more convenient. In 1967, at a time when the credit card was flexing greater muscle in consumer purchasing, teams such as the Minnesota Twins found that accepting plastic for ticket purchases brought a "response beyond expectation," and the club had brought a computer into its front office to handle accounting chores, with a secondary task of statistical analysis possibly being delegated to the new machine.[52]

An advertisement was taken out by Computer Sciences Corporation, and its Computicket subsidiary announced in September 1967 the imminent demonstration of "the first ticket distribution and control system for the sports and entertainment industries."[53] Retail outlets such as supermarkets, banks, and department stores would be equipped with consoles linked to a pair of IBM 360-40 mainframes—one for primary processing, the other serving in a backup capacity—enabling the box office at an arena or stadium to be extended much closer to fans.

Slated to come online in the spring of 1968, Computicket outlets would initially serve fans in Los Angeles and then spread to New York and other major cities. The terminal setups, which included the ticket printer, cost $7,000 apiece, and customers had the option of paying "on the spot by cash, check or that other marvel of modern science—the credit card." The expansion Montreal Expos took advantage of the opportunity to market seats at Jarry Park via a company called Ticket Reservation Systems in early 1969, and that summer its corporate subsidiary, Ticketron, was offering the same service in the greater New York metropolitan area, with banks, transportation hubs, and travel agencies also providing outlets.[54]

Baseball and its calm, pastoral traits stood in contrast to its faster-paced competitors of football, basketball, hockey, and auto racing, and the tempo of the national pastime was not likely to change. Indeed, as baseball moved beyond the 1960s, games once played at efficient two-hour gallops began increasingly to consume more and more time. Longer games meant fans spent more time at the ballpark, generating more chances for the sale of concessions, but rather than growing completely bored by drawn-out contests, fans were also being entertained by another electronic device finding its way into stadiums, especially the newer ballparks, that was slowly replacing its manually operated forebears.

Electronic Scoreboards

As modern stadiums began to open in the 1960s, it was only natural that the latest technology would be built into them. The 1964 debut of Shea Stadium inaugurated the use of an oversized electronic scoreboard seven stories in height and operated from a space in the press box outfitted with a computer terminal. Messages entered into the system were reviewed for accuracy and could be stored for future use or displayed immediately. The following year, as the Los Angeles Angels were soon to segue to their new home in Anaheim, the club unveiled plans for a gigantic twenty-three-story, A-shaped structure featuring a sixty-by-fifty-four-foot scoreboard. The Angels' "electronic cheerleader" was controlled by a computer system with the capacity to hold one thousand preprogrammed messages, plus "its own special brand of animated antics and bouncing letters" along with "animation [that] will enliven game action," while homers struck by the home team would prompt the computer operator to activate the seventy-foot-wide halo at the top of the A to illuminate it "in a scintillating burst of incandescence."[55] Such accoutrements were tailored to the Angels in the same manner that the Astrodome scoreboard gave a nod to its Texan heritage.

In 1966 the scoreboard at new Busch Memorial Stadium had a console of 273 buttons, switches, and other controls used in its operation, but not all teams were enthusiastic about some of the information conveyed via the latest technology. In the summer of 1967, the Baltimore Orioles allowed—on a trial basis—an IBM messaging system operated by a model 1130 computer to display data from a forty-foot van equipped with a retractable scoreboard. The computer manufacturer's van was first used earlier that year in conjunction with the Professional Golfers Association tour, and the 1130 was capable of creating messages of combined statistical data and character text. Some of the Orioles blanched when their unflattering batting averages were flashed on the seven-thousand-light board for all to see, but when Brooks Robinson clouted a home run during the van's visit, the crowd was instantly—and pleasantly—informed that the third baseman had just tied the club record of 142 set by Gus Triandos.

Apparently satisfied with the functioning of the 1130 computer, the Oakland Athletics used it to power the pair of $1 million scoreboards that were in operation for the team's opening in 1969. The board's internal system was built in part by Information Concepts Incorporated, who delivered Macmillan's *The Baseball Encyclopedia*, and had much instantaneous programming built into it. When the third out of an inning was entered into the 1130, according to a contemporary account, "[the computer] recognizes that the side has been retired. It automatically resets the ball-strike section of the scoreboard to zero. It updates the inning-by-inning score. It updates [the last batter's] batting average. It updates the pitcher's statistics for later display. It provides the name and batting average of the next batter. And it does all this in less than one second."[56] As this statistical wizardry was taking place on one scoreboard, fans could be entertained on the other by a cartoon version of owner Charlie Finley's famed mascot, the mule Charley-O. Such animation was a labor of love, however: Six to seven weeks of programming was required to produce a sixty-second clip. But another practical feature of the computer's work behind the scenes was its generation of a postgame report, which was then distributed to the media, with the most up-to-date statistics.

At Cincinnati's new Riverfront Stadium, the twenty-five-hundred-car garage built as part of the stadium's complex used a different kind of scorekeeping. The four levels of the garage had electronic vehicle counters to track the number of vacant parking spots and when none were available "[relay information] to central traffic computers in order to re-route traffic to downtown locations immediately," but in the stadium proper, "an electronic typewriter [was] used to punch tapes that will be fed through a computer and ultimately display messages on the board."[57] The Reds' venue actually featured a three-part messaging system, with a main scoreboard and animation board inside Riverfront plus a message board on the outside of the stadium.

The Pirates' Three Rivers Stadium claimed to feature the most sophisticated scoreboard at the time of its opening in 1970, and, as was the case in Anaheim, the firm of Stewart-Warner was contracted to program its operating system. Besides the messaging component, the computer in Pittsburgh also contained "an optical element called a 'graphic reader,'" which allowed the operator to "instantly flash a pictorial likeness of [an] individual on the scoreboard."[58] Generation of up-to-the-minute statistics was a part of the Three Rivers system as well.

Embedded in a cauldron of circuitry, the computer's processing unit was making obsolete not only the time-honored manually operated scoreboard but even some of the more recent electronic versions such as the one at Shea Stadium, which displayed panels of lights that showed only individual letters and numbers. For better or worse, animation became a new standard feature by the end of the 1960s, but the functionality of the computer to handle vast amounts of message information and statistics made for alluring entertainment at the ballpark and kept fans better informed.

Giving the Fans a Vote

In the summer of 1956, five members of the Cincinnati Redlegs were selected to start for the National League All-Star squad, while three of their teammates were chosen as reserves by manager Walter Alston.[59] Fans at the time had the privilege to vote for the starters, but such a preponderance of Redlegs earning honors drew suspicion and prompted a call to change the voting system, though no amendments materialized. This unwelcome pall not only lingered for another year but drew unvarnished outrage when the All-Star Game balloting for 1957 revealed that seven Cincinnatians had been voted as NL starters, prompting commissioner Ford Frick to make immediate roster adjustments and further strip fans of the privilege to choose the starting players.

With major-league players, coaches, and managers empowered to select the starters, there would no longer be a "deluge" of votes from the Queen City—or anywhere else, for that matter—to taint the All-Star rosters of either league. Suffering from a bit of punisher's remorse, perhaps, Frick investigated the possibility of employing computers to tabulate punch-card ballots for the 1964 contest. In late 1963 an accounting firm in Detroit, Sommers Business Service, suggested allotting one hundred thousand cards per major-league city that fans could use to vote for their desired players. Company president Joseph L. Sommers promoted the idea as economical—assuming a corporate sponsor would underwrite the estimated $25,000 cost of the campaign—and fair because "the electronic voting system is completely equitable and no [single city's players] can dominate."[60]

While this idea did not bear immediate fruit, the secretary of the Baseball Writers' Association of America announced in early 1964 that voting for the Hall of Fame had been reduced from "an all-day job for eight men" to a much simpler two-hour process thanks to assistance from an IBM computer.[61] At this time, another All-Star voting proposition was advanced by a Minneapolis-based computer company in which players' names would be accompanied by a three-digit code to be used by fans to indicate their choices.

But in May, Frick declined to return balloting to the fans because of concern over printing the computer cards too early in the season, a fault whereby some deserving players' names might be omitted. Time would also be required to distribute ballots across the nation—rather than limiting them only to major-league cities—in order to maximize participation. In the meantime, Frick was comfortable with maintaining the status quo allowing players to choose their peers in the wake of the Cincinnati imbroglio: "The team[s] chosen by the players in the past few years have been regarded as truly representative."[62]

Upon Bowie Kuhn's arrival as commissioner in February 1969, the decade-long policy of Frick's initiative was soon to be abandoned. Kuhn was fervent in his desire to let the fans have their say, and although he admitted that "there would be some howls" over the selection of some of the players, the commissioner defended his reversal of the Frick edict because "fan voting made too much marketing sense to ignore."[63] There was no time available to renew fan voting for that season's Midsummer Classic, but after the Gillette Company was named as the sponsor, the logistics were put in place for the 1970 contest.

Twenty-six million punch-card ballots were distributed nationwide to 75,000 retail outlets and to 150 minor- and major-league teams for use during the voting period of May 30 through June 28. But the inaugural cards immediately drew the rebuke Kuhn had feared: Several players who were performing splendidly early in the 1970 campaign were left off the ballots that listed a total of forty-eight men from both the American and National leagues. Among them were Al Kaline of the Tigers, who as of mid-May was Detroit's best hitter and run-producer, and Atlanta's Rico Carty, who was batting well over .400 as voting was about to open. Catcher Jim Price of the Tigers, who was among the player representatives and managers charged with nominating those whose names would be printed on the ballot—six catchers, six at each infield position, and eighteen outfielders—vented his spleen when he learned that Kaline did not make the cut. "How can you select who's going to be on the All-Star team during spring training?" fumed Price about the early printing deadline.[64] The insult of omission was compounded by the injury of the inclusion of disabled players such as Mike Shannon of the Cardinals, who did not appear in a game until May 14, and Ken Harrelson of the Indians, who had been out of action for almost the entire season after breaking a leg in mid-March.

Fans nonetheless had the opportunity to take matters into their own hands, albeit on a limited basis. Space was provided on the punch card to allow for write-in candidates, and ballots containing such players would be tallied separately rather than being processed directly by computer. Those entrusted with counting the ballots claimed that a large number of write-in votes would not be problematic as long as they were confined to only a few positions, such as Carty's outfield slot and possibly the National League third-base position, whose selections included rookie Coco Laboy of the expansion Montreal Expos but not the Dodgers' hot-hitting rookie, Billy Grabarkewitz. One fan proposed a ballot in the future that included the regular position players for every team, but this would have been nearly impossible given the limitations of the Hollerith cards on which the ballots were configured.[65]

The uneven start to the resumption of fan voting via computer forced Kuhn to look askance at criticism levied against the program. The commissioner admitted that the new system was not perfect, but in his memoir he declared victory: "Far from damaging the process, [fan balloting] fostered fierce debates and actually popularized the new voting." Also endorsing the renaissance was the *Sporting News*, which editorialized that stars selected by the fans closely matched those chosen in an unofficial poll—in twelve of sixteen instances—and, while not mentioning Carty's name, noted that "write-ins were permitted" and "it's hard to quarrel with the popular choices."[66]

Little could be done in the future to prevent unforeseen flaws that could arise, yet the prescience of putting the write-in option on the ballot offered some degree of justice to slighted players. However, the broader issue of Kuhn's desire to generate interest in the All-Star Game could not have become a reality without the aid of the modern machinery that read and sorted the millions of ballots cast.

It's Only a (Simulated) Game

Predating the earliest versions of computerized baseball games by many decades, the table game of Parlour Base-Ball originated in 1866, and in the ensuing century other board and card games were created to allow participants the chance to claim victory on an imaginary diamond. The computer enabled future generations to re-create baseball action as well as that of other sporting events.

In the summer of 1965, when Tommy John was in his first season with the Chicago White Sox, the young southpaw faced off against several Hall of Fame hurlers, with the home field—of sorts—being the circuitry of an IBM 1620 computer. At the time, John was a part-time mathematics major at Indiana State University, and in conjunction with his instructor, he devised a ball game played on the computer using statistics derived from his former team, the Cleveland Indians, and those of past great ballplayers. In a series of contests that lasted about eight minutes each, John pitched against Bob Feller, Lefty Grove, and Christy Mathewson, coming out on the short end in most of the matchups. Presaging his real-life mound appearances, in which he became notorious for using a scuffed ball, John admitted he could rig the simulation "by giving the computer bad information," and confessed that in some circumstances, "I had to cheat. It was my only chance."[67]

When the 1965 World Series was being played in reality, radio station WFIL in Philadelphia staged a computer simulation of games in which teams of all-time great players from the American and National leagues squared off. Data gleaned from the *Sporting News* were "fed into the computer at the Franklin Institute and the high-speed machine took just 12 seconds per game to digest the information and bat out a play-by-play account."[68] The Nationals prevailed, taking four of six games.

Just as the 1970 regular season was opening, NBC announced plans to sponsor a computer tournament seeded by eight great teams of yesteryear and the very recent past. On the strength of their upset World Series victory, the 1969 New York Mets had vaulted into ostensible immortality along with their miraculous companions, the 1951 New York Giants, both chosen by the tourney organizers, while the other six teams were included based on a vote of fans taken by the network. After the games were played on a computer, NBC replayed them accompanied by actual game footage—where available—between the real-life contestants. The finalists, perhaps not surprisingly, were the 1927 New York Yankees and their 1961 Bronx brethren, with the former club reigning in the finale on the strength of a tenth-inning home run by Lou Gehrig.

Eldon and Harlan Mills, the brothers who introduced the player win averages statistic, were integral to the project's success as the computer masterminds of the game simulation, and they in turn availed themselves of a marketing opportunity by linking the NBC broadcasts with their new book. For less than five dollars, fans could purchase a copy of *Player Win Averages* and a printout detailing the staged contests. "The book tells how, using the same computer baseball program that NBC used, Player Win Averages—a new clutch baseball statistic—is developed," their company's advertisement claimed, and to emphasize the validity of the results, the Mills brothers stressed that readers would learn about the "Hidden Heroes" whose low batting averages were transformed into value-laden return due to impressive clutch performances.[69]

"There isn't in existence a complete roster of the major league players for all time, unless some sterling collector is hiding under a bushel. . . . The time probably will never come when everything will be known about baseball as it has been exemplified in the major leagues and the time certainly will never come when everything that has happened in the minor leagues will be catalogued and ready for the seeker of information."[70] One can easily sense the resignation in Ernest J. Lanigan's voice as he worked to assemble his *Baseball Cyclopedia*, yet Lanigan had no way of foretelling a time well in the future when machines, with their capacity to store and process many gigabytes of information, would become a fixture of everyday life not just in business but in the home.

The boom in computer innovation continues unabated to this day, and each new application seems to become obsolete with the introduction of the next new application—until it also is quickly surpassed. When Macmillan's *The Baseball Encyclopedia* burst onto the scene in 1969, it was a marvel to behold and the first attempt during the computer age to assuage Lanigan's frustration, but that tome and its later editions would themselves become victims of technological advancement. Why run to a six-plus-pound book for answers when the same information—and more—can be found on your cell phone?

As surely as flannel baseball uniforms yielded to those made of polyester, the old-fashioned age of manual processing ceded its place throughout society to the computer, not all at once, but in an inexorable manner over many years. Baseball, too, was swept along in the tide of bits and bytes that steeped it further in the digital era.

Afterword

Major League Baseball crossed an important threshold in 1968 and reached a new frontier the following year with budding success, which is not to state flatly that all went smoothly. That the national pastime not only surmounted its growing pains but also prospered in the ensuing years stands as testimony to its resilience. As baseball emerged from the potentially damaging swoon of second-class status, it brought into its fold new fans in distant outposts—albeit an accomplishment attended by more than a modicum of angst—while at the same time retaining the qualities that make the game so attractive in the first place.

Having slowly gained the confidence of baseball's labor force—which is to say, the players—Marvin Miller delivered increasing salaries and improved benefits to the union membership not just through tenacious bargaining but by also instilling in the players confidence in their ability to stand up collectively for their rights, a characteristic virtually nonexistent before Miller became the director of the players' association. Tainted by rising levels of animosity as the financial stakes also rose in succeeding years, player clashes with team ownership would grow more raucous, even after the reserve clause was struck down. But Miller's tactics were instructive and began to demonstrate that the players as well as the team magnates could prosper in baseball's new, changing economy.

American society and culture were in flux, and baseball was affected by the changes in a country growing evermore restive with a stubborn war in Southeast Asia. The nation's landscape was scarred by assassination and marked by the fallout of peace protests, drug use, and mutinous behavior by the younger generation, the same generation that supplied baseball with the players who toiled on its diamonds. Casting a wary eye on "the Establishment," youth in the

249

United States had kindred spirits among baseball players whose own mindsets were informed by current events swirling around them. As older players left the game, the turnover in baseball rosters allowed the first of the Baby Boomers to fill the void, and the departure of the old guard also meant that those newer players would be characterized by a different attitude toward their employers, a trait working in concert with Miller's efforts.

New expansion teams gave birth to divisions in each league, and the World Series was no longer baseball's sole October attraction. When expansion joined with revisions to the strike zone and the height of the pitching mound, the changes imparted freshness to a sport in need of rejuvenation. The venues that hosted games were undergoing modern transformation in stadium design and construction, which were further augmented by the flourishing of computer technology that in turn was delivering greater amounts of information and new applications to fans and big-league front offices.

Acting as the captain guiding baseball's ship through demanding and uncertain waters was a new commissioner, far more knowledgeable than his predecessor and better qualified to extract the game from the lethargic state into which it had meandered. Like William Eckert before him, Bowie Kuhn would later fall out of favor with the club owners who held the fate of his employment as commissioner. But Kuhn passed his screen test in 1969, to the pleasure of the moguls, and the executive branch of the game's governing body was then solidified by an enthusiastic official sensitive to the issues of baseball's greatest concern. The luster of Kuhn's reign would diminish, but at the time of his installation he proved to be a sage choice to lead the national pastime beyond its stodgy ten-team leagues and into a new modern era.

It is difficult to choose a single salient aspect of this period that was more important than any other in contributing to baseball's long-term prosperity. Rather, it may be more appropriate to view an amalgamation of these factors working together to position the game for profit—economically, and by becoming more attractive so as to broaden its fan base—as baseball crossed the divide from the 1960s into the 1970s. Subjects of this book's chapters and subtopics, those features brought forth a very early version of a national pastime now updated to move into succeeding decades. The growing pains of two new franchises stumbling out of the starting gate, as well as indignation at the labor movement because of a perceived danger that the players' union would ruin the game, detracted from baseball's mission to strengthen itself. Although these perils came with the territory of operating the enterprise, they proved to be obstacles that could be surmounted.

This book's relatively narrow timeframe invites further exploration of the topics contained herein because these pages emphasize, as much as possible, the two crucial years of 1968—the end of the old game, in a manner of speaking—and 1969, at which time the divisional era was born. That birth, attended by a new commissioner and seminal rule changes, expedited a process that extricated baseball from its slumber and reset its course on a path to regaining ground it had lost to professional football. Facing the challenges of revision and modernity in the context of the age, baseball in the late 1960s became a proving ground for how well its stamina and character would hold up in the years to come.

Notes

Preface

1. Oscar Kahan, "Baseball Groping for New Direction," *Sporting News*, December 21, 1968, 25.

Chapter 1

1. Denny McLain with Eli Zaret, *I Told You I Wasn't Perfect* (Chicago: Triumph Books, 2007), 84–85.
2. Jack Lang, "Recuperating Gil Steps Up His Exercise Program," *Sporting News*, December 7, 1968, 38.
3. Bob Gibson, quoted in Joseph Durso, "Umpire Cautioned Schoendienst," *New York Times*, October 7, 1968.
4. Leonard Koppett, quoted in Jerome Holtzman, *The Commissioners: Baseball's Midlife Crisis* (New York: Total Sports, 1998), 131.
5. Mark Kurlansky, *1968: The Year That Rocked the World* (New York: Ballantine Books, 2004), 382.

Chapter 2

1. John Drebinger, "American League, in '61, to Add Minneapolis and Los Angeles," in *The New York Times Book of Baseball History* (New York: Arno Press, 1975), 217.
2. Paul Hensler, *The American League in Transition, 1965–1975: How Competition Thrived When the Yankees Didn't* (Jefferson, NC: McFarland, 2012), 158–60.

3. Joe McGuff, "Sporting Comment," *Kansas City Star*, October 17, 1967; Jerome Holtzman, "AL Vote to Expand Marks 1967 History," in Chris Roewe and Oscar Kahan, eds., *Official 1968 Baseball Guide* (St. Louis: Sporting News, 1968), 176.

4. John R. Cauley, "Jabs Finley in Senate," *Kansas City Star*, October 20, 1967.

5. Dick Young, "Young Ideas," *Sporting News*, November 11, 1967, 14.

6. Jerome Holtzman, "Expansion, Canadian Club, Feature 1968," in Chris Roewe and Paul MacFarlane, eds., *Official 1969 Baseball Guide* (St. Louis: Sporting News, 1969), 174; Joseph Durso, "National League Adds Montreal and San Diego," in *The New York Times Book of Baseball History*, 277.

7. Lou Chapman, "No NL Team for City," *Milwaukee Sentinel*, May 28, 1968, 1.

8. Tommy Mercer, quoted in Holtzman, "Expansion, Canadian Club, Feature 1968," 176.

9. "Legislature and Buffalo Group Okay Terms of Stadium Lease," *Sporting News*, June 1, 1968, 38; Dick Kaegel, "Sweating, Waiting . . . As N.L. Debated," *Sporting News*, June 8, 1968, 5.

10. Bob Broeg, "Cards' Toomey Suggests Three Majors in '70," *Sporting News*, June 1, 1968, 30.

11. "Surprise in Montreal—What Next?" *Sporting News*, July 20, 1968, 14; Holtzman, "Expansion, Canadian Club, Feature 1968," 179.

12. Calvin Griffith, quoted in Jon Kerr, *Calvin: Baseball's Last Dinosaur—An Authorized Biography* (Dubuque, IA: William C. Brown, 1990), 80.

13. Minutes, Executive Council meeting, June 26, 1968, Papers of Bowie K. Kuhn, BAMSS100, National Baseball Hall of Fame Library, National Baseball Hall of Fame, Cooperstown, NY, Series I, Sub-Series 1, Box 1, Folder 2, Executive Council Meetings March 20, 1968–October 19, 1970; Cronin, quoted in Dick Kaegel, "Cool It! That's What Club Brass Will Do in Wake of Big Fuss," *Sporting News*, June 15, 1968, 4.

14. M. Donald Grant, quoted in "Two-Division Plan for N.L.," *Sporting News*, June 29, 1968, 14.

15. Jim Bouton, *Ball Four*, ed. Leonard Shecter, 20th anniversary ed. (New York: Wiley, 1990), 19; "Electronic System to Aid A.L. Draft," *Sporting News*, October 12, 1968, 31.

16. Jack Lang, "Hill Gems Scarce, Expos, Padres Discover," *Sporting News*, October 26, 1968, 11.

17. "Who Are the Real Culprits?" *Sporting News*, April 20, 1968, 16.

Chapter 3

1. Paul O'Boynick, "American League Owners Put Welcome Mat Out for Kauffman," *Kansas City Times*, January 12, 1968; "Kauffman Heads Kansas City Club," *New York Times*, January 12, 1968.

2. Anne Morgan, *Prescription for Success: The Life and Values of Ewing Marion Kauffman* (Kansas City: Andrews & McMeel, 1995), 17, 46.

3. Morgan, *Prescription for Success*, 53; Don Kowet, *The Rich Who Own Sports* (New York: Random House, 1977), 144.

4. Morgan, *Prescription for Success*, 117.

5. Ewing Kauffman, quoted in "Kauffman Heads Kansas City Club," *New York Times*, January 12, 1968; Kauffman, quoted in Joe McGuff, "Team Is Here to Stay," *Kansas City Times*, January 12, 1968; Sid Borman, "Score Runs High in Selection of Kauffman," *Kansas City Times*, January 12, 1968; Burke, quoted in O'Boynick, "American League Owners Put Welcome Mat Out for Kauffman."

6. Phil Koury, "Kauffman Puts Winning Record on Line," *Kansas City Star*, January 14, 1968.

7. Editorial cartoon, *Kansas City Star*, January 14, 1968; editorial cartoon, *Kansas City Times*, March 4, 1968; Jim Lapham, "Ranged Far on Ball Team Name," *Kansas City Star*, March 24, 1968; "So It's Kansas City Royals," *Kansas City Star*, March 22, 1968.

8. Dutton Brookfield, "As I See '68 . . . ," *Kansas City Star*, January 14, 1968; *1969 Kansas City Royals Media Guide*, 2.

9. Jean Wuellner, "Royals Win Fans and Game in Opener," *Kansas City Times*, April 9, 1969; Paul O'Boynick, "Gordon Lays Plans for 1970," *Kansas City Star*, October 2, 1969; "Royal Memories for October-Time," *Kansas City Times*, October 4, 1969.

10. Morgan, *Prescription for Success*, 253.

11. Bill Mullins, *Becoming Big League: Seattle, the Pilots, and Stadium Politics* (Seattle: University of Washington Press, 2013), 10.

12. Mullins, *Becoming Big League*, 12.

13. Mullins, *Becoming Big League*, 48.

14. John Owen, "A Day to Remember!" *Seattle Post-Intelligencer*, October 18, 1967; Lenny Anderson, "League OKs Team If City Has Stadium," *Seattle Post-Intelligencer*, October 19, 1967.

15. Mullins, *Becoming Big League*, 61.

16. Mullins, *Becoming Big League*, 63.

17. Larry Claflin, "Pilots Select Vets, Royals Corral Kids," *Sporting News*, October 26, 1968, 11.

18. Mullins, *Becoming Big League*, 148.

19. United Airlines advertisement, *Seattle Post-Intelligencer*, April 10, 1969.

20. Mullins, *Becoming Big League*, 115; Jim Bouton, *Ball Four*, ed. Leonard Schechter, 20th anniversary ed. (New York: Wiley, 1993), 145.

21. John Owen, "Let's Call a Spade a Shovel," *Seattle Post-Intelligencer*, October 1, 1969.

22. Photograph by Doug Wilson, *Seattle Post-Intelligencer*, October 3, 1969.

23. Owen, "Let's Call a Spade a Shovel."

24. Mullins, *Becoming Big League*, 233.

Chapter 4

1. Bob Ortman, "Scouts Are No. 1 on Bavasi's List of Musts," *Sporting News*, June 22, 1968, 9.

2. Melvin Durslag, "The O'Malley Eyes Completely Dry at Bavasi's Departure," *Sporting News*, June 22, 1968, 9; *1969 San Diego Padres Media Guide*, 9.

3. Ortman, "Scouts Are No. 1 on Bavasi's List of Musts," 9.

4. Paul Cour, "Padres Set Goal of 4,000 Season Ducats," *Sporting News*, December 28, 1968, 43.

5. Emil Bavasi, quoted in Phil Collier, "Padres Were Born with Deathbed Commitment," in Jim Enright, ed., *Trade Him! 100 Years of Baseball's Greatest Deals* (Chicago: Follett, 1976), 228.

6. Bill Swank, *Baseball in San Diego: From the Padres to Petco* (Charleston, SC: Arcadia, 2004), 72.

7. "Major League Baseball Expanding to Montreal," *Montreal Gazette*, May 28, 1968.

8. Danny Gallagher and Bill Young, *Remembering the Montreal Expos* (Toronto: Scoop Press, 2005), 12; Ted Blackman, "Montreal Team's Backers Demand Action on Stadium," *Sporting News*, July 13, 1968, 27.

9. Gallagher and Young, *Remembering the Montreal Expos*, 20.

10. *Le magazine Expos 1980* (vol. 1): 14.

11. "Backers of Montreal Bid Launch a Counterattack," *Sporting News*, May 18, 1968, 18; Blackman, "Montreal Team's Backers Demand Action on Stadium," 27.

12. Ted Blackman, "New Feather in Cap of Montreal Mayor," *Sporting News*, June 15, 1968, 5.

13. Ted Blackman, "Montreal Fans Clamor for Season Tickets," *Sporting News*, August 31, 1968, 7.

14. Jean-Louis Lévesque, quoted in Ted Blackman, "Montreal Will Sign McHale as G.M.," *Sporting News*, June 22, 1968, 30.

15. Donn Clendenon, quoted in John Robertson, "One Trade Akin to Leaving a Monastery," in Enright, *Trade Him!*, 164.

16. Robertson, "One Trade Akin to Leaving a Monastery," 165.

17. Spec Richardson, quoted in Jerome Holtzman, "Two Divisions, Rules, Player Demands, Etc.," in Paul MacFarlane, Chris Roewe, and Larry Wigge, eds., *Official 1970 Baseball Guide* (St. Louis: Sporting News, 1970), 274.

18. Clendenon, quoted in Robertson, "One Trade Akin to Leaving a Monastery," 166.

19. Ted Blackman, "Wise Expos Will Avoid Clash with Hockey," *Sporting News*, November 16, 1968, 38.

20. Edgar Munzel, "A 13-Hour Meeting; The Result: Nothing," *Sporting News*, January 4, 1969, 41.

21. Ray Boetel, "Cozy Camp: Braves Share Drill Facilities with Expos," *Sporting News*, March 1, 1969, 7; Dan Turner, *The Expos Inside Out* (Toronto: McClelland & Stewart, 1983), 15.

Chapter 5

1. Jerome Holtzman, *The Commissioners: Baseball's Midlife Crisis* (New York: Total Sports, 1998), 15.

2. Fred Saigh, quoted in Holtzman, *The Commissioners*, 87.

3. Holtzman, *The Commissioners*, 98.

4. "Fetzer First to Interview Eckert, Game's New Boss," *Sporting News*, December 4, 1965, 4; "A New Hand at Baseball's Helm," *Sporting News*, November 27, 1965, 14.

5. Holtzman, *The Commissioners*, 122.

6. William Eckert, quoted in Barney Kremenko, "'I'll Call the Signals,' Eckert Promises," *Sporting News*, December 4, 1965, 3.

7. Dick Young, "Young Ideas," *Sporting News*, December 25, 1965, 14.

8. William Eckert, quoted in "Eckert Favors Orderly Expansion," *Sporting News*, June 11, 1966, 16.

9. Leonard Koppett, "Eye on Eckert," *Sporting News*, December 25, 1965, 25.

10. Brian McKenna, "William Eckert," BioProject of the Society for American Baseball Research, accessed October 5, 2016, http://sabr.org/bioproj/person/4691515d; Holtzman, *The Commissioners*, 123, 125.

11. William Eckert, quoted in Tom Kelly, "Get-Acquainted Junket Keeping Eckert on Move," *Sporting News*, March 19, 1966, 7.

12. John Underwood, "Progress Report on the Unknown Soldier," *Sports Illustrated*, April 4, 1966.

13. Leonard Koppett, "New Eckert Era—The First 275 Days," *Sporting News*, September 3, 1966, 5; Underwood, "Progress Report on the Unknown Soldier."

14. Jerome Holtzman, "$8 Million Scheduled for Players' Pension Plan in '67 and '68," *Sporting News*, September 10, 1966, 8.

15. Marvin Miller, *A Whole Different Ball Game: The Sport and Business of Baseball* (New York: Birch Lane Press, 1991), 161.

16. William Eckert, "Eckert Offers '67 Progress Report," *Sporting News*, January 13, 1968, 34.

17. Joe King, "Eckert Strategy Map Gives Priority to Fan," *Sporting News*, March 9, 1968, 5.

18. Minutes, Executive Council meeting, March 20, 1968, Papers of Bowie K. Kuhn, BAMSS100, National Baseball Hall of Fame Library, National Baseball Hall of Fame, Cooperstown, NY, Series I, Sub-Series 1, Box 1, Folder 2, Executive Council Meetings March 20, 1968–October 19, 1970.

19. Memo from Joseph Reichler to George E. Arnstein, May 7, 1968, Papers of Bowie K. Kuhn, BAMSS100, National Baseball Hall of Fame Library, National Baseball Hall of Fame, Cooperstown, NY, Series VI, Sub-Series 3, Box 14, Folder 9, Misc. Attendance Data & Analysis 1969.

20. C. C. Johnson Spink, "We Believe . . . ," *Sporting News*, June 22, 1968, 14; Dick Young, "Young Ideas," *Sporting News*, June 22, 1968, 14.

21. Jim Murray, "Murray's Best," *Sporting News*, September 14, 1968, 32; McKenna, "Willian Eckert."

22. Dick Young, "The Hoffberger Gang's Revolt—End of an Era," *Sporting News*, December 21, 1968, 25, 46; Minutes, Executive Council meeting, December 3, 1968, Papers of Bowie K. Kuhn, BAMSS100, National Baseball Hall of Fame Library, National Baseball Hall of Fame, Cooperstown, NY, Series I, Sub-Series 1, Box 1, Folder 2, Executive Council Meetings March 20, 1968–October 19, 1970.

23. Young, "The Hoffberger Gang's Revolt," 46.

24. Oscar Kahan, "Baseball Groping for New Direction," *Sporting News*, December 21, 1968, 25; Leonard Koppett, interviewed by Gabriel Schechter, June 16, 1992, SABR Oral History Project; Joe Falls, *Sporting News*, December 21, 1968, 2.

25. Spink, "We Believe . . . ," 14; Leonard Koppett quoted in Holtzman, *The Commissioners*, 131.

26. Dave Nightingale, "Baseball's Smashing Revival," *Cleveland Press*, October 16, 1969.

27. Leonard Koppett, "Baseball Owners Must Face Major Challenges to Achieve Modernization," *New York Times*, December 8, 1968.

28. "Crisis of the Old Order," *Sporting News*, December 21, 1968, 14.

29. William Leggett, "Court-martial for a General," *Sports Illustrated*, December 16, 1968, 51.

30. Holtzman, *The Commissioners*, 134.

31. Bowie Kuhn, *Hardball: The Education of a Baseball Commissioner* (New York: Times Books, 1987), 34; Milton Richman, "Today's Sports Parade," February 7, 1969; Bowie Kuhn Scrapbook, 1969, BASCR234, National Baseball Hall of Fame Library, National Baseball Hall of Fame, Cooperstown, NY.

32. William Leggett, "The Big Leagues Select a Fan," *Sports Illustrated*, February 17, 1969.

33. Jerome Holtzman, "Two Divisions, Rules, Player Demands, Etc.," in Paul Mac-Farlane, Chris Roewe, and Larry Wigge, eds., *Official 1970 Baseball Guide* (St. Louis: Sporting News, 1970), 266.

34. Alexander Edelman, "Ken Harrelson," BioProject of the Society for American Baseball Research, accessed October 5, 2016, http://www.sabr.org/bioproj/person/442 dbc70.

35. "The Hawk Is Mighty Sharp," *Sporting News*, May 19, 1969, 14.

36. "'Just Want to Do My Thing For Indians,' Crows Hawk," *Sporting News*, May 3, 1969, 13; Holtzman, "Two Divisions, Rules, Player Demands, Etc.," 277; Kuhn, *Hardball*, 50.

37. Memo of proposed realignment of major league baseball teams, June 19, 1969, Papers of Bowie K. Kuhn, BAMSS100, National Baseball Hall of Fame Library, National Baseball Hall of Fame, Cooperstown, NY, Series I, Sub-Series 2, Box 6, Folder 5, Three Division Play 1969, 1971.

38. Memo of proposed realignment of major league baseball teams, June 19, 1969.

39. Bowie Kuhn, quoted in Mark Mulvoy, "Baseball Booms Again," *Sports Illustrated*, August 4, 1969.

40. Bowie Kuhn, quoted in Stanley Frank, "Greed Is the Name of the Game," *TV Guide*, August 9, 1969, 9.

41. Minutes of Joint Meeting, August 12, 1969, Papers of Bowie K. Kuhn, BAMSS100, National Baseball Hall of Fame Library, National Baseball Hall of Fame, Cooperstown, NY, Series III, Sub-Series 2, Box 1, Folder 7, Joint Meetings May 28, 1968–December 6, 1969.

42. Mulvoy, "Baseball Booms Again."

43. Memo from Carl Lindemann Jr. to Bowie Kuhn, May 8, 1969, Papers of Bowie K. Kuhn, BAMSS100, National Baseball Hall of Fame Library, National Baseball Hall

of Fame, Cooperstown, NY, Series IV, Sub-Series 2, Box 10, Folder 8, TV Committee 1969; memo from Jack Singer to Bowie Kuhn, June 26, 1969, Papers of Bowie K. Kuhn, BAMSS100, National Baseball Hall of Fame Library, National Baseball Hall of Fame, Cooperstown, NY, Series IV, Sub-Series 2, Box 10, Folder 8, TV Committee 1969.

44. Draft memo to Bowie Kuhn, n.d., Papers of Bowie K. Kuhn, BAMSS100, National Baseball Hall of Fame Library, National Baseball Hall of Fame, Cooperstown, NY, Series VI, Sub-Series 3, Box 14, Folder 9, Misc. Attendance Data & Analysis 1969 (This missive may have been written by publicist Joseph Reichler in early 1969.); draft memo to Bowie Kuhn, September 22, 1969, Papers of Bowie K. Kuhn, BAMSS100, National Baseball Hall of Fame Library, National Baseball Hall of Fame, Cooperstown, NY, Series VI, Sub-Series 3, Box 14, Folder 9, Misc. Attendance Data & Analysis 1969.

45. Memo from Pete Rozelle to Bowie Kuhn, Papers of Bowie K. Kuhn, BAMSS100, National Baseball Hall of Fame Library, National Baseball Hall of Fame, Cooperstown, NY, Series VII, Box 17, Folder 9, Correspondence.

46. *Proposed Reorganization of Professional Baseball*, Wharton School of Finance and Commerce, Papers of Bowie K. Kuhn, BAMSS100, National Baseball Hall of Fame Library, National Baseball Hall of Fame, Cooperstown, NY, Series I, Sub-Series 2, Box 5, Folder 8, Restructuring/Reorganizing of Professional Baseball 1968–1971.

47. *Proposed Reorganization of Professional Baseball*.

48. *Proposed Reorganization of Professional Baseball*; Kuhn, *Hardball*, 67.

49. Planning Committee Commentary on the Wharton Report, January 8, 1970, Papers of Bowie K. Kuhn, BAMSS100, National Baseball Hall of Fame Library, National Baseball Hall of Fame, Cooperstown, NY, Series I, Sub-Series 2, Box 5, Folder 9, Restructuring/Planning—Wharton Notes 1968–1971. This document contains Kuhn's handwritten notes of this meeting.

50. Kuhn, *Hardball*, 35, 36.

Chapter 6

1. Leonard Koppett, interviewed by Gabriel Schechter, June 16, 1992, Society for American Baseball Research Archives, Phoenix, AZ.

2. Koppett, SABR interview.

3. Ed Edmonds, e-mail correspondence with author, June 11, 2015.

4. Brian McKenna, "Robert Cannon," BioProject of the Society for American Baseball Research, accessed October 5, 2016, http://sabr.org/bioproj/person/a7414ea2.

5. Jim Bouton, interviewed by Gabriel Schechter, August 12, 1992, Society for American Baseball Research Archives, Phoenix, AZ; McKenna, "Robert Cannon," emphasis added.

6. Koppett, SABR interview; Bouton, SABR interview.

7. Marvin Miller, *A Whole Different Ball Game: The Sport and Business of Baseball* (New York: Birch Lane Press, 1991), 7; John Helyar, *Lords of the Realm: The Real History of Baseball* (New York: Ballantine Books, 1994), 15.

8. Marvin Miller, interviewed by Fay Vincent, May 26, 2004, National Baseball Hall of Fame Library, National Baseball Hall of Fame, Cooperstown, NY.

9. Miller, Hall of Fame interview.

10. Dick Hall, interviewed by Gabriel Schechter, August 20, 1992, Society for American Baseball Research Archives, Phoenix, AZ.

11. Miller, Hall of Fame interview.

12. Miller, Hall of Fame interview.

13. Lee Lowenfish, *The Imperfect Diamond: A History of Baseball's Labor Wars* (Lincoln: University of Nebraska Press, 2010), 202; Miller, *A Whole Different Ball Game*, 45.

14. Miller, Hall of Fame interview.

15. Helyar, *Lords of the Realm*, 85.

16. Miller, *A Whole Different Ball Game*, 57; Bouton, SABR interview; James B. Dworkin, *Owners versus Players: Baseball and Collective Bargaining* (Boston: Auburn House, 1981), 36; Miller, Hall of Fame interview.

17. Koppett, SABR interview.

18. "Collective Bargaining: A New Threat?" *Sporting News*, April 9, 1966, 16.

19. Hall, SABR interview; Tom Haller, interviewed by Gabriel Schechter, July 8, 1991, Society for American Baseball Research Archives, Phoenix, AZ.

20. Hall, SABR interview.

21. "Minimum-Pay Hike in Order," *Sporting News*, April 23, 1966, 14.

22. Joe King, "New Contract Form and Reserve Clause Sought by Players," *Sporting News*, August 12, 1967, 4.

23. Marvin Miller, quoted in Dick Kaegel, "Player-Owner Friction Mounting Rapidly," *Sporting News*, December 16, 1967, 32; Warren Corbett, *The Wizard of Waxahachie: Paul Richards and the End of Baseball as We Knew It* (Dallas: Southern Methodist University Press, 2009), 317, 316.

24. Paul Richards, quoted in Dick Kaegel, "Miller's Blast 'Shocks, Angers' Moguls, But They Cool Off Fast," *Sporting News*, December 16, 1967, 31; Kaegel, "Player-Owner Friction Mounting Rapidly," 32.

25. "Let's Get Down to Business," *Sporting News*, December 16, 1967, 14.

26. Oscar Kahan, "Agreement Claimed On $10,000 Salary In 'Stalling' Debate," *Sporting News*, February 3, 1968, 22.

27. Joe King, "$10,000 Minimum Pay Okayed; Player-Owner Treaty Is Likely," *Sporting News*, February 10, 1968, 30.

28. "Agreement Signed for Minimum Pay," *Sporting News*, March 9, 1968, 23.

29. Miller, *A Whole Different Ball Game*, 97.

30. Helyar, *Lords of the Realm*, 91.

31. Marvin Miller, quoted in Jerome Holtzman, "Expansion, Canadian Club, Feature 1968," in Chris Roewe and Paul MacFarlane, eds., *Official 1969 Baseball Guide* (St. Louis: Sporting News, 1969), 190; Miller, *A Whole Different Ball Game*, 98.

32. Miller, *A Whole Different Ball Game*, 99; Haller, SABR interview.

33. Holtzman, "Expansion, Canadian Club, Feature 1968," 191; Agreement between The Major League Baseball Television Committee and NBC News, February 14, 1969, Bowie K. Kuhn Collection, BAMSS100, National Baseball Hall of Fame Library, National Baseball Hall of Fame and Museum, Cooperstown, NY, Series IV, Sub-Series 2, Box 6, Folder 5, MLB & NBC News Agreement and Supplement 1968, 1969.

34. Miller, *A Whole Different Ball Game*, 101; Bob Locker, interviewed by Gabriel Schechter, June 16, 1992, Society for American Baseball Research Archives, Phoenix, AZ; Minutes of Joint Meeting, February 27, 1969, Bowie K. Kuhn Collection, BAMSS100, National Baseball Hall of Fame Library, National Baseball Hall of Fame and Museum, Cooperstown, NY, Series III, Sub-Series 2, Box 1, Folder 7, Joint Meetings May 28, 1968–December 6, 1969, emphasis added.

35. Holtzman, "Expansion, Canadian Club, Feature 1968," 191.

36. Miller, *A Whole Different Ball Game*, 96, 103.

37. Holtzman, "Expansion, Canadian Club, Feature 1968," 192.

38. Corbett, *The Wizard of Waxahachie*, 322; Holtzman, "Expansion, Canadian Club, Feature 1968," 193.

39. Gary Bell, quoted in Jim Bouton, *Ball Four*, ed. Leonard Shecter, 20th anniversary ed. (New York: Wiley, 1990), 196; Bouton, *Ball Four*, 195–96.

40. Holtzman, "Expansion, Canadian Club, Feature 1968," 194.

41. Koppett, SABR interview.

42. Russ Gibson, interviewed by Gabriel Schechter, August 4, 1992, Society for American Baseball Research Archives, Phoenix, AZ.

43. Miller, *A Whole Different Ball Game*, 105; Bowie Kuhn, *Hardball: The Education of a Baseball Commissioner* (New York: Times Books, 1987), 40.

44. Bouton, *Ball Four*, 273, 283, 314.

45. Bouton, *Ball Four*, 284.

46. Exhibit A, "Historical Development of the Reserve Clause," April 21, 1970, Bowie K. Kuhn Collection, BAMSS100, National Baseball Hall of Fame Library, National Baseball Hall of Fame and Museum, Cooperstown, NY, Series II, Sub-Series 4, Box 12, Folder 1, Flood Trial.

47. Lowenfish, *The Imperfect Diamond*, 16.

48. Joe Schultz, quoted in Bouton, *Ball Four*, 313; Stew Thornley, "The Demise of the Reserve Clause," *Baseball Research Journal* (Society for American Baseball Research) 35 (2007): 115.

49. Kuhn, *Hardball*, 19.

50. Lowenfish, *The Imperfect Diamond*, 175.

51. Mitchell Nathanson, "Dick Allen Preferred Not To: A Reconsideration of Baseball's Bartleby," *NINE: A Journal of Baseball History and Culture*, 22, no. 2 (spring 2014): 5.

52. Memo from Lou Krems, May 19, 1970, Bowie K. Kuhn Collection, BAMSS100, National Baseball Hall of Fame Library, National Baseball Hall of Fame and Museum, Cooperstown, NY, Series II, Sub-Series 4, Box 12, Folder 5, Bowie K. Kuhn Subpoena and Material 1970.

53. Brad Snyder, *A Well-Paid Slave: Curt Flood's Fight for Free Agency in Professional Sports* (New York: Plume, 2007), 2.

54. Miller, Hall of Fame interview.

55. Miller, Hall of Fame interview.

56. Snyder, *A Well-Paid Slave*, 80.

57. Miller, Hall of Fame interview. Use of an impartial arbitrator was achieved later in 1970.

58. Clark Griffith, quoted in Harold Seymour, *Baseball: The Early Years* (New York: Oxford University Press, 1960), 111.

59. Curt Flood, quoted in Lynn Hudson, "90G Still Slave, Sez Flood," *New York Sunday News*, January 4, 1970; *Flood v. Kuhn, et al.*, 309 F. Supp. 793, accessed October 5, 2016, http://casetext.com/case/flood-v-kuhn.

60. Miller, Hall of Fame interview; Marvin Miller memo, "Joint Study of the Reserve Clause," June 27, 1969, Bowie K. Kuhn Collection, BAMSS100, National Baseball Hall of Fame Library, National Baseball Hall of Fame and Museum, Cooperstown, NY, Series II, Sub-Series 4, Box 12, Folder 9, Joint Study of the Reserve Clause.

61. Memo from Monte Irvin to Bowie Kuhn, April 9, 1970, Bowie K. Kuhn Collection, BAMSS100, National Baseball Hall of Fame Library, National Baseball Hall of Fame and Museum, Cooperstown, NY, Series II, Sub-Series 4, Box 12, Folder 1, Flood Trial.

62. Snyder, *A Well-Paid Slave*, 216.

63. *Flood v. Kuhn, et al.*, 309 F. Supp. 793; Questioning of Bowie Kuhn, April 21, 1970, Bowie K. Kuhn Collection, BAMSS100, National Baseball Hall of Fame Library, National Baseball Hall of Fame and Museum, Cooperstown, NY, Series II, Sub-Series 4, Box 12, Folder 1, Flood Trial; *Flood v. Kuhn, et al.*, 443 F. 2d 264, accessed October 5, 2016, http://caselaw.lp.findlaw.com/us-supreme-court/407/258.html.

64. *Flood v. Kuhn, et al.*, 407 U.S. 258, accessed October 5, 2016, http://caselaw.lp.findlaw.com/us-supreme-court/407/258.html.

65. Miller, *A Whole Different Ball Game*, 240.

66. Snyder, *A Well-Paid Slave*, 229.

67. David A. Bohmer, "Marvin Miller and Free Agency: The Pivotal Year, 1969," in William M. Simons, ed., *The Cooperstown Symposium on Baseball and American Culture, 2011–2012* (Jefferson, NC: McFarland, 2013), 88.

68. Joe Cronin, quoted in Holtzman, "Expansion, Canadian Club, Feature 1968," 195, 196.

69. Holtzman, "Expansion, Canadian Club, Feature 1968," 196.

70. Holtzman, "Expansion, Canadian Club, Feature 1968," 196.

71. Bohmer, "Marvin Miller and Free Agency," 93.

72. Mark Armour, "A Tale of Two Umpires," *Baseball Research Journal* (Society for American Baseball Research) 38, no. 2 (fall 2009): 128.

73. Armour, "A Tale of Two Umpires," 129; Bohmer, "Marvin Miller and Free Agency," 96.

74. Miller, *A Whole Different Ball Game*, 413.

75. Bouton, SABR interview.

76. Jim Bunning, quoted in Dick Kaegel, "Player Owner Friction Mounting Rapidly," *Sporting News*, December 16, 1967, 31.

Chapter 7

1. Jules Witcover, *The Year the Dream Died: Revisiting 1968 in America* (New York: Warner Books, 1997), 112; Gordon Carruth, *The Encyclopedia of American Facts and Dates*, 9th ed. (New York: HarperCollins, 1993), 668.

2. David Fleitz, "Cap Anson," BioProject of the Society for American Baseball Research, accessed October 5, 2016, http://www.sabr.org/bioproj/person/9b42f875.

3. "New Horizons for the Negro," *Sporting News*, May 28, 1966, 14.

4. Emmett Ashford, quoted in Joe McGuff, "Sporting Comment," *Kansas City Star*, March 3, 1968.

5. Mitchell Nathanson, "Dick Allen Preferred Not To," *NINE: A Journal of Baseball History and Culture*, 22, no. 2 (spring 2014), 18.

6. John N. Ingham, "Managing Integration: Clemente, Wills, 'Harry the Hat,' and the Pittsburgh Pirates' 1967 Season of Discontent," *NINE: A Journal of Baseball History and Culture*, 21, no. 1 (fall 2012), 87, 88.

7. Warren Corbett, *The Wizard of Waxahachie: Paul Richards and the End of Baseball as We Knew It* (Dallas: Southern Methodist University Press, 2009), 310; Hank Aaron with Lonnie Wheeler, *I Had a Hammer: The Hank Aaron Story* (New York; Harper Perennial, 1991), 261–63.

8. Jackie Robinson, quoted in "Robinson Backs Defense of Black Group, But Mrs. Basie Defers," in Thomas W. Zeiler, *Jackie Robinson and Race in America* (Boston: Bedford/St. Martin's, 2014), 125.

9. "Mays Has Answer for Robinson," *Kansas City Times*, March 16, 1968.

10. James S. Hirsch, *Willie Mays: The Life, The Legend* (New York: Scribner, 2010), 474; Ernie Banks, quoted in "Ernie Banks, the Eternally Hopeful Mr. Cub, Dies at 83," *New York Times*, January 23, 2015.

11. Mark Kram, "Discord Defied and Deified," *Sports Illustrated*, October 5, 1970.

12. Bob Gibson with Lonnie Wheeler, *Stranger to the Game* (New York: Viking, 1994), 187.

13. Les Biederman, "Buccos, Steelers Cheer Start of New Stadium," *Sporting News*, May 11, 1968, 15; "The Commissioner's Wise Choice," *Sporting News*, September 7, 1968, 14.

14. Dave DuPree, "Blacks Big in Baseball," *Seattle Post-Intelligencer*, April 11, 1969; Curt Blefary, interviewed by Dave Bergman, July 10, 1992, Society for American Baseball Research Archives, Phoenix, AZ.

15. Brooks Robinson, quoted in John Eisenberg, *From 33rd Street to Camden Yards: An Oral History of the Baltimore Orioles* (New York: Contemporary Books, 2001), 163.

16. Mark Kram, "Discord Defied and Deified."

17. Tommy Davis, quoted in Jim Bouton *Ball Four*, ed. Leonard Shecter, 20th anniversary ed. (New York: Wiley, 1990), 285.

18. Bouton, *Ball Four*, 334.

19. Richard O. Davies, *Sports in American Life: A History*, 2nd ed. (Malden, MA: Wiley-Blackwell, 2012), 287.

20. Aaron, *I Had a Hammer*, 4, 19; Jackie Robinson, quoted in "Robinson Backs Defense of Black Group, But Mrs. Basie Defers," 126.

21. Anthony H. Pascal and Leonard A. Rapping, "Racial Discrimination in Organized Baseball," Rand Corporation, Santa Monica, CA, December 1970, 7, accessed October 5, 2016, http://www.rand.org/content/dam/rand/pubs/research_memoranda/2008/RM6227.pdf. The actual figures show 116 U.S. blacks and 58 Latin blacks, which, when totaled, comprise 22 percent of all major-league players in 1968. Al Downing, quoted in "Are Whites Retaking Baseball?," *Ebony*, July 1981, 81; Pascal and Rapping, "Racial Discrimination in Organized Baseball," 49–50.

22. Flood's biographer indicates that the painting was not the work of Flood. See Brad Snyder, *A Well-Paid Slave: Curt Flood's Fight for Free Agency in Professional Sports* (New York: Plume, 2007), 9.

23. Aaron, *I Had a Hammer*, 232, 267, 269.

24. Gibson, *Stranger to the Game*, 199; Pascal and Rapping, "Racial Discrimination in Organized Baseball," 29–30.

25. Rod Carew and Ira Berkow, *Carew* (New York: Simon & Schuster, 1979), 150.

26. Floyd McKissick, quoted in Abraham Iqbal Kahn, *Curt Flood in the Media: Baseball, Race, and the Demise of the Activist-Athlete* (Jackson: University Press of Mississippi, 2012), 130.

27. Frank Robinson, quoted in Joseph Durso, "Indians Plan to Drop Pilot; Yank Game Off," *New York Times*, September 28, 1974.

28. James T. Patterson, *The Eve of Destruction: How 1965 Transformed America* (New York: Basic Books, 2012), 89.

29. Aaron, *I Had a Hammer*, 131.

30. Carew and Berkow, *Carew*, 52.

31. George Gmelch, "Tiger Town: Spring Training, 1966," *NINE: A Journal of Baseball History and Culture* 22, no. 1 (fall 2013), 123.

32. William Leggett, "Some Hot Rookies for a New Season," *Sports Illustrated*, March 11, 1968.

33. Leo Durocher, quoted in Doug Feldmann, *El Birdos: The 1967 and 1968 St. Louis Cardinals* (Jefferson, NC: McFarland, 2007), 87.

34. Roy Gleason with Mark Langill, *Lost in the Sun: Roy Gleason's Odyssey from the Outfield to the Battlefield* (Champaign, IL: Sports Publishing, 2005), 207; "Vietnam War Deaths," Baseball's Greatest Sacrifice, accessed October 5, 2016, http://www.base ballsgreatestsacrifice.com/vietnam_war.html.

35. Jim Fregosi, quoted in Ross Newhan, "Fregosi Shaken to Bootstraps after Visiting War Casualties," *Sporting News*, January 6, 1968, 51.

36. Ron Kline, quoted in Les Biederman, "Kline Brings Back Messages from Wounded GIs," *Sporting News*, November 30, 1968, 53; Ernie Banks, quoted in Stan Isle, "Vietnam Soldiers Cheers Banks, No. 1 Morale Booster," *Sporting News*, December 14, 1968, 31.

37. George Vecsey, "Swoboda Encounters 'Real Thing' in Ballplayer's Odyssey in Vietnam," *New York Times*, December 15, 1968.

38. "World Series Notes," *Sporting News*, November 1, 1969, 6; Bowie Kuhn, quoted in James Tuite, "War Casualties Demand Full-Staff Flag at Shea," *New York Times*, October 16, 1969.

39. With the exception of note 40 below, quotes in the following summary of Kuhn's trip are extracted from the Bowie Kuhn Diary, Saigon, November 1969, Papers of Bowie K. Kuhn, BAMSS100, National Baseball Hall of Fame Library, National Baseball Hall of Fame, Cooperstown, NY, Series V–Official Trips and Tours, Box 1, Folder 1.

40. Kuhn, *Hardball*, 64.

41. Wilbur W. Evans, "Armed Forces Professional Entertainment—Consolidated Attendance and Final Itinerary Report," November 22, 1969, National Archives and Records Administration.

42. Robert S. Wicks, "'Major League Baseball Centennial Showcase'—After-Action Report," January 2, 1970, National Archives and Records Administration; Milt Pappas, "Entertainment Unit Manager's Report," November 21, 1969, National Archives and Records Administration.

43. Evans, "Armed Forces Professional Entertainment"; Wicks, "'Major League Baseball Centennial Showcase.'"

44. Denny McLain with Eli Zaret, *I Told You I Wasn't Perfect* (Chicago: Triumph Books, 2007), 143.

45. Richard Riis, Facebook correspondence with author, June 8, 2015.

46. David Maraniss, *Clemente: The Passion and Grace of Baseball's Last Hero* (New York: Simon & Schuster, 2006), 221.

47. "Phils Nix LA Tuesday Opening," *Baltimore Afro-American*, April 9, 1968, 17.

48. "The Fight for Racial Equality," *Sporting News*, April 20, 1968, 16, emphasis added.

49. Letter from Monte Irvin to Dr. William A. Rutherford, January 2, 1969, Martin Luther King Jr. East/West Baseball Classic, BAMSS168, National Baseball Hall of Fame Library, National Baseball Hall of Fame, Cooperstown, NY, General Correspondence, Folder 5.

50. Witcover, *The Year the Dream Died*, 263.

51. Gibson, *Stranger to the Game*, 188.

52. Bill Fleischman, "The Aftermath—Baseball Takes a Beating," *Sporting News*, June 22, 1968, 4; Ed Kranepool, quoted in George Vecsey, *Joy in Mudville* (New York: McCall, 1970), 155.

53. Thomas Rogers, "Baseball Mourns Kennedy; Yankees Offer Bat Day Refunds," *New York Times*, June 10, 1968.

54. Fleischman, "The Aftermath," 34; "A Kennedy Aide Sends His Thanks to Players," *Sporting News*, June 22, 1968, 34.

55. Letters of Bucky Denniston, Gregory Price, Wesley Tom, and Mrs. Philip King, "Voice of the Fan," *Sporting News*, June 29, 1968, 6.

56. Leonard Koppett, interviewed by Gabriel Schechter, June 16, 1992, Society for American Baseball Research Archives, Phoenix, AZ.

57. Executive Council Meetings, September 12, 1968, Papers of Bowie K. Kuhn, BAMSS100, National Baseball Hall of Fame Library, National Baseball Hall of Fame, Cooperstown, NY, Series I, Sub-Series 1: Executive Council, Box 1, Folder 2, emphasis added.

58. "Star-Spangled Banner—José Feliciano (story and 1968 video)," accessed October 5, 2016, https://www.youtube.com/watch?v=8lVqlVKNrug.

59. John Gettings, "Star-Mangled Banner," Infoplease, accessed October 5, 2016, http://www.infoplease.com/spot/starmangledbanner.html.

60. Matt Gold, "Voice of the Fan," *Sporting News*, October 26, 1968, 6; Joe Cory, "Voice of the Fan," *Sporting News*, October 26, 1968, 6; Letters of Murphy L. Tamkersley, James Sanford Hill, Clayton M. Bergman Jr., Joseph D. Guidry, and Rev. J. P. Scherer, "Voice of the Fan," *Sporting News*, October 26, 1968, 6; José Feliciano, quoted in "Fans Protest Soul Singer's Anthem Version," *New York Times*, October 8, 1968.

61. Jama Lazerow, "1960–1974," in Stephen J. Whitfield, ed., *A Companion to 20th-Century America* (Malden, MA: Blackwell, 2007), 96, 97.

62. Patterson, *The Eve of Destruction*, 18.

63. Ken Harrelson, quoted in William Leggett, "Hawk Baby is Big in Boston," *Sports Illustrated*, September 2, 1968.

64. Tom Clark, *Champagne and Baloney: The Rise and Fall of Finley's A's* (New York: Harper & Row, 1976), 48.

65. Steve Hovley, quoted in Bouton, *Ball Four*, 319.

66. Marty Appel, "Remembering Baseball's Chipmunks," *Memories and Dreams: The Official Magazine of the National Baseball Hall of Fame* 38, no. 2 (2016): 34, 35.

67. Bill Freehan, *Behind the Mask: An Inside Baseball Diary* (New York: World, 1970), 6, 32, 33, 204.

68. Leo Durocher, quoted in David Claerbaut, *Durocher's Cubs: The Greatest Team That Didn't Win* (Dallas: Taylor, 2000), 30.

69. Roger I. Abrams, "Alcohol, Drugs and the National Pastime," *University of Pennsylvania Journal of Labor and Employment Law* 8, no. 4 (summer 2006): 861.

70. Will Carroll with William L. Carroll, *The Juice: The Real Story of Baseball's Drug Problem* (Chicago: Ivan R. Dee, 2005), 35.

71. Carroll, *The Juice*, 75.

72. Bouton, *Ball Four*, 81, 157, 351.

73. Aaron, *I Had a Hammer*, 268; Carroll, *The Juice*, 79.

74. Elliott J. Gorn and Warren Goldstein, *A Brief History of American Sports* (Urbana: University of Illinois Press, 2004), 243.

75. Allan Doherty, "General William D. Eckert," Steroids in Baseball, accessed October 5, 2016, http://www.steroidsinbaseball.net/commish/eckert.html.

76. Carroll, *The Juice*, 39.

77. Doherty, "General William D. Eckert"; Carroll, *The Juice*, 39.

78. Tom House, quoted in "Former Pitcher Tom House Describes Past Steroid Use," *USA Today*, May 3, 2005, accessed October 5, 2016, http://www.usatoday30.usatoday.com/sports/baseball/2005-05-03-steroids-house_x.htm#.

79. David Halberstam, *The Fifties* (New York: Villard Books, 1993), 184–85.

80. Roone Arledge, quoted in Randy Roberts and James Olson, "The Impact of Roone Arledge on Televised Sports," in Steven A. Riess, ed., *Major Problems in American Sports History* (Boston: Wadsworth, 1997), 418.

81. Vince Lombardi and Walter O'Malley, quoted in William Johnson, "TV Made It All a New Game," *Sports Illustrated*, December 22, 1969.

82. Johnson, "TV Made It All a New Game."

83. Richard Nixon note, White House and MLB Correspondence, BAMSS49, National Baseball Hall of Fame Library, National Baseball Hall of Fame, Cooperstown, NY, Box 1, Folder 9.

84. Harold Peterson, "Baseball's Johnny Appleseed," *Sports Illustrated*, April 14, 1969; William Leggett, "One Hundred One," *Sports Illustrated*, April 14, 1969.

85. For the complete rosters with runners-up, see Merrell Whittlesey, "'Greatest Ever' . . . Cheers Ring Out for All-Timers," *Sporting News*, August 2, 1969, 5; Aaron, *I Had a Hammer*, 276; Jane Leavy, *The Last Boy: Mickey Mantle and the End of America's Childhood* (New York: HarperCollins, 2010), 291.

86. Leonard Koppett, "All-Star Game Tuesday Night Caps Washington Gathering of Baseball Greats," *New York Times*, July 20, 1969; "A Feast Before the Game," *New York Times*, July 22, 1969.

87. Marty Appel, "Baseball's Centennial 'Greatest Players Ever' Poll," The National Pastime Museum, accessed October 5, 2016, http://www.thenationalpastimemuseum.com/article/baseballs-centennial-greatest-players-ever-poll.

88. Mark Mulvoy, "Baseball Booms Again," *Sports Illustrated*, August 2, 1969.

89. Letter from Bowie Kuhn to Richard Nixon, BAMSS49, National Baseball Hall of Fame Library, National Baseball Hall of Fame, Cooperstown, NY, Series VII, Correspondence, Box 17, Folder 7; letter from Bowie Kuhn to Pope Paul VI, BAMSS49, National Baseball Hall of Fame Library, National Baseball Hall of Fame, Cooperstown, NY, Series VII, Correspondence, Box 16, Folder 1.

90. Arthur Daley, "Centennial Celebration," *New York Times*, July 25, 1969.

91. Tony Kubek, quoted in "Fans Protest Soul Singer's Anthem Version," *New York Times*, October 8, 1968.

Chapter 8

1. Jim Hawkins, *Al Kaline: The Biography of a Tigers Icon* (Chicago: Triumph Books, 2010), 152.

2. Denny McLain with Eli Zaret, *I Told You I Wasn't Perfect* (Chicago: Triumph Books, 2007), 114. Contac was a popular over-the-counter medication for the relief of colds, flu, and allergies.

3. Bill Freehan, *Behind the Mask: An Inside Baseball Diary* (New York: World, 1970), 222; Al Kaline, quoted in Hawkins, *Al Kaline*, 200.

4. Bob Gibson with Lonnie Wheeler, *Stranger to the Game* (New York: Viking, 1994), 206.

5. Brad Snyder, *A Well-Paid Slave: Curt Flood's Fight for Free Agency in Professional Sports* (New York: Plume, 2007), 6.

6. Neal Russo, "Redbird Express Blew Boiler Early," in Paul MacFarlane, Chris Roewe, and Larry Wigge, eds., *Official 1970 Baseball Guide* (St. Louis: Sporting News, 1970), 135.

7. Mike Lamey, "Fiery Martin Led Twins to West Flag," in MacFarlane, Roewe, and Wigge, *Official 1970 Baseball Guide*, 39.

8. Hank Aaron with Lonnie Wheeler, *I Had a Hammer: The Hank Aaron Story* (New York: Harper Perennial, 1991), 273.

9. Aaron, *I Had a Hammer*, 272.

10. Warren Corbett, *The Wizard of Waxahachie: Paul Richards and the End of Baseball as We Knew It* (Dallas: Southern Methodist University Press, 2009), 330.

11. William Leggett, "Lights in the Met Cellar," *Sports Illustrated*, May 6, 1968.

12. Dan Murr, "Fourth-Place J-Mets Kayo Int Playoff Foes," *Sporting News*, October 5, 1968, 55.

13. Joseph Reichler, "When Tommie Agee Shattered the Cubs," in Doris Townsend, ed., *This Great Game* (New York: Rutledge Books, 1971), 142.

14. William Leggett, "Maybe It's Time to Break Up the Mets," *Sports Illustrated*, September 22, 1968.

15. Joseph Durso, "Mets Win 5–3, Take the Series," in *The New York Times Book of Baseball History: Highlights from the Pages of the New York Times* (New York: Arno Press, 1975), 289.

16. Joe Gergen, quoted in George Vecsey, *Joy in Mudville* (New York: McCall, 1970), 192.

17. Randy Hundley, quoted in David Claerbaut, *Durocher's Cubs: The Greatest Team That Didn't Win* (Dallas: Taylor, 2000), 34.

18. Fergie Jenkins with Lew Freedman, *Fergie: My Life from the Cubs to Cooperstown* (Chicago: Triumph Books, 2009), 96; Gene Oliver, quoted in Robert H. Boyle, "Leo's Bums Rap for the Cubs," *Sports Illustrated*, June 30, 1969.

19. Jenkins, *Fergie*, 97; J. C. Martin, quoted in Mort Zachter, *Gil Hodges: A Hall of Fame Life* (Lincoln: University of Nebraska Press, 2015), 326.

20. Mort Zachter, "If Gil Hodges Managed the Cubs and Leo Durocher the Mets in 1969, Whose 'Miracle' Would It Have Been?" in *The National Pastime*, ed. Stuart Shea (Phoenix: Society for American Baseball Research, 2015).

21. John Eisenberg, *From 33rd Street to Camden Yards: An Oral History of the Baltimore Orioles* (New York: Contemporary Books, 2001), 185.

22. Stephen J. Walker, *A Whole New Ballgame: The 1969 Washington Senators* (Clifton, VA: Pocol Press, 2009), 19.

23. Ed Brinkman, quoted in Ben Bradlee Jr., *The Kid: The Immortal Life of Ted Williams* (New York: Little, Brown, 2013), 549.

24. William Leggett, "A Jam-up of Talent at Third," *Sports Illustrated*, April 28, 1969.

25. Tony Conigliaro, quoted in Mark Mulvoy, "Now Playing in Right Field . . . ," *Sports Illustrated*, April 7, 1969.

26. Tony Conigliaro with Jack Zanger, *Seeing It Through* (London: Macmillan, 1970), 218.

27. McLain, *I Told You I Wasn't Perfect*, 175.

28. Mickey Mantle, quoted in Jane Leavy, *The Last Boy: Mickey Mantle and the End of America's Childhood* (New York: HarperCollins, 2010), 292.

29. Roger Maris, quoted in Neal Russo, "'Well, So Long, Rog, It's Been Great,'" *Sporting News*, October 12, 1968, 3, emphasis added.

Chapter 9

1. John Thorn, "Our Game, Part 3," Our Game (blog), August 5, 2015, accessed August 5, 2015, https://ourgame.mlblogs.com/our-game-part-3-f35bf0da0948; Joe King, "Baseball Never Changes . . . Does It?" *Sporting News*, April 20, 1968, 29.

2. Leonard Koppett, *All About Baseball* (New York: Quadrangle, 1974), 333; Leonard Koppett, *A Thinking Man's Guide to Baseball* (New York: Dutton, 1967), 266.

3. Frank Lane, quoted in Lou Hatter, "Lane Suggests a Lower Mound to Help Hitters," *Sporting News*, April 20, 1968, 18.

4. "The Voice of Experience," *Sporting News*, June 1, 1968, 14; Mayo Smith, quoted in Bob Addie, "Addie's Atoms," *Sporting News*, June 1, 1968, 14; Rex Lardner, "The Pitchers Are Ruining the Game," *New York Times*, June 16, 1968.

5. Mark Mulvoy, "Sore Spots in a Big-Arm Year," *Sports Illustrated*, August 26, 1968.

6. Minutes of Executive Council meeting, September 12, 1968, Papers of Bowie K. Kuhn, BAMSS100, National Baseball Hall of Fame Library, National Baseball Hall of Fame, Cooperstown, NY, Series I, Sub-Series 1, Box 1, Folder 2, Executive Council Meetings.

7. Bill Kinnamon, quoted in Larry R. Gerlach, *The Men in Blue: Conversations with Umpires* (Lincoln: University of Nebraska Press, 1980), 242.

8. Leonard Koppett, "Hitters Scrape Bottom, Figures Show," *Sporting News*, October 19, 1968, 27. The data cited in this paragraph is derived from this article.

9. Koppett, "Hitters Scrape Bottom, Figures Show," 27; "What's Behind Swat Decay?" *Sporting News*, October 26, 1968, 14.

10. Bill James and Rob Neyer, *The Neyer/James Guide to Pitchers* (New York: Fireside, 2004), 9, 10, 39; John Thorn, *The Relief Pitcher: Baseball's New Hero* (New York: Dutton, 1979), 158.

11. Leonard Koppett, "Larger Strike Zone Key to Batting Famine," *Sporting News*, October 26, 1968, 15.

12. Leo Durocher, quoted in "New Rule Won't Stop Spit Balls—Leo," *Kansas City Times*, March 14, 1968.

13. John Thorn and John Holway, *The Pitcher* (New York: Prentice Hall, 1987), 172.

14. Bob Gibson with Lonnie Wheeler, *Stranger to the Game* (New York: Viking, 1994), 209.

15. Thorn and Holway, *The Pitcher*, 14; Richard Dozer, "Pitchers Ready for New Setup, Lopez Says," *Chicago Tribune*, January 7, 1969; John Rosengren, *The Fight of Their Lives: How Juan Marichal and John Roseboro Turned Baseball's Ugliest Brawl into a Story of Forgiveness and Redemption* (Guilford, CT: Lyons Press, 2014), 158; Camilo Pascual, quoted in William Leggett, "From Mountain to Molehill," *Sports Illustrated*, March 24, 1969.

16. J. Temple Black, letter to the editor, *Sports Illustrated*, January 13, 1969. In his biography of Richards, Warren Corbett cites a backward mound movement of two feet, but Thorn and Holway note a five-foot displacement. See Warren Corbett, *The Wizard of Waxahachie: Paul Richards and the End of Baseball as We Knew It* (Dallas: Southern Methodist University Press, 2009), 322; Thorn and Holway, *The Pitcher*, 13.

17. Kinnamon quoted in Gerlach, *The Men in Blue*, 255.

18. Doug Harvey and Peter Golenbock, *They Called Me God: The Best Umpire Who Ever Lived* (New York: Gallery Books, 2014), 140; Will Carroll with William L. Carroll, *The Juice: The Real Story of Baseball's Drug Problem* (Chicago: Ivan R. Dee, 2005), 218; Leggett, "From Mountain to Molehill."

19. Ray Sadecki, quoted in Mark Mulvoy, "Here Come the Hitters—Maybe," *Sports Illustrated*, May 12, 1969.

20. Paul MacFarlane, Chris Roewe, and Larry Wigge, eds., *Official 1970 Baseball Guide* (St. Louis: Sporting News, 1970), 292–93. Averages per team offer a valid comparison from 1968 to 1969 because of the increase from twenty to twenty-four teams due to expansion.

21. Average home run output per American League team went from 110.4 in 1968 to 137.4 in 1969; in the National League the averages soared from 89.1 in 1968 to 122.5 in 1969.

22. Memo from Cal Gauss to Bowie Kuhn, October 23, 1969, Papers of Bowie K. Kuhn, BAMSS100, National Baseball Hall of Fame Library, National Baseball Hall of Fame, Cooperstown, NY, Series VI, Sub-Series 1, Box 9, Folder 7, Playing Rules, December 1969.

23. Joseph Reichler memo to Bowie Kuhn, November 21, 1969, Papers of Bowie K. Kuhn, BAMSS100, National Baseball Hall of Fame Library, National Baseball Hall of Fame, Cooperstown, NY, Series VI, Sub-Series 1, Box 9, Folder 7, Playing Rules, December 1969.

24. Undated memo, Papers of Bowie K. Kuhn, BAMSS100, National Baseball Hall of Fame Library, National Baseball Hall of Fame, Cooperstown, NY, Series VI, Sub-Series 3, Box 14, Folder 9, Miscellaneous Attendance Data and Analysis, 1969. This appears to be a draft memo likely written by Joseph Reichler in early June 1969.

25. Duke Snider, quoted in Jack Lang, "Alter Pinch-Hit Rules to Hypo Hitting—Duke," *Sporting News*, September 28, 1968, 19.

26. Joe Cronin, quoted in Edward Prell, "Cronin Doesn't Like 10th Man," *Chicago Tribune*, March 14, 1969; Bowie Kuhn, *Hardball: The Education of a Baseball Commissioner* (New York: Times Books, 1987), 55; Dewey Soriano, quoted in "Pinch Hitter for Pitcher Plan Adopted on Coast," *Chicago Sunday Tribune*, March 5, 1961.

27. Al Lopez, quoted in Richard Dozer, "Sox, Cub Pilots Rap Experimental Spring Rules," *Chicago Tribune*, March 6, 1969; Leo Durocher, quoted in Jerome Holtzman, "Lip Ecstatic Over Cubs' Speedy Gamble," *Sporting News*, March 22, 1969, 5; Leo Durocher, quoted in George Langford, "Experimental Rules Rouse Durocher Ire," *Chicago Tribune*, March 12, 1969.

28. Bob Addie, "Addie's Atoms," *Sporting News*, April 5, 1969, 14; Memo from Joe Reichler to Bowie Kuhn, March 28, 1969, Papers of Bowie K. Kuhn, BAMSS100, National Baseball Hall of Fame Library, National Baseball Hall of Fame, Cooperstown, NY, Series VI, Sub-Series 3, Box 14, Folder 9, Miscellaneous Attendance Data and Analysis, 1969.

29. Memo from Harry Simmons to Bowie Kuhn, May 5, 1969, Papers of Bowie K. Kuhn, BAMSS100, National Baseball Hall of Fame Library, National Baseball Hall of Fame, Cooperstown, NY, Series VI, Sub-Series 3, Box 14, Folder 9, Miscellaneous Attendance Data and Analysis, 1969.

30. William Leggett, "Rx: A DH Factor for Baseball Ills," *Sports Illustrated*, August 11, 1969; MacFarlane, Roewe, and Wigge, *Official 1970 Baseball Guide*, 405.

31. David Condon, "In the Wake of the News," *Chicago Tribune*, November 13, 1969.

32. Memo from Charlie Finley to Michael Burke, November 15, 1969, Papers of Bowie K. Kuhn, BAMSS100, National Baseball Hall of Fame Library, National Baseball Hall of Fame, Cooperstown, NY, Series VI, Sub-Series 1, Box 9, Folder 7, Playing Rules, December 1969; Memo from Michael Burke to Charlie Finley, November 19, 1969, Papers of Bowie K. Kuhn, BAMSS100, National Baseball Hall of Fame Library,

National Baseball Hall of Fame, Cooperstown, NY, Series VI, Sub-Series 1, Box 9, Folder 7, Playing Rules, December 1969.

33. Chris Roewe and Paul MacFarlane, eds., *Official 1969 Baseball Guide* (St. Louis: Sporting News, 1969), 203; William Curran, *Strikeout: A Celebration of the Art of Pitching* (New York: Crown, 1995), 183.

34. *1969 Minnesota Twins Press Radio TV Guide*, 7.

35. John D. Allen, "The History of Professional Baseball Rule Changes," Master's thesis, University of Wisconsin, 1971, 146–47.

36. Memo from Joseph E. Cronin to American League Managers, November 13, 1968, Papers of Harry Dalton, 1960–1993, BAMSS40, National Baseball Hall of Fame Library, National Baseball Hall of Fame, Cooperstown, NY, Box 8, Folder 7, General Managers Meetings, 1965–1994. The recipient title of "To: American League Managers" was certainly intended to mean "*General* Managers."

37. MacFarlane, Roewe, and Wigge, *Official 1970 Baseball Guide*, 277.

38. Saul Wisnia, "Jim Lonborg," BioProject of the Society for American Baseball Research, accessed February 14, 2016, http://www.sabr.org/bioproj/person/8eb88355.

39. Roewe and MacFarlane, *Official 1969 Baseball Guide*, 203.

40. King, "Baseball Never Changes . . . Does It?" 29.

Chapter 10

1. "Gate in 1960s Nears 200 Million," *Sporting News*, January 11, 1969, 33.

2. Philip J. Lowry, *Green Cathedrals: The Ultimate Celebration of All 271 Major League and Negro League Parks Past and Present* (Reading, MA: Addison-Wesley, 1992), 248.

3. Richard O. Davies, *Sports in American Life: A History*, 2nd ed. (Malden, MA: Wiley-Blackwell, 2012), 231.

4. Doug Feldmann, *El Birdos: The 1967 and 1968 St. Louis Cardinals* (Jefferson, NC: McFarland, 2007), 25; "New Parks Herald Speedup of Play," *Sporting News*, July 9, 1966, 14.

5. Rory Costello, "Jarry Park (Montreal)," Society for American Baseball Research, accessed March 6, 2016, http://www.sabr.org/bioproj/park/be7dd3d0.

6. "White Sox Sprucing Up Park," *Hartford Courant*, February 11, 1969.

7. Robert A. Caro, *The Power Broker: Robert Moses and the Fall of New York* (New York: Vintage Books, 1975), 829; Robert Moses to William Shea, May 31, 1960, New York World's Fair 1964–1965 Inc. series, Robert Moses papers, New York Public Library, Astor, Lenox, and Tilden Foundations.

8. Robert Moses to James A. McCarthy, October 14, 1960, New York World's Fair 1964–1965 Inc. series, Robert Moses papers, New York Public Library, Astor, Lenox, and Tilden Foundations; Stuart Constable, quoted in Newbold Morris to Robert Moses, October 19, 1960, New York World's Fair 1964–1965 Inc. series, Robert Moses papers, New York Public Library, Astor, Lenox, and Tilden Foundations (Morris served as the commissioner of the Department of Parks for the City of New York.); Robert Moses to William Shea, October 20, 1960, New York World's Fair 1964–1965 Inc. series, Robert Moses papers, New York Public Library, Astor, Lenox, and Tilden Foundations.

9. *30 Years of Progress, 1934–1964*, Report to the Mayor and the Board of Estimate, New York City Department of Parks, June 9, 1964, 67, 68, www.nycgovparks.org/sub_about/parks_history/library/pdf/thirty_years_of_progress.pdf. Viewed March 2, 2016; Carl Lundquist, "Roof on Shea by '66, Sports Boss Forecasts," *Sporting News*, June 5, 1965, 7.

10. Hank Aaron with Lonnie Wheeler, *I Had a Hammer: The Hank Aaron Story* (New York; Harper Perennial, 1991), 247.

11. Judge Roy Hofheinz, quoted in Tex Maule, "The Greatest Showman on Earth, and He's the First to Admit It," *Sports Illustrated*, April 21, 1969; Liz Smith, "Giltfinger's Golden Dome," *Sports Illustrated*, April 22, 1965, 45.

12. Clark Nealon, "The Curve Ball Curves in Domed Arena, *Sporting News*, February 20, 1965, 7, emphasis added; "The AstroDome—A Symbol of Progress," *Sporting News*, April 24, 1965, 14.

13. Roger Angell, quoted in C. C. Johnson Spink, "We Believe," *Sporting News*, May 28, 1966, 14.

14. John Wilson, "Judge Ready to Give Refunds If Games Had Proved Farce," *Sporting News*, April 24, 1965, 10.

15. Mary Bellis, "The History of Astroturf," ThoughtCo., accessed March 30, 2017, https://www.thoughtco.com/history-of-astroturf-1991235.

16. Gene Bossard, quoted in Edgar Munzel, "Chisox Groundskeeper Cites Advantages of AstroTurf at White Sox Park," *Sporting News*, August 9, 1969, 11; Danny Murtaugh, quoted in Michael Gershman, *Diamonds: The Evolution of the Ballpark* (Boston: Houghton Mifflin, 1993), 198.

17. Monsanto advertisement, *Sports Illustrated*, April 13, 1970, 40–41. The Cincinnati Reds claimed a maximum of three hours for such a conversion. See "Riverfront Stadium Features AstroTurf," *Cincinnati Riverfront Stadium Opening Souvenir Magazine* (1970), 11, 13.

18. Ed Sudol, quoted in Larry R. Gerlach, *The Men in Blue: Conversations with Umpires* (Lincoln: University of Nebraska Press, 1980), 229; "Riverfront Stadium Features AstroTurf," 13.

19. "Riverfront Stadium Features Comfortable and Contoured Seating," *Cincinnati Riverfront Stadium Opening Souvenir Magazine* (1970), 19.

20. Richie Hebner quoted in Lowry, *Green Cathedrals*, 75.

21. Matthew W. Mihalka, "From the Hammond Organ to 'Sweet Caroline': The Historical Evolution of Baseball's Sonic Environment" (PhD diss., University of Minnesota, 2012), 71–72.

22. Caption of photograph of Nancy Faust, *Sporting News*, May 23, 1970, 37.

23. "How a Loser Is Really a Winner," *Nation's Business*, n.d., found in *The Stadium Industry, Its Economic and Related Impacts*, Real Estate Research Corporation for Minneapolis, April 1978, 6–62.

24. "How a Loser Is Really a Winner," 6–62.

25. Jim Schottelkotte, "Riverfront Stadium: Fruition of a Dream," *Cincinnati Riverfront Stadium Opening Souvenir Magazine* (1970), 5, 7.

26. Ritter Collett, "Ohio's No. 1 Sports Fan—Fast-Moving Gov. Rhodes," *Sporting News*, December 28, 1968, 21. At the time, the park was simply being referred to as an uncapitalized "riverfront stadium."

27. Minutes of General Managers meeting, December 5, 1969, Papers of Bowie K. Kuhn, BAMSS100, National Baseball Hall of Fame Library, National Baseball Hall of Fame, Cooperstown, NY, Series III, Sub-Series 1, Box 1, Folder 1, General Managers Meetings—1969; Earl Lawson, "Some Weeds Already Sprouting in Reds' Infield," *Sporting News*, January 17, 1970, 40.

28. *1971 Cincinnati Reds Media Guide*, 7; "Riverfront Stadium Fact Sheet" *Cincinnati Riverfront Stadium Opening Souvenir Magazine* (1970), 9.

29. "Green 'Grass' Grows All Around," *Three Rivers Stadium Souvenir Book* (1970), 19; Burrell Cohen, "Three Rivers Stadium: Pittsburgh Goes Big League," *Three Rivers Stadium Souvenir Book* (1970), 5, 7.

30. Dahlen K. Ritchey, "Designing the Stadium," *Three Rivers Stadium Souvenir Book* (1970), 13.

31. Lee Vilensky, quoted in Mitchell Nathanson, *God Almighty Hisself: The Life and Legacy of Dick Allen* (Philadelphia: University of Pennsylvania Press, 2016), 66.

32. Allen Lewis, "Philly Voters Approve Extra Stadium Funds," *Sporting News*, June 3, 1967, 15.

33. Rich Westcott, *Veterans Stadium: Field of Memories* (Philadelphia: Temple University Press, 2005), 7.

34. Allen Lewis, "Philly Voters Approve Extra Stadium Funds," *Sporting News*, June 3, 1967, 15.

35. David M. Jordan, *Occasional Glory: The History of the Philadelphia Phillies*, 2nd ed. (Jefferson, NC: McFarland, 2003), 120; Allen Lewis, "Philly Stadium Like a Dream Fulfilled," *Sporting News*, April 24, 1971, 5.

36. *1970 Philadelphia Phillies Radio TV Press Guide*, 4.

37. This section draws from a consultant's report, *The Stadium Industry*.

38. *The Stadium Industry*, 5–33.

39. *The Stadium Industry*, 6–29.

40. *The Stadium Industry*, 6–47.

41. *The Stadium Industry*, 6–26.

42. Andrew Thompson, "Guess How Much Money We Still Owe for Building Veterans Stadium," *Philadelphia*, June 14, 2013, accessed April 16, 2016, http://www.phillymag.com/news/2013/06/14/paying-building-now-demolished-vet.

43. Philip Bess, *City Baseball Magic: Plain Talk and Uncommon Sense About Cities and Baseball Parks* (St. Paul: Knothole Press, 1999), 18; Robert Baade and Richard Dye, quoted in *City Baseball Magic*, 20.

44. Aaron, *I Had a Hammer*, 285.

45. Janet Marie Smith, "Ballpark or Stadium: Does It Matter?" *NINE: A Journal of Baseball History and Culture* 23, no. 1 (fall 2014): 112.

Chapter 11

1. James T. Patterson, *Grand Expectations: The United States, 1945–1974* (New York: Oxford University Press, 1996), 8–9.

2. "Test by Electric Brain Supports Rickey in Complicated Player-Rating Formula," *Sporting News*, March 23, 1955, 32.

3. "'Brain' Picks Tigers, Brooks," *Sporting News*, April 25, 1956, 30.

4. Dan Daniel, "Daredevil Dan Foresees Yank-Brave Repeat," *Sporting News*, December 31, 1958, 7; Joe King, "Univac Tosses Curve to Dr. King," *Sporting News*, August 5, 1959, 2.

5. Dan Daniel, "Over the Fence," *Sporting News*, May 28, 1958, 12.

6. Bob Joyce, "'Electronic Manager' Proves Real Whiz in Strategy Quiz," *Sporting News*, June 15, 1960, 36; Paul Richards, quoted in C. C. Johnson Spink, "We Believe," *Sporting News*, January 15, 1966, 14.

7. "Ours Is a Wonderful Idea," *Sporting News*, May 6, 1967, 14. The paper did credit United Press International for being more judicious with their box scores but was particularly harsh on the Associated Press.

8. "IBM System/360," Wikipedia, accessed June 20, 2016, http:://en.wikipedia.org/wiki/IBM_System/360.

9. LaSalle Extension University advertisement, *Sporting News*, November 4, 1967, 48.

10. William D. Smith, "Controls Haven't Caught Up to Boom in Computers," *New York Times*, February 22, 1970.

11. Harold Seymour, quoted in Alan Schwarz, *The Numbers Game: Baseball's Lifelong Fascination with Statistics* (New York: St. Martin's Press, 2004), 12.

12. Al Elias, quoted in Schwarz, *The Numbers Game*, 41.

13. Jerry Kirshenbaum, "His Word Is the Law of Averages," *Sports Illustrated*, August 18, 1969.

14. Andy McCue, "Allan Roth," *Baseball Research Journal* (Society for American Baseball Research) 43, no. 1 (2014): 7, 8, emphasis added.

15. Bill James, quoted in McCue, "Allan Roth," 12.

16. Leonard Koppett, *All About Baseball* (New York: Quadrangle, 1974), 336.

17. Alan Kornspan, "A Historical Analysis of the Chicago Cubs' Use of Statistics to Analyze Baseball Performance," *NINE: A Journal of Baseball History and Culture* 23, no. 1 (fall 2014), 22.

18. Bob Sudyk, "Computer Picks Top Clutch-Hitters," *Sporting News*, April 16, 1966, 13.

19. Spink, "We Believe," 14; Earnshaw Cook with Donald L. Fink, *Percentage Baseball and the Computer*, 3rd ed. (Baltimore: Waverly Press, 1971), 7, 8. The first two editions of this book were published in 1964 and 1966, respectively.

20. Earnshaw Cook, quoted in Spink, "We Believe," 14.

21. Harvey E. Cohen, "Formula Pinpoints Offensive Skill, and Computer Ranks Top Players," *Sporting News*, January 18, 1969, 6.

22. William Elenko, "Sports Editor's Mailbox," *New York Times*, November 9, 1969; Pete Palmer, "Player Win Averages," *Baseball Research Journal* (Society for American Baseball Research) 45, no. 1 (spring 2016): 25.

23. Eldon G. Mills and Harlan D. Mills, *Player Win Averages: A Computer Guide to Winning Baseball Players* (New York: A. S. Barnes, 1970), 13.

24. Mills and Mills, *Player Win Averages*, 20.

25. Mills and Mills, *Player Win Averages*, 35, 43, 47, 51, 55.

26. Advertisement, *Sporting News*, February 14, 1970, 35; John Thorn, "Surprise Postseason Heroes," Our Game (blog), November 23, 2015, accessed November 23, 2015, https://ourgame.mlblogs.com/surprise-postseason-heroes-c024e6823858.

27. Hy Turkin and S. C. Thompson, *The Official Encyclopedia of Baseball*, Jubilee ed. (New York: A. S. Barnes, 1951), vii.

28. Joe Reichler, ed., *Ronald Encyclopedia of Baseball* (New York: Ronald Press, 1962), xiv; A. S. Barnes was on to a sixth edition of *The Official Encyclopedia of Football*, also priced at $9.75 and featured in the same advertisement on page 17 of the December 21, 1968, edition of the *Sporting News*, all well placed in time for Christmas shopping.

29. Seymour Siwoff, ed., *The Book of Baseball Records*, 1972 ed. (New York: Seymour Siwoff, 1972), 2.

30. Schwarz, *The Numbers Game*, 94.

31. Schwarz, *The Numbers Game*, 104.

32. "Decisions of the Special Baseball Records Committee," *The Baseball Encyclopedia*, 1st ed. (New York: Macmillan, 1969), found at John Thorn, "Why Is the National Association Not a Major League . . . and Other Records Issues," Our Game, accessed May 4, 2015, https://ourgame.mlblogs.com/2015/05/04/why-is-the-national-association -not-a-major-league-and-other-records-issues; *The Baseball Encyclopedia*, 1st ed., 8.

33. Clifford S. Kachline, "Phantom Ballplayers," found at Our Game, accessed May 13, 2015, http://ourgame.mlblogs.com/2014/07/17/phantom-ballplayers.

34. David Neft, quoted in Christopher Lehmann-Haupt, "You Could Look It Up," *New York Times*, September 5, 1969.

35. Robert Creamer, "Get Your Names, Numbers, BAs, RBIs, BBs, ERAs, Etc. of All the Players," *Sports Illustrated*, October 13, 1969; advertisement for *The Baseball Encyclopedia*, *Sporting News*, June 28, 1969, 13 (Shipping of the books was free as long as buyers checked a box at the bottom of the ad's order coupon before mailing it in.); Lehmann-Haupt, "You Could Look It Up," 35.

36. Memo from Rose Mary Woods to Bowie Kuhn, October 1, 1969, Papers of Bowie K. Kuhn, BAMSS100, National Baseball Hall of Fame Library, National Baseball Hall of Fame, Cooperstown, NY, Series VII, Box 17, Folder 7, Correspondence; Schwarz, *The Numbers Game*, 108.

37. Advertisement, *Sporting News*, May 16, 1970, 9. Macmillan was teaming up with ICI to produce a similar book for all major-league teams.

38. Robert C. Berring, "The Macmillan *Baseball Encyclopedia*, the West System, and Sweat Equity," *Baseball Research Journal* (Society for American Baseball Research) 39, no. 2 (2010): 83.

39. Earl Weaver with Terry Pluto, *Weaver on Strategy* (New York: Collier Books, 1984), 139.

40. "Electronic System to Aid A.L. Draft," *Sporting News*, October 12, 1968, 31.

41. Spink, "We Believe," 14.

42. Doug Brown, "Dave Johnson Looks for Computer's Help on Oriole Problems," *Sporting News*, January 25, 1969, 42.

43. Al Harvin, "Koosman Makes Computer Pitch," *New York Times*, October 28, 1969. Even in their earliest years, the Dallas Cowboys of the National Football League

became the vanguard of computer usage. See Tex Maule, "Make No Mistake about It," *Sports Illustrated*, January 29, 1968.

44. John Wilson, "DiLauro Is an Astro On Tip by Computer," *Sporting News*, March 14, 1970, 26.

45. Bill Cutler, quoted in Edgar Munzel, "Want Headache? Try to Make Up Major Schedule," *Sporting News*, September 26, 1964, 5. Cutler may have meant August 6, which was a Thursday, as the end date of the second section. Teams began series with new opponents on Friday, August 7, which would have been a logical beginning point for the last third of the season.

46. Fred Fleig, quoted in Bob Wolf, "N.L. Fires Volley at Veeck's Expansion View," *Sporting News*, January 8, 1966, 11; Jerry Green, "Big Checkerboard Helps Solve NFL's Knotty Sked Problems," *Sporting News*, May 6, 1967, 47.

47. Oscar Kahan, "Reds to Open National League Schedule on April 6," *Sporting News*, March 14, 1970, 19.

48. COM/PAIR advertisement, *Sporting News*, July 15, 1967, 32.

49. "Push-Button Gimmick Which Nixes Use of Coins in Pay-TV to Be Tested," *Sporting News*, January 10, 1962, 8. Other buttons on the box were intended to be used for "mass education programs" delivered to the home and "direct selling" of goods found in retail stores, thereby creating a televised shop-at-home service.

50. Bob Hunter, "O'Malley Taps New Mother Lode—Fee Teevee," *Sporting News*, August 1, 1964, 2; Melvin Durslag, "STV Expects Subscribers to Run Up Average Monthly Bill of $15," *Sporting News*, August 4, 1964, 2.

51. Wells Twombly, "Players Flash Green Light on Astroturf," *Sporting News*, April 2, 1966, 10.

52. Max Nichols, "Minnesota Fans Buy Tickets on Credit," *Sporting News*, February 25, 1967, 23.

53. Computicket advertisement, *Sporting News*, September 2, 1967, 28.

54. John Hall, "You'll Soon Buy Sports Ducats at Computer in Supermarket," *Sporting News*, March 2, 1968, 20. At the time only the Yankees were on board for electronic sales; the Mets joined at a later date.

55. "Angel Scoreboard: A 23-Story Giant," *Sporting News*, September 11, 1965, 19.

56. "Athletics Hope Fans Will Get Many Kicks Out of Lavish New Computer Scoreboard," *New York Times*, April 6, 1969.

57. "Facts about the Cincinnati Riverfront Stadium Scoreboard," *Cincinnati Riverfront Stadium Opening Souvenir Magazine* (1970), 25, 17.

58. "This Scoreboard Does Everything!" *Three Rivers Stadium Souvenir Book* (1970), 17.

59. The Cincinnati team was known as the Redlegs between 1954 and 1958, then rechristened the Reds in 1959.

60. Michael Strauss, "Frick Sidetracks Three Redlegs after Avalanche of Ohio Votes," in *The New York Times Book of Baseball History: Highlights from the Pages of The New York Times* (New York: Arno Press, 1975), 197; Joseph L. Sommers, quoted in "Computer Plan Suggested for All-Star Vote," *Sporting News*, December 28, 1963, 22.

61. "IBM Machines Employed to Tabulate Shrine Votes," *Sporting News*, February 1, 1964, 14.

62. Ford Frick, quoted in "All-Star Voting to Remain With Players—Frick," *Sporting News*, May 23, 1964, 24.

63. Bowie Kuhn, *Hardball: The Education of a Baseball Commissioner* (New York: Times Books, 1987), 52.

64. Jim Price, quoted in "Fans to Begin Balloting for the All-Star Teams," *Sporting News*, May 23, 1970, 37.

65. Each card could hold 80 characters of data, and the programming to count votes for each position while also determining invalid ballots, such as those containing multiple votes for one position, had to have been enormous in scope.

66. Kuhn, *Hardball*, 53; "Fans' Verdict Confirmed," *Sporting News*, July 18, 1970, 20.

67. Jerome Holtzman, "Chisox' John Duels Feller, Matty in Computer Battles," *Sporting News*, August 28, 1965, 17.

68. "All-Time, All-Star Teams Meet in Computer Games," *Sporting News*, October 16, 1965, 25.

69. Advertisement for Computer Research in Sports, *Sporting News*, May 16, 1970, 18.

70. Ernest J. Lanigan, *Baseball Cyclopedia* (1922; reprint, New York: Horton, 1988), 59.

Bibliography

Books

Aaron, Hank, with Lonnie Wheeler. *I Had a Hammer: The Hank Aaron Story*. New York: Harper Perennial, 1991.

Balzer, Howard, ed. *Official 1979 Baseball Register*. St. Louis: Sporting News, 1979.

The Baseball Encyclopedia. 1st ed. New York: Macmillan, 1969.

The Baseball Encyclopedia. 9th ed. New York: Macmillan, 1993.

Bess, Philip. *City Baseball Magic: Plain Talk and Uncommon Sense about Cities and Baseball Parks*. St. Paul: Knothole Press, 1999.

Bouton, Jim. *Ball Four*. Edited by Leonard Schecter. 20th anniversary ed. New York: Wiley, 1990.

Bradlee, Ben, Jr. *The Kid: The Immortal Life of Ted Williams*. New York: Little, Brown, 2013.

Branch, Taylor. *At Canaan's Edge: America in the King Years, 1965–1968*. New York: Simon & Schuster, 2006.

Carew, Rod, and Ira Berkow. *Carew*. New York: Simon & Schuster, 1979.

Caro, Robert A. *The Power Broker: Robert Moses and the Fall of New York*. New York: Vintage Books, 1975.

———. *The Years of Lyndon Johnson: The Passage of Power*. New York: Alfred A. Knopf, 2012.

Carroll, Will, with William L. Carroll. *The Juice: The Real Story of Baseball's Drug Problem*. Chicago: Ivan R. Dee, 2005.

Carruth, Gordon. *The Encyclopedia of American Facts and Dates*. 9th ed. New York: HarperCollins, 1993.

Center, Bill. *Padres Essential: Everything You Need to Know to Be a Real Fan*. Chicago: Triumph Books, 2007.

Claerbaut, David. *Durocher's Cubs: The Greatest Team That Didn't Win*. Dallas: Taylor, 2000.

Clark, Tom. *Champagne and Baloney: The Rise and Fall of Finley's A's.* New York: Harper & Row, 1976.

Conigliaro, Tony, with Jack Zanger. *Seeing It Through.* London: Macmillan, 1970.

Cook, Earnshaw, with Donald L. Fink. *Percentage Baseball and the Computer.* 3rd ed. Baltimore: Waverly Press, 1971.

Corbett, Warren. *The Wizard of Waxahachie: Paul Richards and the End of Baseball as We Knew It.* Dallas: Southern Methodist University Press, 2009.

Curran, William. *Strikeout: A Celebration of the Art of Pitching.* New York: Crown, 1995.

Davies, Richard O. *Sports in American Life: A History.* 2nd ed. Malden, MA: Wiley-Blackwell, 2012.

Douchant, Mike, and Joe Marcin, eds. *Official 1976 Baseball Register.* St. Louis: Sporting News, 1976.

Dworkin, James B. *Owners versus Players: Baseball and Collective Bargaining.* Boston: Auburn House, 1981.

Eisenberg, John. *From 33rd Street to Camden Yards: An Oral History of the Baltimore Orioles.* New York: Contemporary Books, 2001.

Enright, Jim, ed. *Trade Him! 100 Years of Baseball's Greatest Deals.* Chicago: Follett, 1976.

Feldmann, Doug. *El Birdos: The 1967 and 1968 St. Louis Cardinals.* Jefferson, NC: McFarland, 2007.

Freehan, Bill. *Behind the Mask: An Inside Baseball Diary.* New York: World, 1970.

Gallagher, Danny, and Bill Young. *Remembering the Montreal Expos.* Toronto: Scoop Press, 2005.

Gerlach, Larry R. *The Men in Blue: Conversations with Umpires.* Lincoln: University of Nebraska Press, 1980.

Gershman, Michael. *Diamonds: The Evolution of the Ballpark.* Boston: Houghton Mifflin, 1993.

Gibson, Bob, with Lonnie Wheeler. *Stranger to the Game.* New York: Viking, 1994.

Gillette, Gary, and Pete Palmer. *The ESPN Baseball Encyclopedia.* 4th ed. New York: Sterling, 2007.

Gleason, Roy, with Mark Langill. *Lost in the Sun: Roy Gleason's Odyssey from the Outfield to the Battlefield.* Champaign, IL: Sports Publishing, 2005.

Gordon, Lois, and Alan Gordon. *American Chronicle: Year by Year Through the Twentieth Century.* New Haven, CT: Yale University Press, 1999.

Gorn, Elliott J., and Warren Goldstein. *A Brief History of American Sports.* Urbana: University of Illinois Press, 2004.

Gruver, Ed. *Hairs vs. Squares: The Mustache Gang, the Big Red Machine, and the Tumultuous Summer of 1972.* Lincoln: University of Nebraska Press, 2016.

Halberstam, David. *The Fifties.* New York: Villard Books, 1993.

Harvey, Doug, and Peter Golenbock. *They Called Me God: The Best Umpire Who Ever Lived.* New York: Gallery Books, 2014.

Hawkins, Jim. *Al Kaline: The Biography of a Tigers Icon.* Chicago: Triumph Books, 2010.

Helyar, John. *Lords of the Realm: The Real History of Baseball.* New York: Ballantine Books, 1994.

Hensler, Paul. *The American League in Transition, 1965–1975: How Competition Thrived When the Yankees Didn't.* Jefferson, NC: McFarland, 2012.

Hirsch, James S. *Willie Mays: The Life, The Legend.* New York: Scribner, 2010.

Holtzman, Jerome. *The Commissioners: Baseball's Midlife Crisis.* New York: Total Sports, 1998.

James, Bill, and Rob Neyer. *The Neyer/James Guide to Pitchers.* New York: Fireside, 2004.

Jenkins, Fergie, with Lew Freedman. *Fergie: My Life from the Cubs to Cooperstown.* Chicago: Triumph Books, 2009.

Jordan, David M. *Occasional Glory: The History of the Philadelphia Phillies.* 2nd ed. Jefferson, NC: McFarland, 2003.

Kahn, Abraham Iqbal. *Curt Flood in the Media: Baseball, Race, and the Demise of the Activist-Athlete.* Jackson: University Press of Mississippi, 2012.

Kerr, Jon. *Calvin: Baseball's Last Dinosaur—An Authorized Biography.* Dubuque, IA: William C. Brown, 1990.

Koppett, Leonard. *All About Baseball.* New York: Quadrangle, 1974.

———. *A Thinking Man's Guide to Baseball.* New York: Dutton, 1967.

Korr, Charles P. *The End of Baseball as We Knew It: The Players Union, 1960–1981.* Chicago: University of Illinois Press, 2002.

Kowet, Don. *The Rich Who Own Sports.* New York: Random House, 1977.

Kuhn, Bowie. *Hardball: The Education of a Baseball Commissioner.* New York: Times Books, 1987.

Kurlansky, Mark. *1968: The Year That Rocked the World.* New York: Ballantine Books, 2004.

Lane, F. C., ed. *The Pocket Cyclopedia of Major League Baseball.* New York: Al Munro Elias Baseball Bureau, 1938.

Lang, Jack, and Peter Simon. *The New York Mets: Twenty-five Years of Baseball Magic.* New York: Holt, 1986.

Lanigan, Ernest J. *Baseball Cyclopedia.* 1922. Reprint, New York: Horton, 1988.

Leavy, Jane. *The Last Boy: Mickey Mantle and the End of America's Childhood.* New York: HarperCollins, 2010.

Lowenfish, Lee. *The Imperfect Diamond: A History of Baseball's Labor Wars.* Lincoln: University of Nebraska Press, 2010.

Lowry, Philip J. *Green Cathedrals: The Ultimate Celebration of All 271 Major League and Negro League Parks Past and Present.* Reading, MA: Addison-Wesley, 1992.

MacFarlane, Paul, Chris Roewe, and Larry Wigge, eds. *Official 1970 Baseball Guide.* St. Louis: Sporting News, 1970.

Manchester, William. *The Glory and the Dream: A Narrative History of America, 1932–1972.* New York: Bantam Books, 1974.

Maraniss, David. *Clemente: The Passion and Grace of Baseball's Last Hero.* New York: Simon & Schuster, 2006.

McLain, Denny, with Eli Zaret. *I Told You I Wasn't Perfect.* Chicago: Triumph Books, 2007.

McNeil, William F. *The Evolution of Pitching in Major League Baseball.* Jefferson, NC: McFarland, 2006.

Miller, Marvin. *A Whole Different Ball Game: The Sport and Business of Baseball.* New York: Birch Lane Press, 1991.

Mills, Eldon G., and Harlan D. Mills. *Player Win Averages: A Computer Guide to Winning Baseball Players.* New York: A. S. Barnes, 1970.

Morgan, Anne. *Prescription for Success: The Life and Values of Ewing Marion Kauffman.* Kansas City: Andrews & McMeel, 1995.

Mullins, Bill. *Becoming Big League: Seattle, the Pilots, and Stadium Politics.* Seattle: University of Washington Press, 2013.

Nathanson, Mitchell. *God Almighty Hisself: The Life and Legacy of Dick Allen.* Philadelphia: University of Pennsylvania Press, 2016.

The New York Times Book of Baseball History: Highlights from the Pages of the New York Times. New York: Arno Press, 1975.

Palmer, R. R., Joel Colton, and Lloyd Kramer. *A History of the Modern World.* 10th ed. New York: McGraw-Hill, 2007.

Papucci, Nelson. *The San Diego Padres, 1969–2002: A Complete History.* San Diego: Big League Press, 2002.

Patterson, James T. *The Eve of Destruction: How 1965 Transformed America.* New York: Basic Books, 2012.

———. *Grand Expectations: The United States, 1945–1974.* New York: Oxford University Press, 1996.

Reichler, Joseph L. *The Baseball Trade Register.* New York: Macmillan, 1984.

———, ed. *Ronald Encyclopedia of Baseball.* New York: Ronald Press, 1962.

Riess, Steven A., ed. *Major Problems in American Sports History.* Boston: Wadsworth, 1997.

Roewe, Chris, and Oscar Kahan, eds. *Official 1968 Baseball Guide.* St. Louis: Sporting News, 1968.

Roewe, Chris, and Paul MacFarlane, eds. *Official 1969 Baseball Guide.* St. Louis: Sporting News, 1969.

Rosengren, John. *The Fight of Their Lives: How Juan Marichal and John Roseboro Turned Baseball's Ugliest Brawl into a Story of Forgiveness and Redemption.* Guilford, CT: Lyons Press, 2014.

Schoor, Gene. *Seaver.* Chicago: Contemporary Books, 1986.

Schwarz, Alan. *The Numbers Game: Baseball's Lifelong Fascination with Statistics.* New York: St. Martin's Press, 2004.

Seymour, Harold. *Baseball: The Early Years.* New York: Oxford University Press, 1960.

Simons, William M., ed. *The Cooperstown Symposium on Baseball and American Culture, 2011–2012.* Jefferson, NC: McFarland, 2013.

Siwoff, Seymour, ed. *The Book of Baseball Records.* 1972 ed. New York: Seymour Siwoff, 1972.

Snyder, Brad. *A Well-Paid Slave: Curt Flood's Fight for Free Agency in Professional Sports.* New York: Plume, 2007.

Swank, Bill. *Baseball in San Diego: From the Padres to Petco.* Charleston, SC: Arcadia, 2004.

Thorn, John. *The Relief Pitcher: Baseball's New Hero.* New York: Dutton, 1979.

Thorn, John, and John Holway. *The Pitcher.* New York: Prentice Hall, 1987.

Townsend, Doris, ed. *This Great Game*. New York: Rutledge Books, 1971.

Turkin, Hy, and S. C. Thompson. *The Official Encyclopedia of Baseball*. Jubilee ed. New York: A. S. Barnes, 1951.

———. *The Official Encyclopedia of Baseball*. 5th rev. ed. New York: A. S. Barnes, 1970.

———. *The Official Encyclopedia of Baseball*. 10th rev. ed. Garden City, NY: Doubleday/ Dolphin, 1979.

Turner, Dan. *The Expos Inside Out*. Toronto: McClelland & Stewart, 1983.

Vecsey, George. *Joy in Mudville*. New York: McCall, 1970.

Walker, Stephen J. *A Whole New Ballgame: The 1969 Washington Senators*. Clifton, VA: Pocol Press, 2009.

Weaver, Earl, with Berry Stainback. *It's What You Learn after You Know It All That Counts*. Garden City, NY: Doubleday, 1982.

Weaver, Earl, with Terry Pluto. *Weaver on Strategy*. New York: Collier Books, 1984.

Wendel, Tim. *Summer of '68: The Season That Changed Baseball, and America, Forever*. Philadelphia: Da Capo Press, 2012.

Westcott, Rich. *Veterans Stadium: Field of Memories*. Philadelphia: Temple University Press, 2005.

Whitfield, Stephen J., ed. *A Companion to 20th-Century America*. Malden, MA: Blackwell, 2007.

Wing, Jeff. *Major League Baseball's Greatest 150 Individual Pitching Seasons*. New York: Authors Choice Press, 2001.

Witcover, Jules. *The Year the Dream Died: Revisiting 1968 in America*. New York: Warner Books, 1997.

Zachter, Mort. *Gil Hodges: A Hall of Fame Life*. Lincoln: University of Nebraska Press, 2015.

Zeiler, Thomas W. *Jackie Robinson and Race in America*. Boston: Bedford/St. Martin's, 2014.

Special Collections

Kuhn, Bowie K. Papers. National Baseball Hall of Fame Library. National Baseball Hall of Fame, Cooperstown, NY.

Moses, Robert. Papers. Manuscripts and Archives Division. New York Public Library, New York. Astor, Lenox, and Tilden Foundations.

Records of US Forces in Southeast Asia. USO Tours, Major League Baseball Centennial Showcase, November 8, 1969. Record Group 472. National Archives, College Park, MD.

Documents

Allen, John D. "The History of Professional Baseball Rule Changes." Master's thesis, University of Wisconsin, 1971.

Becker, Charles Porter. "A Chronology of Changes in Major League Baseball Pitching Rules." Master's thesis, Sacramento State College, 1971.

Brown, Robert S. "The Assassination of Martin Luther King, Jr. and the Opening of the 1968 Baseball Season." Paper presented at the 24th Cooperstown Symposium on Baseball and American Culture, Cooperstown, NY, May 30–June 1, 2012.

Glanville, Douglas M. "Transportation Feasibility Study For 30th Street Baseball Stadium." 2001. MFF277. National Baseball Hall of Fame Library. National Baseball Hall of Fame, Cooperstown, NY.

Mendonca, Lenny. "Racial Discrimination in Major League Baseball." March 23, 1983. National Baseball Hall of Fame Library. National Baseball Hall of Fame, Cooperstown, NY.

Mihalka, Matthew W. "From the Hammond Organ to 'Sweet Caroline': The Historical Evolution of Baseball's Sonic Environment." PhD diss., University of Minnesota, 2012.

Richards, Brian J. "Half-Broken Barriers: Frank Robinson, Major League Baseball, and American Race Relations in the 1970s." Master's thesis. State University of New York at Oneonta, 2007. National Baseball Hall of Fame Library. National Baseball Hall of Fame, Cooperstown, NY.

The Stadium Industry, Its Economic and Related Impacts. Real Estate Research Corporation for Minneapolis, April 1978.

30 Years of Progress, 1934–1964. Report to the Mayor and the Board of Estimate. New York City Department of Parks, June 9, 1964. Accessed March 2, 2016. http://www .nycgovparks.org/sub_about/parks_history/library/pdf/thirty_years_of_progress.pdf.

Articles

Abrams, Roger I. "Alcohol, Drugs and the National Pastime." *University of Pennsylvania Journal of Labor and Employment Law* 8, no. 4 (summer 2006).

Appel, Marty. "Remembering Baseball's Chipmunks." *Memories and Dreams: The Official Magazine of the National Baseball Hall of Fame* 38, no. 2 (2016).

Armour, Mark. "A Tale of Two Umpires." *Baseball Research Journal* (Society for American Baseball Research) 38, no. 2 (fall 2009).

Berring, Robert C. "The Macmillan *Baseball Encyclopedia*, the West System, and Sweat Equity." *Baseball Research Journal* (Society for American Baseball Research) 39, no. 2 (2010).

Gmelch, George. "Tiger Town: Spring Training, 1966." *NINE: A Journal of Baseball History and Culture* 22, no. 1 (fall 2013).

Ingham, John N. "Managing Integration: Clemente, Wills, 'Harry the Hat,' and the Pittsburgh Pirates' 1967 Season of Discontent." *NINE: A Journal of Baseball History and Culture* 21, no. 1 (fall 2012).

Kornspan, Alan. "A Historical Analysis of the Chicago Cubs' Use of Statistics to Analyze Baseball Performance." *NINE: A Journal of Baseball History and Culture* 23, no. 1 (fall 2014).

McCue, Andy. "Allan Roth." *Baseball Research Journal* (Society for American Baseball Research) 43, no. 1 (2014).

Nathanson, Mitchell. "Dick Allen Preferred Not To: A Reconsideration of Baseball's Bartleby." *NINE: A Journal of Baseball History and Culture* 22, no. 2 (spring 2014).

Palmer, Pete. "Player Win Averages." *Baseball Research Journal* (Society for American Baseball Research) 45, no. 1 (spring 2016).

Smith, Janet Marie. "Ballpark or Stadium: Does It Matter?" *NINE: A Journal of Baseball History and Culture* 23, no. 1 (fall 2014).

Thornley, Stew. "The Demise of the Reserve Clause." *Baseball Research Journal* (Society for American Baseball Research) 35 (2007).

Zachter, Mort. "If Gil Hodges Managed the Cubs and Leo Durocher the Mets in 1969, Whose 'Miracle' Would It Have Been?" In *The National Pastime*, edited by Stuart Shea. Phoenix: Society for American Baseball Research, 2015.

Baseball Team Publications

Cincinnati Riverfront Stadium Opening Souvenir Magazine. 1970.

East-West Major League Baseball Classic. Game program, March 28, 1970.

Introducing the Luxurious Superboxes. Brochure. Philadelphia Veterans Stadium, 1970.

Le magazine Expos 1980.

Three Rivers Stadium Souvenir Book. 1970.

1969 Kansas City Royals Media Guide.

1969 Minnesota Twins Press Radio TV Guide.

1969 Montreal Expos Press Radio TV Guide.

1969 San Diego Padres Media Guide.

1969 Seattle Pilots Log Book.

1970 Kansas City Royals Media Guide.

1970 New York Mets Media Guide.

1970 Philadelphia Phillies Radio TV Press Guide.

1970 Pittsburgh Pirates Press TV-Radio Guide.

1970 San Diego Padres Media Guide.

1971 Cincinnati Reds Media Guide.

1971 Philadelphia Phillies Radio TV Press Guide.

Periodicals

Baltimore Afro-American
Chicago Daily News
Chicago Tribune
Cleveland Press
Ebony
Kansas City Star

Kansas City Times
Los Angeles Times
Miami Herald
Milwaukee Sentinel
Minneapolis Tribune
Montreal Gazette
New York Daily News
New York Sunday News
New York Times
Seattle Post-Intelligencer
The Sporting News
TV Guide

Web Sites

Appel, Marty. "Baseball's Centennial 'Greatest Players Ever' Poll." The National Pastime Museum. Accessed October 5, 2016. http://www.thenationalpastimemuseum.com/article/baseballs-centennial-greatest-players-ever-poll.

Bellis, Mary. "The History of Astroturf." ThoughtCo. Accessed March 30, 2017. https://www.thoughtco.com/history-of-astroturf-1991235.

Costello, Rory. "Jarry Park (Montreal)." Society for American Baseball Research. Accessed March 6, 2016. http://www.sabr.org/bioproj/park/be7dd3d0.

Doherty, Allan. "General William D. Eckert." Steroids in Baseball. Accessed October 5, 2016. http://www.steroidsinbaseball.net/commish/eckert.html.

Edelman, Alexander. "Ken Harrelson." BioProject of the Society for American Baseball Research. Accessed October 5, 2016. http://www.sabr.org/bioproj/person/442dbc70.

Feliciano, José. Video. Accessed October 5, 2016. http://www.youtube.com/watch?v=8lVqlVKNrug.

Fleitz, David. "Cap Anson." BioProject of the Society for American Baseball Research. Accessed October 5, 2016. http://www.sabr.org/bioproj/person/9b42f875.

"Former Pitcher Tom House Describes Past Steroid Use." *USA Today*. May 3, 2005. Accessed October 5, 2016. http://www.usatoday30.usatoday.com/sports/baseball/2005-05-03-steroids-house_x.htm#.

Gettings, John. "Star-Mangled Banner." Infoplease. Accessed October 5, 2016. http://www.infoplease.com/spot/starmangledbanner.html.

"IBM System/360." Wikipedia. Accessed June 20, 2016. http:://en.wikipedia.org/wiki/IBM_System/360.

Kachline, Clifford S. "Phantom Ballplayers." Found at Our Game. Accessed May 13, 2015. http://ourgame.mlblogs.com/2014/07/17/phantom-ballplayers.

McKenna, Brian. "Robert Cannon." BioProject of the Society for American Baseball Research. Accessed October 5, 2016. http://sabr.org/bioproj/person/a7414ea2.

———. "William Eckert." BioProject of the Society for American Baseball Research. Accessed October 5, 2016. http://www.sabr.org/bioproj/person/4691515d.

Pascal, Anthony H., and Leonard A. Rapping. "Racial Discrimination in Organized Baseball." RAND Corporation, Santa Monica, CA, December 1970, 7. Accessed October 5, 2016, http://www.rand.org/content/dam/rand/pubs/research_memo randa/2008/RM6227.pdf.

Thompson, Andrew. "Guess How Much Money We Still Owe for Building Veterans Stadium." *Philadelphia*. June 14, 2013. Accessed April 16, 2016. http://www.philly mag.com/news/2013/06/14/paying-building-now-demolished-vet.

Thorn, John. "Our Game, Part 3." Our Game (blog). August 5, 2015. Accessed August 5, 2015. https://ourgame.mlblogs.com/our-game-part-3-f35bf0da0948.

———. "Surprise Postseason Heroes." Our Game (blog). November 23, 2015. Accessed November 23, 2015. https://ourgame.mlblogs.com/surprise-postseason-heroes c024e6.

———. "Why Is the National Association Not a Major League . . . and Other Records Issues." Our Game (blog). May 4, 2015. Accessed May 4, 2015. https://ourgame. mlblogs.com/2015/05/04/why-is-the-national-association-not-a-major-league-and -other-records-issues.

"Vietnam War Deaths." Baseball's Greatest Sacrifice. Accessed October 5, 2016. http:// www.baseballsgreatestsacrifice.com/vietnam_war.html.

Wisnia, Saul. "Jim Lonborg." BioProject of the Society for American Baseball Research. Accessed February 14, 2016. http://www.sabr.org/bioproj/person/8eb88355.

Index

Owens, Jesse, 113
Oyler, Ray, 148

Paige, Satchel, 168
Palmer, Jim, 154, 182, 185, 230
Pappas, Milt, 122, 123, 128, 129, 156
Parlour Base-Ball, 247
Parrott, Harold, 31, 32
Pascual, Camilo, 185
Patek, Freddie, 22, 25, 170
Patterson, James, 132, 219
Patti, Tudie, 18
Paul, Gabe, 21, 31, 72
Pelekoudas, Chris, 184
Penn State University, 238
Pepitone, Joe, 135, 137
Perez, Tony, 38, 165, 166
Perranoski, Ron, 155
Perry, Gaylord, 184, 193
Perry, Jim, 155, 156
Peters, Joseph D., 126
Petrocelli, Rico, 122
Philadelphia 76ers, 238
Philadelphia Eagles, 211–212
Philadelphia Phillies, 61, 97, 125, 159, 211–213, 221
Piniella, Lou, 22, 23
Pinson, Vada, 97, 113, 151
pitching mound, 177, 182, 184–186
Pitt Stadium (Pittsburgh), 210
Pittsburgh Pirates, 110–111, 125, 128, 147, 165, 210–211
Pittsburgh Plate Glass, 211
Pittsburgh Steelers, 215
Pizarro, Juan, 71
player: attitudes, 131–136; trade rule, 193; win average, 230, 248
Podres, Johnny, 173
Polo Grounds (New York), 197, 198, 200
Pope Paul VI, 144
Powell, Boog, 154
Powles, George, 97, 113
Praeger-Kavanaugh-Waterbury, 201
Price, Jim, 246

Professional Golfers Association, 243
Pruitt, Bob, 20

racial issues, 108–117; black–Latino tension, 110–111; blacks in management, 112, 116–117; decline of blacks in baseball, 115; integration of baseball, 108–109
Rader, Doug, 114
RAND Corporation, 115
RCA computer, 220, 221
Reach, Albert, 225
Reed, Ron, 157
Reese, Rich, 155
Reeves computer, 220
Regan, Phil, 163, 184
Reichler, Joseph, 58, 60, 61, 63, 188, 190, 232
Reilly, Dr. Raymond, 24
Renko, Steve, 48
reserve clause, 95–103
Resinger, Grover, 135
Reynolds, Jack, 104
RFK Stadium (Washington), 198
Rhodes, James A., 208
Rice University, 214
Richards, Paul, 88, 93, 156–157, 177, 185, 203, 223
Richardson, Spec, 48, 128
Richert, Pete, 121, 154
Richman, Milt, 3
Rickey, Branch, 38, 109, 194, 201, 220, 226
Rigney, Bill, 156
Ritter, Lawrence S., 236
Riverfront Stadium (Cincinnati), 204, 208–210, 214–215, 244
Roberts, Robin, 82, 83
Robinson, Brooks, 113–114, 120, 154, 243
Robinson, Frank, 97, 112, 113–114, 115, 116–117, 126, 154, 183
Robinson, Jackie, 43, 56, 80, 108–109, 111, 112, 114, 115

About the Author

Paul Hensler received his master's degree in history from Trinity College in Hartford, Connecticut, and is a member of the Society for American Baseball Research as well as the Phi Alpha Theta National History Honor Society. The author of *The American League in Transition, 1965–1975: How Competition Thrived When the Yankees Didn't*, Hensler has lectured on baseball in the 1960s and presented papers at the annual Cooperstown Symposium on Baseball and American culture. His essays and book reviews have appeared in SABR's *Baseball Research Journal* and *NINE: A Journal of Baseball History and Culture*. For more information, please visit www.paulhensler.com.